Publications of the
CENTRE FOR REFORMATION AND RENAISSANCE STUDIES

Essays and Studies, 27

SERIES EDITOR   KONRAD EISENBICHLER

Victoria University
in the
University of Toronto

Marriage in Premodern Europe: Italy and Beyond

Edited by

JACQUELINE MURRAY

Toronto
Centre for Reformation and Renaissance Studies
2012

CRRS Publications
Centre for Reformation and Renaissance Studies
Victoria University in the University of Toronto
Toronto, Ontario M5S 1K7, Canada
Tel: 416/585–4465   Fax: 416/585–4430
Email: crrs.publications@utoronto.ca   Web: www.crrs.ca

National Library of Canada Cataloguing in Publication

Marriage in premodern Europe : Italy and beyond / Jacqueline Murray, editor.
(Essays and studies ; 27)
Includes bibliographical references and index.
Issued also in an electronic format.
ISBN 978-0-7727-2122-8

1. Marriage—Europe—History. 2. Women—Europe—History. 3. Europe—History—1492–. I. Murray, Jacqueline, 1953– II. Victoria University (Toronto, Ont.). Centre for Reformation and Renaissance Studies III. Series: Essays and studies (Victoria University (Toronto, Ont.). Centre for Reformation and Renaissance Studies) ; 27.

HQ611.M375 2012
306.81094   C2012-901487-7

Cover image: Raphael, *The Marriage of the Virgin* (detail), 1504. Brera, Milano. Ⓓ Wikipedia Commons.

Typesetting, cover design, and production: Iter Inc.

Contents

Images and Ideologies

Acknowledgments

This collection of essays emerged from the conference *To Have and to Hold: Marriage in Premodern Europe, 1200–1700* organized under the aegis of the Centre for Reformation and Renaissance Studies of Victoria College in the University of Toronto. The CRRS has achieved a well-deserved reputation for excellence in many areas, not the least for its splendid international conferences and the collections of essays that emanate from those conferences. The Director to the Centre, Olga Pugliese and the Assistant to the Director, Stephanie Treloar provided support for this conference at every step of the way. We benefited in particular from Dr Treloar's logistical expertise that ensured a seamless and harmonious meeting for all.

The Social Science and Humanities Research Council of Canada generously provided a grant to support the conference. SSHRC's ongoing funding of conferences is critical to maintain a national and international dialogue about the premodern world. We were also fortunate to receive generous financial support from various constituencies of the University of Toronto including the Office of the Vice President, the Deans of Graduate Studies and of Arts and Science, the Centre for Medieval Studies, the Division of Humanities at the University of Toronto Scarborough, the Department of History, and the Toronto Renaissance and Reformation Colloquium.

One of the great strengths of the CRRS and the whole of the premodern studies community in Toronto is the strong ties that stretch from academia into the community. These warm collaborative relationships were evident throughout the conference. The Bata Shoe Museum provided conference participants with a splendid reception and the opportunity to view their unique collection. The Istituto Italiano di Cultura also provided conference delegates with a warm welcome and excellent reception at the Institute. These gestures of hospitality enhanced the experience of people who came from far and near to attend the conference, and who left with a firm understanding of the interrelationships that support scholarship at the CRRS.

People are always central to the success of any scholarly meeting and there was a tremendous team of students who helped to staff the registration and other aspects of the meeting. During the preparation of this volume I benefited from the assistance of Jack Mallon and Kirk Goodlet.

Above all, however, I want acknowledge my co-organizers of this conference, Konrad Eisenbichler and Nick Terpstra. We three have been friends and colleagues for longer than any of us would admit. Over these many years, my respect for Konrad and Nick only increases. Their collegiality and scholarship, their originality and wisdom, are inspirational and treasured. It is a wonderful experience to work with such scholars and gentlemen. Thanks guys!

JACQUELINE MURRAY
UNIVERSITY OF GUELPH

ILLUSTRATIONS

1.1   Marriage flow chart.

3.1   Detail showing the Ducal Palace in Mantua with the addition of the *Palazzina* Paleologa, built by Giulio Romano, from a modern reproduction of the map of Mantua engraved by Pierre Mortier in Amsterdam, 1704. Photo: author.

3.2   One lira coin, issued 1562, Casale Monferrato, with the portraits of Guglielmo Gonzaga and Margherita Paleologa, in widow's veil, inscribed "MARG ET GVL DVCES MANT ET MAR MONT F." Motto on verso: "NON IMPROVIDIS ." By permission: Dr. Roberto Maestri, Circolo Culturale i Marchesi di Monferrato. "I Marchesi di Monferrato," (html//www.marchimonferrato.com).

7.1   Selected genealogy of the Durante branch of the Scolari family.

7.2   Selected genealogy of the Giannozzo branch of the Cavalcanti family.

7.3   Selected genealogy of the Filippo branch of the Melanesi da Prato family.

7.4   Selected genealogy of the Mannini family.

9.1   Domenico Ghirlandaio (student of), *Rape of the Sabine Women.* Galleria Colonna, Rome, Italy. By permission: Alinari/Art Resource, NY.

9.2   Domenico Ghirlandaio (student of), *Peace Between the Romans and the Sabines.* Galleria Colonna, Rome, Italy. By permission: Alinari/Art Resource, NY.

12.1   Bartolomeo Passerotti, *Family Portrait* (ca. 1575). Gemäldegalerie Alte Meister, Dresden, Germany. By permission.

CONTRIBUTORS

P. RENÉE BAERNSTEIN is Associate Professor of History at Miami University in Oxford, Ohio. She holds degrees from Cornell University and Harvard University. She is the author of *A Convent Tale: A Century of Sisterhood in Spanish Milan* (Routledge, 2002). Her current project is a study of gender and marriage in Baroque Rome.

ELENA BRIZIO earned a PhD in Medieval History from the University of Florence. She has published on the sociological, political, institutional and legal history of the Trecento. Her current research focuses on the cultural, economic and social power of women in the Renaissance. She is Research Fellow and Vice Director at The Medici Archive Project in Florence.

ERSIE C. BURKE earned her PhD from Monash University where she is now Adjunct Research Associate in the School of Philosophical, Historical and International Studies. Her research focuses on Venetian Greek immigration, settlement and community; Greco-Venetian social networks; and the Venetian Stato da Mar.

ERIN J. CAMPBELL is Associate Professor of Early Modern European Art in the Department of History in Art, University of Victoria. Her research interests include cultural representations of old age, cross-cultural connections in European art, and the material culture of the early modern domestic interior.

MAURO CARBONI is Assistant Professor of Economic History at the School of Economics at the University of Bologna. He holds a PhD from Michigan State University. His research has focused on various subjects related to credit, family, and charitable institutions in early modern Italy, with particular reference to Bologna and the Papal States.

JENNIFER MARA DESILVA is Assistant Professor of History at Ball State University and has published articles on ritual, politics, and patronage in Renaissance Italy in *Renaissance Studies*, *The Journal of Early Modern History*, and *The Catholic Historical Review*.

SALLY HICKSON is Associate Professor of Art History at the University of Guelph. Her research interests include female patrons and publics in Renaissance Mantua, religious and secular, as well as the history of collecting and antiquarianism.

SHENNAN HUTTON received her PhD in medieval history from the University of California, Davis. She teaches courses at a number of universities in northern California, including UC Davis and University of the Pacific. She is program coordinator for the California History-Social Science Project, a collaboration between academic historians and K–12 history teachers. She has published *Women and Economic Activities in Late Medieval Ghent*, and her current research examines gender in the Flemish medieval wool cloth industry.

REINIER LEUSHUIS is Associate Professor of French and Italian at Florida State University. He specializes in early modern dialogue, the literary treatment of marriage and friendship and Franco-Italian literary connections. He is the author of *Le Mariage et l'amitié courtoise dans le dialogue et le récit bref de la Renaissance*.

JACQUELINE MURRAY is Professor of History and Director of First-Year Seminars at the University of Guelph. She was an historical consultant in the cases that challenged and ultimately led to the abolition of laws prohibiting same-sex marriage in Ontario and Canada. She has published *Love, Marriage and the Family in the Middle Ages*.

HEATHER PARKER is a doctoral candidate in History at the University of Guelph. Her research lies broadly in the history of family, kinship and social structures in medieval Scotland and her dissertation examines the formation of marriage in Scotland from 1350 to 1600. She co-edited *The Shaping of Scottish Identities: Family, Marriage, and the Worlds Beyond*.

LESLEY PETERSON completed her PhD at the University of Alberta. She is Associate Professor of English at the University of North Alabama where she teaches (and sometimes directs) early modern drama. She recently edited *The Mirror of the Worlde* by Elizabeth Cary and is currently co-editing Tennyson's *The Devil and the Lady*.

KATALIN PRAJDA earned her PhD from European University Institute, Florence. She is currently a Research Fellow at the New Europe College – Institute for Advanced Study, Bucharest. Her research focuses on social networks in late medieval Florence. She is the author of "The Florentine Scolari Family at the Court of Sigismund of Luxemburg in Buda" (*Journal of Early Modern History*, 2010/6) and "Fra Filippo Lippi's *Portrait of a Woman and a Man at a Casement*" (Metropolitan Museum Journal, forthcoming).

JAMIE SMITH earned a PhD in History from the University of Toronto. She has published on the socio-economic and legal history of the family in fourteenth and fifteenth century Genoa. Her current projects focus on exile and the family.

WILLIAM E. SMITH III recently completed his PhD in Religious Studies at Indiana University. His research interests include mysticism, marriage, and the history of Christianity, in particular how bigamy inhabits the imagination and lives of premodern European Christians.

MATTEO SORANZO is Assistant Professor of Italian at McGill University. He holds a Laurea in Lettere from the Università degli Studi di Padova and a PhD in Italian from the University of Wisconsin. His research focuses on the literature and society of Quattrocento Naples and especially on the relationship between poetic writing and identity formation.

ELENA CRISLYN WOODACRE recently completed her doctoral studies at Bath Spa University. Her thesis focused on the queens regnant of Navarre, examining issues surrounding female succession, marital diplomacy and the personal and political partnership between ruling queens and their male consorts.

Introduction:
Marriage in Times of Change

Jacqueline Murray

Marriage is once again at the forefront of scholarly consideration. From the late 1960s to the 1980s, the study of the history of marriage and family was central to the enterprise of social history. Gradually, however, attention shifted away from marriage, as the study of gender and sexuality began to dominate scholarly consciousness. There are myriad explanations for the ebb and flow of topics that dominate historical discourse. Certainly, we might posit that as a social institution and religious sacrament marriage was increasingly marginalized in the western world. As fewer people married and as churches gradually emptied, there was less urgency and less cachet for the study of an institution that was viewed as increasingly marginalized and perhaps irrelevant.

The scholarly landscape changed, however, suddenly and dramatically, when the controversy surrounding same-sex marriage started to dominate the headlines and the courts, and became a feature of everyday life, at least in Canada and some other western countries. Society, the general public, wanted to know how marriage could be valid between two men or two women. "Wait!" people objected, "Marriage was created in the Garden of Eden, by God, for Adam and Eve, *not* Adam and Steve." One of the single most important factors to bring the history of marriage to the forefront for scholars and the general public alike, was the publication of John Boswell's *Same-Sex Unions in Premodern Europe* (1994).

Even before its publication, *Same-Sex Unions* was controversial. Garry Trudeau devoted a week of his famous comic strip, *Doonesbury*, to a discussion of the Christian Church's ancient support of same-sex marriage "according to a famous Yale historian," as Boswell was identified obliquely. The comic strip series was a sensation: it was discussed on the front pages of some newspapers while others cancelled their subscriptions to *Doonesbury* or refused to publish those particular instalments.[1] Due to widespread public demand, Boswell's book was rushed to bookstores some three weeks

---

[1] See, for example, *The Toronto Star*, 7–11 June 1994.

in advance of its formal publication date. Media stories abounded and historians were thrust into the limelight to discuss the pros and cons of Boswell's linguistic and paleographical skills, not to mention his interpretation of evidence. Theologians from across the faith spectrum jumped into the fray, mostly condemning, very occasionally supporting Boswell's argument. Suddenly, the history of marriage mattered again.

The scholarly controversy about the meaning and import of those ancient ceremonies of same-sex union, and whether they were comparable to marriage, continued to preoccupy historians, theologians, and contemporary polemicists ranging from the editors of *The Advocate* to televangelist Jerry Falwell. As a result of all this attention to the institution of marriage, the public became aware of something of which scholars had long been aware: marriage is a mutable social institution that changes over time and across cultures. For many, this spelled the potential demise of one of the last "foundations" of society. For others, it meant new possibilities for the legalization and legitimization of their affective domestic arrangements.

In Canada, two groups were moving in parallel to challenge exclusionary marriage laws. One group argued that excluding gay and lesbian people from marriage was discriminatory and thus launched a court challenge based on the Canadian Charter of Rights and Freedoms. A second group took quite another tack, focusing on marriage as a religious institution. In Ontario, the usual means to marry legally involved applying for a marriage license and subsequently registering the marriage with provincial authorities. It was at the point of application that clerks were refusing marriage licenses for same-sex couples. A second, lesser known marriage provision, dating from the nineteenth-century, endured in Ontario law. This process invoked the roots and traditions of marriage as a Christian sacrament. If the banns had been proclaimed three times, and a priest or minister had presided at a marriage ceremony, the officiant could then supply the appropriate documentation to the province and the marriage would be registered and recognized under the law.

On 14 January 2001, in the Metropolitan Community Church in Toronto, the Reverend Brent Hawkes, wearing a bullet proof vest under his ecclesiastical vestments, presided at the marriage of two same-sex couples, Kevin Bourassa to Joe Varnell, and Elaine Vautour to Anne Vautour. The banns had been proclaimed on the preceding three Sundays as the press widely reported. When Hawkes tried to register the marriages, the officials refused to do so, and another court case ensued. In a complicated series of decisions and appeals, involving both provincial and federal jurisdictions, during which the rights-based case and the religiously-based case became intertwined, same-sex marriage was upheld. The courts found that the laws that prohibited marriage between people of the same sex violated the Canadian Charter of Rights. The first legal civil union in Canada occurred in 2003, after the original case had worked its way through the various levels of appeal. Adam and Eve were now joined by Adam and Steve.

What is perhaps both startling and fascinating is that reading the banns — a legal innovation from late twelfth-century England that was subsequently implemented across Christendom by the Fourth Lateran Council (1215) and reaffirmed by the Council of Trent (1563) — was central to effecting change to twenty-first-century marriage law. Moreover, the scholarship of John Boswell played a significant role in the affidavits submitted by historians of marriage in support of the application to strike down the exclusionary laws.[2] Whether scholars agreed or disagreed with the finer points of evidence and interpretation, Boswell marshalled sufficient evidence to challenge the notion of marriage as an immutable institution.

The arguments and issues found in the same-sex marriage debates underscore aspects of marriage that are found in the past. Marriage was a flexible institution, then as now. The values and customs surrounding marriage, the institutional structure and purpose of marriage differed across time and culture. In the essays collected here, there are examples of marriage heavily controlled for political and economic reasons or marriage as a source of tension between secular and religious society. We find marriages in which the bride remained a stranger in a strange household and others in which the bride was fully integrated as a trusted member of her new family. Sometimes families controlled the marriage of their children, other times children rebelled. There were economic and political consequences as well as unintended consequences. Nevertheless, although theory and practice could diverge, and there were frequent points of tension between secular and

---

[2] This discussion is based upon personal knowledge as one of the historians who participated in the debates by publishing opinion pieces in the national press that set out the mutability of marriage. In addition, I provided an affidavit, on behalf of the Metropolitan Community Church, that outlined the development of marriage in western history and how it changed over time.

religious values, there was also an underlying foundation provided by the Church and the theology of marriage as a sacrament.

In the premodern world, the formation of the marriage bond required, at its most minimal, only the freely exchanged consent of the couple to marry each other, in words spoken in the present tense. The external manifestations of that consent, which Church and society alike expected to accompany legitimate and socially-sanctioned unions, were summarized and solidified by the Fourth Lateran Council (1215). While upholding the fundamental principle that the consent of the couple alone was the only requirement for a valid and indissoluble marriage, the Council required that the banns be read on three consecutive Sundays in order that friends and family could reveal any impediments to the union and to halt a couple from entering into a false union. The presence of the priest, to witness the couple's exchange of consent rather than to marry them, the exchange of dowry and marriage gifts, and the approbation of parents and kin and friends were all desirable but ultimately unnecessary.[3] Despite these spare requirements for marriage, both Church and society recognized other ceremonial features that characterized nuptials. As early as the ninth century, in his letter to the Bulgarian ruler, Boris I, Pope Nicholas I (r. 858–867) outlined the ceremonial features of Christian marriage. These included the groom placing a ring on the bride's hand, the reception of a marriage veil, and the blessing of the priest,[4] vestiges of which have endured in the west into the twenty-first century.

The Council of Trent considered the sacrament of marriage in Session 24, on 11 November 1563. Chapter 1 of the canons reaffirms the form of marriage that had been developed by the Fourth Lateran Council.[5] Thus, the thirteenth-century guidelines governing the solemnization of marriage passed from the medieval world into the modern world. There were a number of modifications to the earlier canons as well, modifications that had as much to do with temporal considerations as they did with sacramental theology. For example, no longer would the church permit the remarriage of the innocent spouse in cases of adultery and there was less tolerance of concubinage. Some of the impediments to marriage, prohibitions that had been used to great effect by couples (or their families) who wished to dissolve a union, were

---

[3] Tanner, *Decrees of the Ecumenical Councils*, 257–59.

[4] Murray, *Love, Marriage, and the Family in the Middle Ages. A Reader*, 234–41.

[5] Tanner, *Decrees of the Ecumenical Councils*, 755.

narrowed. Most significantly, however, was the Council of Trent's attempt to suppress clandestine marriage.

The medieval Church had taught that the only thing essential to contract a sacramental bond was the free consent of the bride and groom. For the Lateran fathers, the reading of the banns, the presence of witnesses, and a priest's blessing were all desirable but ultimately not required. Urged by secular forces, especially the French contingent, and by the criticism of Protestants who considered such marriages to be scandalous, the Trent fathers introduced modifications, ostensibly to halt the contracting of clandestine marriage. This was a challenge, because the fundamental theology of marriage rested on free consent, something that would not bear tinkering. The decree *Tametsi* marginalized clandestine unions by making it valid but illegal to marry without the appropriate ceremonials, and by stressing that parental consent was essential. In the end, however, the Council of Trent did not dare to challenge the validity of a clandestine union if it had been contracted by free consent.[6] The belief that free consent of the couple alone was the only requirement for marriage was too deeply embedded in sacramental theology to be removed during a period that was experiencing considerable theological challenges.

While in theory and theology marriage might pertain equally to all Christians, the practice of marriage was influenced by multiple considerations: political and social context, rank and wealth, gender and family status. There is a certain irony that the poor and those of modest rank experienced fewer constraints and enjoyed greater freedom to marry.[7] The higher up the socio-economic ladder, the more marriage was viewed as a matter of family or state, with multiple considerations, the least of which was individual choice or personal desire. Elena Woodacre's exploration of the marriage of queens illustrates how problematic marriage was for those at the political pinnacle. Kingdoms and peoples could rise and fall on the choice of a king's consort. Moving across the premodern world, both temporally and geographically, Woodacre reveals the multiple considerations that would inform the selection of a queen's spouse, whether he were a leader in the kingdom, a rival claimant to the throne, or a foreign monarch. Against this backdrop, the reasons for Elizabeth I's decision not to wed are manifestly apparent. The theoretical

---

[6] Brundage, *Law, Sex, and Christian Society in Medieval Europe*, 563–65.

[7] Sheehan, *Marriage, Family and Law in Medieval Europe*, 211–24.

subjection of every wife to her husband threatened to disempower a queen and could destabilize her realm or lead to domestic rebellion or foreign war.

The marriage celebrations that Jennifer Mara DeSilva examines show more complicated ceremonies that bespeak not only a sophisticated development of liturgy and ceremonial since Pope Nicholas I, but also a more intense social activity that joined houses and lineages, nations and princi-palities. These nuptials were more displays of international diplomacy than individual domesticity and affectivity. This was nowhere more evident than among the circle of friends and relatives with ties to the pope. When a pope's niece/nephew or son/daughter married in the Vatican, it raised interesting challenges for those charged to oversee protocol and ceremonials. DeSilva argues that while the Officers of Ceremonials might treat such events as private, and not part of the Vatican's official ceremonies, nevertheless, everything that involved the pope had a public and official aspect to it. It was the responsibil-ity of the Office to ensure there were no improprieties or breaches of protocol and that the appropriate hierarchy was rigidly maintained, a hierarchy in which the pope was always at the top and in which ecclesiastical status was always privileged over secular status. While the marriages of his relatives ex-tended the pope's political and familial ties, as for any member of the secular elite, the Vatican's bureaucrats needed to ensure that such marriages, which capitalized on proximity to the pontiff, did not taint the sacred aura of the papacy.

Among the elite, marriage involved multiple levels of complex-ity. Sally Hickson traces the intricate marriage negotiations of Federico II Gonzaga (1500–1540), negotiations that reveal the difficulties involved in pursuing political and territorial strategies through marriage contracts. Hickson highlights the obstacles and unforeseen events that could complicate marriage strategies in an era of shifting political alliances, early deaths, and multiple and competing interests. The adult Federico was betrothed to a six-year-old Byzantine princess who would bring an important political alliance. According to the ebb and flow of political fortunes, especially in light of the manoeuvring of the French king and the Emperor, Federico petitioned the pope to dissolve the betrothal, and as the political scene again changed, to reinstate it, only to have the bride die before the marriage was concluded. The shifting marriage strategies, involving a large and diverse group of interested parties, reveals how convoluted marriage negotiations could become when personal desire was irrelevant. In the end, however, Hickson reveals how women, although pawns in this marital chess game, could nevertheless use the opportunities that were presented to maximize their positions as widows and regents.

Women's ability to be active participants in the complex world of marriage and family politics is the focus of Elena Brizio's essay. Taking a case study from sixteenth-century Siena, Brizio plumbs the archives to reveal a woman who took control of her own destiny, choosing and marrying a second husband against the will of her family and community. Not only was Maddalena della Gazzaia flouting the conventions of upper class Sienese society which, like all such elites, used marriage as a political and economic tool, but she also defied Sienese patriotism by choosing a Spaniard, a member of the occupying enemy army. Maddalena's behaviour was by no means the norm for women, but she is an important reminder that women, even as they acquiesced to husbands and fathers, were also making their own decisions. The Church's doctrine of free consent to marriage meant that women could reject an undesirable union but also choose a marriage to which others objected. Maddalena della Gazzaia provides an example of how free consent could work in practice.

The focus on women as independent and competent individuals continues in Jamie Smith's examination of the wealth of domestic information found in Genoese notarial records. Smith moves beyond the formation and dissolution of marriage to tease out what the records reveal about marriages and the activities of husbands and wives. Her study reveals that, in defiance of prevailing Roman law, wives were frequently appointed as guardians of their children while their husbands were overseas. Women were clearly considered to be able and astute administrators. Moreover, because they were outsiders who had married into the family, the preference of wives as guardians over a paternal uncle or grandfather (or in concert with them) reveals that wives were fully incorporated into and trusted by their new extended family. This challenges the view that wives were perpetual outsiders, living as strangers in a lineage of strangers.

Exogamic marriage could have multiple manifestations in the premodern world. Most simply it meant marriage between people separated by geography, but exogamy could also be practiced across social, cultural, and economic boundaries. Shennan Hutton explores marriage between patricians and burghers in fourteenth-century Ghent. In this context, the laws that excluded married women from controlling property had not yet hardened and partible inheritance practices meant that women and men inherited equally. Upon marriage both families provided moveable and immoveable property to the couple, who then owned it jointly. As a result of these property considerations, when a Flemish noble family needed a monetary infusion, it sought a match with a wealthy burgher family. Significantly, this pattern crosses gender lines, with both noble men and women marrying burgher spouses.

Katalin Prajda examines the effect of geographic mobility, specifically that of Florentine merchants active in the Kingdom of Hungary. How did prolonged absences affect traditional patterns of endogamy that characterized marriage among the Florentine elite? Prajda examines the marriage and family patterns of a number of merchants, many working abroad in family groupings. Long distance trade did not always disrupt the embedded preference for endogamous marriage, however, in some cases, exogamy could provide a merchant with an entrée into foreign political and economic circles that would not have otherwise been possible. Thus, Florentines who saw the potential afforded by permanent settlement in the Kingdom of Hungary sought local brides. The majority, however, viewed their time in Hungary as temporary and therefore sought stable alliances in Florence, reinforcing the tradition of endogamy among the Florentine elite.

There were many manifestations of exogamy in the premodern world. Economic and social rank was one marker of difference. So, too, was marrying outside one's city or kingdom. Another area of exogamy was across linguistic, ethnic, and religious boundaries. Opportunities of exogamic marriages between Venetians and inhabitants of their overseas holdings could cross multiple differences: Catholic-Orthodox, Greek-Italian or Venetian with various peoples including Byzantine, Cretan, Cypriot and so on. Ersie Burke traces a number of marriages of Greek women to Venetian men, examining how the linguistic and cultural differences might have been managed and how these women, torn from all that was familiar, coped in a new Italian setting. Most women had at least one other female relative who also had married a Venetian and relocated. These women formed extended families based on female ties, in preference to developing relationships with other members of the expatriate Greek community or with their Italian marital families.

P. Renée Baernstein takes the popularity of the story of the rape of the Sabine women as a starting point to examine the exogamic practice of marriage in sixteenth-century Rome. The ancient story foregrounds the practice of Roman men (ancient and premodern) to marry women from outside, rather than to consolidate local ties, as done so well by, for example, the Florentines. Thus, arguably, the Roman nobility was weakened by its practice of marrying their daughters across Italy and introducing new women into Rome. Baernstein examines the marriage of Costanza Colonna to a minor Lombard nobleman and reveals the stresses and strains that could accompany an exogamic marriage. Removed from her family at a young age, Costanza suffered at the hands of her marital family and unsuccessfully sought release from her marriage. Her ability, and that of many women whose marriages took them far away from their natal kin, to maintain ties with her natal family through letters reveals something of how women coped with distance. The letter writing that accompanied inter-regional marriage also helped, argues Baernstein, to establish webs of relationship formed through correspondence and a peninsular ruling class with a similarity of identity, a phenomenon that may have contributed to the evolution of a distinctly Italian culture.

While the careful employment of exogamous marriage was used by elites throughout the premodern world to increase the wealth or political influence of a family, so, too, endogamy was used to consolidate position. This was done brilliantly by the Florentines, less so by the Roman nobility. Heather Parker examines the marriage patterns of the sixteenth-century Scottish family, the Carnegies. At a time when the roil of Scottish politics and the Reformation made ties with the elite critical for navigating the shifting political landscape, as well as for the common aims to increase land and titles, the Carnegies displayed a definite and anomalous preference for endogamous marriages that consolidated relationships with neighbours and kin. This policy, practiced over many years, eventually led to the family receiving the honours and rank that common wisdom would have said accrued to those who engaged in a concerted effort to marry outward and upward. The Carnegies provide a window onto the web of marital alliances at a tumultuous time in Scottish history.

Erin J. Campbell examines the images of older women portrayed in portraits from multigenerational families in Bologna during the latter half of the sixteenth century. The portraits allow a glimpse into life stages that are usually obscured: menopause, sexual abstinence, grand-parenthood, and widowhood past the age of remarriage. Paintings and other representations of older wives and older widows provided matriarchal symbols to families confronting constricting kinships and truncated longevity. Although such older women were demographically rare, their images perpetuated their idealized place in a multigenerational the family.

The relationship between marriage and literary production is examined by Matteo Soranzo in his study of Pontano's adaptation of the elegy form to praise his own marriage. Set against the changing situation in Naples during the later fifteenth century, a period of dominance by the Aragonese, Pontano, a humanist and government bureaucrat, was able to marry into the Neapolitan elite. In his *De amore coniugali*, Pontano celebrates the joys of marriage and the birth of his son, while simultaneously presenting a new type of scholar and poet, which he himself personifies.

Mauro Carboni explores the relationship between marriage, civic identity, and the endurance of oligarchy among aristocratic families in sixteenth- and seventeenth-century Bologna. Through marriage strategies that privileged endogamy and restricted and controlled access to marriage, Bolognese patricians sought to solidify their lineages and access to power and wealth. Ironically, these very patterns that accounted for the strength and longevity of some families, also led to the extinction of others, as fewer marriages resulted in fewer heirs to continue the lineage. Carboni highlights how marriage strategies could have both strengths and weaknesses for the families that employed them. Just as Roman exogamy might have weakened their elite, the Bolognese elite were weakened by endogamy. Neither marriage pattern necessarily produced the expected results. Context and circumstance influenced the outcome of every marriage policy.

Reinier Leushuis focuses his analysis on the formation of the marriage bond in the novellas of the sixteenth-century author and cleric, Matteo Bandello. Leushuis engages in a close, critical reading of how Bandello portrayed his characters exchanging consent to marry and how their unions were formed. Of particular significance is whether or not there was some action to publicize the marriage, reminding us of the commonplace nature of clandestine marriage in this pre-Tridentine context. Leushuis demonstrates that the novellas reflect a shift in the general understanding of marriage. Rather than being a move away from the ecclesiastical view that consent alone formed the sacramental bond to a more secular understanding of marriage, Leushuis argues that the fundamental change to marriage, prior to the Council of Trent, was focused on a move from private marriage to public contracts. Bandello, then, addressed one of the major secular criticisms of ecclesiastical marriage law since the implementation of consensual marriage at the end of the twelfth century.

Lesley Peterson uses three sixteenth-/seventeenth-century tragedies: Christopher Marlowe's *Tamburlaine the Great Part II*, Elizabeth Cary's *The Tragedy of Mariam*, and William Shakespeare's *Winter's Tale*, to investigate the complicated marital relationships between rulers and their wives, women who occupy the role both of queen and captive. By examining women's bodies, in juxtaposition with women's tombs, and the various ways in which a husband is portrayed to memorialize his dead wife, Peterson presents a provocative discussion of Renaissance theatre. Drama reflected the shifting models of marriage, which were informed by discussions of commemoration and anatomical science. How these tragedies portray the fate of queens consort reminds us of Woodacre's caution about the marital dangers that confronted queens regnant. Marriage could be a dangerous prospect for many premodern women across geography, class, and era, in life as well as in art.

William E. Smith III explores the problematic marriage(s) of Anne Wentworth, as portrayed in several of her spiritual and autobiographical writings. Wentworth was an anomaly. A victim of domestic violence from her unpleasant husband, she may have sought spiritual or psychological relief through a mystical marriage with Jesus. Sadly, by her own account, Jesus, too, was demanding and violent with Wentworth, so divine polyandry scarcely provided a refuge from earthy mistreatment, but it did provide a justification for public preaching. Wentworth provides a glimpse of marriage in turmoil and a society which firmly looked the other way in the face of domestic violence and psychological or spiritual damage. While she lived in a very different world, there is much in her disastrous marriage that would resonate with women from an earlier period, be it Marjorie Kempe, who also sought solace with a heavenly husband, or Godelieve of Ghistelle, canonized as a martyr as a result of violence and brutal murder by her husband.

The essays gathered in this volume reveal premodern marriage in its richness and complexity. Rarely are the situations so simple that marriages conform to the ecclesiastical values of canon law and theology. Similarly, the political or economic marriage strategies deployed by families varied widely and frequently went awry. And despite the concurrence of Church and society, independent-minded people were found following individual desires rather that the prescriptions of family, Church, and society. Therein lies the connection between past and present: marriage was and is a mutable institution that is manifest in myriad forms.

University of Guelph

Cited Works

Boswell, John. *Same-Sex Unions in Premodern Europe*. New York: Villard, 1994.

Brundage, James A. *Law, Sex, and Christian Society in Medieval Europe*. Chicago: University of Chicago, 1987.

Murray, Jacqueline. *Love, Marriage, and the Family in the Middle Ages. A Reader*. Toronto: Broadview Press, 2001.

Sheehan, Michael M. "Theory and Practice: Marriage of the Unfree and the Poor in Medieval Society" in Michael M. Sheehan, *Marriage, Family and Law in Medieval Europe. Collected Studies*, ed. James K. Farge. Toronto: Pontifical Institute of Mediaeval Studies, 1996.

Tanner, Norman P. *Decrees of the Ecumenical Councils*. London: Sheed and Ward, 1990, vol.1.

The Queen's Marriage: Matrimonial Politics in Pre-Modern Europe

Elena Crislyn Woodacre

Matrimonial politics always played a vital role in building alliances and securing the frontiers of a realm, but the marriage of a sovereign, male or female, was an especially significant diplomatic opportunity. It was crucially important for a sovereign to marry in order to ensure dynastic continuity and secure the succession to the realm. In the case of a female sovereign, the process of choosing a marriage partner was charged with additional significance, as there was an expectation, or perhaps a fear, that the queen's husband would wield power and influence in his wife's realm. As Charles Beem notes, "a man would naturally enjoy a position of strength in the royal marriage, in accordance with contemporary understandings of the relations of power between man and wife".[1] Arguably the most important factors in the reign of a female sovereign were her access to and exercise of power, her marriage (with the obvious exception of the unmarried Elizabeth I of England) and the internal and external political situation. These factors were interdependent, as a queen's ability to access and exercise power was profoundly affected by the personal and political relationship that she formed with her king consort. In addition, the selection of the queen's husband was closely linked to the internal and external political situation. Thus, the selection of a king consort could have significant positive or negative consequences for the realm. The right choice could bring considerable benefits such as new territory, a strengthening alliance, a powerful commander for the army and an able partner to rule alongside the queen. The wrong choice, however, could bring disastrous results, for example embroiling the country in war with its neighbours or destabilizing the realm internally, if the husband was unpopular with the queen's subjects or the queen and her consort could not form a harmonious personal and political partnership.

---

[1] Beem, *The Lioness Roared*, 85. See also Sommerville, *Sex and Subjection*, for an excellent discussion of the balance of power between a queen regnant and her consort.

Although marriage in the pre-modern period has been thoroughly explored by such scholars as Georges Duby and Christopher Brooke and the field of queenship studies has produced many valuable insights on the rule of women, the key connection between marriage and queens regnant has not been directly assessed, particularly with regard to diplomatic strategy and the impact of the marriages themselves.[2] This essay bridges the study of marriage and queenship through an exploration of the selection of a queen's husband and a discussion of the accompanying diplomatic strategies. It draws from a wide range of examples from the pre-modern period that highlight some of the ramifications of this important decision.

The selection process for a matrimonial candidate is depicted in the flow chart (Figure 1.1, p. 44), which reveals the important considerations and choices that informed the selection process. The first crucial consideration was whether to seek an internal or external candidate. An internal candidate could help a queen to consolidate her power by forging a marital alliance with another powerful family. One strategy employed during the pre-modern period, was for the queen or heiress to marry a member of a collateral branch of the family, uniting two sometimes opposing claims to the throne. The drawback to this strategy was the likelihood that consanguinity would require a papal dispensation. A further disadvantage was that such a union did not forge a strategic foreign alliance or add additional territory to the realm. However, this endogamous strategy could be successful. One example from the seventeenth century is that of William of Orange and Mary Stuart, where a female heiress married her first cousin, who was the nearest male claimant to the throne. The consolidation of their claims ensured that William would not emerge as a rival if Mary ascended the throne, and it put the couple in a strong position to oust Mary's father, James II, after the controversial birth of her half-brother. Such a strategy was also deployed successfully in cases where there were both male and female claimants to a throne, as in the late-fourteenth-century example of Katherine of Lancaster and Henry III of Castile or the marriage of Henry VII and Elizabeth of York at the end of the

---

[2] Duby's important work on medieval marriage includes *The Knight, the Lady and the Priest* and Brooke's *The Medieval Idea of Marriage* is another insightful examination. Both touch briefly on the marriages of queens but only in the context of their wider discussions of the marriages of heiresses. See also Holt, "The Heiress and the Alien".

fifteenth century.[3] These marriages combined rival claims and brought an end to civil war.

The strategy to unite rival claimants was not universally successful. Giovanna I of Naples was betrothed to her cousin, Andrew of Hungary, in an attempt to unite two branches of the House of Anjou. The marriage ended with Andrew's murder in 1345, in which Giovanna was implicated.[4] In the sixteenth century, Mary Queen of Scots was similarly accused of involvement in the murder of her husband, Lord Darnley, a close cousin with a reasonable claim to both the Scottish and English thrones. This dynastic link had made Darnley a particularly attractive prospect as consort. His dynastic claims dramatically bolstered the rights of both his wife, Mary, and their son, James, both north and south of the border.[5] The cases of Mary and Giovanna highlight one of the problems with this strategy; to marry someone who also had a strong claim to the throne could be dangerous if the relationship between the partners deteriorated, as occurred in these cases. Both consorts were accused of drinking to excess and behaving badly. Moreover, both men were dissatisfied with their position and posed a potential threat to their wife's power. This placed both Mary and Giovanna in a no-win situation, being lumbered with a powerful and poisonous consort, or getting rid of him and coping with the fallout. In Mary's case, the death of Darnley was arguably one of the factors that precipitated the loss of her throne. In Giovanna's case, Andrew's murder triggered war with his brother, Louis of Hungary. Although she was able to hold on to her throne for nearly forty years, Giovanna was reportedly killed by strangulation, exactly as her first husband had been, perhaps as a deliberate allusion to her role in Andrew's death.[6]

---

[3] For the case of Elizabeth of York see, Chamberlayne, "Crowns and virgins," 50–51. Regarding Katherine of Lancaster see O'Callaghan, *Medieval Spain*, 534.

[4] Léonard, *Les Angevins*, 316–320. Many chronicles, such as the *Chronicon Estense* and Domenico da Gravina's *Chronicon de rebus in Apulia gestis* either blatantly accuse or at least allude to Giovanna's involvement in the crime. Machiavelli is perhaps the most direct in his accusation, stating simply that "she caused him to be murdered". See *Chronicon Estense*, 132; Domenico da Gravina, *Chronicon de rebus in Apulia gestis*, 16; and *History of Florence*, Book I, Chapter VI.

[5] Darnley's claim to the Scottish throne was through his father, Matthew Lennox, the 4th Earl of Lennox. Mary's biographer John Guy also discusses the attractiveness of Darnley's English claim in *My Heart is my own*, 194–195, 199 and 201.

[6] Opfell, *Queens*, 13.

The other internal option available to a queen was to marry a member of a noble family within the kingdom. However, while this strategy had the advantage of consolidating power within the realm, it also precluded a strategic foreign alliance or the addition of territory. An added disadvantage was that it might result in jealousy among other noble houses because one family was elevated over the others. This might create factions that could destabilize the realm or lead to civil war. Jean Bodin highlighted this potential danger:

> Should the sovereign princess marry, as she must do to secure the succession, she must marry either a subject or a foreigner. If a subject, it is a great abasement for a princess to marry one other servants, seeing that the greatest sovereign princes in the world have found all sorts of difficulties follow marriage to a subject. There is besides the risk of the envy and jealousy of great and powerful nobles, in the contempt they always feel for men of inferior station, if she insists on marrying the man of her preference …[7]

Opposition to internal matches is seen in the marriage of Mary, Queen of Scots to James Hepburn, the Earl of Bothwell, and also in the resistance to Elizabeth I's apparent desire to wed her childhood friend, Robert Dudley, the Earl of Leicester. Dudley was the focus of repeated literary attacks in such works as "A Treatice of Treasons" (1572), "A Letter of Estate" and "Leicester's Commonwealth #1"(both 1584) which describe him as "a man of such spirit as he is known to be, of so extreme ambition, pride, falsehood and treachery."[8] Even after his death, in 1588, the attacks continued in "News from Heaven and Hell" (1588) and "Leicester's Ghost"(1603).[9] Although Leicester made enemies at court because of his political views, the root cause of the rancour towards him was his position as the Queen's favourite and his ambition to become her consort in fact, instead of merely in rumour. The source of the problem with marriages internal to the realm, was that the queen would nec-

---

[7] Bodin, *Six Books of the Commonwealth*, Book VI, Chapter V.

[8] 'Leicester's Commonwealth', 9.

[9] All of the aforementioned works are mostly likely the work of Edward de Vere, Earl of Oxford. They can be found at The Oxford Authorship Site, http://www.oxfordshakespeare.com/leicester.html.

essarily marry beneath her and, as Margaret Sommerville notes, this would give "excessive influence to a man not born to be king."[10] Indeed, for a reigning queen, hypergamy was virtually impossible, and to marry a man of equal rank, she had only one option, an external match.

The advantages of an exogamous marriage derived from the resultant foreign alliance, which could bring prestige, strength, security and, possibly, additional territory. The negative aspect was that the queen's husband would be a foreigner, who might be viewed with suspicion or outright hostility by the nobility. A common fear, that was often realized, was that a foreign husband might put the needs of his homeland above those of his wife and her country. In 1515 Claude de Seyssel discussed this danger at length and used it as a means to argue against female rule:[11]

> ... for by falling into the feminine line it can come into the power of a foreigner, a pernicious and dangerous thing, since a ruler from a foreign nation is of a different rearing and condition, of difference customs, different language, and a different way of life from the man of the lands he comes to rule. He ordinarily, therefore, wishes to advance those of his nation...he always has more love for and faith in them and so conforms more to their customs and ways than to the customs of the land to which he has newly come, whence there always follows envy and dissension between the natives and the foreigners and indignation against the princes ...[11]

The most prestigious alliance was for a queen to contract with a king, in a marriage of relative equality. However, this type of match usually resulted in the effective merger of two realms which could compromise their individual independence. The advantage of union with a neighbour was the potential to create a larger, more powerful state, as in the case of the marriage between Isabel of Castile and Ferdinand of Aragon in 1469. Their marriage united Spain and, although it was initially controversial, their partnership was successful on a personal as well as a political level, as they negotiated a balance of power, reflected in their motto, ("Tanto monta, monta tanto — Isabel como

---

[10] Sommerville, *Sex and Subjection*, 58.

[11] de Seyssel, *The Monarchy of France*, 48–49.

Fernando", "Each is worth as much as the other — Isabel as Ferdinand").[12] The same strategy had been employed unsuccessfully in Iberia almost four hundred years earlier, when in 1109 Urraca of Léon-Castile married Alfonso of Aragon and Navarre. This strategic marital alliance was intended to unite the Christian kingdoms of Spain but, instead, resulted in a brutal civil war between the spouses. Their marriage had been unpopular with the pope, the Castilian nobility and the queen, herself. After a rocky few years, punctuated by marital disputes, allegations of spousal abuse and homosexuality, in 1112, the couple separated, after a last-ditch attempt to reconcile failed. The former spouses then spent most of the next five years at war to decide which of them would rule the kingdoms they had once ruled together.[13]

Another Iberian example, with mixed results, was the marriage of Juana I, Queen of Navarre to Philip IV of France. Juana had succeeded to the throne of Navarre as an infant, in 1274, but her mother had fled with her to the court of France to escape the dual pressures of internal upheaval and threatening neighbours. A marriage with the son of the French king brought key support, which enabled Juana to retain her throne, and brought to France her Pyrenean kingdom, as well as her large and rich county of Champagne. As Queen of France, however, Juana was not free to return to her own kingdom and Navarre became a French appendage, administered by governors who were directed from Paris, although she did retain some involvement in the governance of Champagne.[14] Navarre became increasingly unhappy under French rule, first by Juana's husband, later by her sons. Ironically, it was the advent of another queen regnant, in 1328, her granddaughter, Juana II, which eventually freed Navarre from French domination.

This case highlights the difficulty of marriage between two sovereigns, but it could pertain whenever a queen regnant married a consort with lands of his own. Ultimately, it was a question of whose lands would receive the bulk of attention and direct administration by the ruling couple. There was no guarantee that a queen's realm would take precedence over her

---

[12] See Weissberger, "Tanto monta" for an in-depth analysis of the use of this motto and the official symbolism of the *Reyes Católicos*. Weissberger argues in this piece that the motto, "*Tanto monta*" did not reflect the reality of the couple's power-sharing dynamic given Isabel clearly had the upper hand as the ruler of the stronger nation, Castile.

[13] Reilly, *Queen Urraca*; see chapters two and three for thorough coverage of the disastrous marriage and the war which followed.

[14] Lalou, "*Le gouvernement*," 16–30.

husband's lands, even if her title and rank were superior. For example, Juana II of Navarre divided her time between her own court, in Pamplona, and the lands of her husband, Philippe, Count of Evreux. To balance the needs of several counties in Northern France with those of a Pyrenean kingdom required the ruling couple to juggle competing priorities, which negated some of the benefits that accrued to the queen from the additional territory that her husband brought to the Navarrese crown.

Even when the additional lands were in close proximity, territorial expansion could bring difficulties, along with prestige and wealth. The matrimonial alliance of the last reigning Queen of Navarre, Catalina, illustrates this problem. Catalina's marriage to Jean d'Albret, in 1484, was unpopular with her Iterian subjects and neighbours, although it significantly increased the frontiers of Navarre. The addition of the Albret holdings swelled the frontiers of the kingdom to approximately 55,000 square kilometres and increased Navarre's size and enhanced its strategic location in the Pyrenees.[15] Although the disparate territories were united under one crown, each continued to prize its regional traditions and independence. Catalina's subjects spoke several different languages and even used different dating systems on either side of the Pyrenees.[16] Ultimately, the Queen was unable to unify her lands, or reconcile the different political goals of her Iberian and French subjects, and the territorial amalgamation became unstable. This weakness was one of the key factors that led to the annexation of the Iberian portion of the kingdom of Navarre (by Ferdinand of Aragon) in 1512.

Given the potential downside of territorial expansion through marriage, it is unsurprising that some queens regnant chose landless husbands. The marriage of Melisende of Jerusalem and Fulk of Anjou, in the mid twelfth century, might well illustrate the ideal arrangement. Fulk's administrative and military experience, as the seasoned ruler of Anjou, were the qualities that recommended him as king consort. William of Tyre described Fulk as "a powerful prince ... very successful in ruling his own people" and acknowledged Fulk to be "an experienced warrior full of patience and wisdom in military affairs."[17] Another important factor was Fulk's diplomatic connections. He had also made a positive impression on the Crusader lords, during his previous stay in the Kingdom of Jerusalem, due to

---

[15] Boissonnade, *Histoire de la Réunion*, 117.

[16] Anthony, "Un élément de critique," 26–32.

[17] Tyre, *Historia*, 512.

his affable personality and his ability to maintain a large retinue. While his experience, wealth and connections were desirable, his lands in far-off Anjou were not. The marriage contract stipulated that Fulk had to transfer his French possessions to his son, Geoffrey, and commit to remaining permanently in the Kingdom of Jerusalem.[18]

Fulk's experience and his diplomatic connections, both in Europe and the Latin East, were key to his suitability as king consort and compensated for the fact that he could not add territories to the Crusader kingdom. A landless husband, without these valuable intangible assets, risked ridicule. Guy de Lusignan, the husband of a later Queen of Jerusalem, Sibylla, was considered a poor choice to be king consort. William of Tyre claims that Sibylla's brother, King Baldwin IV, could have procured a better husband for her, "He [King Baldwin IV] might have found in the kingdom nobles of far greater importance, wisdom and even wealth, both foreigners and natives, an alliance with any one of whom would have been an advantage to the kingdom."[19] Guy, unlike Sibylla's previous husband and carefully selected fiancés, was not a wealthy, powerful and well-connected lord, but only one of the many sons of Hugh le Brun, a middling French baron. Sibylla and Guy's controversial marriage was widely considered to be a waste of the diplomatic opportunity to procure a politically powerful consort, whose accession would have brought political, military, and financial support to shore up the beleaguered kingdom.

The younger sons of a royal or noble house were not always considered a bad match for a queen. Frequently, they were a desirable option, particularly if they brought diplomatic alliances or additional territory, without the imperative to merge with another realm. Freed from the need to govern their own lands, in theory they could help the queen to rule her kingdom, as her personal and political partner. Carlos III of Navarre chose a younger son to marry his daughter and heiress, Blanca, in 1420. The Infante Juan was the second son of the King of Aragon and appeared a good choice to solidify the alliance between Navarre and Aragon. Juan was also heavily dowered with the impressive territories of his mother, the great heiress, Leonor de Albuquerque. These lands bestowed upon him many titles including Duke of Peñafiel, Count of Mayorga, Lord of Medina del Campo, Briones, Castrojeriz, Haró and other important towns, making him a thoroughly respectable

---

[18] Mayer, "Succession," 141.

[19] Tyre, *Historia*, 446.

consort.[20] However, the diplomatic and territorial benefits of this alliance were undone by Juan's actions, when he drew Navarre into a devastating war against Castile, a war that was largely of his own making.

An example of a more helpful younger son, as a queen's consort, is George of Denmark, husband of Anne Stuart, who became Queen of England in 1702. George was unencumbered by his own foreign territories, and was not a likely heir to the Danish throne, key aspects of his suitability as a royal spouse. John Macky has highlighted this, claiming that, "having no dominions of his own to gratify, he [George] would have nothing else in view but the interest of England."[21] George was lacked political ambition and was more than willing to let his wife reign, famously claiming "I am her Majesty's subject...I shall do naught but what she commands me."[22]

Popular disapproval of foreign betrothals for royal heiresses could cause plans for diplomatic alliances and ordered succession to go awry. Louis of Anjou ruled the united kingdoms of Hungary and Poland in the late fourteenth century. Although he was unsuccessful in seizing the kingdom of Naples from his cousin, Giovanna I, he continued to exercise his ambition through matrimonial politics. Louis contracted strategic marriages for all three of his daughters; Catherine was betrothed to Louis of France, Maria to Sigismund of Luxembourg and Jadwiga to Wilhelm of Austria. Sigismund and Wilhelm both traveled to Hungary in order to seal their betrothals formally. Somewhat unusually, both fiancés remained in the Hungarian court, with their future wives, for the duration of their youth.[23] The eldest daughter, Catherine, died in 1378 and, lacking a son to succeed him, Louis designated his other two daughters, Maria and Jadwiga, as his heirs. Louis died in 1382, leaving the future of his two young daughters uncertain. Factions formed, favouring the accession of different princesses, or of alternative dynasties. Although Maria was formally invested with the Hungarian crown, as queen regnant, a group of Hungarian nobles, who opposed her accession and her marriage to Sigismund, summoned her cousin, Charles of Durazzo, to claim the throne. Maria was ousted by her cousin and forced to witness his coronation in 1386.[24] Maria regained her place after Charles was murdered,

---

[20] Highfield, *Spain*, 127.

[21] Macky, "Characters of the Court," 2.

[22] Cockburn, *Essay*, 10.

[23] Opfell, *Queens*, 14.

[24] Wolf, "Reigning Queens ," 173–174.

only to be captured and imprisoned in Dalmatia. By the time she was released, her husband, Sigismund, was entrenched as the ruler of Hungary and Maria "had to make do with the role of queen consort."[25]

In Poland, some nobles favoured the accession of Maria's husband, Sigismund, while others preferred her younger, as yet unmarried sister, Jadwiga. A third party favoured the election of the scion of a rival house.[26] Ultimately, Jadwiga's candidacy was successful: she was crowned in on Wawel Hill in Cracow on 15 October 1384.[27] Although, they had accepted Jadwiga as their queen, the Poles were not universally amenable to her Hapsburg fiancé. Wilhelm's arrival in Cracow was hailed by the German residents of the city, but the Castellan of Cracow castle forcibly prevented him from reaching his bride.[28] The young queen was informed that her betrothal was annulled and she was coerced into marriage with Jagiello of Lithuania, a pagan prince who was three times her age. Their marriage, which took place in 1385, ensured the conversion of Jagiello's subjects to Christianity and formed the basis for the union between Poland and Lithuania, a union that lasted 186 years, despite the fact Jagwiga died young and childless.

Finally, marriage negotiations, in and of themselves, were useful exercises to build diplomatic alliances, even if the marriage did not come to fruition. The most famous example of this tactic is Elizabeth I of England, who used the possibility of her marriage as an effective diplomatic tool for decades. Susan Doran counters the view that the negotiations were a smokescreen, concealing Elizabeth's intention to rule alone.[29] Whatever the queen's personal views towards marriage, Elizabeth was able to counter internal pressure to marry and build diplomatic bridges abroad by conducting a series of marital negotiations. Ultimately, however, the queen remained unmarried, although whether this was due to personal preference, the lack of an ideal candidate or the failure to contract an alliance is open to conjecture.

Elizabeth was not the only master of marital politics. In the twelfth century, the Byzantine emperor, Manuel I Comnenus, made the most of his family gambits, on both the domestic and international marriage markets,

---

[25] Molnár and Maygar, *Hungary*, 55.

[26] Davies, *God's Playground*, 112.

[27] Davies, *God's Playground*, 117.

[28] Opfell discusses a number of different versions of Wilhelm's arrival in various chronicles. See Opfell, *Queens*, 19–20.

[29] Doran, *Monarchy and Matrimony*, 1.

to contract alliances. Manuel's daughter, Maria, was his primary pawn for negotiations, since, for most of her childhood, she was the imperial heiress.[30] A total of five betrothals were made and broken on Maria's behalf, over the course of twenty five years. Nicetas Choniates described the adult Maria as, "The maiden, a princess wooed by many, was like Agamemnon's daughter Electra raving long in the palace and, stately as a white poplar wet with dew, longing for the marriage bed."[31] Manuel rejected the possibility of a domestic match to prevent the imperial throne from passing into the control of another family. However, he pursued a number of different foreign marriage strategies. Overall, Manuel appears to have placed more importance on forming a strategic alliance than on whether the potential bridegroom was an eldest or younger son or had valuable territory. As in the case of Elizabeth, it was the means rather than the end that was important. Manuel used the process of negotiation, often deliberately protracted, as a way to attain his objectives in international relations. Even when negotiations were unsuccessful, the impressive gifts delivered by the Imperial envoys enhanced Manuel's reputation for great wealth and generosity.[32] As the political situation and his own policy objectives changed, he was willing to break off engagements in his search for the best possible alliance for the Empire. Manuel employed this course of action as long as possible, until Maria had lost a great deal of value on the marriage market, being almost thirty and having lost her place as heiress, due to the birth of a younger brother, before she finally married.[33]

Successful matrimonial negotiations resulted in a series of binding legal documents, termed marriage agreements, contracts or capitulations. Negotiations for the marriage of an heiress were often finely balanced on a clear statement of the bride's position as there was a significant difference in the marital value of an heiress as opposed to a princess. During the negotiations of his marriage to Melisende of Jerusalem, Fulk of Anjou demanded that she be officially recognized as her father's heir.[34] Accordingly, Melisende began to appear prominently in the charters of the kingdom as the king's designated

---

[30] Kinnamos, *Deeds*, 94.

[31] Choniates, *Byzantium*, 97.

[32] Ciggaar, *Western Travellers*, 88.

[33] Maria was finally married to Renier of Montferrat in a lavish double wedding with her younger half-brother Alexis and his bride Agnes of France in early 1180.

[34] Mayer, "Succession," 143–144.

heir, listed her as "filia regis et regni Ierosolimitani haeres" ("daughter of the king and heir to the kingdom of Jerusalem").[35]

Another marriage contact, that clearly delineates the position of the bride as the heiress of the realm, was drawn up for the betrothal of Juana of Navarre and Henry, the son of Edward I of England, in 1273.[36] At this point, both children were heirs to their respective kingdoms, and their position is clearly stated in the opening paragraphs. Henry is described as the eldest son and heir: "Henrico, filio primogenito & hæredi præfati Edwardi Regis Angliæ" ("Henry, first born son and heir of the aforesaid Edward King of England"). For his part, Enrique I of Navarre confirmed Juana as the heir to his throne and his French counties of Champagne and Brie: "Johanna, filia nostra nobis succedat, & fit hæres in Regno Navarræ, Comitatibus Campaniæ & Briæ, & in aliis bonis nobis" ("Juana, our daughter will succeed us and is heiress in the Kingdom of Navarre, the Counties of Champagne and Brie and of all our possessions"). Moreover, the contract contained a provision for an alternative monetary dowry for Juana should her father sire a son who would replace her in the line of succession. While Juana did succeed to the throne of Navarre a year later, in 1274, the projected marriage to the English prince never occurred, and Juana eventually married the heir of the King of France.

Another key factor in marriage negotiations was the role that the consort was expected, or not expected, to play in the governance of his wife's kingdom. This was often clearly defined in the marriage contract; however, forcing a consort to adhere to this agreement after the queen's accession was another matter entirely. Giovanna II of Naples attempted to clarify the position of her second husband, Jacques de Bourbon, before their marriage. In 1415, however, once he arrived in Italy, he was quick to press his advantage in an attempt to usurp his wife's authority. As Machiavelli reports:

> [The queen] took for her husband Giacopo della Marca, a Frenchman of the royal line, on the condition that he should be content to be called Prince of Taranto, and leave to her the

---

[35] Röhricht, *Regesta regni Hierosolymitani*, No.137a. Also cited in Mayer, "Succession," 144. Mayer also argues that Fulk's insistence that Melisende was officially recognized as heiress was tied to the similar recognition of the Empress Matilda as Henry I of England's heir (146).

[36] Rymer, *Foedera*, 18 Archivo General de Navarra, Comptos, Cojón 3, no. 65, dated 30 November 1273 at Bonloc.

title and government of the kingdom. But the soldiery, upon his arrival in Naples, proclaimed him king; so that between the husband and the wife wars ensued; and although they contended with varying success, the queen at length obtained the superiority.[37]

In an attempt to avert this kind of martial dispute, the agreements signed before the marriage of Blanca, heiress of Navarre, to Juan of Aragon, in 1420, were thorough and clear on nearly every possible topic.[38] Blanca's position as heiress was strongly reaffirmed, and her father, Carlos III, promised not to sire any other heirs who might take away her position as "heredera universal."[39] The *capitulaciones* stressed that it was Blanca, not Juan, who had the right to inherit the throne; his position as *rey consorte* and an *extranjero* or foreigner was clearly delineated. Moreover, Juan was admonished not go against the wishes of his wife, the Queen, and he was prohibited from giving away castles, fortresses or territories to foreigners or permitting the annexation of the realm. The future succession was also discussed. If Blanca died without heirs, Juan was expressly excluded from succeeding to the crown and would be forced to leave Navarre, presumably to prevent him from attempting rule in his own right. Ironically, a later codicil in Blanca's will allowed Juan to remain on the throne after her death, flouting the marriage agreement and supplanting their three grown children.

Nearly fifty years later, Juan's son from his second marriage, Ferdinand of Aragon, also married a queen regnant, Isabel of Castile. Juan was involved in drafting the capitulations for his son's marriage. These agreements were initially signed in 1469, but were revised twice before the final version was signed, in 1475.[40] Given the fact that both bride and groom were reigning sovereigns, the documents affirmed the individual rights of each spouse, in their own realm, and set specific limits on the powers and rights they would

[37] Machiavelli, *History of Florence*, Bk. 1, chapt. 7. Note that Machiavelli has apparently combined her husband's name and original title (Jacques de Bourbon, Count of La Marche) and given it an Italian equivalent resulting in "Giacopo della Marca".

[38] The *capitulaciones matrimoniales*, Archivo General de Navarra, Comptos, Cajón 105, no. 1-2, were signed on 5 November 1419 at Olite. Castro Alava, "Blanca," 51.

[39] Both Castro Alava and Eloísa Ramírez Vaquero have done a detailed analysis of the capitulations. See Castro Alava, "Blanca," 51–55 and Ramírez Vaquero, *Blanca y Juan*, 69–73.

[40] Weissberger, "*Tanto monta*," 51.

have in their spouse's kingdom. These accords, termed "one of the most famous prenuptial agreements in history," became the foundation of both their marriage and, undoubtedly, their successful political partnership.[41]

The marriage of Isabel and Ferdinand's granddaughter, Queen Mary I of England, was also subject to a complex series of negotiations concerning the position of her husband, Philip of Spain. These negotiations were concluded in November 1553, and Charles Beem argues that the result was "a form of pre-nuptial agreement that sought statutorily to pre-empt Philip's rights to any aspect of his wife's royal prerogative."[42] Philip was barred from many aspects of government, including making appointments, and was specifically prohibited from taking his wife out of England without her consent or taking her jewels.[43] The agreement, however, was not enough to allay public fears about the Queen's marriage to the Spanish prince. Accordingly, Mary's role as hereditary reigning sovereign was further defined and strengthened in the "Act Concerning Regal Power," in early 1554. Ultimately, however, the marriage between Philip and Mary proved to be ill-starred, both personally and politically, although the marriage contract did provide a lasting exemplar which was used as the basis for the negotiations in Elizabeth's subsequent marital diplomacy.[44]

This survey of the marriages of pre-modern queens regnant has examined wide ranging and diverse examples in order to evaluate larger developments in matrimonial diplomacy. Although the experience of queenship itself varied considerably during the time period under consideration, from the early twelfth century to the beginning of the eighteenth century and was significantly influenced by local and regional factors, the fundamental considerations that informed the selection of a husband for a female sovereign applied to each of the queens discussed here. There were a number of diplomatic strategies that could be employed in negotiations for the marriage of a queen, all of which had both pitfalls and advantages: no single strategy was consistently effective. A pre-nuptial contract, that clearly defined the position of the consort in the kingdom, was a key area for negotiation and could allay concerns about the marriage and provide a good foundation for a couple's political partnership. However, even

---

[41] Earenfight, "Two Bodies," 11.

[42] Beem, *Lioness*, 89.

[43] Redworth, "Male and Female Monarchy," 598.

[44] Beem, *Lioness*, 98.

though they were crucially important, matrimonial politics, no matter how effectively conducted, could not guarantee that a female sovereign would enjoy a successful reign. Ultimately, the long term success of the reigns, and of the marriages, of queens regnant was determined by three factors: brokering a beneficial alliance, the internal and external political situation and the personal compatibility of the spouses.

BATH SPA UNIVERSITY

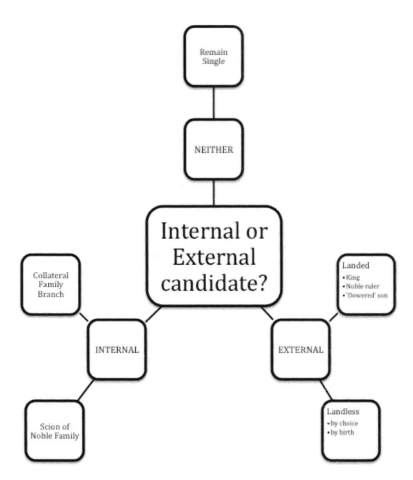

1.1   Marriage flow chart.

CITED WORKS

Anon. *Chronicon Estense, cum additamentis usque ad annum 1478*, eds. Giulio Bertoni and Emilio Paolo Vicini. Rerum Italicum Scriptores, 15:3. 2 vols. Città di Castello: S. Lapi, 1908–37.

Anon., "Leicester's Commonwealth" (1584), "A Treatise of Treasons" (1572), "A Letter of Estate" (1584), "News from Heaven and Hell' (1588), Leicester's Ghost" (1603). Accessed at The Oxford Authorship Site, http://www.oxford-shakespeare.com/leicester.html.

Anthony, R. "Un élément de critique chronologique á propos de documents émanant de la reine de Navarre Catherine de Foix." *Le Moyen Age* 4:1 (1933): 26–32.

Beem, Charles. *The Lioness Roared: The Problems of Female Rule in English History.* New York: Palgrave MacMillan, 2008.

Bodin, Jean. *Six Books of the Commonwealth. (Les Six livres de la République).* Trans. M. J. Tooley. Oxford: Blackwell, 1955. Available electronically at http://www.constitution.org/bodin/bodin_.htm.

Boissonnade, Pierre. *Histoire de la Réunion de la Navarre a la Castille (Essai sur les Relations de prince de Foix-Albret avec la France et l'Espagne).* Geneva: Slatkine-Megariotis Reprints, 1975.

Brooke, Christopher N.L. *The Medieval Idea of Marriage.* Oxford: Oxford University Press, 1989.

Castro Alava, José Ramón. "Blanca de Navarra y Juan de Aragón." *Principe de Viana* 27 (1966): 47–63.

Chamberlayne, Joanna L. "Crowns and virgins: Queenmaking During the Wars of the Roses." In *Young Medieval Women*, eds. Katherine J. Lewis, Noel James Menuge and Kim M. Phillips. Stroud: Sutton Publishing, 1999, 47–68.

Choniates, Nicetas, *O City of Byzantium*, trans. Harry J. Magoulias. Detroit: Wayne State University Press, 1984.

Ciggaar, Krijnie N. *Western Travellers to Constantinople. The West and Byzantium, 962–1204: Culture and Political Relations.* Leiden: E.J. Brill, 1996.

Cockburn, William. *An Essay Upon the Propitious and Glorious Reign of Our Gracious Sovereign Anne.* Printed for the author, and sold by the booksellers of London and Westminster. London, 1710.

da Gravina, Domenico. *Chronicon de rebus in Apulia gestis ab anno MCCCXXXIII usque ad annum MCCCL*, ed. Arbano Sorbelli. Rerum Italicum Scriptores, 21, 24, 70. Città di Castello: S. Lapi, 1903–09.

Davies, Norman. *God's Playground; A History of Poland*. Vol. 1, *The Origins to 1795*. Oxford: Clarendon Press, 1981.

de Seyssel, Claude. *The Monarchy of France*. trans. J.H. Hexter and Michael Sherman, ed. Donald R. Kelley. New Haven: Yale University Press, 1981.

Doran, Susan. *Monarchy and Matrimony. The Courtships of Elizabeth I*. London: Routledge, 1996.

Duby, Georges. *The Knight, the Lady and the Priest; The making of modern marriage in Medieval France*, trans. Barbara Bray. New York: Pantheon Books, 1983.

Earenfight, Theresa. "Two Bodies, One Spirit: Isabel and Fernando's Construction of Monarchical Partnership." In *Queen Isabel I of Castile; Power, Personage, Persona*, ed. Barbara F. Weissberger. Woodbridge: Tamesis, 2008, 3–18.

Guy, John. *My Heart is My Own; The Life of Mary, Queen of Scots*. London: Harper Perennial, 1994.

Highfield, Roger. *Spain in the Fifteenth Century, 1369–1516. Essays and Extracts by Historians of Spain*. London: Harper and Row, 1972.

Holt, J.C. "Feudal Society and the Family in Early Modern England: IV. The Heiress and the Alien." *Transactions of the Royal Historical Society* 35.5 (1985): 1–28.

Kinnamos, John. *Deeds of John and Manuel Comnenus*, trans. Charles M. Brand. New York: Columbia University Press, 1976.

Lalou, Elisabeth. "Le gouvernement de la reine Jeanne 1285–1305." *Cahiers Haut-Marnais* 167 (1986): 16–30.

Léonard, Émile G. *Les Angevins de Naples*. Paris: Presses Universitaires de France, 1954.

Machiavelli, Niccolò. *The History of Florence and of the Affairs of Italy from the Earliest Times to the Death of Lorenzo the Magnificent*. (1525) Full text (English) version online at http://ebooks.adelaide.edu.au/m/machiavelli/niccolo/m149h/.

Macky, John. "Characters of the Court of Great Britain." In *Memoirs of the Secret Services of John Macky, esq. During the Reigns of King William, Queen Anne and George I*. Published from his original manuscript; as attested by his son Spring Macky, Esq London, 1733.

Mayer, Hans Eberard. "The Succession to Baldwin II of Jerusalem: English Impact on the East." *Dumbarton Oaks Papers* 39 (1985): 139–147.

Molnár, Miklós and Maygar, Anna. *A Concise History of Hungary*, trans. Anna Maygar. Cambridge, UK: Cambridge University Press, 2001.

O'Callaghan, Joseph F. *A History of Medieval Spain.* Ithaca, NY: Cornell University Press, 1975.

Opfell, Olga S. *Queens, Empresses, Grand Duchesses and Regents; Women Rulers of Europe AD 1328–1989.* London: McFarland and Company, 1989.

Ramírez Vaquero, Eloísa. *Blanca y Juan II Reyes de Navarra; Reyes Pirenáicos.* Pamplona: Editorial Mintzoa, 2003.

Redworth, Glyn. "'Matters Impertinent to Women': Male and Female Monarchy under Phillip & Mary." *The English Historical Review* 112.447 (1997): 597–613.

Reilly, Bernard F. *The Kingdom of León-Castilla under Queen Urraca, 1109–1126.* Princeton, NJ: Princeton University Press, 1982.

Röhricht, Reinhold. *Regesta regni Hierosolymitani,* New York: B. Franklin, 1960.

Rymer, Thomas. *Foedera, conventiones, literae, et cujuscunque generis acta publica, inter reges Angliae et alios quosvis imperatores, reges, pontifices, principes, vel communitates, ab ineunte saeculo duodecimo, viz. ab anno 1101, ad nostra usque tempora, habita aut tractata: ex autographis, infra secretiores archivorum regiorum thesaurarias per multa saecula reconditis, fideliter exscripta: in lucem missa de mandato Reginae. Tomus II,* London: A & J Churchill, 1705.

Sommerville, Margaret R. *Sex and Subjection. Attitudes to Women in Early Modern Society.* London: Arnold, 1995.

Tyre, William of. *Historia Rerum in Partibus Transmarinus Gestarum (A History of Deeds Done Beyond the Sea),* trans. Emily A. Babcock and A.C. Krey. New York: Columbia University Press, 1943.

Weissberger, Barbara. "*Tanto monta;* The Catholic Monarchs' Nuptial Fiction and the Power of Isabel I of Castile." In *The Rule of Women in Early Modern Europe,* eds. Anne J.Cruz and Mihoko Suzuki. Chicago: University of Illinois Press, 2009, 43–63.

Wolf, Armin. "Reigning Queens in Medieval Europe: When, Where and Why." In *Medieval Queenship,* ed. John Carmi Parsons. Stroud: Sutton Publishing Limited, 1993, 169–188.

'Personal' Rituals:
The Office of Ceremonies and Papal Weddings, 1483–1521

Jennifer Mara DeSilva[1]

On Wednesday, the 13th of the month of November, around the twenty-second hour or thereabouts, Maddalena, daughter of the Florentine citizen Lorenzo de' Medici, entered the city through the Porta Viridaria. Otherwise she is the bride of Francesco Cibo, the son of His Holiness the pope, called the *nipote*. With her mother and many women and attendants, she was received a little way beyond the gate by three or four prelates of the Palace and other ambassadors, who accompanied her all the way to the home of the aforesaid Francesco, located in the Borgo San Pietro, in which previously resided Don Antonio of Forlì, a clerk of the Apostolic Chamber. The procession passed in this order: first rode the household of the aforesaid prelates and the ambassadors, then the attendants of the bride, then Francesco Cibo the groom in between, while on the right was Piero di Lorenzo, the brother of the bride, and Jacopo Salviati to the left. He was followed by the bride between the Lord Archbishop of Cosenza on the right and the Bishop of Orense on the left. Then came Clara (or Clarice), the mother of the bride, in the middle between the Bishop of Bobbio, who was the ambassador of the Duke of Milan, on the right, and the Bishop of Volterra on the left. Prelates and women followed these people along with other people of lesser rank

---

[1] I wish to thank the volume editor Jacqueline Murray and the two anonymous assessors for their valuable comments on this essay, and Konrad Eisenbichler for his editorial expertise.

mixed together without any order. None of our men had been called, and nor was there one of us present.[2]

Johann Burchard, the papal Master of Ceremonies, recorded in his diary this description of Maddalena de' Medici's entry into Rome in 1487. Although this welcome generally conformed to fifteenth-century rituals surrounding exogamic weddings, there are several unusual aspects that deserve deeper analysis. Firstly, the public welcome by elite clergy of a future daughter-in-law of the pope was an unusual event that revealed the participation by members of the papal court in many rituals that might properly be called personal rituals. Secondly, the presence of only certain prelates at the Porta Viridaria reveals the semi-private nature of the welcome, which contrasts with the size of Maddalena's entourage and the stir that they caused. Thirdly, the absence of Burchard, himself, combined with his clear interest in this event, places such personal rituals in a category outside of the ecclesiastical rituals that were his professional responsibility. Using the records from the Office of Ceremonies, this essay explores the entry of Maddalena, along with other wedding events, in order to delineate more fully the ritual life of the early modern papal court and the reconciliation of the pope's relationship with his lay relatives, as seen through the lens of ritual.

Between 1483 and 1521, members of the papal Office of Ceremonies, which was responsible for the direction of the papal chapel and all ritual and liturgical events connected to the pope,[3] recorded fourteen weddings involving members of the papal family (Table 1). Analyzing these events provides a new perspective on the ritual activities of the pope that emphasizes the importance of lay connections in elite Catholic Church leadership.[4] This analysis reveals the increasing involvement of papal ceremonialists in the preparation and supervision of wedding events,[5] highlighting the ceremonialists' own broad definition of their mandate and a pragmatic

---

[2] Burchard, *Liber notarum*, 1:209–210.

[3] Constant, "Les maîtres de cérémonies," 161–229, 319–343.

[4] Barbara McClung Hallman has shown the close links within the College of Cardinals through both blood and marriage between 1492 and 1563; Hallman, *Italian Cardinals*, "Kinship Chart", Illustration 5.1.

[5] The phrase "wedding events" identifies the collection of activities chronicled by the ceremonialists (entry into Rome, movement of spouses through the city, *sponsalia*, banquets) that is distinct from the modern understanding of a Christian wedding (Mass, civil ceremony, banquet). The celebration of early modern unions, especially elite unions,

approach to the boundaries of papal ritual. This pragmatism is an important characteristic in an office whose members felt the weight of history and ritual precedent influencing each event under their direction.[6] As the ritual directors of an elite community preoccupied with ecclesiastical and secular governance, the ceremonialists ensured that the papal court maintained a visible structure through ritual forms that reflected the universal hierarchy led by the pope and the cardinals, while simultaneously incorporating the pope's lay relatives who often played an active role in papal strategies. In the early modern period the marital strategies pursued by individual popes for their lay relatives reveal the mechanics of elite social mobility and the unique situation of the pope as a patron.

The foremost collection of sources for these weddings comes from the diaries kept by the two papal Masters of Ceremonies during this period, Johann Burchard (1483–1506) and Paris de' Grassi (1504–1521). These reports allow a re-interpretation of papal ritual that supports the new category of personal ritual that incorporated aspects of both clerical and secular rituals, and that transcended theological boundaries to meet social and political imperatives. The place and mobility of the family group, or *consorteria*, at the papal court appears clearly through these wedding rituals, dispelling the rigid bounds of lay and clerical status and replacing them with a more universal approach to power-brokering on which early modern Italians depended.

Marriage, Politics and the Papacy

If paper were ducats, the amount of correspondence written by Maddalena de Medici's father, in arranging her marriage to Francesco Cibo, would have made the couple fabulously wealthy. The investment of time, energy and resources in this union, both by Lorenzo de' Medici and his agents in Rome, reflected the contemporary view that a good marriage could bring profit to

---

involved a greater variety of activities that often had a more public character than modern Christian weddings.

[6] Elsewhere I have discussed signs of Paris de' Grassi's pragmatism when dealing with the papal court, which suggest that his reputation for pedantry and a closed mind is not completely correct; DeSilva, "Senators or courtiers," 168–170. On de' Grassi's reputation, see Shearman, "The Vatican *stanze*," 370: "[de' Grassi] belonged to that blessed and maligned breed of men we call pedants, and he was obsessed by the necessity of being understood." As Shearman acknowledges, this obsession over clarity and detail has been a boon to historians.

both families for several generations. Indeed, the bonds of *parentado*, created by this marriage, between Lorenzo and Pope Innocent VIII were the prerequisite for many privileges gleaned by the Medici bank[7] and, most importantly, the elevation of Maddalena's brother, Giovanni, to the cardinalate. As Pope Leo X (r. 1513–1521), Giovanni repaid the favour to his Cibo relatives by elevating Maddalena's son, Innocenzo, to the cardinalate.[8]

Barbara McClung Hallman has noted the early modern Church's acknowledgement of "the over-riding importance of the family" as seen through the effort made by elite clergy to sustain their families through appropriating church offices as private property.[9] There was equal interest in success by clerical or lay relatives, as elite members of each group could influence and access offices in the other group. While this is clear from Giovanni's elevation to the College of Cardinals and the revival of the Medici bank in Rome, Francesco Cibo profited almost as handsomely from this union as did his in-laws. In addition to receiving Maddalena's dowry of 4,000 ducats, Lorenzo arranged for Francesco to receive feudal lands around Cerveteri along with income to support seigneurial aspirations.[10] Although women and children demanded significant organization and financial support from clerical relatives, these two groups represented the continuation of the family name and expansion of its wealth and prestige. Careful management of these relatives, through marriages, offices and noble titles, could effect rapid social advancement and profit for the wider family group.[11]

Hence, the marital alliances pursued by the pope and his family were of great importance. Since, throughout this period, the average length of a pontificate was approximately 8.4 years,[12] there was a strong impetus to establish the family permanently in both clerical and lay offices, from which they would reap benefits that outlasted their papal patron. This acknowledged

---

[7] For the exploitation of these bonds see Bullard, "'Hammering Away at the Pope,'" 383–398.

[8] BAV, Vat. lat. 12275, 62v–63v.

[9] Hallman, *Italian Cardinals*, 147.

[10] Bullard, "In pursuit of *honore et utile*," 136–137; Tomas, *The Medici Women*.

[11] Hallman has charted the acquisition of noble titles in several families within three generations which originated in commerce and offices at the papal court, especially the Cesi; Hallman, *Italian Cardinals*, 133–147.

[12] These data result from calculating the average length in years of a pontificate between Eugenius IV's succession in 1431 and Paul III's death in 1549, which is the period generally considered as the climax of nepotism.

culture of nepotism[13] has challenged many historians to show how early modern contemporaries could balance the rhetoric of the non-generative Vicar of Christ on Earth with concern for familial advancement. While some modern readers struggle with accepting children born to elite clergy in the early modern period in clear contravention of the ecclesiastical injunction to chastity, early moderns could be ambivalent on the subject, censorious in theory but accepting in practice.[14] Nevertheless, the frequent presence of papal relatives, both clerical and lay, in papal government and at the papal court, make plain the need to investigate further the boundaries of acceptance and the function of nepotism in the popes' social and political strategies.

While Irene Fosi and Maria Antonietta Visceglia have shown how complex the negotiation of marital alliances could be for the families of both popes and cardinals,[15] historians have not analyzed the rituals that cemented these alliances. It is commonplace among historians to assert that Rome, and especially the papal court, was the centre of Christian ritual, but the exclusive focus of many modern studies on ceremonies of a religious character might erroneously suggest that that the ceremonial space at the Vatican was essentially liturgical, and its participants exclusively clerical.[16] Any affirmative

---

[13] Between the return of the papacy from Avignon to Rome in 1420 and the close of the Council of Trent in 1563, there were only three popes (Pius III, Adrian VI, and Marcellus II) who did not elevate a nephew, grand-nephew, cousin, son, grandson, or brother to the College of Cardinals or appoint another relative to an elite lay office. These men did not elevate any cardinals and all died within two years of ascending the papal throne. It is important to note that the decrees and concordats of the Council of Constance (1414–1418), which through the fifteenth and early sixteenth centuries provided an ideal standard for the College of Cardinals, allowed a single cardinal nephew to the reigning pope; Thomson, *Popes and Princes*, 65, 68, 70.

[14] In the aptly named section "The Pope and the Man," the historian Ludwig von Pastor explored the reaction of early modern contemporaries and modern historians to Pope Alexander VI Borgia's incorporation of his children into papal government as elite advisors, ambassadors, military leaders and nearly autonomous *signori*. In this case it was the frequency and extraordinarily great financial reward of Borgia nepotism that bothered contemporaries, rather than the basic practice of nepotism that alienated observers; von Pastor, *The History of the Popes*, 6:139–140.

[15] Fosi and Visceglia, "Marriage and politics," 197–224.

[16] The exclusion of the laity from the liturgical business of the papal chapel is evident in Duperac's *Maiestas pontificia* (1578), in which clergy surround the altar and elite laymen either sit on the steps before the papal throne or remain farthest from the altar, behind the benches of the cardinals (*quadratura*) or in the chancel; Rasmussen, "Maies-

judgment on the clerical exclusivity of the papal court would minimize the presence of the many lay people who frequently attended papal rituals. Throughout this period, some of the pope's relatives held clerical or lay offices at the papal court, while other relatives were accepted interlopers, without a traditional title or office. This presented continued challenges to the Office of Ceremonies in the maintenance of a universal hierarchy with the pope at the top, as the celibate Vicar of Christ, removed from earthly concerns.[17]

Papal Weddings, 1483–1521

More than many other events, wedding rituals reveal the inter-dependence between the clerical and lay worlds found at the early modern papal court. Although the weddings described by the two Masters of Ceremonies during this period, Johann Burchard and Paris de' Grassi, vary considerably across nearly four decades and four pontificates, the events all had a distinctly secular tone. The ceremonialists include descriptions of entries into Rome, the solemnization of nuptial vows (*sponsalia*) and wedding banquets. Rarely does the ceremonialist describe all three of the events for a given couple (Table 2). The information is neither exclusively liturgical nor focused solely on clergy. These descriptions read very much like a social register, detailing the attendees, their relationship to each other, seating plans and, finally, describing the event's activities. While the events themselves might include ecclesiastical aspects (for example, a sermon, a blessing) or the presence of the pope, the core of the nuptial event was legal.[18] The purpose of the event was the union of two people and, thus, two families, in a social, financial and political contract. As

---

tas pontificia," 109–148. Visceglia and Brice, *Cérémonial et rituel à Rome*; Burke, "Sacred Rules, Royal Priests," 168–182; Mitchell, *Italian Civic Pageantry*, 111–138.

[17] The position of Captain-General of the Church, the practical leader of the papal armed forces, attracted many papal *nipoti* through this period, including Francesco Cibo, Giovanni Borgia, Cesare Borgia, Francesco Maria della Rovere, Giuliano de' Medici and Lorenzo di Piero de' Medici. The pope bestowed the more ceremonial offices of Gonfaloniere and Prefect of Rome on members of the same group, as well as a larger circle of men whose interest he wished to maintain at the papal court. Tomas' study of Medici women at the papal court provides a fine example of a group with influence but with little official authority; Tomas, *The Medici Women*, especially Chapters 3 and 5.

[18] Unfortunately Christiane Klapisch-Zuber accepts Marco Antonio Altieri at his word that elite Roman weddings necessarily included a wedding mass (*messa del congiunto*). Neither Burchard nor de' Grassi's diaries support this assertion. Klapisch-Zuber, *Women, Family, and Ritual*, 194.

such, the weddings that involved the pope's near relatives provide insight into the social and political strategies pursued by the papal family.

As Table 1 illustrates, the ceremonialists recorded fourteen weddings across the pontificates of Innocent VIII Cibo (r. 1484–1492), Alexander VI Borgia (r. 1492–1503), Julius II della Rovere (r. 1503–1513) and Leo X de' Medici (r. 1513–1521). This table includes twelve weddings that occurred in Rome, one wedding in Naples and one wedding at the French court. There were further weddings arranged by these popes, but which neither Burchard nor de' Grassi noted, and which consequently lie outside the scope of this study.[19] Celebrations for ten of the twelve Roman weddings took place at the Vatican Palace, specifically in the *Sala dei Pontefici*. The two remaining weddings took place in palaces belonging to Roman cardinals, and with relative levels of secrecy, precisely to escape the interest of the papal court.[20] The location of these events suggests that only in a few specific circumstances did the popes feel uncomfortable celebrating the marriages of their kin. Otherwise, they freely appropriated the *Sala dei Pontefici*, a large space often used for Consistory sessions, for the wedding events, which included the *sponsalia* and, afterwards, a banquet or reception with refreshments.

The involvement of the Office of Ceremonies in wedding celebrations from 1493 onwards represents the growth of these events, as well as the increased political value of marriage. Apart from a discussion of liturgical rituals as opposed to personal ones, for practical purposes, the ceremonialist's skills at organizing events and handling large numbers of people were extremely useful. Under Innocent VIII, the largest wedding was probably the union of Francesco Cibo and Maddalena de' Medici, in 1487. Although

---

[19] There are no entries in Paris de' Grassi's diary chronicling the weddings of Lorenzo Salviati and Costanza Conti (1514), Lorenzo Cibo and Riccarda Malaspina (1515) or Lorenzo di Piero de' Medici duke of Urbino and Madeleine de La Tour d'Auvergne (1518). Likewise, de' Grassi was absent from Rome for the first three months of 1515, thus, he also missed celebrations for the marriage between Giuliano de' Medici duke of Nemours and Philiberte of Savoy (February 1515), which occurred in France.

[20] According to contemporaries, the weddings of Lucrezia Borgia to Alfonso d'Aragona (1498) and Felice della Rovere to Giangiordano Orsini (1506) had a furtive quality that was completely at odds with the semi-public display of other weddings. Julius II went so far as to forbid any public celebration in Rome of his daughter's nuptials in order to avoid criticism and comparison to Alexander VI. Sanuto, *Diarii di Marino Sanuto*, 6:347. In his diary, Burchard recorded that Lucrezia's *sponsalia* took place away from the Vatican Palace and "sine pompa solemni sed secrete, omnibus scientibus." Burchard, *Liber notarum*, 2:116.

Burchard does not record the number of guests at the *sponsalia* ceremony, a useful benchmark for comparison of size and, indirectly, political importance is the number of prelates in attendance at any event. Throughout all of the events, both Burchard and de' Grassi were careful to note the names of all elite clergy at each event, from which one can discern the familial connections and political interest in the match (Table 2). There was an increase in elite clerical attendance at papal wedding ceremonies that persisted through the pontificates of Alexander VI and Julius II, following the general increase in size and complexity of weddings, which offers a convincing explanation for the authorized presence and participation of the Office of Ceremonies.[21]

The early absence of the Master of Ceremonies from the Cibo weddings reveals a great deal more about the quality of these events in the eyes of the bride and groom. Maddalena de' Medici's progress through the Eternal City, in 1487, took her to meet her new father-in-law, who would become her father's most important ally[22] but whom, as Pope Innocent VIII, was venerated as the Vicar of Christ on Earth, by all Christendom. Although the couple was of an elite social standing, and accompanied by many prelates on their progress towards the Vatican Palace, they did not demand Burchard's services because most likely they did not view the entry to be a liturgical event or a function of the papal chapel. While prelates and ambassadors viewed the operation of politics with a broad perspective that incorporated manifold events, the pope held a far more circumscribed office. Kin connections remained at the core of papal power relationships, yet theologically, at his election, the pope abandoned his kinship connections and became a father to all of Christendom. Thus, the non-official or personal quality of Maddalena's entry was reinforced by her arrangement to wed the pope's son, who held an essential position, in practical terms, but theologically remained outside of the pope's proper *familia* of elite clergy and office-holders. The division between the papal chapel and the events focusing on papal kin is signalled by the absence of the papal ceremonialist from Maddalena's entry into Rome.

---

[21] The lack of *sponsalia* descriptions from Pope Leo X's pontificate precludes any conclusion about the grandeur of, and papal interest in, Medici weddings.

[22] Bullard, "In pursuit of *honore et utile*," 123–142.

Public, Private, and Personal Rituals

In his foundational essay on papal ritual, Peter Burke identified two categories of rituals: the ordinary and the extraordinary.[23] Yet, in ritual terms, Maddalena de' Medici's entry reveals a combination of religious, political and personal forms and motivations that resonate beyond frequency alone. The papal family's social and political alliances, established through marriage, were not considered to be religious events. Although these alliances could have a significant impact on Italian politics, initially they remained personal acts, outside the responsibility of the *quasi*-public papal chapel and the professional ceremonialist. This initial effort to separate the pope's kinship connections from papal rituals was both artificial and impractical when compared to the combination of rhetorical and practical strategies employed throughout the late Middle Ages. Agostino Paravicini-Bagliani has shown that throughout the eleventh and thirteenth centuries, the person of the pope merged with the figure of the Vicar of Christ and became the embodiment of Christ on Earth, justifying his use of the pontifical power (*plenitudo potestatis*) and his abandoning the generative ability of mortal men.[24] Only in the late fourteenth and fifteenth centuries was there a distinct effort at the pope's death and the transfer of his office to distinguish between the perpetual office and its mortal occupant.[25] Yet, this rhetorical model stands in opposition to the fifteenth- and sixteenth-century practice of power at the papal court. Not only did the weddings perpetuate the familial networks that supported oligarchic power structures within the Italian Church, but also they celebrated the involvement of lay *nipoti* in papal government. Burchard's frustration over Maddalena's disorganized and unsupervised entry, and de' Grassi's desire to arrange seating to depict a consistorial hierarchy, reveals a practical combination of care to maintain a late medieval image of papal authority alongside the early modern demands of elite power-brokering. Strikingly, neither ceremonialist commented on the impropriety of the events, which suggests that the necessity of clerical and lay relatives working side by side was a foregone conclusion.[26]

---

[23] Burke, "Sacred Rules, Royal Priests,"169.

[24] Paravicini-Bagliani, *The Pope's Body*, 59.

[25] For a discussion of this idea as an influence on papal funeral rituals, see Paravicini-Bagliani, *The Pope's Body*, Chapters 4–6.

[26] De' Grassi had significant experience working cooperatively with his brothers, Senator Agamennone and Cardinal Achille, for both personal and political goals. DeSilva,

The distinction between public and private ritual prompts questions about the pope's position. Undoubtedly as the bishop and secular leader of Rome, and as the "living image" of Christ on Earth, the pope occupied a public role. This public role was best emphasized through rituals that incorporated people and places subject to the pope's rule, or reinforcing his position in the universal hierarchy. Julius II's triumphant entries into Rome (1507 and 1511), after returning from campaigns against Bologna, as well as the *possesso* ceremony, which involved traveling to St. John's Lateran cathedral to take possession of the bishopric of Rome,[27] best illustrate how the pope served as a ritualized authority on public display. Public rituals transcended class boundaries purposely, in order to enforce a universal hierarchy that was emphatic and that unarguably established the pope as the ultimate earthly authority beyond the papal court.

Yet, outside of these public responsibilities, the pope participated in daily and cyclical rituals that might properly be considered to be private, except for the fact that the rituals occurred in the same spaces and involved the same participants as the pope's public and formal rituals. In this instance, private ritual is a less exact category, for the papal court was an amorphous entity, with permeable boundaries that could be crossed through wealth, piety, office and nobility. Private ritual, limited by space and authorized attendance, might be defined by the liturgical activities of the papal chapel, which included the calendar of annual feast days and devotional activities that was altered to suit the character and spiritual or institutional connections of each new pope.[28] While many of the chapel's rituals took place outside the relatively closed space of the Vatican Palace, and incorporated certain public participation, the presence of mace-bearers and guards emphasized the selectivity of chapel membership. The private quality of papal chapel rituals is best considered through the various elite and accessible/open characters of its ritual spaces. While members of the papal chapel processed from the Vatican Palace to a variety of Roman churches for specific devotional activities,[29]

"Official and Unofficial Diplomacy," 535–557.

[27] Fosi, "Court and city," 31–52.

[28] For example, Pope Leo X elevated the feast day of Saints Cosma and Damian (27 September) to the papal chapel devotional cycle. DeSilva, "Ritual negotiations," 255–258.

[29] For example, the church of S. Maria sopra Minerva on the feast of St. Thomas Aquinas (28 January); Norman, "In imitation of Saint Thomas Aquinas," 1–42.

entrance to the tiny chapel of San Lorenzo, where the pope often heard daily mass, was necessarily curtailed.

Alongside public and private rituals, the category of personal rituals builds on the criteria of space and personnel/membership to include kinship as the delimiting factor for participation. Personal rituals incorporated events that rightly fell outside the liturgy of the papal chapel and did not emerge from the political necessities of the Papal State. Rather, personal rituals emanated from the activities and responsibilities of the pope that recalled lay or familial life and connections, acknowledging the practical needs of early modern social positioning and the pope's obligations to act as patron towards kin. While properly the category of personal ritual belies the transformation of a cardinal into a pope, abandoning his earthly life for the papal office,[30] the acceptance of these rituals by the papal Master of Ceremonies asserted their existence at the papal court in practice, even if not as a theologically-defined group. Not surprisingly, the papal ceremonial canon, codified by Agostino Patrizi Piccolomini in 1488, does not include provision for the marriage of papal kin, as this event emphasized the transgression of the non-generative papal model.[31] Yet, these weddings reveal an acceptance by pope, ceremonialists and the papal court of the practical demands of leadership and the *consorteria*'s essential role as a bulwark of political support. While the Master of Ceremonies did not explicitly debate the character of personal rituals, there was an on-going concern about the supervision of wedding events. At the core of personal rituals was a concern to structure the papal image and articulate power relationships, according to the current needs and norms, in a manner similar to practical or liturgical rituals.

The Office of Ceremonies and the Image of the Pope

Burchard's interest in the entry of Maddalena de' Medici is tangible, as was his frustration at the exclusion of the Office of Ceremonies from the Cibo weddings. As he recorded in his diary, "none of our men [ceremonialists] had been called, and nor was there one of us present."[32] Strikingly, Burchard expected to be present and direct, or at least advise on, an entry that had

---

[30] Paravicini-Bagliani, *The Pope's Body*, 154–155, 164–165; Bertelli, *The King's Body*, 58–59.

[31] Dykmans, *L'Oeuvre de Patrizi Piccolomini*, vol. 1.

[32] Burchard, *Liber notarum*, 1:210.

no connection with the papal chapel. Although there were many prelates accompanying the bridal couple, the entry's purpose was to raise the social and political profiles of two families, not to fulfill any papal religious goals. Burchard's comment articulates a mandate, expanded beyond Patrizi's ritual canon, to include any event connected with the pope, his family and members of the papal court, both ecclesiastical and secular.

Following the pontificate of Innocent VIII, the diaries of Burchard and de' Grassi reveal both their broadened responsibilities and their concerns regarding personal rituals. The expanded ceremonial mandate is clarified by a discussion from 1514. De' Grassi described how, during Consistory, Leo X charged him with arranging the public reception of Jacopo V d'Appiano, the Lord of Piombino, who would arrive in Rome to wed the pope's niece, Emilia Ridolfi. The discussion recorded by de' Grassi suggests that the pope feared diminished honour, and deferred to the ceremonialist's knowledge of the papal court and organizational skills, in order to ensure an honourable welcome and to mobilize public interest in the wedding.[33] The town of Piombino was of strategic importance to the Medici, as a Tuscan port, but it was of only mild importance to the papal court and the citizens of Rome. The entry of Jacopo d'Appiano needed to reflect its personal quality, the investment that Leo and the Medici had made in the alliance, rather than Piombino's international political importance. By 1514, the ritual needs of the papal family had joined with the Office of Ceremonies' more traditional mandate, as another aspect of managing the papal image and pursuing individual strategies of the papal family.

From the succession of Alexander VI, in 1492, the Office of Ceremonies was involved officially in papal weddings. Although there is no concern in either Burchard or de' Grassi's diaries for the celebration of lay involvement in papal government, there is a continuous and strenuous effort to maintain a formal atmosphere and the universal hierarchy throughout the wedding activities. The Office of Ceremonies' constant desire to assert the pope's superiority likely stemmed from the threat of disorder that wedding ceremonies held. There were many opportunities for papal relatives and *parenti* to transgress social and civil bounds, under the guise of celebration or, more dangerously, to eclipse the pope through pretended authority or magnificence. In 1487, Nofri Tornabuoni, a Medici agent, described

---

[33] BAV, Vat. lat. 12275, 122r–122v.

Maddalena's entry into Rome as carrying "more triumph that one can say,"[34] whereas Burchard lamented the undisciplined crowd that included clergy and women mixed together.[35] Several papal marriages combined newly elite families (for example, the della Rovere) with ancient baronial families (for example, the Colonna and the Orsini) known for their ambitions to political dominance. Hence, throughout the wedding events, the Office of Ceremonies consistently upheld the ritual norms of the papal chapel in which the pope occupied the central focus as chief authority and worshipper, effectively excluding other individuals from positions of power. These efforts are best seen in the use of the hierarchical seating plan (*quadratura*) of Consistory sessions, the practice of kissing the pope's foot (*osculum pedis*) and the prohibition against women dining with the pope. The integration of these three aspects reveals the ceremonialists' attempts to preserve the pope's political and spiritual authority, while accepting his pragmatic responsibility, as a benefactor to his relatives. In essence, the ceremonialist ensured that, even at private wedding activities, the pope would never be the father of the bride, but would remain a patron, bound by the ritual forms of the papal chapel, just as he was at political or liturgical events.

To reinforce this vision of the pope, in the rooms allocated for wedding rituals at the Vatican Palace, both Burchard and de' Grassi established a hierarchical seating plan. In 1505, as de' Grassi arranged benches for the *sponsalia* of Francesco Maria della Rovere and Eleonora Gonzaga, he recalled that the seating, described as *parva quadratura*, reproduced in miniature the arrangement for Consistory sessions.[36] De' Grassi had arranged several benches facing the papal throne and sat the most illustrious guests in decreasing proximity to the pope, in order to reinforce the relative importance of the occasion and the participants:

> There were three benches across from the throne of the pope,
> and afterwards I placed a fourth bench directly and slightly

<hr>

[34] Letter of Nofri Tornabuoni to Lorenzo de' Medici, 16 November 1487, "Arete inteso che la brighata vostra entrò martedì con tanto trionfo quanto si possa più dire"; ASF, Mediceo Avanti il Principato, filza LII, documento 58.

[35] "[H]os sequebantur prelati et mulieres ac alii modici togati mixtim sine ordine;" Burchard, *Liber notarum*, 1:210.

[36] "[E]rat sedes papae parata sicut pro Consistorio, et circu[m] circa erant scabella in parva quadratura"; BAV, Vat. lat. 5635, 87r.

behind the throne of the pope. On the first bench sat the duke of Urbino [Guidobaldo da Montefeltro, uncle to the bridegroom]. On the second bench sat the Prefect of Rome [Francesco Maria della Rovere, the bridegroom and heir of the duke]. On the third bench sat the Prince of Salerno [Antonello Sanseverino, uncle to the bridegroom]. On the fourth bench sat the Magnifico Lord Giovanni Gonzaga, brother to the marquis of Mantova, who came with the mandate to celebrate the said *sponsalia.*[37]

Throughout this period the issue of precedence, and consequently seating arrangements, according to the Church's vision of a universal hierarchy, occupied the full attention of members of the Office of Ceremonies. De' Grassi's diary includes several precedence lists covering both lay and clerical members and all potential visitors to the papal court.[38] The maintenance of hierarchy through seating established a visible structure for privilege and nobility that all participants could observe and absorb. On the occasion of Francesco Maria's *sponsalia*, de' Grassi faithfully reproduced the hierarchical gradations of elite lay guests, all of whom sat in opposition, and in submission, to their spiritual lord, the pope. While all of these men would soon be linked to the pope through marital ties, and thus achieve intimacy as *parenti*, placing each man according to his distinct hierarchical position reminded all the guests of the importance of this match for the prestige of their individual families and, more importantly, of the pope's role as ultimate patron.[39]

The use by Burchard and de' Grassi of the *quadratura* seating plan[40] is closely connected to the Office of Ceremonies' understanding of, and desire to be involved in, these wedding activities. The unions of lay papal relatives fell outside the Office's traditional responsibility for the papal chapel and extraordinary rituals connected with the pope. Yet, the combination of spiritual and political issues that were discussed in Consistory sessions, mirrors the confluence of clerical and lay ambitions that was present in these

---

[37] BAV, Vat. lat. 5635, 87r.

[38] "Ordo Regum [Christ]ianorum"; BAV, Vat. lat. 5635, unpaginated.

[39] Conversely, an alliance with a ruling house, such as the Gonzaga or the Montefeltro, was "the ultimate aspiration for all papal families." Fosi and Visceglia, "Marriage and politics," 219.

[40] Dykmans, *L'Oeuvre de Patrizi Piccolomini*, 1:164–168.

weddings. The incorporation of the ritual of kissing the pope's foot (*osculum pedis*) is one sign of the melding of the lay world of marital alliances with the celibate world of the papal court. In 1505, Paris de' Grassi recorded that, following the union of Niccolò Franciotto della Rovere with Laura Orsini, before the couple and their guests adjourned to dine in the pope's rooms, they reverently kissed Pope Julius' foot.[41] This act was the quintessential display of obedience and fealty to the pope. Included in ecclesiastical ceremonies of clerical elevation, as well as rituals of political obeisance or reconciliation, the prone position reinforced the pope's spiritual and political dominance, while the kiss created a bond of intimacy.[42] Interestingly, in 1505, as well as at the first wedding of Lucrezia Borgia, in 1493, only the female guests performed the *osculum pedis*.[43] Thus, incorporating the *osculum pedis* as a reminder of papal authority underscored the mixed character of these marriages, fully lay in their participants, but deeply invested in the ecclesiastical fortunes of the spouses' *parenti*. Moreover, the *osculum pedis* asserted the pope's leadership role, simultaneously reminding the new papal kin of their powerful relative and the advantages of the marital alliance.

While the ceremonialists recalled the universal hierarchy, through consistorial seating and the *osculum pedis*, with little difficulty, they encountered resistance to the traditional papal prohibition against dining with women. As social historians have consistently noted, one of the fundamental signs of goodwill, familiarity and political trust is the act of sharing a meal and, throughout the early modern period, the wedding banquet was important to establish bonds of kinship and familiarity between the two families.[44] In 1488, Burchard wrote that Peretta Usodimare's banquet

---

[41] BAV, Vat. lat. 5635, 171v.

[42] The *osculum pedis* appears throughout Patrizi's *Caeremoniale romanum*, as an act signalling the kisser's humility before a more elite individual, usually the pontiff or more rarely a cardinal. Frequently, the ritual kiss is found in transformative ceremonies, including the papal and imperial consecration rituals, elevation to or through the ranks of the cardinalate and the creation of apostolic legates and secular nobles.

[43] Burchard, *Liber notarum*, 1:444.

[44] The depiction of wedding banquets in contemporary paintings emphasizes the event as an opportunity to manifest new kinship ties through hospitality and to project an image of magnificence. A good example is Sandro Botticelli's *The Wedding Banquet of Nastagio degli Onesti* (1482–83), which Antonio Pucci commissioned to celebrate his son Gianozzo's wedding to Lucrezia Bini, and which depicts each families' heraldic arms alongside those of Lorenzo de' Medici, who served as the wedding broker. Kent, *Friend-*

"was done against the rules of our ceremonies, which expressly prohibit women from dining with the pontiff."[45] Nonetheless, for five of the ten *sponsalia* ceremonies, the ceremonialists described a banquet or reception for the bridal couple and their guests (Table 2). In moments of uncertainty, the Master of Ceremonies looked to the historical sources for the traditional place of anomalous individuals or unusual events. Chief among these sources were the works of Agostino Patrizi Piccolomini, who had occupied the Office of Ceremonies from 1466 to 1488, and whose texts provided the authoritative standard for papal liturgical ritual. Throughout *Caeremoniale romanum* (1488), Patrizi maintained the laity's subordinate position to the clergy,[46] and explicitly established the dining hall as a clerical space: "Regarding the laity, who are outsiders, we assign nothing, for those who are admitted are accustomed to the will of the pope, and not regular [members of the papal court]."[47] Moreover, Patrizi placed a clear prohibition against women at papal banquets, including both the most illustrious and likely visitors — the Holy Roman Empress and the pope's own female relatives.[48]

Burchard and de' Grassi's repetition of the prohibition against women dining with the pope emphasizes their efforts to enforce the traditional character of the papal court as a non-generative ecclesiastical patriarchy. Yet, the continued celebration of the wedding banquet reveals the ritual compromises inherent in the confluence of clerical and lay objectives. While the pope rarely upheld Patrizi's injunction against female diners, Burchard's description of the distribution of wedding guests, at the wedding

---

ship, Love, and Trust, 132–134; Woods, Richardson and Lymberopoulou, *Viewing Renaissance Art*, 21–23.

[45] "[L]icet contra normam ceremoniarum nostrarum acta sint, que expresse prohibent mulieres esse in convivio cum pontifice"; Burchard, *Liber notarum*, 1:245.

[46] This subordination is manifested through the fact that the layman remained standing throughout the rituals of the papal chapel: "Alii autem preter supra nominatos, quantumcumque nobiles aut graduati sint, non sedent in capella apostolica. Laici stant, clerici togati sedent in terra super panno virides." Dykmans, *L'Oeuvre de Patrizi Piccolomini*, 2:465.

[47] "De laicis, qui sunt extraordinarii, nihil ponimus, nam admitti solent ad voluntatem pontificis, et non ordinarie." Dykmans, *L'Oeuvre de Patrizi Piccolomini*, 1:89.

[48] "Advertendum tamen quod numquam in convivio pontificis admittuntur mulieres, etiam si imperatrix, regina, vel etiam consanguinea pontificis esset." Dykmans, *L'Oeuvre de Patrizi Piccolomini*, 1:91. In 1506, de' Grassi reminded Pope Julius II of Patrizi's prohibition using very similar language: "quia nunq[uam] papa pu[bli]ce comedit, ubi sunt mulieres et[iam] si soror, vel neptis esset, et Regina vel Imperatrix." BAV, Vat. lat. 5635, 235v.

of Peretta Usodimare, accords with Patrizi's own placement of the laity at papal banquets (*convivio solemni*). In *Caeremoniale romanum* Patrizi seated cardinal-bishops and cardinal-priests at one table, cardinal-deacons at a second table, and ambassadors, nobles and office-holders at a third table.[49] At Peretta's banquet, there were three tables that accommodated three groups: the most elite clergy (the pope and two cardinals), the remaining clergy and the laity. The latter three tables acted as a visualized cosmography of the city of Rome, clearly delineating the population divisions and wealth distribution. The first and smallest table included the most powerful wedding guests, while the second table included the first table's entourage and the third table included their lay dependents.[50] The segregation of guests according to hierarchy simultaneously celebrated the achievements of the laity present at the banquet, but also asserted the necessary mediation of elite clerical relatives, upon whose election the alliance hinged.

Conclusion

As Niels Krogh Rasmussen has argued, Patrizi's texts would be "reinterpreted by the *praxis* of the [papal] *Capella* as witnessed by the diaries of the *Magistri Ceremoniarum*".[51] The practical demands of papal government and family strategies urged the ceremonialists to make concessions in rituals, in order to maintain papal authority while accommodating "personal rituals". While the early modern papacy depended upon the services of lay *condottieri* and the governing skills of lay relatives, their presence at the Vatican Palace was supposed to be limited. At his election, the pope was meant to be consecrated as the Vicar of Christ, and to abandon his earthly possessions, interests and connections. In effect, as he abandoned his own blood relatives, he became the Father of all Christians.[52] Nonetheless, the betrothal of Francesco Maria della Rovere, in 1505, illustrates the intimate connections between clerical and lay relatives, seen throughout these wedding events. De' Grassi's seating arrangement placed the elite laymen in opposition to the pope's throne,

---

[49] A further distinction is evident when the pope washes his hands before dining. During this act cardinals and prelates remove their hats and non-prelates along with laymen kneel. Dykmans, *L'Oeuvre de Patrizi Piccolomini*, 1:85, 87.

[50] Burchard, *Liber notarum*, 1:244–245.

[51] Rasmussen, "*Maiestas pontificia*," 114.

[52] Paravicini-Bagliani, *The Pope's Body*.

in order to replicate the universal hierarchy that began with the pontiff and descended from duke to *magnifico*.[53] Yet, even before the ceremony, the pope, the duke of Urbino and the prince of Salerno all shared an interest in their nephew, the bridegroom. Each man hoped that the union of Francesco Maria with the daughter of the marquis of Mantova would bring profit to his territory (the Papal States, Urbino, Salerno) and family (della Rovere, Montefeltro, Sanseverino), all of which were somewhat in competition and yet bound together by marital ties.[54]

Accepting the importance of wedding rituals to the political and social fortunes of the papacy and the pope's family, the ritual character of weddings underlined the need for the Office of Ceremonies to be involved. The ceremonialists had substantial experience with the spaces used and the people who attended these events, and undoubtedly could adapt their skills to the *sponsalia* ritual form. Although there has been substantial debate among modern historians about the precise involvement of the Church in early modern wedding rituals, beyond the use of notaries as officiants, there remained a sense of sacramentality in the *sponsalia*.[55] Just before Lucrezia Borgia departed Rome for Ferrara with her new husband in 1502, Alexander VI mused aloud on the possibility of repeating the vows a second time in Rome. Quickly, the Cardinal of Siena replied that the sacramental quality of the wedding ritual meant that it should not be repeated.[56] While some historians might attribute the expansion of the ceremonialists' mandate to a politicization of the papacy or the diminution of sacramentality, a more holistic judgement rests on the ceremonialists' own acceptance of these new rituals as a combination of spiritual, social and political forms. Like many other aspects of the early modern papacy, these weddings were personal

---

[53] BAV, Vat. lat. 5635, 87r.

[54] This competition between family members and territories for resources and attention is clearly revealed by Francesco Maria's anxiety to save his uncle's duchy of Urbino from Cesare Borgia's soldiers, in 1502–1503, ultimately at the expense of his father's patrimony, the city of Senigallia, and much to the annoyance of his uncle, the future pope. Shaw, *Julius II*, 114.

[55] Elsewhere, Christiane Klapisch-Zuber has identified the "liturgization" of the rites of *verba de praesenti* in medieval France, arguing that the increasing use of the sanctuary and the presence of clergy at these rites denotes increasing clerical control, through liturgical spaces and forms. Klapisch-Zuber, *Women, Family, and Ritual*, 194.

[56] "[R]. d. cardinalis Senensis respondit matrimonium esse sacramentum, propterea non reiterandum"; Burchard, *Liber notarum*, 2:310.

rituals that bound the ruling families of Italy together, in order to strengthen authority and networks of practical power, across secular and ecclesiastical spheres.

BALL STATE UNIVERSITY

APPENDIX

Table 1
Papal Weddings Recorded by Ceremonialists, 1484–1521

Date	Pontificate	Couple	Relationship to Pope	Location	Master of Ceremonies present
13 November 1487	Innocent VIII	Francesco Cibo m. Maddalena de' Medici	Son	Rome Vatican Palace	No
16 November 1488	Innocent VIII	Peretta Usodimare m. Alfonso del Carretto	Grand-daughter	Rome Vatican Palace	No
9 October 1491	Innocent VIII	Pietro Paolo Cesarini m. Ballarda di Conza	unclear	Rome Vatican Palace	No
3 June 1492	Innocent VIII	Battistina Usodimare m. Luigi d'Aragona	Grand-daughter	Rome Vatican Palace	No
9–12 June 1493	Alexander VI	Lucrezia Borgia m. Giovanni Sforza	Daughter	Rome Vatican Palace	Yes
May 1494	Alexander VI	Giuffrè Borgia m. Sancia d'Aragona	Son	Naples	Yes

August 1498	Alexander VI	Lucrezia Borgia m. Alfonso d'Aragona	Daughter	Rome, Palace of Card. S. Maria in Porticu	unclear
10–12 May 1499	Alexander VI	Cesare Borgia m. Charlotte d'Albret	Son	French court	No
September 1502	Alexander VI	Lucrezia Borgia m. Alfonso II d'Este	Daughter	Rome Vatican Palace	Yes
2 March 1505	Julius II	Francesco Maria della Rovere m. Eleonora Gonzaga	Nephew	Sponsalia at Vatican, wedding in Urbino (Dec.1509)	Yes
30 November 1505	Julius II	Niccolò Franciotto della Rovere m. Laura Orsini	Nephew	Rome Vatican Palace	Yes
24 May 1506	Julius II	Felice della Rovere m. Giangiordano Orsini	Daughter	Rome Palazzo della Cancelleria Vecchia	Yes
25 July 1506	Julius II	Lucrezia della Rovere m. Marcantonio Colonna	Niece	Rome Vatican Palace	Yes
22 August 1514	Leo X	Emilia di Piero Ridolfi m. Jacopo V d'Appiano Lord of Piombino	Niece	Rome Vatican Palace	Yes

Table 2
Supplementary Information on the Weddings discussed in the Text

Pontificate	Couple	Event(s) Described by Ceremonialist	No. of Cardinals Present	No. of Archbishops/ Bishops Present
Innocent VIII	Francesco Cibo m. Maddalena de' Medici	Entry into Rome	None	"Three or four palatine clergy"
Innocent VIII	Peretta Usodimare m. Alfonso del Carretto	Sponsalia, Banquet	Two	Two archbishops and more than six bishops
Innocent VIII	Pietro Paolo Cesarini m. Ballarda di Conza	Arrival at the Vatican Palace	lacuna	lacuna
Innocent VIII	Battistina Usodimare m. Luigi d'Aragona	Sponsalia	Three	One archbishop
Alexander VI	Lucrezia Borgia m. Giovanni Sforza	Sponsalia, Sermon, Osculum pedis, Banquet	Ten	Five archbishops and more than three bishops
Alexander VI	Giuffrè Borgia m. Sancia of Aragon	Sponsalia	One	At least one
Alexander VI	Lucrezia Borgia m. Alfonso d'Aragona	Sponsalia	None	None
Alexander VI	Lucrezia Borgia m. Alfonso II d'Este	Sponsalia, Sermon, Reception	Thirteen	At least one
Julius II	Francesco Maria della Rovere m. Eleonora Gonzaga	Sponsalia	Eighteen	No details
Julius II	Niccolò Franciotto della Rovere m. Laura Orsini	Sponsalia, Osculum pedis, Banquet	Seven	"Many prelates and other curialists"

Julius II	Felice della Rovere m. Giangiordano Orsini	Sponsalia	Twelve	"All the palatine clergy"
Julius II	Lucrezia della Rovere m. Marcantonio Colonna	Sponsalia, Osculum pedis, Banquet	Fifteen	No details
Leo X	Emilia di Piero Ridolfi m. Jacopo V d'Appiano Lord of Piombino	Plan for Jacopo's entry into Rome	No details	No details

CITED WORKS

Manuscript Sources

Florence. Archivio di Stato di Firenze (ASF)
Mediceo Avanti il Principato, filza LII, documento 58

Vatican City. Biblioteca Apostolica Vaticana (BAV)
Vat. lat. 5635, *Diarium caeremoniarum Paridis de Grassi (1504-1506)*
Vat. lat. 12275, *Diarium caeremoniarum Paridis de Grassi (1513-1521)*

Printed Sources

Bertelli, Sergio. *The King's Body: Sacred Rituals of Power in Medieval and Early Modern Europe*, trans. R. Burr Litchfield. University Park, PA: Pennsylvania State University Press, 2001.

Bullard, Melissa Meriam. "'Hammering Away at the Pope': Nofri Tornabuoni, Lorenzo's Agent and Collaborator in Rome." In *Florence and Beyond: Culture, Society and Politics in Renaissance Italy. Essays in Honour of John M. Najemy*, eds. David S. Peterson and Daniel E. Bornstein. Toronto: Centre for Reformation and Renaissance Studies, 2008, 383–398.

————. "In pursuit of *honore et utile*: Lorenzo de' Medici and Rome." In *Lorenzo il Magnifico e il suo mondo. Convegno internazionale di studi (Firenze, 9-13 giugno 1992)*, ed. Gian Carlo Garfagnini. Florence: Leo S. Olschki, 1994, 123–142.

Burchard, Johann. *Johannis Burckardi Liber notarum ab anno MCCCCLXXXIII usque ad annum MDVI*, ed. Enrico Celani. 2 vols. Città di Castello: Tipi della Casa editrice S. Lapi, 1907–1914.

Burke, Peter. "Sacred Rules, Royal Priests: Rituals of the Early Modern Popes." In *The Historical Anthropology of Early Modern Italy*. Cambridge: Cambridge University Press, 1987, 168–182.

Constant, G. "Les maîtres de cérémonies du XVIᵉ siècle." *Mélanges d'archeologie et d'histoire, École Française de Rome* 23 (1903): 161–229, 319–343.

DeSilva, Jennifer Mara. "Official and Unofficial Diplomacy between Rome and Bologna: the de' Grassi Family under Pope Julius II, 1503–1513." *Journal of Early Modern History* 14 (2010): 535–557.

_____. "Senators or courtiers: negotiating models for the College of Cardinals under Julius II and Leo X." *Renaissance Studies* 22 (2008): 154–173.

_____. "Ritual negotiations: Paris de' Grassi and the Office of Ceremonies under Pope Julius II & Leo X (1504–1521)." Unpublished Ph.D. dissertation. Toronto, University of Toronto, 2007.

Dykmans, Marc. *L'Oeuvre de Patrizi Piccolomini ou le cérémonial papal de la première Renaissance*, 2 vols. Città del Vaticano: Biblioteca Apostolica Vaticana, 1982.

Fosi, Irene. "Court and city in the ceremony of the *possesso* in the sixteenth century." In *Court and Politics in Papal Rome, 1492–1700*, eds. Gianvittorio Signorotto and Maria Antonietta Visceglia, trans. Thomas V. Cohen. Cambridge, UK: Cambridge University Press, 2002, 31–52.

Fosi, Irene and Visceglia, Maria Antonietta. "Marriage and politics at the papal court in the sixteenth and seventeenth centuries." In *Marriage in Italy, 1300–1650*, eds. T. Dean and K.J.P. Lowe, trans. Anna Teicher. Cambridge, UK: Cambridge University Press, 1998, 197–224.

Hallman, Barbara McClung. *Italian Cardinals, Reform, and the Church as Property, 1492–1563*. Berkeley: University of California Press, 1985.

Kent, Dale. *Friendship, Love, and Trust in Renaissance Florence*. Cambridge, MA: Harvard University Press, 2009.

Klapisch-Zuber, Christiane. *Women, Family, and Ritual in Renaissance Italy*, trans. Lydia G. Cochrane. Chicago: University of Chicago Press, 1985.

Mitchell, Bonner. *Italian Civic Pageantry in the High Renaissance: A Descriptive Bibliography of Triumphal Entries and Selected Other Festivals for State Occasions*. Florence: Leo S. Olschki Editore, 1979.

Norman, Diana. "In imitation of Saint Thomas Aquinas: Art, Patronage and Liturgy Within a Renaissance Chapel." *Renaissance Studies* 7 (1993): 1–42.

Paravicini-Bagliani, Agostino. *The Pope's Body*, trans. David S. Peterson. Chicago: Chicago University Press, 2000.

Rasmussen, Niels Krogh. "*Maiestas pontificia*: A Liturgical Reading of Etienne Duperac's Engraving of the Cappella Sistina from 1578." *Analecta Romana Instituti Danici* 12 (1983): 109–148.

Sanuto, Marino. *Diarii di Marino Sanuto*, ed. G. Berchet, vol. 6. Venice: F. Visentini, 1881.

Shaw, Christine. *Julius II: The Warrior Pope*. Oxford: Blackwell, 1997.

Shearman, John. "The Vatican *stanze*: Functions and Decoration." *Proceedings of the British Academy* 57 (1971): 369–424.

Thomson, John A.F. *Popes and princes, 1417–1517. Politics and polity in the late medieval Church.* London: George Allen & Unwin, 1980.

Tomas, Natalie R. *The Medici Women: Gender and Power in Renaissance Florence.* Aldershot, UK: Ashgate, 2003.

Visceglia, Maria Antonietta and Brice, Catherine. *Cérémonial et rituel à Rome: XVIe–XIXe siècle.* Rome: École Française de Rome, 1997.

von Pastor, Ludwig. *The History of the Popes from the Close of the Middle Ages,* vol. 6, ed. Frederick Ignatius Antrobus. St. Louis, MO: B. Herder, 1923.

Woods, Kim M., Richardson, Carol M., and Lymberopoulou, Angeliki. *Viewing Renaissance Art.* New Haven: Yale University Press, 2007.

The Compromise Bride: The Marriage of Federico II Gonzaga and Margherita Paleologa of Monferrato

Sally Hickson

In 1531, Federico II Gonzaga (1500–40), newly minted Duke of Mantua, married Margherita Paleologa of Monferrato (1510–66), the last princess of the Byzantine Paleologue line.[1] In anticipation of his bride's arrival in the city, Federico's architect, Giulio Romano, worked furiously to complete the building and decoration of the small *palazzina* that had been commissioned in her honour. This palace was built as an extension of the small tower in the medieval castle of St. George, called the tower of San Nicolò, which had once housed the private rooms of Margherita's formidable mother-in-law, Isabella d'Este. The *torretta* was, in fact, the first location of Isabella's famous *studiolo*, with its allegorical paintings by Mantegna and others, and her famous *Grotta*, her small museum of antiquities. After 1519, the year Isabella became a widow and her son Federico assumed the role of Marquis of Mantua, she moved to an apartment on the ground floor of the *Corte Vecchia* wing of the palace, taking with her the paintings, furnishings, decorative fixtures and her famous collection of antiquities.[2] Approximately ten years later, the original locations of her *Grotta* and *studiolo*, superimposed one above the other in the tower, were hurriedly transformed, by Giulio Romano, into a passageway through

---

[1] For the Paleologues in Monferrato see the essays in Maestri, ed., *L'arrivo in Monferrato dei Paleologi di Bisanzio, 1306–2006*. Celebrations marking the 500th anniversary of Margherita Paleologa's birth were held in Mantua and in Monferrato, on 28 November 2009. I thank Dr. Roberto Maestri of the Circolo Culturale i Marchesi di Monferrato for his kind permission to use an image for this article.

[2] For the *torretta* see Cantarelli and Brown, "La torretta di San Nicolò"; the architectural history of both of Isabella's suites in the Ducal Palace is found in Brown, *Isabella d'Este in the Ducal Palace at Mantua*, with Giulio's work summarized at 147–150.

which the new princess could access her private palace.[3] In other words, to arrive at her private suite in the *palazzina*, the new Duchess Margherita was required to pass through the spaces formerly associated with her mother-in-law, who still lived in the same ducal complex. The inscription of the new Duchess onto Isabella's spaces clearly emphasized the importance of female power in Mantua, and drew attention to the fact that the Gonzaga had other claims to royal lineage through the female line, since Isabella d'Este's mother was Eleonora d'Aragona, the daughter of King Ferrante I of Naples. As described by Martha Sue Ahrendt, Margherita's suite in the *palazzina* consisted of three main rooms on the *piano nobile*, and culminated in an attic story that opened onto a rooftop garden, with a view across the lake.[4] When Isabella inspected the suite before Margherita's arrival, she remarked that she never would have left the tower had her own apartments offered her such a wonderful view.[5] Isabella also helped to choose the paintings to be hung in the private *camerino* of the Duchess; these included a *St. Jerome* by Titian, a *Saint Catherine* by Giulio Romano and Mantegna's famous *Foreshortened Christ* (now in the Brera). Ahrendt has pointed out that as a public extension of the formerly closed and private female spaces of the palace, the *palazzina* could be interpreted as an architectural expression of greater female visibility at the Gonzaga court.[6] It is certainly true that the *palazzina* related more explicitly and conspicuously to the city and to the outside world than had Isabella's own spaces, which lay on the inside of the architectural fabric.

Unfortunately, the *palazzina*, which once extended the fabric of the palace toward the Lago di Mezzo and the bridge of San Giorgio, had so deteriorated by the late nineteenth century that it was torn down in 1899. However, again according to Ahrendt, when first completed the exterior façade facing the bridge had been lavishly decorated in fresco designs incorporating the arms of both the Paleologa and Gonzaga families and

---

[3] Preparations for the wedding are briefly discussed in Cartwright, *Isabella d'Este*, 2:337–340, and by Gombrich in *Splendours of the Gonzaga*, 80–81. The *palazzina* is discussed at greater length by Cottafavi, "I gabinetti della 'Paleologa,'" 276–285 and Amadeo Belluzzi, "La Palazzina di Margherita Paleologa nel castello di Mantova," in the exhibition catalogue *Giulio Romano* (1989), 85–87. Documents concerning Giulio's work on the building of the *palazzina* are in Ferrari ed., *Repertorio di fonti documentarie*.

[4] A detailed critical analysis of the *palazzina* in the context of female agency at the Gonzaga court is found in Ahrendt, "Cultural Legacy," 58–125.

[5] Cartwright, *Isabella d'Este*, 2:337; also cited by Ahrendt, "Cultural Legacy," 112.

[6] Ahrendt, "Cultural Legacy," 123.

the *impresa* of Duke Federico.[7] Frederick Hartt remarked that the structure, box-like and wreathed in decorative fresco, was the architectural equivalent of an elaborate marriage *cassone*.[8] To the outside world then, particularly to ambassadors and visitors approaching the city across the San Giorgio bridge, the *palazzina* was an announcement, in architectural form, of the new ducal alliance. However, as a mere annex to the core of the ducal palace, the *palazzina* also mirrored the political situation around Margherita's marriage to Federico II, which was really a rather unhappy and forced alliance of the states of Mantua and Monferrato, themselves geographically separated by the state of Milan. The distance between the two states meant that Mantua maintained only a tenuous hold on Monferrato, a situation that only grew worse after Margherita's death in 1566.[9] In the end, the physical separation of the *palazzina* of the princess from the core of the Gonzaga stronghold was also a reminder that Margherita came to Mantua as Federico's "compromise bride," and a review of the circumstances around their union demonstrates just how complicated Renaissance marriage could be.

As is well-known from the magisterial study by Stefano Davari in the nineteenth century, and the more recent work by Deanna Shemek, Margherita was hardly Federico's first choice of bride.[10] His first choice had been her elder sister Maria Paleologa, and after this union was dissolved he was betrothed, for a brief period of time, to the imperial princess Giovanna of Aragon, after which he reverted back to Maria. It was only after Maria died quite suddenly in 1530 that Federico completed negotiations to marry Margherita. These complex marriage negotiations involved Isabella d'Este and Anna of Alençon, the formidable matriarchs of Mantua and Monferrato, and later extended to include both the emperor and the pope. Margherita's own role in the marriage is seldom considered beyond her arrival in Mantua. However, a rereading of certain primary documents, and a reconsideration of contemporary accounts of the marriage, permit us to shift the emphasis away from Federico's marital politics in order to reconsider Margherita's role as

---

[7] Ahrendt, "Cultural Legacy," 78.

[8] Hartt, *Giulio Romano*, 1:263.

[9] For the politics surrounding the marriage of Mantua and Monferrato, Oresko and Parrot, "The sovereignty of Monferrato and the citadel of Casale as European problems in the early modern period," in *Stefano Guazzo e Casale tra Cinque e Seicento*, 11–86.

[10] Davari, "Federico Gonzaga e la famiglia Paleologa del Monferrato" and Shemek, "Aretino's Marescalco"; also Cartwright, *Isabella d'Este*, 2:322–343.

bride, wife, mother, widow and co-regent, and to highlight her representation and reputation as Mantua's compromise bride. Doing so reveals the many marital identities that Margherita assumed during her years as a wife and mother and, after Federico's death, as a public widow and co-regent of the Gonzaga heirs to the Mantuan state. The evidence suggests that, during the years of her widowhood, Margherita viewed herself as the consort of the state and the public partner of Cardinal Ercole Gonzaga in Mantuan affairs, while remaining the literal embodiment of the state of Monferrato. Furthermore, her status as the last of the Byzantine empresses of the Paleologue dynasty was crucial to legitimating Gonzaga power in Monferrato, a power celebrated through variations on marital iconography employed in Monferrato altarpieces, as well as on the currency of the state. This essay examines the way that Margherita's marriage was constantly reframed within the artistic and material cultures of both states, first throughout her husband's lifetime, next during her co-regency with Cardinal Ercole Gonzaga and, finally, in concert with the ascendance of her son, Guglielmo Gonzaga, to the title of Duke of Monferrato. However, in order to effectively trace these trajectories of Margherita's marital identity, it is necessary to revisit the series of events that led to her union with Federico II Gonzaga in the first place, a saga of broken promises and marital politics unrivalled in the history of Italian dynasty.

Aside from the saga of Henry VIII in England, who was Federico's contemporary, there is probably no other series of engagements and entanglements more convoluted than those surrounding the marriage of Federico II Gonzaga to Margherita Paleologa. In the fourteen years between his betrothal to Maria Paleologa in 1517, and his eventual marriage to her younger sister Margherita in 1531, Federico mixed marriage with politics, openly courting betrothal prospects that would link him to one or the other of the opposing factions of the house of Valois and the Hapsburg Emperor, Charles V. All the while he engaged in an infamous, flagrant and prolonged public affair with his married Mantuan mistress, Isabella Boschetti. Federico's tendencies to flaunt convention in his personal life, and to exploit every opportunity to bargain for political advantage were, undoubtedly, the result of his rather unconventional childhood experiences. In 1509, his father Francesco II Gonzaga, a *condottiere* in the service of the pope during the wars against the League of Cambrai, was taken hostage by the Venetians. To secure Francesco's freedom, Pope Julius II promised the Venetians that he would hold Federico 'hostage' at the papal court against his father's release.[11] The arrangement was encouraged by Isabella d'Este, who saw this as a tremendous cultural and political opportunity for her son. In fact, during his time in Rome, which lasted until just after the death of Julius II in 1513, Federico met Michelangelo and Raphael, and spent his time in the company of powerful prelates and cardinals. In 1515, when the new French victors occupied Milan, Isabella agreed to send Federico to live at the French court, under the watchful eye of Francis I, where he once again mingled with a courtly society far beyond the circumscription of the Mantua milieu. These experiences were crucial to the formation of Federico's future tastes as a privileged patron, and allowed him to witness at first-hand the workings of papal and princely power, lessons he never forgot. As an adult, Federico was to become one of the most important of the Italian princely allies to Emperor Charles V, a decision predicated, one assumes, on his intimate familiarity with the French and papal opponents to imperial power.[12]

In 1517, while he was still residing at the French court in Milan, arrangements were made between the Gonzaga and Paleologue families for Federico to travel to Monferrato, where he was introduced to the six-year-old Byzantine princess Maria. Their ensuing 'marriage', which Federico agreed to without, it seems, considering the long-term implications, took place during this visit, and was peculiar even by Renaissance standards. According to Stefano Davari and to Deanna Shemek, the ceremony that took place observed "both civil and ecclesiastical norms"; the couple exchanged vows in front of witnesses, the bride received a ring, and the arrangement was evidently sealed with a kiss.[13] There is some question, however, of whether, under canon law,

---

[11] Cartwright, *Isabella d'Este*, 2:44–79.

[12] Federico's own political formation has never been completely studied, nor has there been any comprehensive study of his artistic patronage; for his period in Rome see Luzio, "Federico Gonzaga ostaggio alla corte di Giulio II"; for his time in Milan, Tamalio, *Federico Gonzaga alla corte di Francesco I*.

[13] Shemek, "Aretino's Marescalco," 374. Davari, "Federico Gonzaga," quotes from the report filed in Casale on 15 April 1517 regarding the ceremony: "Ill.re S.r Federico, seti content pigliare per vostra legittima sposa et mogliera Mad.a Maria de Monferrato qua presente, e per parola de presente secundo che comanda la santa roman chiesa? Alla qual interogatione epso S.r Federico respose publicamente, et audiente li infrascripti testimonij astanti, per parole, liberum consensum de presenti exprimente, monsignor si…" according to Davari "in sala deaurata arcis civitatis Casalis. Ex rogit. Ambro. De Turri de Ripalta, notarij Casalen. Ac marchio. Secret.," 433. There was much discussion at the marriage

the couple was actually married or whether the Monferrato ceremony was a contract for future marriage. As Brundage reports, in Italy during the late medieval period the exchange of vows, and even the giving of the ring to the bride to indicate her status as a *sponsa*, were all acts of betrothal; the crucial act of sexual intercourse was required to consummate the marriage.[14] Nevertheless, the betrothal vows constituted a legal obligation between the parties which could only be broken, and often was, when one or the other of the parties could demonstrate that they had secretly married someone else.[15] Shortly after Federico's ceremony in Monferrato in 1517, Protestant and Catholic Reformers alike placed the whole notion of marriage under new scrutiny. Protestants questioned the status of marriage as a sacrament, and the legality of the mere act of consent, emphasizing the necessity for parental consent. In response, the final edicts of the Council of Trent actually reiterated that under canon law the free exchange of consent between the parties did constitute marriage.[16] In the case of Federico's betrothal to Maria, the union was questionable under canon law, which usually stipulated boys had to be fourteen and girls at least twelve for any such contract to be legal.[17] Maria, of course, was only six at the time of the Monferrato ceremony. It was therefore agreed that the betrothal would be finalized with the necessary physical consummation which would take place in 1524, when Maria would be delivered to Mantua at the age of fifteen.[18] This left five years for Federico to further contemplate the pros and cons of the Paleologue arrangement, which promised him an opportunity to elevate the status of the Gonzaga through the reflected glory of Byzantine imperial power. His time in Rome, and later in the company of Francis I, fed Federico's aspirations to princely status and

---

conference about consent and ritual and the legal definitions of marriage in the Italian Renaissance; for an examination of the instability of the verbal troth, which asserted "the enduring power of words over people and things," see Nelson, "Doing Things with Words," 373. Marriage is, of course, a major subject for Brundage, *Law, Sex and Christian Society*. On the general question of the ceremonies of marriage see also Deborah L. Krohn, "What constituted marriage in the Italian Renaissance?" in *Art and Love in Renaissance Italy*, 11–13.

[14] Davari, "Federico Gonzaga," 431.

[15] Brundage, *Law, Sex and Christian Society*, 497 and, for clandestine marriages as a means to dissolve unwanted betrothals, 501–502.

[16] Brundage, *Law, Sex and Christian Society*, 563.

[17] Brundage, *Law, Sex and Christian Society*, 433.

[18] Davari, "Federico Gonzaga," 430.

by 1518, it seems that Maria's father had been prepared to insure that she would inherit the state of Monferrato but died before he could formalize these arrangements. Accordingly, Maria's brother, Bonifacio VI, inherited his father's title, with his mother acting as regent until he could reach the age of majority.[19] With Monferrato slipping from his grasp, Federico seems to have begun contemplating the legal loopholes that might free him from his promised marriage to Maria Paleologa.

When Francesco II Gonzaga died in 1519, Federico turned his attention to his new duties as Marquis of Mantua, and to his new romantic liaison with Isabella Boschetti, the wife of Giovanni Calvisano of Mantua. The affair was notoriously public; Paolo Giovio wrote about Isabella d'Este's misfortune in having a son whose "*innamorata*" walked haughtily around Mantua accompanied by a crowd of admirers.[20] By 1524, Maria Paleologue was still in Monferrato, presumably because of Federico's public dalliance with Boschetti. Whether or not the luxurious rooms of the Palazzo del Te, transformed by Giulio Romano into Federico's private pleasure palace and featuring lascivious frescoes of the loves of the gods centred on the wedding celebrations between Venus and Mars, were really intended to mirror the liaison between Federico and Boschetti remains somewhat problematic.[21] Nevertheless, the images speak to Federico's hedonistic side, quite well known to Giulio and to the poet Pietro Aretino who, having been expelled from Rome with Giulio for their collaboration on the pornographic prints and verses of the sex manual *I Modi*, willingly took refuge in Mantua and fed Federico's appetites.[22] Guido Rebecchini cites a letter that Aretino wrote to Federico from Venice, in 1527, offering to send him a Venus made by Jacopo Sansovino, "so true and alive that she fills with lust whoever looks at her."[23]

---

[19] Summarized by Shemek, "Aretino's Marescalco."

[20] Shemek indicates Giovio's reference to the affair, citing his *Imprese*, via Luzio, "Aretino's Marescalco," 373; the whole passage is found in Paolo Giovio, *Delle imprese* (Lyon: Giulio Roviglio, 1559), 123–125.

[21] Verheyen supported this view in his *Palazzo del Te in Mantua* (1977); the premise is questioned by Charles Davis, review of Verheyen in the *Journal of the Society of Architectural Historians* 38/1 (March 1979), 56–58.

[22] Cartwright rather archly claims that Federico's hedonistic tastes had developed during his time in Rome when he was exposed to "orgies of Cardinals and monkish buffoons," *Isabella d'Este*, 2:80.

[23] Rebecchini, "Exchanges of works of art at the court of Federico II," 383.

Now an ambitious young man in his early thirties, Federico had been in charge of Mantua since 1519, and was anxious for political advancement. Accordingly, he seized on the opportunity to exploit the conflict between France and the Emperor that had destabilized the Italian peninsula by siding with Charles V. Seeing greater possibilities for himself beyond the marriage to Monferrato, Federico appealed to Pope Clement VII to annul his marriage to Maria, which had not been consummated. The pope, rendered helpless by the Sack of Rome, granted his petition in 1529.[24] Given a new lease on his ambition, Federico considered other marriage candidates, which were proposed to him both by the French, who still hoped to sway him against Charles, and by the Emperor. In recognition of the importance of Federico's endorsement of imperial power in Italy, Charles V made him Duke of Mantua and offered him the imperial princess, Giulia of Aragon, daughter of Frederick IV, the deposed King of Naples. Since Giulia was already thirty-eight, Charles further agreed that, should she be unable to produce a Gonzaga heir, he would exercise his power of juridical recognition as Emperor to legitimize the son that Federico already had with Isabella Boschetti.[25] Having secured the Emperor's support, the stage was set for Charles' famous visit to Mantua, in March of 1530, during which he was entertained by the vistas, views and the dazzling display of the wedding banquet of Cupid and Psyche in the luxurious accommodations offered at the Palazzo del Te.

However, in June of 1530 Federico's circumstances suddenly changed. Bonifacio VI Paleologo, heir to the duchy of Monferrato, was accidentally killed in a hunting accident. Monferrato passed to Bonifacio's uncle Gian Giorgio Paleologo who, without heirs and on the brink of death from a fatal disease, declared that Monferrato be designated a *feudo femminino*, allowing rulership to pass to the eldest female descendant of the family, Maria Paleologa. Now seeing a clear opportunity to successfully annex Monferrato to Mantua, Federico became anxious to reassert the legality of his betrothal to Maria and approached the pope again, this time asking him to reverse the earlier annulment. Clement, undoubtedly exhausted by Federico's constant changes of mind, quietly acquiesced to the demand.[26] In the meantime, of

---

[24] The *breve* issued on 6 May 1529, declared the marriage "*rato e non consumato in causa della minore età della sposa*," Davari, "Federico Gonzaga," 433.

[25] Oresko and Parrot, *Stefano Guazzo*, 17.

[26] According to a *breve* of 20 September 1530, the marriage that Clement had declared "*nullo e invalido*" in 1529 was now "*valido e indissolubile*," Davari, "Federico Gonzaga," 433.

course, Federico had also to reverse his promise to marry Giulia of Aragon, an offense that Charles V seems to have taken rather personally, since in 1533 the matter would again become a matter of some contention.

Unfortunately, in the midst of preparing for her triumphant departure to Mantua, Maria Paleologa promptly died, leaving her younger sister, Margherita Paleologa, heir to the state of Monferrato and the sudden object of much marital competition in Italy. At this point, Anna of Alençon, regent of Monferrato since her husband's death in 1518, entered into the fray by advocating that Margherita marry Federico.[27] Her endorsement of Federico at this point in the proceedings seems rather unlikely, given his failure to carry through with his original marriage, but Federico evidently strong-armed her by implicating her in an intricate plot (probably largely invented) to poison his mistress, Isabella Boschetti.[28] For his part, Federico was also being pushed towards marriage by his own mother. Isabella d'Este wanted to make sure that Federico's illegitimate son with Boschetti, a boy named Alessandro, who had come dangerously close to legitimacy under the Emperor's marriage plan, be supplanted by legitimate Gonzaga heirs.[29] Isabella saw marriage to Margherita Paleologa, who was only twenty, as the most immediate and advantageous strategy for solving the problem of Gonzaga inheritance. Supported by Isabella d'Este, negotiations between Anna d'Alençon and Federico began in earnest. That Federico's involvement with Boschetti continued to be a major impediment to sealing the deal is revealed in an inventory of the legal documents that Margherita Paleologa left behind when she died in 1567. Along with the concession granted by the Pope for her marriage to Federico, the papers also include a declaration made by Federico, dated April 1531, stating that he had no legal marriage contract with anyone else, and a further declaration, signed by Isabella Boschetti, that she had not legally married anyone after the death of her own

[27] Davari remarks, rather chillingly, that "Maria's body was still warm" when these negotiations started, "Federico Gonzaga," 49.

[28] Davari, "Federico Gonzaga," 432–433, Shemek, "Aretino's Marescalco," 374.

[29] Shemek, "Aretino's Marescalco," 375, says that Isabella managed to nullify the agreement to legitimate Alessandro Gonzaga, and cites Luzio, "Isabella d'Este e il sacco di Roma," 105. In fact, Isabella's continued preoccupation with Alessandro's status is expressed in the terms of her will of 1539, in which she specified that any inheritance would pass only to Federico's legitimate and natural first-born son; this will is completely transcribed in my forthcoming *Women and Art and Architectural Patronage in Renaissance Mantua: Widows, Mystics and Matrons* (Ashgate, 2011).

husband, Francesco Gonzaga of Calvisano.[30] Calvisano had already been neatly disposed of, probably at Federico's order, as part of the poisoning plot against Boschetti. These denials of any clandestine marriage on the part of either party were undoubtedly demanded by Anna d'Alençon and especially by Isabella d'Este.

The wedding between Federico and Margherita finally took place in Monferrato and the new Duchess traveled to Mantua to take up residence in the new *palazzina*. An unexpected complication arose soon afterward, however, when in April of 1533 Alfonso I d'Este, Duke of Ferrara, arranged a marriage between the rejected Giulia of Aragon and Margherita's ailing uncle, Gian Giorgio Paleologo, a move approved by Charles V, who agreed that if the union failed to produce heirs, Monferrato would finally be given to Federico II.[31] Given Gian Giorgio's dire state of health (in fact, he died just eight days after the wedding) and the age of the bride, an heir was frankly impossible. At this point, Giulia's age made her rather more of a burden than an asset in the imperial marriage game, and it is entirely possible that the union was arranged by Charles V expressly so that Giulia could receive some kind of support from the Paleologue family. In fact, Margherita's documents include records of payments made to Giulia. [32]

The saga of the Gonzaga-Paleologa marriage usually ends with Margherita's arrival in Mantua. The wedding ceremonies having duly taken place, Margherita proved to be the perfect compromise bride. For the nine years of her marriage, she produced a succession of male heirs, guaranteeing the Gonzaga succession. By the time Federico died in 1540, Margherita was left with five children, four of them boys. The eldest, Francesco, was only six years old. Her biographer, Giuseppe Betussi, summed up her situation, writing: "having no desire to enjoy the embraces of a new husband, she

---

[30] ASMn, Magistrato Camerale, BBII, 1558–1704, among the list of documents in Casale Monferrato, 8 February 1567: "*Una patente dell'Ecc.mo Sr. Duca Federico del primo d'Aprile 1531, per la quale dichara non haver contratto matrimonio alcuno,*" followed by "*Un'altra fede fatta per la S.ra Isabella Boschetti per(?) in carta pecorina di non haver contratto matrimonio dopo morte de Mx. Francesco Gonzaga da Calvisano.*"

[31] Oresko and Parrot in *Stefano Guazzo*, 19.

[32] ASM, Magistrato Camerale BBII, 1558–1704, 8 February 1567, contains an undated note (probably referring to a payment date in the 1540s, as per the dating of other documents on the sheet) which reads: "*Una copia di mandati di danari pagati all'Ill.ma S.ra Donna Giulia di Aragona, per li scuti xiii.m et insieme altri danari et argenti mandati a Casale per la somma de scuti 14705 in copia.*"

remained the governess of her son Francesco," a duty which she shared with her brother-in-law, Cardinal Ercole Gonzaga, and his brother, the *condottiere* Ferrante Gonzaga.[33] Betussi continues, "Modesty was in her heart and in her actions, her children were her spouse, companion, sustenance and consolation in her widowhood."[34] The description explicitly cancels out any desirability that Margherita might have had as a thirty-year-old widow, and puts the emphasis squarely on her obligations to the state. Furthermore, he implies that, as regent over her children, Margherita was really still married. Because Ferrante's military duties kept him away from Mantua, Margherita and Ercole effectively became co-regents of the state and governed together. It is this period that is particularly interesting in terms of Margherita's status as the bride of the state, because she had so many roles to fulfill; she remained the public face of Mantua in Monferrato, while functioning essentially as the public consort of the Mantuan state in partnership with Cardinal Ercole.

As regent of her young sons, and a ruler with an active political role to play, Margherita could not choose, as many widows did in this period, to retire to a monastery and leave public life — although an inventory of her personal documents, made shortly after her death, shows that some time after 1559, a brief was issued to her by Pope Paul IV which allowed her to enter the Clarissan monastery of Santa Paola in the city, where her sister-in-law, Suor Paola Gonzaga, was abbess.[35] In her early widowhood, however, Margherita lived in a state of constant compromise between her public duties as regent, especially as Marchesa of Monferrato, where she was indeed the ruler of the state, and her more private, pious inclinations. Under the tutelage of Cardinal Ercole, Margherita also cultivated a carefully managed persona as a pious widow. In fact, Cardinal Ercole commissioned the Mantuan court artist Fermo Ghisoni to paint versions of the *Pietà*, the *Crucifixion* and the *Woman of Samaria*, all of them based on drawings made by Michelangelo for the most famous pious widow of this era, the poet and reformer, Vittoria Colonna. As part of a circle of Roman reformers around Colonna, Cardinal Ercole had

---

[33] Betussi, "Margherita Paleologa Marchesana di Monferrato, et Duchessa di Mantova," in his *Libro delle donne illustri* (1545), 205r – 206v. Some aspects of Margherita's regency in partnership with Cardinal Ercole are discussed in Murphy, *Ruling Peacefully*.

[34] Betussi, *Libro delle donne illustri*, 205v.

[35] ASM, Magistrato Camerale BBII, 1558–1704, 8 February 1567, "*Copia d'una comissione fatta per Pio 4 a Mad.ma Ex.ma di potere entrare nel monasterio di S.ta Paola*."

obtained copies of these gift drawings, which circulated in this group.[36] The Cardinal's gift to Margherita encouraged her to identify with Colonna.[37]

When Margherita's eldest son, Francesco, suddenly died in 1550, having been Duke for only one year, she resumed her role as co-regent, in partnership with Cardinal Ercole, until her second son, Guglielmo, officially assumed his duties as Duke, in 1556. During this period, Margherita performed administrative duties in partnership with Cardinal Ercole, acted as custodian of the Gonzaga assets and was employed as a public symbol of the continuing Paleologue dynasty in Monferrato. It was Guglielmo, with the support of the humanist, Stefano Guazzo, a native of Monferrato, former secretary to Margherita and a supporter of the unpopular Gonzaga princely rule, who first clearly asserted the male Gonzaga patrimony over his mother's state.[38] A coin issued by the *zecca* in Monferrato is stamped with double profile portraits, the young Guglielmo in the foreground and his mother Margherita, in widow's veil, behind him. The visual pairing shows the extent to which Gonzaga authority in Monferrato was only permissible under the aegis of the Byzantine imperial authority, embodied by Margherita herself. This kind of double-portrait coin harkens back to Byzantine traditions, in which coins were struck when an *augusta*, a female member of the Imperial line, conferred imperial power to a new emperor through marriage. The title of *augusta* had been conferred on imperial wives since the reign of Augustus and Livia, and appears on coins from the time of Claudius (41–54); it was eventually extended to other women in the imperial family, including the mothers and daughters of emperors.[39] When the Emperor Theodosios II

---

[36] For some discussion of the copies after the Colonna drawings that Cardinal Ercole commissioned from Fermo Ghisoni, see Brown, "Paintings in the Collection of Cardinal Ercole Gonzaga," 203–207.

[37] For Colonna's role as an exemplar to other women involved in Reform see Brundin, *Vittoria Colonna and Spiritual Poetics*, especially 63–65; she also discusses Colonna's *Canzoniere Spirituale* for Michelangelo and his reciprocal drawings, 67–100; also Monica Bianco and Vittoria Bianco, "Vittoria Colonna e Michelangelo," in the catalogue *Vittoria Colonna e Michelangelo*, 145–164. For Paleologa's ties to Counter-Reform circles in Mantua see Bugatti, "Orizzonti spirituali," 6–22.

[38] For Guazzo see G. Patrizi, "Guazzo, Stefano," *DBI*, 60:534–538.

[39] It is worth noting that the inventories of Isabella d'Este show that she owned an exquisite cameo depicting Augustus and Livia, for a long time identified with a cameo in Vienna (Kunsthistorisches Museum), now more commonly thought to depict Ptolemy II Philadelphus and his sister Arsinoë; and the so-called "Gonzaga Cameo" in Saint Peters-

died without heirs, in 450, his sister Pulcheria (who had been designated an *augusta*) married Marcian, making him the successor to the imperial throne. To celebrate the marriage, a coin was issued with a reverse depicting Marcian and Pulcheria being blessed by Christ.[40] In late Byzantium, these double portrait coins were frequently used to convey "imperial unity" but also, as Brubaker and Tobler point out, especially when "the role of the empress increased." Double portrait and *augusta* coins continued to be issued in the later Byzantine period to legitimate the continuity of empire through the female line.[41] There are few, if any, precedents for such jugate iconography being employed to depict mothers and sons in the Italian context, but the Margherita-Guglielmo double-portrait coin, of which there are at least two variants, must certainly have been intended to confer on Margherita the status of *augusta* and to legitimate Guglielmo's rule of Monferrato. The use of these images on common currency, in Monferrato, speaks to Guglielmo's desire to publically reinforce his authority by stressing his direct descent from Byzantine imperial ancestry. [42] In fact, in 1567, the year after his mother died, an attempt was made on Guglielmo's life, in Casale Cathedral.[43] His rule was officially accepted in Casale only in 1569 and he officially became duke of Monferrato in 1573.[44] While Margherita was alive, Guglielmo's ascendency was negotiated through the presence of his mother, using her status as the last empress of the Byzantine Paleologue dynasty to assert his sovereignty over the reluctant state of Monferrato, by pairing their portraits on common currency. When she arrived in Mantua, as the bride to Federico II Gonzaga,

---

burg (State Hermitage Museum); although there is still some debate about the identities of the figures portrayed, both were, at one time, thought to represent Alexander and Olympias. See Brown, "Isabella d'Este Gonzaga's Augustus and Livia Cameo and the "Alexander and Olympias" Gems in Vienna and St. Petersburg," in *Engraved Gems*, 85–108.

[40] Brubaker and Tobler, "The Gender of Money," 581–82. I want to thank Dr. Myra Nan Rosenfeld for her helpful comments on the significance of Byzantine coins in the context of these representations of Margherita.

[41] Brubaker and Tobler, "The Gender of Money," 86. See also Cormack, *Writing in Gold*, for an early eighth-century gold coin with a double portrait of Justinian II and his designated heir Tiberios on the reverse, 98.

[42] See also Ahrendt's discussion of Margherita's image on the currency of Monferrato, "The Cultural Legacy," 183–228. She connects jugate portraits of mothers and sons to female rulers of ancient Greece, like Cleopatra Thea, 213–215.

[43] Fenlon, *Music and Patronage in Sixteenth-Century Mantua*, 2:82.

[44] Oresko and Parrot, in *Stefano Guazzo*, 21.

Margherita's role as the liaison between two states was visually and even spatially symbolized through the annexation of her *palazzina* Paleologa to the existing Gonzaga palace. In her widowhood, the conjoined images of mother and son were designed to remind an unwilling populace of the marriage bond that legitimated Gonzaga rule.

After Margherita's death, Guglielmo continued to assert his mother's presence throughout Monferrato, by commissioning altarpieces like the *Madonna of the Rosary*, made for a church in Occimiano, in the province of Alessandria in Piedmont, around 1580. In this altarpiece, beneath the image of the enthroned Madonna, the painter, Ambrogio Oliva, included a number of portraits, among which art historians have tentatively identified Margherita Paleologa, her mother, Anna d'Alençon, the humanist, Stefano Guazzo, Pope Pius V, the Emperor Charles V and, finally, Guglielmo Gonzaga and his sister Isabella d'Este, whose piety during her own widowhood caused her to be venerated almost as a saint after her death, in 1579.[45] Among these figures from Monferrato's political and pious past and present, Federico II Gonzaga is conspicuously absent, his role in the marriage superseded by the political, papal and imperial powers that brought the marriage to fruition, and through which Guglielmo inherited the right to rule Monferrato.

Through her marriage, Margherita Paleologa became princess, duchess, wife, widow, co-regent, public consort of Mantua's cardinal-ruler, mother to and partner with her son, Guglielmo, and protector and symbol of an imperial alliance that both stabilized and destabilized the Gonzaga legacy for succeeding generations. Although it seems that Margherita had very little agency in the matter of her marriage to Federico II Gonzaga, circumstances

---

[45] V. Natale, "Vicende di un'iconografia pittorica," in *Pio V e Santa Croce di Bosco*, 399–443, and see cat. 8, *Madonna of the Rosary*, attributed to Ambrogio Oliva, c. 1580, Chiesa del SS. Nome di Gesù, Occimiano, Italy, 436. The portraits in the lower quadrant of the altarpiece are identified as Margherita Paleologa, Anna d'Alençon, unidentified female profile, the Emperor Charles V, the humanist Stefano Guazzo, Pope Pius V, Bishop Ambrogio Aldegatto of Casale, Cardinal Ercole Gonzaga, Guglielmo Gonzaga and his sister, Isabella Gonzaga d'Avalos, in Grignolio and Angelino, *I tesori delle chiese del Monferrato* — 2, 72–73. The altarpiece is described at Associazione Casalese Arte e Storia, "Monferratoarte." http://artestoria.net/ Indici/Bancadati.php (accessed July 4, 2009). For the veneration of Isabella Gonzaga d'Avalos after her death at Casalmaggiore 1579, see my forthcoming *Women and Religious Patronage in Sixteenth-Century Mantua*.

conferred on her many different identities, as well as varying degrees of visibility and invisibility, as Mantua's compromise bride.

UNIVERSITY OF GUELPH

CITED WORKS

Abbreviations

DBI   *Dizionario Biografico degli Italiani.* 71 vols. to date. Rome: Istituto della Enciclopedia Italiana, 1960– .

Manuscript Sources

Mantua. Archivio di Stato di Mantova (ASM)
    Archivio Gonzaga, Magistrato Camerale, BBII, 1558–1700

Printed Sources

Ahrendt, Martha Sue. "The Cultural Legacy and Patronal Stewardship of Margherita Paleologa (1510–1566), Duchess of Mantua and Marchesa of Monferrat." PhD. diss., Washington University, 2002.

L'arrivo in Monferrato dei Paleologi di Bisanzio, 1306–2006. Studi sui Paleologi di Monferrato, ed. Roberto Maestri. Alessandria: Circolo culturale i marchesi del Monferrato, 2007.

Art and Love in Renaissance Italy, ed. Andrea Bayer. New York: Metropolitan Museum of Art, 2008.

Betussi, Giuseppe. *Libro delle donne illustri.* Venice: 1542.

Brown, Clifford M. "Isabella d'Este Gonzaga's Augustus and Livia Cameo and the "Alexander and Olympias" Gems in Vienna and St. Petersburg," in *Engraved Gems: Survivals and Revivals*, ed. Clifford Malcolm Brown, 85–108. Washington, National Gallery of Art, 1997.

Brown, Clifford M. *Isabella d'Este in the Ducal Palace at Mantua. An Overview of her Rooms in the Castello di San Giorgio and the Corte Vecchia.* Rome: Bulzoni, 2005.

_____. "Paintings in the Collection of Cardinal Ercole Gonzaga." In *Giulio Romano: Atti del Convegno Internazionale di Studi su Giulio Romano e l'espansione europea del Rinascimento*, ed. Oriana Baracchi et al., 203–226. Mantua: Accademia Nazionale Virgiliana, 1991.

Brubaker, Leslie and Helen Tobler. "The Gender of Money: Byzantine Empresses on Coins (324–802)." *Gender & History* 12:3 (2000): 572–594.

Brundin, Abigail. *Vittoria Colonna and the Spiritual Poetics of the Italian Reformation*. Aldershot, UK: Ashgate, 2008.

Brundage, James A. *Law, Sex and Christian Society*. Chicago: Chicago University Press, 1987.

Bugatti, Vera. "Orizzonti spirituali nella trattatistica dedicata alla Paleologa." *Civiltà Mantovana* 41:121 (2006): 6–22.

Cantarelli, Vincenzo and Clifford M. Brown. "La torretta di San Nicolò nel Palazzo di San Giorgio a Mantova (c.1395–1530). Fra ipotesi e certezza." *Quaderni di Palazzo Te* 10 (2000): 78–91.

Corrispondenza Gonzaghesca. Copialettere di M. Paleologa, ed. Maria Luisa Aldegheri with the collaboration of Sonia Gialdi. Mantua: Archivio di Stato, 1994.

Cottafavi, Clinio. "R. Palazzo Ducale di Mantova. I gabinetti della 'Paleologa." *Bolletino d'arte*, ser. 1, vol. 9, fasc. 6 (1929): 276–285.

Davari, Stefano. *"Federico Gonzaga e la famiglia Paleologa del Monferrato." Giornale linguistico dì archeologia, storia, e belle arti*, 17–18, fasc. 11–12 (1890): 421–469; 18, fasc. 1–2 (1891): 40–76; 18, fasc. 3–4 (1891): 81–109.

Fenlon, Ian. *Music and Patronage in Sixteenth-Century Mantua*. 2 vols. Cambridge and New York: Cambridge University Press, 1980–82.

Giovio, Paolo. *Dialogo dell'imprese militari et amorose*. Lyon: Giulio Roviglio, 1559.

Grignolio, I. and L. Angelino. *I tesori delle chiese del Monferrato — 2*. Villanova Monferrato: 1994.

Hartt, Frederick. *Giulio Romano*. 2 vols. New Haven: Yale University Press, 1958.

Luzio, Alessandro. "Federico Gonzaga ostaggio alla corte di Giulio II." *Archivio della Società Romana di Storia Patria* 9 (1887): 502–582.

Luzio, Alessandro. "Isabella d'Este e il Sacco di Roma." *Archivio Storico Lombardo*, series 4, 10 (1908): 5–107, 361–425.

Murphy, Paul V. *Ruling Peacefully. Cardinal Ercole Gonzaga and Patrician Reform in Sixteenth-Century Italy.* Washington: The Catholic University of America Press, 2007.

Nelson, T.G. A. "Doing Things with Words. Another Look at Marriage Rites in Renaissance Drama and Fiction." *Studies in Philology* 95:4 (1998): 351–373.

Pio V e Santa Croce di Bosco. Aspetti di una committenza papale, eds. Carlenrica Spantigati and Giulio Ieni. Rome: Orso, 1985.

Rebecchini, Guido. "Exchanges of works of art at the court of Federico II Gonzaga with an appendix on Flemish art." *Renaissance Studies* 16:3 (2002): 381–391.

Romano, Giulio. *Saggi di Ernst H. Gombrich ...* [et al]. Milan: Electa, 1989.

_____. *Repertorio di fonti documentarie,* ed. Daniela Ferrari. 2 vols. Rome: Ministero per i Beni Culturali e Ambientali, Ufficio Centrale per i Beni Archivisti, 1992.

Shemek, Deanna. "Aretino's Marescalco: Marriage Woes and the Duke of Mantua." *Renaissance Studies* 16:3 (2002): 366–380.

Splendours of the Gonzaga. Catalogue edited by David Chambers and Jane Martineau. London: Victoria & Albert Museum, 1982.

Stefano Guazzo e Casale tra Cinque e Seicento. Atti del convegno di studi nel quarto centenario della morte, Casale Monferrato, 22–23 ottobre 1993, ed. Daniela Ferrari. Rome: Bulzoni, 1997.

Tamalio, Raffaele. *Federico Gonzaga alla corte di Francesco I di Francia, nel carteggio privato con Mantova 1515–1517.* Paris: Champion, 1994.

Verheyen, Egon. *Palazzo del Te in Mantua: Images of love and politics.* Baltimore: Johns Hopkins University Press, 1977.

Vittoria Colonna e Michelangelo, ed. Pina Ragionieri. Florence: Mandragora, 2005.

Internet Sources

Associazione Casalese Arte e Storia. "Monferratoarte." http://artestoria.net/Indici/Bancadati.php (accessed July 4, 2009).

Bugatti, Vera. "Martha Sue Ahrendt, *The Cultural Legacy and Patronal Stewardship of Margherita Paleologa (1510-1566), Duchess of Mantua and Marchesa of Monferrat.* Ann Arbor, Mich., Univ. of Microfilms, 2002." Review, *Venezia Cinquecento* (24 July 2004).

http://www.veneziacinquecento.it/Segnalibro/ahrendt.htm

Circolo Culturale i Marchesi di Monferrato. "I Marchesi di Monferrato." html//www.marchimonferrato.com (accessed July 3, 2009).

"Since She Was Determined to Have Him for Her Husband." A Sienese Woman Who Chose for Herself

Elena Brizio

In the mid-sixteenth century, as a consequence of the various European wars that were fought on Italian soil, the Republic of Siena suffered a series of political crises that, inevitably, affected its social life and political structures. The turmoil that disrupted daily life in the city and its environs had many negative results for both men and women, but it also created loopholes in the social fabric that allowed some women, in particular, to exercise a small amount of agency and personal independence in areas that, otherwise, were simply not available to them. One of these areas was marriage which, for upper class Sienese women, was generally a matter strictly handled and governed by their male kin. In Siena, as in many other Italian states, the regulations and practices governing the marriage of upper-class, moneyed citizens were strictly controlled. In this tense social and political situation, suddenly a Sienese noblewoman decided to choose for herself and, going against the wishes of her family, the interests of her class and the atmosphere in her city, fought hard to marry not only a foreigner, but a soldier from the occupying army.

This article will follow the case of Maddalena della Gazzaia (or Agazzari) and her successful bid to leave her Sienese husband and marry her Spanish lover. Maddalena broke established conjugal bonds, acted contrary to current social practices and demonstrated a level of female agency that was rare in Siena or elsewhere in Italy at that time. Her unusual case, which came before the courts of the occupied city of Siena in 1557, demonstrates that some women did have the strength and initiative to affirm their own autonomy even in matters as fraught with politics and social expectations as marriage.

Maddalena's story can be pieced together through several surviving documents in Florentine and Sienese archives. In none of these documents can one hear her direct 'voice,' but only what is reported about her by men (whether public officers, the Florentine governor, ecclesiastical authorities or the male plaintiffs). Not surprisingly, these documents seem to mask or omit many details of the intriguing story so as not to highlight Maddalena's disruptive behaviour. The role of her first husband's family, the Placidi, is especially 'visible' because more documents related to this politically and economically powerful family do survive, but much less is apparent about her birth family or about her second husband. One hope that, in the course of future research, additional documents will be uncovered that will help to provide a more nuanced and in-depth picture of Maddalena's life and choices. Even in its outlines, however, Maddalena's story is a powerful and important example of how a determined woman could, if she wanted, chose for herself.

Maddalena belonged to a prominent and rich Sienese family, the Agazzari and was married to the scion of an equally important family, the Placidi. Born in 1523, she was presumably the only child of her late father, Rinaldo (b. 1463). Rinaldo married at least twice: in 1505 to Antonia di Pietro Pecci and in 1508 to Girolama di Alessandro di Pietro Sozzini.[1]

In 1539, Maddalena married Marcantonio di Aldello Placidi, older than her by two years and brought him a dowry of 5,000 florins. Marcantonio's mother was Niccola, the daughter of the jurist Bartolomeo Sozzini. In 1531, already a widow, Niccola was mother, guardian and trustee ("mater, tutrix et curatrix testamentaria") of her son, Marcantonio, who was still a ward. It is quite probable that the marriage between Marcantonio and Maddalena was arranged within the Sozzini family, to which both the mothers, Niccola and Girolama, belonged. This, then, illustrates the important role that women played in arranging marriages, a role that is also evident in the case of the Florentine wife and then widow, Alessandra Macinghi Strozzi.

The scandal involving Maddalena revolved not around her first marriage, but around her decision to remarry and, more specifically, to

---

[1] One of Rinaldo's testaments, drawn in 1519, when he claimed to be sick, is a notarial form, only partially filled. No children whatsoever were recorded and the will stipulated only that a large sum be given to the church of Santa Maria degli Angeli, where Rinaldo had his tomb. "... pateat omnibus evidenter qualiter nobilis vir Raynaldus Celidonii de Agazaria civis senensis, sanus Dei gratia mente et intellectu licet corpore languens ... imprimis quidem omnipotenti Deo semperque matri Viriginis Marie gloriose devotissimeque animam suam commendavit et quando ei de presenti vita transmigrare contigerit mandavit corpum suum sepellire apud ecclesiam sancte Marie Angelorum extra et prope portam novam civitatis Senarum in eius tumulo, ubi elegit sui corporis sepulturam ...", ASS, Conventi 2611, fol. 63v.

marry a Spanish soldier living in Siena with whom, as Governor Niccolini informed Duke Cosimo, she had already had an affair while still married to Marcantonio Placidi.

One reason why Maddalena's decision created such a scandal was because it disrupted the well established pattern of endogamous marriage, that is, of marriage within the same social and political level. This was the dominant practice in mid-sixteenth-century Italy because it safeguarded and sustained the current social and political structure. In the crisis years that eventually led to the collapse of the republic of Siena and its incorporation into the dual duchy of Florence and Siena, endogamy was also a means to defend and sustain the local elite against interference from foreigners, in particular Florentines. Maddalena's marriage to a Spaniard aroused animosity in Siena toward both Florentine and Spanish outsiders, while also raising questions about female autonomy.

After the fall of Florence into Medici and Spanish hands in 1530, Spanish troops began to infiltrate Sienese territory. In Siena itself the Spanish were able to use local political dissention to their advantage in order to influence and control local government and even impose the presence of a Spanish garrison in the city. This, in turn, divided the Sienese ruling elite: many supported the Spanish/Imperial presence, but many opposed it and sought French support in their effort to liberate the city from foreign domination. Not only Sienese men, but women as well were caught in the middle of these tensions and, often following their family's choices, sided with one or the other party.

Sienese dislike for the conquering Florentines was so high, even two years after the siege (1554–55), that almost all the Sienese documentation on this case strongly emphasizes opposition to the Florentine conquerors and their Spanish troops. Following the coronation of Emperor Charles V, in Bologna in 1530 and the renewal of war against the French on Italian soil, the strategic position of Siena in the military scenario had become extremely important. Located halfway between Charles's Milanese duchy and his Neapolitan kingdom, torn between internal factions and continuous fighting between the factions of Noveschi and Popolari, Siena was described by the emperor's Spanish envoy as a place where no justice was administered and where the competition between factions impeded daily life.[2] Moreover, opposition from a part of the Sienese government limited the readmission of

---

[2] Hook, "Siena" 108–109

exiles belonging mainly to the faction of the Noveschi. This coupled with years of internal wars and, more recently, with Sienese resistance to the building of a fortress, which the emperor judged to be absolutely necessary, had led to the imperial decision to send a large number of Spanish troops to control the city.

The Sienese considered the Spanish to be invaders and the building of the fortress evidence of imperial disregard, not to say betrayal, of Siena's long-standing adherence to the Ghibelline side. It was no surprise, then, that when the attacking Florentine/Spanish forces were defeated at the Battle of Porta Camollia in 1552 and the Spanish garrison was expelled from the city, the detested Spanish fortress was torn down. Emperor Charles V and his ally, Duke Cosimo I de' Medici, made it a point of honour to reconquer Siena, which in turn sought help from the French king, Henri II, who was married to Caterina de' Medici, Cosimo's cousin and his enemy. As a result of French military aid in its fight against the Spanish during the last three years of its independence (1552–55) Siena, in mid-century, found itself with a constantly growing number of either Spanish or French troops within its walls.

In contemporary Sienese literature and documents, Spaniards were described as "bombastic, emphatic, ceremonious, vain and bragging."[3] We might add destructive and thievish, if we were to believe the chronicles, which report many acts of violence against goods and people. On the other hand, there is one Sienese report, Montalvo's *Relazione*, that is pro-Spanish and it suggests that not all Sienese were anti-Spanish and that many, fearing social and political disapproval, hid their true feelings towards the Spaniards.

After the Florentine capture of Siena in 1555 and while fighting with the "rebels" barricaded in Montalcino continued, King Philip II of Spain appointed Duke Cosimo I to reorganize the Sienese government. Cosimo did not officially change the political structure of the city, but rather sent a legal representative to Siena who, with the title of Governor, was placed in charge of the legal and political administration of the city. When Maddalena's story reached the courts, the Governor was Agnolo Niccolini.

The soldier Maddalena wanted to marry was not, presumably, lower-class; in his letter to Florence, Governor Niccolini reported the man's last name as Luigi Carovagial.[4] Thus, Luigi probably belonged to the Spanish

---

[3] "pomposo, enfatico, cerimonioso, vanitoso, adulatore, fanfarone", D'Amico, "Nemici," 109.

[4] "Alli giorni passati venne qui un Luigi Carovagial spagnuolo ...", ASF, MdP 1864, fol. 267r. In ASS, Notarile antecosimiano 2799, the name is reported as "Aloysius Diegi de

Carvajal family that, in those same years, gave the Catholic Church the bishop of Sovana, Carvajal de Simoncellis (1535–1596), the Dominican preacher Gaspar Carvajal, who was in Peru with Pizzarro and possibly Francisco de Carvajal, who served under Charles V's principal commanders in the Italian wars. At the beginning of the fifteenth century, the family had had a bishop, Juan Carvajal, who was the auditor of the Rota, the papal court, in Rome, and served as papal legate for popes Eugenius IV and Callistus III and he also was a friend of Pope Pius II Piccolomini. Thus Magdalena's Spanish suitor was well connected in his own right.

"The family is disgraced and the entire city is worried and ashamed,"[5] wrote Niccolini to Cosimo, but Maddalena was undeterred. The description of Maddalena that Governor Niccolini gave in his report is particularly intriguing: "The woman is almost thirty [in fact she was almost 34], without children and, they say, that between legal assets and dowry she had about 15 to 20,000 ducats; she belongs to the very noble Gazzaia family, her husband was Marcantonio Placidi [...] the most handsome and honoured young man of this city."[6] Governor Niccolini continued: "he [Marcantonio] died in Naples, sent there by the Cardinal of Burgos, in August of last year when already, the woman recalled, her affair with the Spaniard had begun."[7] At thirty-four years of age, Maddalena was considered old for the time; the fact that she had not had any children suggests that she was, or was presumed to be, barren; she did, however, belong to a noble family and she was rich. Curiously, Niccolini says nothing about her appearance. Marcantonio, on the other hand, is reported to have been very handsome, the most honoured "young man" of the city, his family was very important, his death far away from home, presumably while he was in exile, terrible, aggravated, as it was, by the fact that while he was still alive his wife, back in Siena, was having an affair with a Spanish soldier,

---

Caravagial d'Avela".

[5] "Li parenti tutti rimoreggiono et l'universale della città ne mostra molto dispiacere et vergogna", ASF, MdP 1864, fol. 267r.

[6] "La donna è di circa trent'anni, non ha figliuoli et dicano che fra heredità et dota ha xv o xx^m ducati; è di casa della Gazzaia nobilissima, il marito fu Marcantonio//Placidi ... il più bello et più honorato giovane di questa città", ASF, MdP 1864, fol. 267r-v.

[7] "... morì in Napoli mandatovi dal cardinale di Burgos d'agosto fece l'anno che di già secondo l'attestatione della donna era cominciato la pratica con lo spagnolo", ASF, MdP 1864, fol. 267v. No official reference to the legal "impedement of crime" (X.4.7.1 "De eo qui duxit", fol. 1: "Propositum" and fol. 6: "Significasti") is indicated, but we can presume this was the main point of the scandal.

perhaps the worst insult in a city which had not yet recovered from having been conquered by Florentine/Spanish forces. In short, Marcantonio died far away while being betrayed with the enemy by his wife at home.

It is difficult to imagine Maddalena. Only a few scattered documents refer to her, such as the tax report filed in 1549. These tax reports were filed by every head of a household and supposedly included every item of property (whether houses, lands, livestock, rents, shops and so on), as well as every debt that the head of the family, as its legal representative, owed. In 1549, Maddalena filed her own tax record as heir of her father, Rinaldo and produced a list of all her properties, both in the city and in the countryside, from which she collected rents, wheat and livestock. "I owe my husband Marcantonio 4,500 florins for the remainder of my dowry,"[8] she noted among her debts, without too much emphasis. In his own tax record, while referring to the same dowry money, Marcantonio seemed more worried, perhaps, for the sake of his family: "Because I am childless, it might happen that I have to return it."[9]

Maddalena reported her properties for the tax evaluation, indicating the positive income she garnered from them, but she also emphasized the negative, trying perhaps to downplay her wealth, as was usual when filing one's taxes. She reported, for example, that among her many lands, the property outside the Porta Nuova, close to the city, "gave us more expenses than income."[10] In Maggiano, she rented a piece of land close to the one at Porta Nuova, but "the whole thing is unstable and unclear."[11] This last piece of property, for which Maddalena paid rent, belonged to the Cistercian abbey at Quarto; we know, through a notarial record, that that same year, 1549, Maddalena still owed the legal representative of the abbey more than 90

---

[8] "Dinanzi a voi Signori alliratori si proponchano [sic] da me Madalena della b. m. di Renaldo Achazzari e donna di Marcantonio Placidi l'infrascritti beni e cioè … so debitrice a Marcantonio mio marito di fiorini 4500 per conto delle mie dote" ASS, Lira 242, fol. 4r–v.

[9] "… trovomi credito con l'erede di Renaldo Achazzari mio suociero per resto di mie dote di [proposed reading: fiorini] 4500 quali per non avere io figli può ochorire d'averli a restituire e per dir meglio a scancellar tal credito ogni giorno", ASS, Lira 242, fol. 3v.

[10] "una posessione fuor della porta nuova … invero per più respetti ci dà magior spese che entrate …", ASS, Lira 242, fol. 4r.

[11] "una perpetua d'un altra [sic] posessione continchua [sic] a la detta posta nel comuno di Maggiano … è cosa [cancelled: molto] poco ferma e stabile", ASS, Lira 242, fol. 4r.

florins.[12] In the countryside of Torrita, the peasants' houses "are rented out so as to preserve them, because they are old and threaten to collapse"[13] while the cultivated lands are "places meagre and weak."[14] On a more positive note, she also reported owning two shops close to piazza del Campo that were rented out, that she had 700 florins of credit on the Monte del Sale (a credit bank), that she owned other lands with vines, livestock, trees and wheat and that some money was owed to her by the Commune.

Temporarily housed in a nunnery while she was interrogated (it is unclear if the interrogations were held in a civil or ecclesiastical court), Maddalena showed no hesitation in telling the Captain of Justice and other representatives of the government that she wanted to remain married to the Spaniard.[15] We can imagine that the legal issue at stake here was her previous sexual relationship with Carvajal while Marcantonio Placidi was still alive, albeit exiled, in Naples. According to Governor Niccolini, "She confessed to everything proudly and gave even more information than she was asked, declaring that she still wanted and desired the same thing."[16] Her new husband Luigi, however, seemed more hesitant about the liaison — or perhaps about Maddalena's feelings. He seemed more worried about the general opinion the families (both Agazzari and Placidi) and the city had of him. "He showed me a note written by her [reporting] that more than once she had consummated the marriage: however, if Maddalena had no longer the same feelings, he [Luigi] would not care. But, if she still had, I [the Governor] should discover it, through my authority with more certainty and with less pain for the relatives."[17] Governor Niccolini was thus being asked by Carvajal ascertain

---

[12] AAS, Cause civili 4714, *ad nomen*.

[13] "… tre casette da comtadini chontichue le quali s'apigionano per mantenerle in piè, che sonno vechie e minacciano ruina …", ASS, Lira 242, fol. 4r.

[14] "sonno luochi magri e debili …" ASS, Lira 242, fol. 4r.

[15] "Però ordinai che la donna andassi in uno di questi monasteri honorati, dove fu esaminata dal Capitano di giustizia et per maggiore giustificatione pubblica volsi v'intervenissino duoi di Balia insieme con il notario et altre persone del munistero", ASF, MdP 1864, fol. 267r.

[16] "Confessò ogni cosa arditamente et molto più che non se li domandava, mostrando che di presente ancora voleva et desiderava il medesimo", ASF, MdP 1864, fol. 267r.

[17] "… mi mostrò haver contratto matrimonio molti mesi sono con una madonna Maddalena della Gazzaia: fecemi vedere una polizza di mano di lei et che haveva consumato più di una volta il matrimonio, nondimeno offeriva che se hora la non era più del

what Maddalena's true feelings might be and to find out what exactly she wanted.

The city was totally involved in this scandal, which quickly transformed into a political matter. On 27 November 1557, the Balìa, the small group at the head of the government delegated to make the toughest decisions, planned to write to Duke Cosimo. "We ask your most illustrious Excellency for suggestions and support in the cause of the supposed wedding of Maddalena Agazzari with a private Spanish soldier, so that no difficulties with relatives and the whole city will ensue." The Balìa planned to give Cosimo all the information they could, "as soon as they were well informed."[18] Presumably an investigation was underway.

Some days later, they had clearly reached an impasse; after carefully considering what to do, the Balìa decided to seek advice from the duke and for his authority in settling this matter that was upsetting Maddalena's relatives and the entire city. The also asked the four Balìa representatives to confer with the Governor to increase the punishments levelled against adultery and clandestine marriage (this is the term used in the Balìa document) that were already present in the city's statute.

The statute of 1544, to which the Balìa specifically referred, punished adultery with a fine of 1,000 lire, while the punishment for a violent rape (where rape meant sexual intercourse) was death.[19] The statute made no specific reference to clandestine marriage, but it is possible that the general feeling to which the Balìa referred was that this marriage was decided and organized by Maddalena alone, without the support of her family or relatives. To complicate matters, the Council of Trent was meeting in these same years. While the holiness and the unity of the marriage bond were clearly defined by the Council only after 1562, clandestine marriage was already widely criticised and strongly opposed by the Church. The Balìa presumably considered the

---

medesimo animo non se ne curava, se la era ch'io ci interponessi la mia authorità per scoprirlo con più sicurezza loro et minore travaglio de parenti", ASF, MdP 1864, fol. 267r.

[18] "... havendo havuto fra di loro maturo discorso et essamine deliberorno che li due sottoscritti del collegio faccino scrivare all'illustrissimo et eccellentissimo signor Duca nostro signore //domandando da Sua Eccellenza Illustrissima conseglio e favore in la causa dell'asserto maritaggio di Maddalena Agazzari con un privato soldato spagnuolo acciò non segui annate [sic] con dispiacere de suoi parenti, e de tutta la città, dando a sua Eccellenza piena informatione di questo caso come bene informati", ASS, Balia 169, fols. 103v–104r [27 Nov. 1557].

[19] Dist. III.76 "De poena adulterii, stupri et raptus", in *L'ultimo statuto*, 315.

fine set by the city's statute to be too small for a case such as Maddalena's — the scandal had to be prosecuted and punished more rigorously. The reaction to the Balìa's actions in this case, and the city's criticism of Maddalena's second marriage, clearly indicate that this had not been a marriage organized to appease either the Sienese or the occupying powers, politically or socially.

After taking all the legal actions he could, including setting an unusually high bail for Maddalena, Governor Niccolini set Maddalena free and left the matter in the hands of the ecclesiastical court. He reported to Cosimo that, "we will leave the whole matter to the ecclesiastical court, if someone on Maddalena's behalf wants to dispute it, given her determination that she wanted the soldier for her husband."[20] No specific documents in the archiepiscopal archive in Siena related to a possible marriage litigation between Maddalena and the Placidi have, however, been uncovered to date.

In the wake of the scandal, Marcantonio's relatives sought to complicate Maddalena's and Luigi's lives.[21] In 1559 the Placidi family had not yet returned Maddalena's dowry to her and she was obliged to ask for it, but apparently without success. At about the same time, the Placidi family presented a request in the ecclesiastical court for the restitution of some books "in vernacular, Latin and other writings"[22] which had belonged to Marcantonio but remained among Maddalena's property. It seems that Maddalena had tried to use the books as leverage in her attempt to recover her dowry. In two different petitions presented to the Florentine governor, Agnolo Niccolini, Maddalena and Luigi both asked for his help in dealing with the Placidi family.

A relative of Marcantonio even tried to take outright possession of some of Maddalena's property. From a complaint lodged by Luigi, we discover that Aldello Placidi stole some of Marcantonio's account books and was now managing some goods belonging to Maddalena as if they were his own or as if he were the legal representative of her husband.[23] Husbands, in

---

[20] "Di poi si licenzierà la donna del monasterio et si lascierà la causa al foro spirituale se sia dalla parte di lei chi la voglia disputare, stando ella ferma nel medesimo proposito di volerlo per marito", ASF, MdP 1864, fol. 275r.

[21] No notarial record reporting the wedding contract has been found yet.

[22] ASS, Cause civili 4726, *ad nomen*.

[23] "Luigi Caravagial spagnolo dolendosi che dal capitano Aldello Placidi è stato levato a Torrita certo libro di Marcantonio Placidi che teneva Federigo suo ministro e levatoli ancora il grano spettante alla consorte di detto Luigi, che ha riscosso il predetto Aldello …", ANCF, Suppliche 28, fol. 97r.

turn, were the legal representatives of their wives and managed their wives' goods and property as if they were their own. On these grounds, Aldello had appropriated and was now managing property that, in these account books, was apparently not specifically separated as belonging to either Marcantonio or Maddalena,.

Aldello was also threatening Luigi's — and consequently Maddalena's — workers and administrators. In 1559, a copy of trial records, forwarded to the duke because of the importance of Maddalena's status as a Sienese noblewoman, offered another hint of the difficult times and the excessive conflict that was spreading in the city between the opposing families. On behalf of his wife, Maddalena, Luigi again petitioned the Governor, in May 1560, to help him recover some wheat that had been stolen from Maddalena.[24]

In January 1561, Maddalena wrote to Cosimo I, through Governor Niccolini, lamenting that her dowry, as well as her personal properties and the interest they produced, were still being withheld from her by the Placidi. It is unclear whether, before Marcantonio's death, Maddalena, as heir to her father, had completely paid to her husband all the instalments of her dowry. If her dowry had been paid in full, she would then have been entitled to recover it in full upon her husband's death. It is also possible that she paid only a part of the dowry: the words "le mie dote," as Maddalena described it, are almost always plural in the Sienese sources and referred to all the belongings that a wife brought into a marriage, including personal items. Maddalena explained very clearly that the Placidi family was trying to steal her revenues by nominating one of Marcantonio's nephews as his heir. Apparently, the plan was to have the boy inherit the wealth, then take religious vows and use the ecclesiastical court, instead of the civil court, to retain the inheritance. Maddalena went on to explain, in very clear terms, that the Placidi were also trying to arrange for a possible trial in a foreign court, "in the Roman court or elsewhere," in order to "tire her and not meet their obligations."[25] She then asked the duke for his help in making sure that his subjects were not obliged to appear in court in a foreign city in order to obtain justice at home.

---

[24] "… ancora minaccia come si dice di volere fare li ricolti delle possessioni spettanti alla medesima consorte di Luigi con dire che si appartengono a lui, et di più usa villane parole verso li ministri et contadini del sudetto Luigi", ANCF, Suppliche 28, fol. 97r.

[25] " … in el foro romano o altrove … così da defatigarlla … et non far el dovere", ANCF, Suppliche 234, *ad nomen*.

Like the majority of Sienese women, Maddalena appears almost by chance in the documents. For many years after the legal battles with her former kin, Maddalena disappears from the records. She lived with Luigi at least until 1573, when Luigi again represented her in court, but then she fades again into obscurity.[26] It is difficult to find the exact date of death for Sienese residents, both men and women, because, unlike in the case of births, the city did not keep official records of deaths.

In 1587, at the age of 67, Maddalena married for a third time. On this occasion she wed a Sienese widower belonging, like her first husband and like herself, to a rich and noble local family — Cornelio di Cesare Marsili (b. 1527) — and brought him a dowry of 7,000 florins.[27] In 1598, again widowed, Maddalena took care of the marriage of Virginia Agazzari, a sister of the famous musician Agostino Agazzari, whose relationship to Maddalena remains unclear.[28] Virginia married Teucro, the scion of another branch of the Agazzari and her dowry was fixed at 2,000 scudi. The largest portion of this sum, 1,500 scudi, was paid directly by Maddalena, who added another 200 scudi to be paid after her death.[29]

Why did Maddalena decide, in the central years of her long life, to make the disruptive choice to marry a foreigner and an enemy of her city and thus attract the disapproval of her clan and of her fellow citizens? Perhaps this was her way of rebelling against a controlling marital family; perhaps it was an expression of her wish for personal freedom and of her need for independence. Or, perhaps, it was just plain true love.

---

[26] "… circa quadam sequestrationem fructuum et bestiaminum predicte honestissime domine Magdalene q. Raynaldi de Agazzaria et domini Aloysii Caravagillis [sic] hyspani eius viri existentium in curia Turrite et Ciliani respective …", ASS, Notarile antecosimiano 2796, fol. 24v.

[27] "die 17 iunii 1588 per scriptura privata manu Bernardi Camilli de Cionis fuit denuntiatum qualiter d. Cornelius de Marsiliis dedit anulum d. Magdalene q. Rainaldi de Agazzaria die 17 iunii cum dote florenorum septemmille [sic] de libris quatuor", ASS, Gabella 411, fol. 153v.

[28] "Virginia's dowry was fixed at 2000 scudi, 1500 of which were to be paid outright by a certain Maddalena, widow of Cornelio Marsili and daughter of Rinaldo Agazzari", Reardon, *Agostino Agazzari*, 10.

[29] "pariter de Agazzariis … Et pro dote predicte domine Virginie nobilis, et egregia mulier d. Magdalena filia magnifici q. domini Raynaldi de eadem familia Agazzarios, viduaque novissime relicta magnifici domini domini Cornelii de Marsiliis presens omnibus suprascriptis…Scutos mille septingentos monete ad rationem libras septem denariorum pro quolibet scuto more senense …", ASS, Notarile postcosimiano protocolli, 178.

Like many other Sienese women, Maddalena was clearly strong and determined. Her temperament, but also her wealth and her nobility, had a strong influence on her case and its outcome. We know about Maddalena because she broke the rules. As such, she serves as an example for other women in early modern Italy who sought to exercise greater agency and claim their personal independence.

THE MEDICI ARCHIVE PROJECT — FLORENCE

CITED WORKS

Manuscript Sources

Florence. Archivio di Stato di Firenze (ASF)
    Mediceo del Principato, 1864

Florence. Archivio Niccolini di Camugliano (ANCF)
    Suppliche, 28, 234

Siena. Archivio Arcivescovile (AAS)
    Cause civili, 4714, 4726

Siena. Archivio di Stato di Siena (ASS)
    Balia, 169
    Conventi, 2611
    Gabella, 327, 330, 411
    Lira, 242
    Notarile antecosimiano, 2796, 2799
    Notarile postcosimiano protocolli, 178

Printed Sources

D'Amico, Juan Carlos. "Nemici e libertà a Siena: Carlo V e gli spagnoli." In *L'ultimo secolo della Repubblica di Siena. Politica e istituzioni, economia e società*. Eds. Mario Ascheri and Fabrizio Nevola. Siena: Accademia senese degli Intronati, 2007, 107–139.

Hook, Judith. "Siena and the Renaissance State." *Bullettino senese di storia patria* 87 (1980): 107–122.

Montalvo, Antonio di. *Relazione della guerra di Siena*. Turin: Vercellino, 1863.

Reardon, Colleen. *Agostino Agazzari and Music at Siena Cathedral, 1597–1641*. Oxford: Clarendon Press, 1993.

L'ultimo statuto della Repubblica di Siena (1545). Ed. Mario Ascheri. Siena: Accademia senese degli Intronati, 1993.

Keeping It Together:
Women, Marriage, and the Family in
Late Fourteenth-Century Genoa

Jamie Smith

In his 1491 exhortation to widows to embrace the opportunity that widow-hood provided to devote themselves fully to God, Savonarola lists no fewer than seven compelling reasons for women to shun remarriage.[1] His argu-ments largely rest on the burdens that wives assumed during marriage, such as raising children, managing a household and honouring husbands in both dress and conduct. While his examples of wifely duties are far from compre-hensive, the Dominican friar recognizes in his admonition the vital role of women during marriage and their responsibilities for maintaining the family.

Most historical studies concerning marriage have surveyed the making and breaking of unions, which is the natural result of the extant sources. For instance, scholars have considered carefully the effect the Roman dotal regime had on marriage in premodern Europe.[2] They have paid equal attention to the autonomy and authority, or often lack thereof, accorded to widows.[3] These studies have painted a vivid picture of the opportunities and frustrations women faced on account of their sex and their subsequent role in the marriage market. This study asks: what happened during marriage? What was a woman's role once she married and entered her new lineage? Importantly, might a woman's expected role during marriage affect the choice of a marriage partner for both parties?

---

[1] Savonarola, "On the Life of a Widow," 193–195.

[2] Hughes, "From Brideprice to Dowry," 262–296. Dowry studies are numerous for Italy. See for example, Chojnacki, "Power of Love," 126–148; Kirshner and Molho, "The Dowry Fund," 403–438; Klapisch-Zuber, "The Griselda Complex," 213–246; Queller and Madden, "Father of the Bride," 685–711.

[3] See Blom, "The History of Widowhood," 191–210 and Kalas, "The Noble Widow's Place in the Patriarchal Household," 519. Klapisch-Zuber, "The 'Cruel Mother,'" 117–131, has asserted an important corrective for the young widow, or the "cruel mother," who could be forced by her family to re-marry, often leaving her children with their paternal relatives to begin a new family with her next husband.

Examples from the notarial records from late fourteenth-century Genoa highlight some of the responsibilities Genoese wives assumed during, and on account of, their marriages. The sources for this study are Genoese legal records that do not involve dowry contracts or cases of dowry restitution, in part because the latter have received extensive attention in recent years. The more critical reason, however, is that dotal agreements and restitutions often represent the bookends of a marriage: the creation and the dissolution. This investigation seeks to understand what happened in the middle, which remains a rather murkier picture than that of the beginning or end of marriage.

Although some cynics, both contemporary and modern, have concluded that a woman's worth was tied to her dowry, women were not the sum of their dowries, as notarial evidence proves. An examination of non-dotal records demonstrates the critical role that women played in maintaining their families. The wifely duties in question go beyond attending to household chores, nurturing children, and maintaining a good reputation, which were the foci of many contemporary manner books and sermons. The notarial records demonstrate that further skills were required of Genoese wives, usually resulting from the mercantile activity of their husbands. In fact, Boccaccio offers a hint of this necessity in the *Decameron* in the penultimate story on the second day when he has the Genoese merchant, Bernabò Lomelini, brag to his compatriots in Paris about his wife, claiming that she had all the "wifely" attributes of their wives, but that she could also "sit a horse, handle a falcon, read, write and keep the accounts better than any merchant."[4] Notarial records show that Genoese wives were investors in their marital and natal kinsmen's business ventures; they were appointed as legal agents (known as procurators) for their husbands and immediate kin; they were also legal guardians (known as tutors) for their children.[5]

In direct contrast to the pictures that have emerged from other studies, which highlight the uncertainty of women's lives once they were traded into another lineage, this study emphasizes the pivotal part that many

---

[4] Boccaccio, *The Decameron*, 147.

[5] While many medievalists have used the extensive Genoese notarial records for economic investigations, prosopographic studies for Genoa exist only in later periods. At present, we do not know a great deal about most medieval Genoese. Petti Balbi, *Simon Boccanegra* and Wardi, *Le Strategie* (Antoniotto Adorno) offer studies of two fourteenth-century doges.

women played in their new families.[6] First, we will probe deeper into the significance of the legal guardian, the tutor. Recent studies have highlighted how frequently women assumed the position, although those works focus on widows rather than wives.[7] In Genoa, as a direct result of the itinerant nature of mercantile life, many mothers assumed the legal care of their children while the father lived. Evidence suggests that members of the wives' marital kin supported wives taking this position, which leads to the conclusion that these women were an accepted and integral part of their married families. The second part of the investigation similarly argues that marital kin supported their female in-laws in the latter's attempts to protect the family. A case of suspected collusion underscores the importance of the greater kin network although the case raises another question about marital patterns given that it involves endogamy within the great Genoese lineages.

The evidence suggests that historians should question what predictive assessments went into choosing a marriage partner. Savvy families would surely think through possible outcomes and select their marriages carefully, which may have taken on heightened importance in the post-plague world. As the Genoese struggled to survive the many hardships that befell their city during the fourteenth century, families served as the first line of defence. It took the cooperation of all members, including wives, to plot a healthy and profitable course.

A Picture of Genoa

To understand the pre-modern Genoese family, one needs to consider the environment that shaped daily life.[8] To approach Genoa from the sea would be to recognize the critical role that the Mediterranean has always played in the city's history and the identity of its inhabitants. Nestled in what little space exists between the sea and Apennines in north-western Italy, Genoa horseshoes its deep harbour. Little arable land and limited access to inland cities forced the Genoese to look to the sea for their survival and livelihood. Tales from the city's early history recall the long tradition of men leaving their

---

[6] Foundational is Klapisch-Zuber, "The "Cruel Mother."

[7] Calvi, "Widows, the State and Guardianship of Children," 209–219; Coolidge, "Neither Dumb, Deaf, nor Destitute of Understanding," 673–693; Coster, "'To Bring them up in the Fear of God,'" 9–32; Renzo Villata, "Note per la storia della tutela" and La tutela.

[8] The best overview of the history of Genoa is Epstein's Genoa and the Genoese.

homes daily, sometimes returning in the evening and other times journeying afar. As in the other maritime capitals (Venice, Pisa, and Amalfi), mercantile activity shaped the medieval city.

Despite the rampant factionalism that characterized the city—as it did most Italian communes—Genoa was at the pinnacle of power at the end of the thirteenth century, controlling the Tyrrhenian and Black Seas and conducting more trade through Pera than Constantinople itself (Pera was the name of the Genoese-held land across the Bosphorus Strait from the Byzantine capital). The Genoese had temporarily defeated the Venetians and claimed naval supremacy as well. Economic success was both a blessing and a curse as the commune proved unable to support all of its *oltremare* activities. Since many Genoese families had personal interests in keeping and expanding their colonies, agreements between the commune and groups of merchants (in this case the merchants comprised both nobles and *popolari*) arose. This was the birth of the *maone* (or *mahone*)—loosely defined as a chartered company.[9] Genoese families gained increasing power and prominence in the wider Mediterranean communities, a reality that often benefited individual families, as well as the commune, though it forced families to adjust their routines as many male members needed to stay abroad to oversee their affairs.

In fact, as a result of trade and war, a significant number of men were away from the commune at any given time. The effect of this phenomenon on political structures and the economy has been studied; how it affected the family has not. Importantly, while the patriarchal model may have been the ideal, it was certainly not the reality for significant periods of time for many Genoese families. While their heads of household sailed the perilous waters of the Mediterranean, wives and elder sons navigated the often tricky, albeit metaphorical, waters at home. The law provided important protections for families in these situations. There were provisions that men could take before leaving, and there were safety nets available during male absence.[10] One such preparatory measure would be to appoint a legal guardian for one's children. Similarly, if a legal guardian had not been appointed, but was

---

[9] Argenti, *The Occupation of Chios*, 116–117. The *maone* benefited both the commune and the individual families: the structure allowed the commune to keep the *imperium* of the place while the members of the *maona* reaped the financial rewards of a trading post.

[10] Smith, "Navigating Absence."

deemed necessary, the court could provide one. It is to the legal guardian that we now turn.

The Tutela

Although Roman law accorded little authority to women, their capabilities were expanded during the Middle Ages. A meaningful example of this transition is the office of tutor.[11] William Durandus (1235? –1296) described the situation for women in Roman law in his *Speculum Iuris*. While initially Roman law had forbidden women to serve in capacity of tutor because the *tutela* was a public office, Durandus related that women gained the ability to be tutors for their children through the influence of canon law. He credits the predominant medieval jurist, Azo of Bologna (d. ca.1230) for asserting that despite classical injunctions, a magistrate could confirm a mother or grandmother as tutor.[12] Durandus further added that: "[t]oday in fact a mother is preferred first and after the grandmother to all the legitimate and given tutors, but not the ones appointed by testament."[13] Genoese practices corroborate Durandus's observation.

Notarial records collect the legal dealings of the *tutelae* and, therefore, are useful to reconstruct the activities of tutors. To understand the responsibilities of wives while they held these positions, we will examine *tutelae* from two families in detail. The first case is useful to evaluate what factors, apart from political and economic alliances, went into arranging a marriage. How would each party identify and handle the trust and risk issues that could easily be predicted to accompany a marriage in which the husband traveled extensively? The second example's value lies in the rare opportunity to examine an extant book that contains all the initial notarial actions of a *tutela*. Evaluating the movement of the tutors at each stage highlights the skills necessary for a wife and the approval she must have had from the greater family to succeed in her endeavours. Both cases provide further

---

[11] Before 390 AD, women were not appointed tutors since it was deemed "man's work." However, after 390 widowed grandmothers and mothers who vowed to remain celibate could be appointed if there was no testamentary or legitimate tutor. Berger, *Encyclopedic Dictionary of Roman Law*, s.v. "Tutor."

[12] Durandus, *Speculum iuris*, 1. 3. *de tutore* (ed. cit. I. 246a).

[13] "Hodie vero praefertur mater primo & post avia omnibus tutoribus legitimis & datis, non tamen testamentaris." Durandus, 1. 3. *de tutore* (ed. cit. I. 247a).

insight into how women negotiated the marital waters and prove that they were valued for more than their dowries and the more feminine qualities of beauty, chastity and domesticity. The first example comes from the Pallavicino family and the second from the Squarciafico family. Both were prominent members of the city and headed their own *albergo*.[14] The mercantile activity of the families is well attested and many members found themselves traveling from the commune.[15] In both cases, as in the many other examples that fill late medieval notarial records in Genoa, wives played a prominent role in forming marriages and shaping marriage practices.

The first example, which highlights the social networking between *alberghi*, concerns the marriage of Gabriele Pallavicino to Petra Lomellino. Like the Pallavicino, the Lomellino also headed their own *albergo* and had family members scattered around the Mediterranean. Notarial records show that the family of Gabriele Pallavicino had to contend with his many absences during the last two decades of the fourteenth century. His risky business ventures meant that he, or other members of his family, dealt with the courts on a regular basis. A noteworthy series of events, including emancipations, coming of age petitions, arbitrations and assignments of agent, involved an extended list of family members who substituted for the oft-absent Gabriele. While it is true that historians have the advantage of hindsight, Gabriele's activities were common and predictable. Therefore, we can presume that when his father Cristoforo sought an advantageous match for his son, he had in mind a woman who could serve his son and his future grandchildren in her husband's absence.

Cristoforo found a good match in Antonio Lomellino's daughter Petra. We can conclude that he was satisfied with Petra's abilities to perform within the marriage since, in his testament in April of 1390, Cristoforo appointed his daughter-in-law Petra to be the legal guardian for his grandchildren.[16] Although the appointment was technically illegal (Roman law forbade a grandfather passing over his son if his son still lived), Petra assumed the office of tutor for her children without protest from either side. Objections from either Petra's marital or natal kin could have ranged from concerns over a

---

[14] See below for a discussion of the Genoese *alberghi* and their functions.

[15] See, for example, Petti Balbi, *Simon Boccanegra*.

[16] ASG, NA Cartolare 447, Oberto Foglieta, fol. 212r–v. (12 August 1390). Foglieta recorded Petra's petition to accept the position during which time he noted the testament that had been created with another notary earlier in the month.

woman holding a public, and therefore male, office, to removing children from the power of a competent and living father, to Petra surrendering the legal benefits accorded to her on account of her sex. This last point is worth considering in light of how it affected a woman's legal status and perhaps how it could factor into marital negotiations.

Classical Roman law protected women, who were considered to be weaker than men. Christian jurists followed suit and maintained the premise that just as every wife needed the physical protection of her father and husband, so, too, did she need the legal protection of both. But, what of women who needed protection from their protectors? Worried that wives could fall prey to unscrupulous or manipulative relatives, including their husbands, the Roman Senate passed a law that came to be known as the Velleian decree (*senatusconsultum Velleianum*). This law sought to dissuade women from interceding legally on someone else's behalf. The result was that any transaction involving women in this capacity could be invalidated.[17] Concern that women would invoke the Velleian decree to defraud creditors resulted in mothers having to renounce their rights to it in order to accept the position of legal guardian. When the Genoese magistrate appointed Petra as tutor, she was required to "concede the benefit of the Senatus Consultum and all other laws and benefits in favour of women."[18] Therefore, accepting the position of tutor to help her family placed Petra in a disadvantageous legal position, and left her vulnerable to manipulation from the men around her.

This was a risk Petra was willing to accept. Having conceded her rights, she took up the responsibilities of legal guardianship. She ordered an inventory of her late father-in-law's property and goods that her children stood to inherit; she accepted rents, paid debts and sold property. Importantly, Petra performed her duties as legal guardian even after her husband Gabriele had returned home. For instance, in February of 1392, Petra sold some property that her children had inherited to a relative. Gabriele served as a witness to this transaction, but since his wife was his children's legal guardian, his presence was neither central to nor required for the sale.

Petra also appointed a procurator for herself during her husband's absence. Although when governing their own affairs Genoese laws demanded that wives have the permission of both husband and father, Petra was able to

---

[17] Grubbs, *Women and the Law*, 55–60.

[18] ASG, NA Cartolare 447, Oberto Foglieta, fol. 213r. '... dicta Petra beneficio Senatus Consulti omnibusque aliis juribus et beneficiis in favorem mulierum concessit.'

make the appointment in Gabriele's absence because a recent law, promulgated
a only two decades earlier, allowed wives to act on their own behalf with
the permission of their fathers, if their husbands were expected to be away
from the commune for more than six months and if they could produce two
relatives of the husband to attest to his lengthy absence.[19]

What is striking is not that Petra, or others like her, appear as important
actors in the legal records; that was routine in late medieval Genoa. Rather,
historians should consider the implications that the behaviour of Petra and
other wives may have had on marriage practices. In some ways, both families
risked their well-being when wives were placed in these roles. For instance,
when Antonio Lomellino married Petra into the Pallavicino family, he would
have known that it was possible that Petra would be forced to renounce the
protection afforded to her sex in order to be a good wife to her husband. This
concession could harm Petra if members of the Pallavicino family or *albergo*
were to manipulate the situation. On the other hand, Cristoforo Pallavicino
would also have wondered if the young Lomellino daughter would be able to
manage the affairs of the family on behalf of his son. Moreover, he could also
have been concerned that her natal kin would have more sway over her during
Gabriele's absences because the law stipulated that she would no longer need
her husband's permission to act on her own behalf if he stayed away longer
than six months. Therefore, families exchanged a significant amount of trust
upon marriage.

Another case, involving the Squarciafico family, highlights how wives
were integral in maintaining the family. The Squarciafico lived with the noble
families of Fieschi, Marocello, di Negro, Mari and de Marini in the *compagna*
of San Lorenzo and had formed their *albergo* in the mid-thirteenth century.[20]
Members of the lineage populated and were involved in the commerce of
the eastern colonies of Caffa, Chios and Pera.[21] When Pietro Antonio
Squarciafico died intestate, it was his mother Isabella who stepped in to assist
his infant heir. This case merits discussion in detail for a few reasons. First, it
is known from one of the few extant collections of acts from a *tutela* that are

---

[19] *Leges Genuenses*, col. 877.

[20] Cattaneo, *I "Politici,"* 188.

[21] Balard, *La Romanie génoise*, 235, 236, 250. The prominence of the Squarciafico
family in the administration of the commune faded during the fifteenth century as fewer
served as public officials. They did not retain an independent albergo during the restruc-
turing in the mid-sixteenth century. Cattaneo, *I "Politici" del Medioevo Genovese*, 50.

self-contained. Most acts appear in the Genoese notarial records on an *ad hoc* basis. The book of the *tutela* allows a rare view into the intricate burdens legal guardians assumed. The second reason, which is closely related to the first, is that since a wife accepted these duties, the book of the *tutela* demonstrates the duties that a wife might expect during marriage. Third, the details provide insight into how the formation and negotiation of a *tutela* involved many members of the family, not only those who were appointed to the position. Significantly, the case underlines the influence women exercised in their new lineage when their marital kin accepted them as assets to the greater family.

Isabella, wife of Giovanni Squarciafico, approached the civil court judge on 10 April 1389 to record that her son, Pietro Antonio, had died intestate, leaving his infant son as sole heir.[22] She submitted a petition to the magistrate to appoint a legal guardian for her grandson. Several anomalies appear in this petition, although they are easily reconciled when it is contextualized. First, according to Roman legal practices governing the *pater familias* (head of the family) and his *potestas* (power), Pietro Antonio's death did not affect the legal guardianship of his son. As *pater familias*, Giovanni had always had control over his children and their children. In other words, Giovanni was Jacopo's legal guardian. Why would Giovanni's wife petition to remove that power? Second, although it was common for widowed mothers or grandmothers to assume the position of tutor, Isabella was not a widow; her husband Giovanni lived. Third, Giovanni was present in Genoa when Isabella submitted the petition, therefore, not even his absence can explain these actions. Moreover, in contrast to Durandus's portrayal and the preference stated by the Genoese statutes that the mother was preferred first before the grandmother, Jacopo's mother Marieta did not appear in the petition. While Jacopo remained physically with his mother (a fact revealed in a later petition in which the grandmother, Isabella, limited the amount of support Marieta could receive from Jacopo's estate), his mother had no legal voice in the affairs regarding her infant son.[23]

Importantly, Isabella appeared before the judge with two male members of her kin network, Jacopo Scarampo and Dorino Usodimare. Although the Genoese statutes allowed a woman to hold the office of tutor

---

[22] ASG, NA Filza 415, Revellino, Cristoforo, 10 April 1389.

[23] Since the notarial records are silent on ages, one supposition could be that Marieta was no more than a child herself, which would be in keeping with Italian marriage practices.

by herself, lawmakers preferred that she share the duties with male relatives.[24] Jacopo Scarampo was the son-in-law of Giovanni and Isabella Squarciafico. Dorino Usodimare was possibly a maternal relative of the young Jacopo. The three petitioned the judge to appoint a tutor for Pietro Antonio's son since the infant stood to inherit a substantial and intricate patrimony.

Following Genoese legal prescriptions, six names were offered as tutors, three from the maternal side and three from the paternal side. Of the three petitioners, Dorino Usodimare's name is the only one on the list. Isabella's husband Giovanni and his son Gerardo made the cut for the paternal side along with perhaps another son or brother Gregorio. Nominees from the maternal side included Dorino, Jacopo and Giovanni Usodimare, although the record contained no description of consanguinity.

It is necessary to follow the procedure closely because each step highlights the way in which the law protected families. Tutors commanded a great deal of power when their charge possessed land or goods. Property transfers, including those through inheritance, were sensitive issues due to the value of property and the opportunities for fraud. Therefore, the laws demanded that the greater kin network be notified of the initial petitions for the position. Since the petitioning trio followed protocol, the greater kin network became informed of their intentions. Immediately after the petition had been filed, the public crier performed his duty by citing the six individuals who should appear before the judge within three days if they were willing to accept a position in the *tutela*. After time had expired without anyone stepping forward, the judge gave the public crier a new order for a general announcement in the neighbourhoods, providing the opportunity for anyone appropriate to appear. The second proclamation had the same result: no one solicited the judge. Although this seems like a minor point, it is telling. The fact that no one else came forward to accept the office of tutor or to object to any of the petitioners proves that the greater family supported the appointment of three petitioners.

Therefore, on 14 April in the home of Isabella and Giovanni Squarciafico, the judge confirmed the three petitioners as co-tutors (*con-tutores*).[25] Each tutor took the oath of office and each also offered another

---

[24] *Leges Genuenses*, col. 895.

[25] ASG, NA Filza 415, Revellino, Cristoforo, 10–14 April 1389. The record of their appointment rehearses the standard provisions of the statutes concerning co-tutors. The tutors should be in agreement, one could not act on his or her own concerning any ad-

person as *fideiussor* (guarantor), in accordance with the Genoese statutes. Her husband stood for Isabella, Bartolomeo Scarampo for Jacopo and Nicolò Spinola for Dorino. Moreover, Gianotto Squarciafico and Manuele Squarciafico swore to the veracity of the fact that Pietro Antonio died intestate. Thus, it took eight people from the greater family to assure the judge that the family believed young Jacopo would be in good hands.

Although three were appointed, it is clear in the notarial records that Isabella took the lead. When the tutors desired to appoint actors to assist them in managing the inheritance, the group met the notary in Isabella's house. She appeared as first actor in the early records. For some of the acts, the notary listed Isabella's husband Giovanni as a witness to the proceedings. At other times, the notary recorded Giovanni's absence. Giovanni's absences explain why the family by-passed his legal standing as *pater familias* and appointed alternate legal guardians for the young Jacopo.

Managing Jacopo's estate was a complex affair. Isabella and her co-tutors needed to be knowledgeable of the family's business abroad to appoint the appropriate people to oversee the needs of their ward. On the day of their appointment, the three tutors assigned Bartolomeo Scarampo as an actor and procurator on behalf of the *tutela*.[26] The mandate, though a general one, also included a specific task: to track down any goods related to Jacopo's inheritance, which the tutors noted were scattered around the world (*per diversas mundi partes*). Thus, Bartolomeo acted as the traveling *tutela*. Eight days later, without removing Bartolomeo, the co-tutors added Manfredo Salnaygus, Cristoforo Vento and Martino Leonaldo as additional actors.[27]

The tutors needed the greater family again when they desired to sell some of the inheritance to pay off creditors. Out of concern for fraud, Genoese lawmakers required the permission and direction (*auctoritas et mandatus*) of a judge before tutors could alienate goods pertaining to a *tutela*. Two relatives from each side of the family stood before the judge to support the tutors' intention to sell some of the inheritance and to place the remaining

---

ministration. However, two tutors could complete an act without the third. If any of the tutors needed to be removed or excused for any reason, it was that person's responsibility to arrange for the appointment of a substitute. *Leges Genuenses*, col. 902.

[26] ASG, NA Filza 415, Revellino, Cristoforo, 14 April 1389.

[27] ASG, NA Filza 415, Revellino, Cristoforo, 22 April 1389. This follows the Roman law model laid out in the Digest that the first procurator to act be given preference above the others. *Dig.* 3.3.32.

proceeds in the public debt of the city, stating that this action would benefit the young Jacopo.[28]

An anomaly of activity appeared within a month of the appointment. On 11 May, Isabella approached the judge by herself in the name of the *tutela*. She submitted a petition to limit the supplement (*taxatio alimentarum*) that Jacopo's mother Marieta could receive for her son's wet-nurse (*alompne*).[29] Although it is clear that the family supported her since otherwise the *taxatio* would not have been applied, Isabella's actions contradicted the tenor of the statutes that mandated at least two actors agree when three had been appointed. Nevertheless, both the judge and the greater family accepted this petition to protect Jacopo's inheritance.

Trouble arose a few weeks later, however, when the two uncles appeared as the main actors in a petition to appoint another actor, Ambrosio Squarciafico, a paternal relative. In fact, there is an interesting discrepancy in the original document. The notary initially wrote "in the presence of the said Isabella, wife of Giovanni Squarciafico, the third tutor of the said Jacopo and not agreeing but entirely contradicting..."[30] Later, he crossed out this sentence and wrote above it and in the margin of the sheet "in the absence of the third tutor of the said Jacopo, Isabella, wife of Giovanni Squarciafico, nevertheless legitimately cited and requested and mandated by the Lord Vicar of the Lord Podestà of the city of Genoa..."[31] Jacopo Scarampo and Dorino Usodimare continued without Isabelle and appointed Ambrosio Squarciafico as an actor for the *tutela*.

The crossed out lines raise, but the rest of the record does not answer, important questions about what happened in the course of the proceedings and why one of the three tutors disagreed with the precedent and rather

---

[28] *Leges Genuenses*, cols. 873–874. As with any transaction that involved Jacopo's inheritance, these actions needed to be recorded in a public instrument and copies kept with the cartulary that contained all the acts of the tutors as well as with the magistrate who appointed the tutors. *Leges Genuenses*, col. 899; ASG, NA Filza 415, Revellino, Cristoforo, 17 May 1389.

[29] I thank Diane Owen Hughes for the definition of "alompne".

[30] ASG, NA Filza 415, Revellino, Cristoforo, 26 May 1389. "Presente dicta Isabella uxore Johnis Squarzafici tertia tutrice dicti Jacobi et non concenciente sed omnino contradicente..."

[31] ASG, NA Filza 415, Revellino, Cristoforo, 26 May 1389. "abstente tertia Isabella uxore Johanis Squarzafici tutrice dicti Jacobi pupili tamen legipmte citata et requisitio demandato domini vicarii domini potestatis civitatis Janue ..."

mundane appointment of yet another actor for the *tutela*. Nevertheless, the appointment stood; unlike Isabella's previous actions with the taxatio, the appointment of Ambrosio was legal since two tutors could act as three if the third had been cited and was aware of their intentions.[32] Isabella disappeared from the record for the next six and a half months, while Jacopo and Dorino maintained their oversight of the estate.

In early December, Isabella, who had communicated with her husband during the interim, re-emerged. She presented letters (no longer extant) from her husband to the judge, which stated Giovanni's preference that his wife abrogate her position in the *tutela*.[33] Giovanni's letters explained that his concern was for "decency" regarding the administration of the *tutela*, and that since his wife had been appointed as his substitute, he had the right to ask for her removal. Unfortunately, the historical record does not state the specific cause of Giovanni's offense to the actions regarding the *tutela*. Without more information it is impossible to conclude if gender, economics, or family politics was the source of affront.

The family, specifically the other tutors, disagreed with Isabella's request. Jacopo and Dorino at first suggested that the judge should not grant her resignation.[34] They invoked the notion of a specific partnership, known as a *societas*, claiming that she could not break the agreements of the partnership on her own. Their arguments were unsound since partners in a *societas* were bound through consent (*consensus*), which could be dissolved through death, bankruptcy or by one partner withdrawing (*renuntiatio*).[35]

The next step for the two tutors, who argued that they could not operate the *tutela* on their own despite six months of evidence to the contrary, was to ask the judge to replace Isabella so that they would still be three. They stood on firmer ground with this request since both the statutes and their appointment mandated this procedure. Therefore, the judge granted Isabella her resignation and requested three names as potential replacements. He was given Gregorio and Gerardo Squarciafico, who were solicited initially, and Antonio Gandico, whose relation to Jacopo was not stated. Repeating the

---

[32] ASG, NA Filza 415, Revellino, Cristoforo, 14 April 1389.

[33] ASG, NA Filza 415, Revellino, Cristoforo, 9 December, 1389.

[34] Justinian made it very difficult for tutors to resign their posts, but the Genoese statutes simply insisted that the tutor who stepped down provided the funds to find and install a substitute.

[35] Berger, *Encyclopedic Dictionary*, s.v. "Societas."

process, the judge ordered the public crier to inform the cited men, then when no one accepted the position, the public crier made a general announcement. Unfortunately, it is here that the book of the *tutela* ends.[36]

The office of tutor carried great responsibility. It was not uncommon in late fourteenth-century Genoa to see mothers and grandmothers assuming the burdens of the office for their children. Moreover, in Genoa, the office became an added obligation of some marriages before it became a duty of widowhood. Both Petra and Isabella substituted for their itinerant husbands to preserve the family. Importantly, in each case, the husband could have appointed another person to perform the task, but instead chose his wife. Moreover, no objections arose from the family, which signifies the approval of the greater kin network. These wives were trusted and integral members of their marital lineage. They had the skills necessary, or the means to acquire them, to oversee the needs of the family. Genoese notarial records add weight to Boccaccio's portrayal of Genoese wives and suggest to historians that they played important and respected roles in their families.

A Case of Collusion

The final example also involves protecting children, albeit in a manner differing from that of a legal guardian. In April of 1396, Sobrana Doria took responsibility for protecting her family by negotiating the quandary in which her son-in-law's suspicious activities placed the Doria family. While initially it appeared as if Sobrana sued her son-in-law, a closer investigation that follows the case outside of the courts and into arbitration, reveals that her actions protected her itinerant kinsman as well as the Doria family name and fortune.[37] Given the status of the Doria family in the commune, Sobrana sought to avoid public knowledge of their spurious activities and to safeguard her natal and marital clan.

---

[36] A *tutela* for the young Jacopo reappears in the records fourteen months later. By February of 1391, Isabella, who was by now a widow, had assumed the role of tutor, this time with her son Gerardo. ASG, NA Cartolare 417, Cristoforo Revellino, fols. 60v–61v (25 February 1391). Jacopo no longer had a maternal relative in charge of his legal well being.

[37] The arbitration case involving Sobrana Doria and her family offers a warning to historians who read case material as strictly adversarial; while Sobrana essentially sued her son-in-law, she did so to protect him and their family.

The Doria were not just any family. During the thirteenth century, they joined with the Spinola family to lead the commune as captains of the people. Despite being nominally pushed out of the government by a popular leadership in the middle of the fourteenth century, the Doria remained politically influential and certainly economically dominant. Importantly, the Doria and Spinola were the first families to start building *alberghi* in the thirteenth century; by the end of the fourteenth century, they seem to have begun a new trend: that of endogamy. Unheard of in the High Middle Ages, examples of inter-lineage marriages among the Spinola and Doria are found throughout the late fourteenth-century notarial and financial records. While historians have concluded exogamic practices initially strengthened ties within the Genoese commune, it is possible that the end of the fourteenth century presented these families with a very different set of circumstances that led them to change their marital conventions.

Internal strife, which led to fifteen different dogeships and sixteen years of foreign leadership during the fourteenth century, prevented the continuity necessary for the economy to recover and society to stabilize. Further exacerbated by plague, poor economic conditions encouraged families to band together for strength and survival. Genoese families created formal alliances, known as *alberghi*, which reflected their lineage ties and spatial connections within the city. Taking the name of the strongest family in the alliance, each *albergo* functioned as a city within the city, possessing its own well, bakers, garbage removal system and many included a parish church. They fortified their domains, with some *alberghi* gaining political or military clout while others increased their economic output. By the early sixteenth-century, in order for a family to be considered noble, they needed to be part of an *albergo*.[38]

Initially, the trend of intra-*albergo* marriage is said to have strengthened ties within the city. Indeed, Emmanuel Wardi highlights this tendency in his study of the marriage strategy of one of Genoa's most exciting doges, Antoniotto Adorno.[39] Nevertheless, fourteenth-century notarial records reveal families choosing marriage and business partners within the albergo, sometimes even within their own lineage. This conservative marriage

---

[38] Hughes, "Urban Growth," 28. Heers, "Urbanisme et structure sociale," 388, has characterized them as "petits bourgs féodaux au coeur de la cité, domaines particuliers du clan familial, on pourrait dire de la tribu."

[39] Wardi, *Le Strategie familiari.*

practice parallels Benjamin Kedar's findings for business practices in general at this time.[40]

The case under investigation here involved arbitration among members of the Doria *albergo*. Sobrana Doria, daughter of Ansaldo Doria, married Pietro de Mari; after his death, she married Paolo Doria. Sobrana married her daughter, Nicolosia, to one Banaraschus Doria. Sobrana also had a son Napoleone, who was left as heir when his sister Nicolosia died. Like all husbands, Banaraschus controlled his wife's monies. Inconveniently for Napoleone, his brother-in-law was out of town on business. Therefore, in April of 1396, Napoleone submitted two requests to the civil court judge.[41] First, he wished to make a claim against his sister's goods as his inheritance. Since he stepped forward as an heir, the judge needed to issue a general call for all creditors of Nicolosia to appear before him in order to establish what remained for him to inherit. Second, Napoleone asked to have a curator appointed for Banaraschus's goods so that he could extract the amount to which he was entitled. The second petition was common in the Genoese notarial records given how often men traveled for extended periods of time. Lawmakers ensured the flow of commerce by enacting legal procedures to work around absence.

A few days after the court appointed the curator general (a city official who accepted the curatorial duties when no kinsmen would), Martino Gavi, to oversee Banaraschus's goods, Sobrana summoned the same notary to her house to appoint her brother, Cazano Doria, as procurator for Napoleone and herself.[42] Her reason for doing so emerged two weeks later when the notary composed an arbitration agreement (*compromissum*) between Cazano Doria and Martino Gavi.[43] As the decision (*laudum*) of the arbitrators (Nicolò Sauli and Lodisio Doria) details, there was far more to Napoleone's inheritance request than an outsider would have assumed. The decision also reveals why Sobrana and kin preferred that their requests be treated out of court.

Cazano, acting his own behalf as well as for Sobrana and Napoleone, presented Martino Gavi with eight separate claims against the goods of Banaraschus. Significantly, only two of the eight petitions pertained to the late Nicolosia (the original reason for Gavi's appointment). The remaining

---

[40] Kedar, *Merchants in Crisis.*

[41] ASG, NA Filza 421, Revellino, Cristoforo, 13–17 April 1396.

[42] ASG, NA Cartolare 422, Cristoforo Revellino, fol. 151r–v (21 April 1396).

[43] ASG, NA Cartolare 422, Cristoforo Revellino, fols. 164r–165r (5 May 1396).

six specify money that the trio, at one point in time or another, lent their kinsman, Banaraschus, as personal favours or as investors. Some were straightforward debts, like the 175 GL for wool Banaraschus owed Cazano or Sobrana's earned proceeds from an overseas venture. Since the creditors, Cazano and Sobrana, could produce verifiable evidence of their legitimate claim, the arbitrators instructed Gavi to turn over the requisite sum. For others, such as Napoleone's claim that Banaraschus borrowed some cash for which the former could only give an oath, the arbitrators withheld judgment.

The fifth petition submitted was more complicated but revealing. In order to prove his claim against the 300 GL that he had invested with Banaraschus in an *accomendatio* contract, Napoleone produced the contract that noted he would be owed profits. Napoleone's only proof that his brother-in-law was indeed profiting from this investment, however, were letters that described his ship's behaviour as "*in modo pirratico*" in the Dardanelles Straits.

This petition immediately suggests why arbitration might be preferred, although historians need to be wary of anachronistic analysis. In the Middle Ages, piracy was in the eye of the beholder, and the line between trade and piracy or warfare and piracy was thin or even blurred. Yet, piracy did interrupt trade and jeopardize diplomatic relations. If the city had a peace agreement with another state and it came to light that someone of the Doria family was subverting it, there could be harsh consequences for the family.

A more convincing explanation to the question of arbitration is to query the original petition, which was Napoleone's innocuous inheritance claim, that installed a curator general for Banaraschus's goods. Napoleone never made a public claim against his brother-in-law; his petition cited only his sister's goods. The judge summoned creditors for Nicolosia, not her husband. Yet, once the court had appointed a curator general, the family had the opportunity to seek restitution on their debts without notifying other creditors. In this way, the greater Doria family protected themselves. The petitioning trio recovered their due while also safeguarding their debtor by keeping their actions out of the public eye. Their actions are understandable given that the other party to the case was also a relative. Therefore, this example should serve as a warning to historians that the adversarial structure of the courts system may reflect a non-existent animosity.

More important for the current discussion, this case may explain why families sought closer alliances rather than wider ones. Involving a family outside of, or unsympathetic to, the Doria clan may have resulted in far greater public knowledge of Banaraschus's debts and behaviour. Instead, the Doria family used legitimate legal actions to secure their own interests. The role that Sobrana played was perhaps less troublesome to her marital kinsmen since she simply moved between branches of the greater lineage.

The late fourteenth century may have been a turning point for marriage practices. Faced with increased hardships, as a result of political turmoil within the city and challenges to their dominance in the Mediterranean, some Genoese families chose to close ranks rather than expand their networks in the city. It is plausible to conclude from the evidence that, given some families' circumstances, the search for brides would take into consideration the duties wives would need to perform during marriage and how much the brides' families would be involved in their business. With the ever-increasing uncertainty at the close of the fourteenth century, is it any wonder that we see Genoese marriage practices opting for endogamy? Despite the changes to marriage practices, however, the role of the wife does not appear to have diminished. Genoese wives remained vital to maintaining the family.

Conclusions

This examination of what a few Genoese women experienced during and on account of their marriages demonstrates that wives were integral to preserving the family. The evidence encourages historians to bear in mind that families may have considered the managerial abilities of a bride and the predicted travel of the groom, along with political and economic factors, to determine the most suitable match. The choice of bride was more complicated than the size of the dowry or her family's political affiliation. Families would search for a trustworthy and capable woman since she might have authority in family affairs. These examples also demonstrate that wives were included in negotiations beyond those issues that concerned their dowries.

The legal records of Genoa reveal another side to premodern women's lives and their roles during their marriages. They are powerful proof that women played integral roles in their new families. As these cases demonstrate, women did not need to be involved in the activities that they oversaw. No dowry money was at stake for the female actors, therefore, the laws did not mandate their presence. Male members of the family could have easily handled the situations without input from these women. Yet, each of the wives not only played an important role in the proceedings, but also appeared as the main actor. Procedural law dictated that the greater kin network must agree to women serving as agents of the family, which demonstrates that male members of the family trusted the women enough to assign them the roles. It is evident that the greater kin group respected the ability of wives to keep the family together.

INDEPENDENT SCHOLAR

CITED WORKS

Manuscript Sources

Genoa. Archivio di Stato di Genova (ASG)
Notai Antichi

Filza 415	Cristoforo Revellino
Cartolare 417	Cristoforo Revellino
Filza 421	Cristoforo Revellino
Cartolare 422	Cristoforo Revellino
Cartolare 447	Oberto Foglieta

Printed Sources

Agosto, Aldo. "Nobili e popolari: l'origine del dogato." In *La storia dei Genovesi, atti del convegno di studi sui ceti dirigenti nelle istituzioni della Repubblica di Genova*. Vol. 1, 91–120. Genoa: L'Associazione, 1980.

Argenti, Philip P. *The Occupation of Chios by the Genoese and Their Administration of the Island, 1346–1566*. Cambridge, UK: Cambridge University Press, 1958.

Balard, Michel. *La Romanie génoise: XIIe–début du XVe siécle*. Rome: École française de Rome, 1978.

Berger, Adolf. *Encyclopedic Dictionary of Roman Law*. Transactions of the American Philosophical Society 43:2. Philadelphia, PA: American Philosophical Society, 1953.

Blom, Ida. "The History of Widowhood: A Bibliographic Overview." *Journal of Family History* 16:2 (1991): 191–210.

Boccaccio, Giovanni. *The Decameron*. Translated by Guido Waldman with an introduction and notes by Jonathan Usher. Oxford: Oxford University Press, 1993.

Calvi, Giulia. "Widows, the State and Guardianship of Children in Early Modern Tuscany." In *Widowhood in Medieval and Early Modern Europe*. Edited by Sandra Cavallo and Lyndan Warner, 209–19. Women and Men in History. London: Longman, 1999.

Cattaneo Mallone di Novi, Cesare. I *"Politici" del Medioevo Genovese (ricerche d'archivio): Il Liber Civilitatis del 1528*. Genoa: s.n., 1987.

Chojnacki, Stanley. "Power of Love: Wives and Husbands in Late Medieval Venice." In *Women and Power in the Middle Ages*. Edited by Mary Erler and Maryanne Kowaleski, 126–148. Athens, GA: University of Georgia Press, 1988.

Coolidge, Grace E. "Neither Dumb, Deaf, nor Destitute of Understanding": Women as Guardians in Early Modern Spain." *Sixteenth Century Journal* 36: 3 (2005): 673–693.

Coster, W. "'To Bring them up in the Fear of God': Guardianship in the Diocese of York, 1550–1668." *Continuity and Change* 10 (1995): 9–32.

The Digest of Justinian. English translation edited by Alan Watson. Latin text edited by Theodor Mommsen with the aid of Paul Krueger. Vols. 1–4. Philadelphia, PA: University of Pennsylvania Press, 1985.

Durantus, William. *Speculum iuris...Gul. Durandi Aureum repertorium*. Frankfurt: Sumptibus haeredum A. Wecheli & J. Gymnici, 1592.

Epstein, Steven A. *Genoa and the Genoese, 958–1528*. Chapel Hill, NC: University of North Carolina Press, 1996.

Heers, Jacques. "Urbanisme et structure sociale à Gênes au Moyen-Age." In *Studi in onore di Amintore Fanfari*. Vol. 1, 371–412. Milan: Giuffrè, 1962.

Hughes, Diane Owen. "Domestic Ideals and Social Behavior: Evidence from Medieval Genoa." In *The Family in History*. Edited by Charles E. Rosenberg, 115–143. Philadelphia, PA: University of Pennsylvania Press, 1975.

_____. "From Brideprice to Dowry in Mediterranean Europe." *Journal of Family History* 3:3 (1978): 262–296.

_____. "Kinsmen and Neighbors in Medieval Genoa." In *The Medieval City*, edited by Harry A. Miskimin, David Herlihy, and Adam L. Udovitch, 95–111. New Haven, CT: Yale University Press, 1977.

_____. "Urban Growth and Family Structure in Medieval Genoa," *Past and Present* 66 (1975): 3–28.

Grubbs, Judith Evans. *Women and the Law in the Roman Law: A Sourcebook on Marriage, Divorce and Widowhood*. New York: Routledge, 2002.

Kalas, Robert J. "The Noble Widow's Place in the Patriarchal Household: The Life and Career of Jeanne de Gontault." *Sixteenth Century Journal* 24:3 (1993): 519–539.

Kedar, Benjamin. *Merchants in Crisis: Genoese and Venetian Men of Affairs and the Fourteenth-Century Depression*. New Haven, CT: Yale University Press, 1976.

Kirshner, Julius and Anthony Molho. "The Dowry Fund and the Marriage Market in Early *Quattrocentro* Florence." *Journal of Modern History* 50 (1978): 403–438.

Klapisch-Zuber, Christiane. "The "Cruel Mother": Maternity, Widowhood, and Dowry in Florence in the Fourteenth and Fifteenth Centuries." In *Women, Family, and Ritual in Renaissance Italy*, translated by Lydia G. Cochrane. Chicago, IL: University of Chicago Press, 1985, 117–131.

_____. "The Griselda Complex: Dowry and Marriage Gifts in the Quattrocentro." In *Women, Family, and Ritual*, 213–246.

Leges Genuenses: Historia Patriae Monumenta. Vol. 18. Turin, 1901.

Queller, Donald E. and Thomas F. Madden, "Father of the Bride: Fathers, Daughters, and Dowries in Late Medieval and Early Renaissance Venice." *Renaissance Quarterly* 46:4 (1993): 685–711.

Petti Balbi, Giovanna. *Simon Boccanegra e la Genova del '300*. Genoa: Marietti, 1991.

Renzo Villata, Maria Gigliola di. "Note per la storia della tutela nell'Italia del Rinascimento." In *La Famiglia e la vita quotidiana in Europa dal '400 al '600: fonti e problemi; atti del convegno internazionale, Milano, 1–4 dicembre, 1983*. Rome, 1986.

_____. *La tutela: Indagini sulla scuola dei glossatori*. Milan: Giuffrè, 1975.

Savonarola, Girolamo. "On the Life of a Widow." In *Girolamo Savonarola, A Guide to Righteous Living and Other Works*. Translated by Konrad Eisenbichler. Toronto: Centre for Reformation and Renaissance Studies, 2003, 191–226

Smith, Jamie. "Navigating Absence: Law and the Family in Genoa, 1380–1420." Ph.D. diss., University of Toronto, 2007.

Wardi, Emanuel. *Le Strategie familiari di un doge di Genova: Antoniotto Adorno 1378–1398.* Turin: Scriptorium, 1996.

Mixed Marriages:
Family Strategies Across the Noble-Burgher and Rural-Urban Divides

Shennan Hutton

In 1349, the noble Jean d'Oisy sold a house and city lot in the Flemish city of
Ghent to a burgher named Willem Bette.[1] The property, located in the city's
best neighbourhood, had originally belonged to Justaes Passcharis, a Ghent
patrician who was probably Sir Jean's father-in-law.[2] By the unwritten legal
custom of Ghent, sales of city lots, as immovable property, were usually performed in person before the aldermen who governed the city. For reasons
which are not explained, Sir Jean instead sent a chirograph (a legal document
on parchment) which the clerk recorded in the aldermen's register, one of the
oldest surviving from Ghent.[3] The clerk "flemishized" the seller's name to "my
lord Jan van Hoysy, knight" (*mijn heer Jan van Hoysy ridder*), and wrote that,
"my lord Jan promises that he will come into Ghent and will bring with him
my lady, his wedded wife, and that they both will perform the legal sale of the
house and city lot to William."[4] The chirograph was a preliminary advisement
to the aldermen of the sale, which would be properly and ritually performed,

---

[1] This article is based on research conducted at the City Archives of Ghent (*Stadsarchief Gent*) and funded by a Fulbright grant.

[2] Blockmans, *Stadspatriciaat* (City Patriciate), 187, 446–449, 547.

[3] SAG, series 301, no. 1, fol. 62r, act no. 1, 16 Apr. 1350. Both Justaes Passcharis
and Jan van Hoysy are identified by the title *mijn heer* (my lord), but the addition of the
word *ridder* (knight) identifies van Hoysy as a lesser noble. Clerks sometimes identified
patricians as *mijn heer*, but it is possible that Justaes Passcharis was regarded as a noble as
well. A Jan Passcharis was lord of Oudenaarde and Pamele from the 1360s through 1382.
Buylaert, "Eeuwen van ambitie (Centuries of Ambition)," Appendix 2: Database Vlaamse
Adel (Flemish Nobility Database). However, Justaes (or Eustasse) was the first name of
several Passcharis men listed by Blockmans as patricians. Blockmans, *Stadspatriciaat*, 80,
99, 446–449, 509.

[4] SAG, series 301, no. 1, fol. 62r, act no. 1: "ende vort heift miin heer Jan vors. gheloft
dat hij commen sal binnen Ghend ende sal met hem bringhen miir vrouwen siin wettelike
wijf ende dat zij beede den vors. Willem wettelike te sinen coepe van den huus en herve
vors. doen sullen" (and so my lord Jan has promised that he will come to Ghent and will

according to custom, by both husband and wife, before the aldermen, at some future date. The clerk also noted the names of two local men, Diederic van der Leyen, a burgher moneychanger, and Maes Passcharis, who both stood as surety for Sir Jean's act.

Although on the surface this property sale seems to have little to do with marriage, it actually exemplifies the nature of mixed marriages in fourteenth-century Flanders. By mixed marriages, I mean marital alliances between nobles and burghers (urban commoners), in families who held property in both urban and rural areas. Mixed marriages offer an avenue to consider two distinct strands in the historiography of the family in Northern Europe. The first involves the noble family, largely based on rural estates, and began with Georges Duby's argument that, in the twelfth century, noble families became patrilineal and agnatic structures, meaning that kinship, property and status passed down only through a single line of male descendants.[5] Although daughters were still important to secure alliances, they were given dowries in movable property — that is, cash, furnishings, or annuities — rather than inheriting a share of the family land, or "patrimony." Daughters' descendants were not considered to be part of the family, according to Duby. In recent years, Evergates, LoPrete and others have levelled serious challenges to Duby's construction of the patrilineal noble family, showing that throughout thirteenth-century France noble women held fiefs — immovable property, patrimonial land inherited from their natal families.[6] While less work has been done on the fourteenth century, it seems clear that the "power of women through the family," typical in early medieval and Carolingian times, lasted throughout the Central Middle Ages in France and in Flanders, its northern-most province.[7]

The second historiographical strand focuses on the burgher family, either as merchants, patricians, or craft guild artisans, located in late medieval cities. Scholars first looked at the origins of inheritance and marital property practices from Germanic custom or Roman law and the tension between the nuclear household and the extended family. They tried to specify the myriad

---

bring with him my lady his legal wife and they both will perform legally the sale of the house and city lot to the aforesaid William.)

[5] Duby, *Medieval Marriage.*

[6] Evergates, *Aristocratic Women*; LoPrete, "Women, Gender and Lordship" among others.

[7] McNamara and Wemple, "Power of Women."

distinct practices particular to each city and region, while still drawing useful conclusions for burgher families as a whole.[8] For the Low Countries, at least, they concluded that the burgher family was largely cognatic, that is, that kinship, property and status passed down on both sides of the family.[9] Those scholars who have crossed the divide between noble and burgher (as social groups in the past and also as modern historiographical categories) have examined mixed marriages in terms of social mobility and displays of social status, particularly among the office-holders in the Burgundian state of the fifteenth and sixteenth centuries.[10] Mixed marriages in fourteenth-century Flanders remain largely unexplored, especially in terms of actual family strategies and property arrangements.

Focusing on mixed marriages allows us to re-examine what the reified categories of "noble" and "burgher" held in common and in what areas their fundamental differences lay. Although specific tactics varied widely among families, I found that there was very little difference in global marital strategies between late medieval noble and burgher families in Flanders. Both wanted their children to marry within their own social group or into a higher group and negotiated marital accords with an eye to preserve and increase family property, to conclude political and factional alliances and to maintain status and honour, just as their counterparts did elsewhere. Moreover, close study of the records of property transactions from mixed marriages show that both burgher and noble families in Flanders were cognatic, with kinship, status and property flowing through both the maternal and paternal sides of the family. One of the repercussions of this powerful family dynamic was an extra scope of activity allowed to married women as defenders of their natal family's interests. As a result, noblewomen often managed family property, sometimes sending representatives, or appearing in court themselves, in order to defend their own, their husband's, or their family's interests.

These conclusions are shaped by the sources which survive: contracts, lawsuit records and inheritance agreements heard before the aldermen of Ghent, from 1339 through 1361, and recorded in their registers. The aldermen

---

[8] Herlihy, *Medieval Households*.

[9] Howell, *Marriage Exchange*, and "From Land to Love"; Prevenier, *Marriage and Social Mobility*; Kittell and Suydam, *Texture of Society*; Nicholas, *Domestic Life*; Carlier and Soens, *Household*.

[10] Blockmans and Janse, *Showing Status*; Dumolyn, "Nobles, Patricians and Officers."

of the *Keure* were one of two boards of magistrates who governed Ghent.[11] In accordance with the city's customary law, the aldermen of the *Keure* judged disputes and some criminal offenses, promulgated ordinances and validated contracts, mostly concerning property and debts. A second board, the aldermen of the *Gedele*, supervised orphans' property and inheritance. There were few marriage contracts or wills in the annual registers kept by the aldermen's clerks, because the city's inheritance and marital property customs were strictly enforced by the aldermen, who would not let them be put aside by any agreement.[12] Both boards of aldermen validated contracts and private agreements, first by witnessing the principals performing the act, and then by affixing their seal to a parchment sheet, called a chirograph, which contained a summary of the act. Besides making copies of the chirograph for all parties, the aldermen's clerk would, for an extra fee, copy the contract or settlement into the aldermen's annual register. These registers are thus rather like a combination of a notarial register and a court roll. The sources for this study are the earliest surviving annual registers of the aldermen of the *Keure*, which date from 1339 through 1361.[13]

The acts in these registers are terse summaries, but some, like the sales contract of Sir Jean d'Oisy, reveal useful information about property, family and gender roles. The clerk's method of identification signals that Sir Jean came from a noble family, while he identified Sir Jean's wife only by her title "my lady" (*mijn vrouw*) and her marital connection to Sir Jean. The way that the clerk identified the property, however, indicates that, before she became "my lady," his wife was probably a commoner from the patrician Passcharis family.[14] The last owner of the house and city lot was the deceased Justaes Passcharis. The act does not say, as do others, that Passcharis had sold the house and city lot to Sir Jean.[15] The distinction between the house and

---

[11] Decavele, "Bestuursinstellingen," 277–321.

[12] Godding, *Le Droit privé*, 288.

[13] SAG, series 301, no. 1 contains fragments of the annual registers from 1339–40, 1343–44 and 1345, and four complete annual registers, from 1349–50, 1353–54, 1357–58 and 1360–61. For further analysis on the database of more than 1,500 legal acts from these registers, see the larger study, Hutton, *Women and Economic Activities*.

[14] Patricians were the highest non-noble group. They were elites, but within the cities. A woman from a patrician family would have high social status, but she would not be considered noble.

[15] See as examples, SAG, series 301, no. 1, fol. 40r, act no. 1, 27 Nov. 1349; fol. 124r, no. 4, 10 Mar. 1354.

the land on which it stood was important because Flemish custom regarded land as immovable property while the houses on it were movable property. The aldermen's clerks paid careful attention to identifying ownership of immovable property, particularly if that property was a city lot, or *erf*. When the city of Ghent had received its original charter of privileges from the count of Flanders, citizenship and the right to participate in the government of the city went to the men who owned city lots.[16] These men, the wealthiest merchants of the eleventh and twelfth centuries, became the patricians, and their descendants held special status and privileges in the city. Even though, by the fourteenth century, city lots were often bought and sold in a quite commercialized property market, ownership of a city lot was still a matter of some importance. The aldermen of the *Keure* required that all sales of city lots had to be done before them, or recorded by them. Because Sir Jean did not have the right to sell the property alone, he was not the heir of Justaes Passcharis. His promise that both he and his wife would perform the sales ritual together likely indicates that the house and city lot that Sir Jean was selling was the inheritance of his wife.[17]

In mid-fourteenth-century Ghent, the principle that a husband should have authority over his wife and her property was not as strong as the principle that property should be transmitted to the proper side of the family. Although the customary law, first written down in the sixteenth century, stated that married women were legally incapable and under the control of their husbands, the custom of the fourteenth century was much more fluid.[18] The strict and equal division of property, according to the city's custom, outweighed other considerations.[19] The completely partible inheritance custom of Ghent, and the rest of Flanders, meant that sons and daughters

---

[16] Godding, *Le Droit privé*, 165; Blockmans, *Stadspatriciaat*, 52–55, 320–324.

[17] It is possible, but in my view unlikely, that Sir Jean's wife was only to appear to give her consent to the sale of community property or that it was Sir Jean's personal property. The clerks used a different legal formula when a wife renounced her right to a dower (*bilevinge*) from her husband's personal property or their community property, for example: "Joncvr. Lijsbette vors. heift quite ghescolden … alle de bilevinghe ende recht dat so namaels hebben mochte an dit vors. land. (Joncvrouw Lijsbette aforesaid has declared quit/renounced … all the dower and right that she ever might have on the aforesaid land.)" SAG, series 301, no. 1, fol. 58v, act no. 2, 5 Mar. 1350.

[18] Gheldolf, Du Bois, De Hondt, eds., "Coutume Homologuée," in *Coutume de la ville de Gand*, [hereafter: *Coutume Gand*], rubric XX, no. 3, 1:86.

[19] Hutton, "On Herself," 325–349.

could inherit equal amounts of property from their parents. When a couple married, rather than making provisions for dowry and dower, each family gave a marriage portion, some or all of that child's share of the inheritance from both parents.[20] Some parents gave daughters both movable and immovable property when they married.[21] Other parents waited until they died to transfer immovable property to their children. In the end, however, all the immovable property, with the exception of fiefs, was divided equally among all sons and daughters, without regard for sex or birth order. "My lady" was not necessarily an heiress with no brothers; in fact, it is likely that the Maes Passcharis, who was a surety for Jean d'Oisy, was her brother. Either when she married, or when Justaes Passcharis died, she had inherited the house and city lot as her portion of her father's estate.

Even though every Fleming, noble or burgher, would have agreed that her husband, Sir Jean d'Oisy, had the right to govern his wife and enjoy the profits from her family's property, they would never have considered him to be the owner of that property. Under Ghent custom, when a couple married, all of their movable property became "community property," owned by both and managed by the husband during the marriage.[22] Each spouse retained ownership of their "personal property" (*eigen goed*), the immovable property they owned before the marriage or inherited during it. When one spouse died, the other received half of the community property outright, with full rights to dispose of it as he or she wished. The other half of the community property, and all the deceased's personal property, went to the heirs, his or her children, or if there were no children, members of his or her natal family.[23] The surviving spouse also received the profits from half of the deceased's personal property and half of the heirs' portion of the community property. This usufruct, the right to the income from the property but not the right to own or sell it, is sometimes translated from Middle Dutch into English as dower or dowry (*bilevinge* or *duwarie*), but in Ghent it was not gender-

---

[20] Meijers, *Oost-Vlaamsche erfrecht* (East Flemish Inheritance Law), 52–53.

[21] SAG, series 301, no. 1, fol. 225r, act no. 1, 1360–61. Hutton, *Women and Economic Activities*, 59–79.

[22] Godding, *Le Droit privé*, 266.

[23] Meijers, *Oost-Vlaamsche erfrecht*, 56–59.

specific.[24] The surviving spouse, widow or widower, received the same profits and rights and held the same responsibilities for debts and obligations.[25]

The logic of this inheritance custom, and the similar customs of other Flemish cities and regions, was that the children of sons and daughters became members of the extended family and rightful heirs of its patrimony — the fundamental component of the cognatic family system. If Sir Jean and "my lady" had children, they would inherit the house and city lot as heirs of the Passcharis family. But if "my lady" died with no surviving children, the city lot, as immovable property, was to return to her family. To insure this, the mid-fourteenth-century customary reasoning held that Sir Jean could only sell the property together with his wife, never by himself. This logic was not so much designed to protect her rights as it was to protect her family's rightful possession of that property.

Sir Jean d'Oisy also owned personal property, some of it likely held in fief. Land held in fief was the one exception to the universal partible inheritance custom of Flanders. In the eleventh and twelfth centuries, the Flemish counts had led a movement to turn the rural land holdings of the noblemen and knights, who comprised their fighting force, from partible inheritances into fiefs to be inherited by the eldest son.[26] The counts were motivated by the desire to ensure an adequate economic base to support their vassals, and noble families, represented by both male and female members, cooperated to preserve a core of property as a patrimony. Counts and nobles gradually worked out methods to insure portions for younger sons and support for widows, while still dedicating most of the land held in feudal tenure to the eldest son. Widows did not inherit fiefs, but were given lifetime use of one-half of the profits from their late husband's fiefs, which would ultimately go either to his son or back to his family. These arrangements were very similar to English, Norman and French noble patrimonial strategies, and they developed during the same time period (1000–1200) Duby highlighted

---

[24] Godding, Le Droit privé, 292–293, 302–305 and 311–312.

[25] This is a significant difference from both Douai, where a widow could flee her late husband's estate (but only if the couple had a marriage contract [*ravestissement par lettre*] that gave them that right) and Bruges, where creditors were paid only after the widow was given her portion of the community property. Howell, *Marriage Exchange*; Murray, "Family, Marriage and Moneychanging;" *Coutume Gand*, rubric XX, no. 20, 1:92.

[26] Heirbaut, "Weduwen, erfgenamen en lenen (Widows, Heirs and Fiefs)," 7–26.

for similar transformations in the Mâconnais region.[27] However, while Flemish noble families were trying to preserve a core of family property for a single male heir, as the economy became increasingly commercialized, these twelfth-century arrangements became much less relevant to noble marital strategies.

Flemish nobles began to seek out mixed marriages when they needed more money to buy horses, armour and other accoutrements required to maintain their status, while, at the same time, urban burghers were growing increasingly wealthy. This process happened throughout northern Europe, but it was accelerated in Flanders. Flanders was the first region of northern Europe to develop a commercialized economy based more on trade and wool cloth production in urban centers, than on agriculture. Although the Flemish cities were smaller than Venice, Florence and Genoa, Ghent was larger than any city in the north, except Paris and perhaps London.[28] In addition, the density of urbanization and the interpenetration of city and countryside in Flanders resembled that of north-central Italy.[29] In Flanders as in Italy, the distance between average nobles and the most elite burghers was not as great as in rural areas of Europe. Favoured by geographic location and liberal policies from the Flemish counts, merchants, shippers and cloth wholesalers, from the Flemish cities of Ghent, Bruges, Ypres, Douai and Lille, grew immensely wealthy from profits on the production and trade of wool cloth, which reached its peak in the 1270s. By contrast, Flemish farmland was of poor quality, and peasants held it in *cheins* tenure at rents fixed in the twelfth century.[30] In the increasingly monetized economy of the late Middle Ages, the real value of a Flemish noble's fiefs fell at a more precipitous rate than the value of lands held by his more fortunate counterparts in England or elsewhere in France. Flemish nobles were very likely to need infusions of cash from marriage alliances with burgher families, who were even wealthier than their peers elsewhere in northern Europe.

Nevertheless, the distinction between a noble and a burgher was clear in the eyes of contemporaries. Noble status was connected to family background, exercise of banal feudal justice and recognition of that status by

---

[27] Duby, *La Société aux XIe et XIIe siècles dans la région mâconnaise*.

[28] Prevenier and Boone, "City-State Dream," 81–105.

[29] Nicholas, *Growth of the Medieval City*, 112–114.

[30] Godding, *Le Droit privé*, 163–164.

fellow nobles.[31] Method of address in the city's legal documents exhibits the careful distinction between "my lord Jan van Hoysy, knight" and "the lord Gillis Rijnvisch" (*der [de heer] Gillis Rijnvisch*), the patrician who was the chief alderman of the *Keure* in 1349–50.[32] In many cases, a noble title for one member of a family did not convey noble status on the entire family. However, Flemish nobles were more likely to be involved in trade, albeit at a safe distance from shopkeeping or manual labour, than nobles elsewhere. For example, the Vaernewijc family of Ghent held a fief just south of the city and were always identified as nobles, but members of that family held offices in city government, invested in city lots, urban property and annuities and engaged in commercial deals with patricians and burghers.[33]

Burghers (*poorters*), themselves, were divided into different status groups. The most prestigious group, closest to nobles in status, were the patricians, who had begun buying rural land and intermarrying with the nobility in the thirteenth century. By the fifteenth century, many had become nobles, but they did not abandon the city and commercial enterprises, but instead combined their traditional urban base with noble contacts and rural investments. [34] Just below the patricians in status were burgher families, who had risen to wealth and power through guild leadership, trade and banking in the thirteenth and fourteenth centuries.[35] Comparable to the "new men" of the Italian city-states, these elite burghers maintained power bases in the guilds, finance or trade, but also diversified their investments among urban and rural land, annuities and commerce. The wealthiest and most prominent guild leaders formed a social group of guild elites, led by the most powerful men in the weavers and the provisioning guilds. Below these elite groups of burghers, there were thousands of middling tradesmen and artisans, who did not possess sufficient wealth to attract noble marriage proposals.

The distinction between the noble-dominated countryside and the burgher-dominated city, never strong in Flanders, was breaking down rapidly by the mid-fourteenth century. Patricians and elite burghers combined urban commercial interests and rural property ownership, and fiefs were bought, sold and leased, to nobles, patricians or burghers, just as any other commercial

---

[31] Buylaert, "Eeuwen van ambitie," 18–53.

[32] SAG, series 301, no. 1, fol. 62r, act no. 1, 16 Apr. 1350.

[33] SAG, series 301, no. 1, fol. 52r, act no. 3; fol. 115v, act no. 5, and fol. 140r–v.

[34] Boone, *Gent en de Bourgondische hertogen*, 36, 39–40, 122, 159.

[35] Howell and Boone, "Becoming Early Modern," 302–303.

property. Social networks also combined urban and rural connections among nobles, patricians and burghers, as Sir Jean d'Oisy's sales contract exemplifies. Sir Jean's sureties were a Ghent moneychanger and a patrician with the same surname as his wife. Scholars track medieval Flemish social networks, in part, by looking at which people acted as sureties for each other — since acting as a surety meant putting one's own honour and money on the line for the good behaviour of another.[36] The persons Sir Jean relied upon were burghers, in a social network either created or reinforced by his marriage alliance with a Ghent patrician family.

Nobles were also attracted to Ghent and other Flemish cities because the cities were semi-autonomous political entities, which competed with the Count of Flanders for noble allegiance. Because of the privileges the counts of Flanders had conceded to the cities since the twelfth century, the three leading cities — Ghent, Bruges and Ypres — were far more powerful than the local nobility, and often challenged the count himself.[37] Particularly noted as the "rebellious city," for its many uprisings against any centralizing efforts by the Flemish counts and, after 1384, the Burgundian dukes, Ghent controlled a huge hinterland, one-third of the county, as its "quarter." Many nobles, who held fiefs in Ghent's quarter, fought on the city's side during rebellions against the count. Some also became Ghent citizens, in order to profit from the judicial privileges of the city.

When nobles became "outside citizens" (*buitenpoorters*) of Ghent, the city's aldermen controlled the division of their estates. Although the aldermen upheld the primogeniture of fiefs, they did not honour marriage contracts or wills which reserved other types of property for the male or female family line. In 1353, the aldermen rejected the special provisions of a marriage contract between a noble citizen of Ghent, Roeger Brysteet, and his wife, Kateline van Reckam.[38] Authorized and sealed at the comital feudal court at Courtrai, the marriage contract specified a fixed dower for Kateline and confirmed her right to her clothing and bedroom furnishings. The aldermen threw out these provisions because they violated Ghent custom. The property Roeger held in fief went to his heir, and Kateline received half the profits for her lifetime, the traditional dower provision from feudal custom. Lady Kateline could not claim her clothing or furniture as her own. Instead, as movable property, it

---

[36] Haemers, *For the Common Good*, 5–10, among many others.

[37] Prevenier and Boone, "City State Dream."

[38] SAG, series 330, no. 2, fols. 32–33, published in *Coutume Gand*, 529–540.

was divisible between her and the heirs, according to Ghent burgher custom. Even though both spouses were nobles, who likely held property all over Flanders, the aldermen's adherence to Ghent custom overrode their marriage contract. Despite the fact that the aldermen's motivation was more likely to enforce their jurisdiction, at the expense of the feudal courts and the count's authority, rather than to deal with the specific issues of the case, the effect was that nobles often had to comply with urban legal customs, based on a cognatic family structure, in their property arrangements.

Noble families in the city's orbit, who had intermarried with patricians and elite burghers for generations and were embedded in urban social networks, probably followed the aldermen's lead in considering their families to be cognatic structures. Mixed marriages were quite common, not only between noblemen and burgher heiresses, but also between noblewomen and burgher men. The noble woman could retain her title in a mixed marriage to a burgher. At several points between 1349 and 1354, a Bruges patrician, Clais Alverdoe (no title), appeared before the Ghent aldermen to manage the personal property of his wife, identified as "my lady Agnes van Brakele, Lady of Zonnemare."[39] Since the property came from Agnes's side of the family, the aldermen considered her its true owner. Even as the clerk recorded that Clais Alverdoe was acting "in the name of and as guardian of Lady Agnes," the clerk emphasized that Agnes was the owner and rightful manager of a plot of moorland:

> The aldermen ... declared that ... **the lady** should have peaceful use of the moor, and if **my lady** sold, or wanted to sell, or will sell the moor ... [that] ... **my lady** has sold [that moor legally] without hindrance.[40]

---

[39] SAG, series 301, no. 1, fol. 31v, act no. 2: "Claise Alverdoe in den name ende alse vogt van mirer vrouwen Agneesen van Brakele vrauwe van Sonnemare sinen wetteliken wive. (Clais Alverdoe in the name of and as guardian of my lady Agnes van Brakele, lady of Sonnemare, his legal wife.)"

[40] SAG, series 301, no. 1, fol. 133r, act no. 4, 30 May 1354: "der vors. vrauwen tfors. moure zouden paysivel doen ghebruken ende waerd dat miin vrauwe den vors. mour vercocht hadde ofte vercoepen wilde ofte vercochte dat zij elken wettelec doen ten vors. moure die min vrauwen vors. vercocht sal hebben zonder belet. (the aforesaid lady would have peaceful use of the aforesaid moor and if my lady had sold or wanted to sell or sold the aforesaid moor that she in each case would be performing legal actions regarding the moor which my lady would have sold without hindrance."

Agnes had inherited immovable land from her noble family of origin, which her patrician husband managed for her. Regarding her as the legitimate representative of her noble family's interests, the aldermen explicitly gave the power to use and sell the property to Agnes, and not to her and her husband together.

Clais Alverdoe did not always act for Agnes, as her husband and guardian. She performed a legal act to manage her property, filing a lawsuit against a fellow noble over property use, by herself, in an act dated just one month after the one quoted above. In that act, the clerk did not even mention Agnes's husband's name nor the fact that she was a married woman. He did note, however, that she was the owner of the land in question and the person who had brought the suit.[41] Clais Alverdoe's claim of acting as his wife's "husband and guardian" was, in fact, the exception rather than the rule for Ghent acts involving married women in the mid-fourteenth century.

Ghent burgher and patrician women routinely performed legal acts to manage their personal property in the mid-fourteenth century. In my larger research database of the more than 1,500 economic acts in the surviving aldermen's registers from 1339 to 1361, one in four acts contains at least one woman acting in her own name.[42] This means that the clerk recorded that the woman was the active party, without using language that would indicate her dependence on anyone else. A further nine percent of the total acts include husbands and wives acting together, again without language of dependence, while only three percent of the acts include a man acting as a guardian of his wife or an adult woman. Of the 491 women who performed legal economic acts — buying, selling, loaning, borrowing, bringing or answering lawsuits — 26 were clearly noble, 133 had patrician surnames and 85 had the same surnames as elite burghers. Noble and patrician status did not prevent a woman from publicly performing legal acts concerning her personal property, and sometimes even community property, without male representation.

Although most noble, patrician and burgher women seem to have cooperated with their families, sometimes women insisted on managing their own property against the wishes of a male relative. When a patrician wife, Kateline Borluut, died, her husband, Jan Criekersteen, tried to get his sister-in-law, Eleene Borluut, to let him continue to control the property the sisters had together inherited from their brother, Pieter. The clerk recorded that, "Jan wanted to use the gift in the same way with *Joncvrouw* Eleene in

---

[41] SAG, series 301, no. 1, fol. 136r, act no. 3, 1 July 1354.

[42] Hutton, *Women and Economic Activities*, 43 and 47.

place of *Joncvrouw* Kateline, his late wife."[43] Eleene protested, however, and the aldermen upheld her claim. Eleene acted in her own self interest and in defiance of her brother-in-law's wishes, but her actions were aligned with the strategic considerations of the cognatic family. While the circumstances of the "gift" from her brother are not explained, by cognatic logic, her family expected Eleene to defend that property for them.

Some women did choose to let male relatives handle their affairs in the aldermen's court. After the death of her husband, the "noble and worthy lady" Lijsbette van Leuwerghem, leased all of her usufruct and property rights throughout Flanders to her son-in-law and daughter in exchange for an annual payment of fourteen pounds groot.[44] Lijsbette included protective clauses fining them if they were late in making a payment, of course, but otherwise the agreement shows her stepping back from involvement in favour of her son-in-law. In six acts from the aldermen's registers, husbands, noble and burgher, acted for married noblewomen, in the same way that Clais Alverdoe had managed Lady Agnes' personal property as her "husband and guardian." Noble women hired representatives in another seven acts. However, in twenty-six acts, noble women appeared themselves before the aldermen to manage legal and economic affairs. These women were exercising power deriving from urban customary law, but also from an understanding of their responsibility to the cognatic family.

While they probably had very little choice about whether or not they would be married to a noble, patrician, or elite burgher, noblewomen could use urban customs and cognatic family ideologies to extend their control over property, even while they were married. This can be seen in the public activities of Lijsbette (or Isabelle) van Lierde, Lady of Zomergem, one of the spouses in the most prominent mixed marriage in fourteenth-century Ghent. Lijsbette van Lierde was an exceptional woman by her birth, her mixed marriage, her wealth and the extent of the documentation about her actions. She was a liminal noblewoman, the illegitimate half-sister of the count of Flanders, Louis of Nevers. Louis of Nevers arranged her marriage to one of

---

[43] SAG, series 301, no. 1, fol. 137v, act no. 2, 18 July 1354: "Welke ghifte de vors. Jan wilde ghebruuken ghelijc Joncvr. Eleenen vors. in de stede van Joncvr. Kateline vorseid zinen wijve was. (which gift the aforesaid Jan wanted to use in the same way with Joncvrouw Eleene in the place of Joncvrouw Kateline aforesaid, who was his wife.)" Joncvrouw was a title denoting social status, not age or marital status.

[44] SAG, series 301, no. 1, fol. 84r–v, 4 Aug. 1350.

his most important supporters, a financier named Simon de Mirabello or van Halen.[45] Simon de Mirabello came from an Italian banking family which had emigrated from Lombardy to Brabant around 1300, and operated a bank with branches in many cities of Brabant and Flanders.[46] Simon ran the Ghent branch of the family banking house, and rapidly built an even greater fortune through making large loans to Count Louis of Nevers, and serving as his financier, tax farmer and receiver. Simon's marriage to Lijsbette gave him access to the count's family circle, and from the marriage onwards, documents identify him as "my lord van Halen" (*mijn heer van Halen*), a noble. Simon was an early example, therefore, of a financial expert who rose from burgher origins to nobility through state service. He departed from the model, however, when the anglophile cities rebelled against francophile count, in the opening manoeuvres of the Hundred Years' War. Count Louis fled to France, but Simon chose to join Ghent and the rebels, who appointed him regent of Flanders. In 1346, as the rebel regime was losing, he was murdered by supporters of Count Louis.[47]

Simon de Mirabello or van Halen was an extremely wealthy man. In addition to his interests in the family bank, he personally owned extensive rural property in Flanders and Brabant, as well as houses, real estate and annuities in many cities.[48] Prominent men owed him large sums of money, including Edward III, his largest debtor, Count Louis and the dukes of Brabant and Clèves. Lijsbette and he had had no children, but he had two daughters, another Lijsbette and Kateline, from a previous marriage. Simon had married his daughter, Lijsbette, to the noble Ywein van Vaernewijc, from the local noble family which already straddled both the urban-rural and noble-burgher boundaries. Simon had married his second daughter, Kateline, first to a Ghent patrician, Gherem Uten Swane, and second, to the noble Philip van Massemine, Lord of St. Joris. Kateline had children by both husbands. Since Simon had no living legitimate sons, he had to look to his daughters and their children to continue his family line. He married each daughter into a solidly noble family which had connections to the city of Ghent, thereby insuring the noble status of his descendants, even though he had lost the count's favour.

---

[45] Kusman, "Jean de Mirabello," 843–931; Rogghé, "Mirabello," columns 709–712.

[46] Kusman, "Jean de Mirabello," 887.

[47] Prevenier and Boone, "City State Dream," 86; Kusman, "Jean de Mirabello," 902.

[48] Kusman, "Jean de Mirabello," 881–895.

After Simon's death, the division of his estate between his widow, Lijsbette van Lierde, and his heirs, represented by his sons-in-law, the nobles Ywein van Vaernewijc and Philip van Massemine, generated many legal acts recorded in the aldermen's registers.[49] As the surviving spouse, Lijsbette received outright ownership of half of the community property, and usufruct of half of Simon's personal property and half of the heirs' half of the community property. She controlled, therefore, three-quarters of Simon's huge estate. While she could have retired and let her sons-in-law manage the estate and pay her an income, Lijsbette chose a more active role. She quickly remarried a Brabantine nobleman, Arnold van Horne, Lord of Rummen, but she did not rely upon him to manage her property or legal affairs. Instead, she used her status as the "noble and worthy Lady Lijsbette, widow of my lord Simon van Halen, now legal wife of my lord Arnold van Horne, Lord of Rummen," to negotiate strenuously and tenaciously with her sons-in-law and her first husband's creditors, to extract every penny owed to her.[50] Lijsbette van Lierde represented herself on at least nine occasions before the aldermen, swore oaths, negotiated agreements and sold property. Arnold's name never appears in the acts, beyond the introduction. He was probably not even present, and he certainly took no active role, in the proceedings. The aldermen treated Lijsbette as a fully capable legal person, and in every legal act, the clerk identified her (rather than Arnold and her) as the owner and manager of the property.

Another striking feature of Lijsbette's activities is that she appealed to a network of Ghent burghers from patrician families, all male, to act as sureties, receivers and arbiters for her.[51] The man she chose most often was Simon SerThomaes, a Ghent patrician, wine merchant and former

---

[49] SAG, series 301, no. 1, fol. 13v, act no. 2, fol. 47r, act no. 3, fols. 50v–51r; fol.52r, act no. 1, fol. 58v, act no. 3, fol. 59r, acts no. 2 and 3, fol. 72r–v, fol. 77r, act no. 2, fol. 85v, act no. 1, fol. 107r, act no. 2, fol. 124r, act no. 4, fol. 130r, act no. 5; series 330, no. 1¹, fols. 13r–14r, fol. 56r–v, fol. 128r; no. 1, fol. 16r; no. 2, fol. 75r.

[50] SAG, series 301, no. 1, fol. 47r, act no. 3, 29 Jan. 1350: "ene edele vrouwe ende werde vrouwe Lijsbette mijne her Symoens wijf was van Halen nu wettelike wijf mijn her Arnoude van Huerne her van Rommene. (a noble lady and a worthy lady Lijsbette, who was the wife of my lord Simoen van Halen, now legal wife of my lord Arnold van Horne, Lord of Rummen.)"

[51] Besides Simon SerThomaes, her sureties and receivers were Jan van den Wallekijne, Pauwels de Blende and Bertram van Lovendeghem. SAG, series 330, no. 1¹, fols. 56r–57v, Dec. 1350 — Jan., 1351; fol. 58v, act no. 3, 15 Aug. 1351.

alderman.[52] These ties show that Lijsbette operated within a network of men who were closely tied to the political and economic power holders of the city. This was undoubtedly a network she inherited from her husband, and she was certainly, to some extent, dependent on their financial backing and subject to their demands. But in the larger sense, Lijsbette did what any man would have done in her circumstances. She chose supporters from among her networks of kin and associates to stand as her sureties, loan her money, represent her and receive for her when she was out of town and act as arbiters for her side in legal disputes. What is most interesting about Lijsbette's use of a network is how much she acted as a man would, and how she crossed boundaries between rural nobles and urban burghers to do so.

In fourteenth-century Flanders, noble, patrician and wealthy burgher families used marriage for social mobility, economic security and advancement, family alliance and social networking. While the social divide between noble and burgher was real, families regularly contracted marriages across status and rank. Cognatic families were useful in a contentious, commercial, urbanized county. But in the cognatic family system, under partible inheritance customs, a woman was more than a passive transmitter of property or holder of a dowry. In the eyes of her contemporaries, a woman was a legitimate representative of her natal family's interests, which gave her the opportunity to choose to manage her personal property. In turn, her family relied upon her to protect their interests. Her management of property helped her family preserve and extend the property holdings which comprised its "patrimony." In later centuries, a noble family, like the Vaernewijcs or the Massemines, would focus on the glorious accomplishments of their illustrious warrior progenitors but, in reality, the survival of their families in the fourteenth century depended just as much on their burgher, urban and female ancestors.

California History Social Science Project
University of California, Davis

---

[52] In 1352–53, Simon SerThomaes served as the first seat on the board of the aldermen of the *Keure* and held tax farm of the wine assize in 1349 and 1352 and the assize of the gates in 1349. De Pauw and Vuylsteke, *Rekeningen* (Accounts), 1:2 and 24; 2:36 and 155; Van Werveke, *Stadsrekeningen* (City Accounts), 16; Blockmans, *Stadspatriciaat*, 350, 438–447, 465; SAG, series 301, no 1, fol. 47r, act no. 3, 29 Jan. 1350, fol. 59r, acts nos. 2 and 3, 10 Mar. 1350, fol. 107r, act no. 2, 24 Sep. 1353; series 330, no. 1¹, fols. 56r–57.

CITED WORKS

Manuscript Sources

Gent. Stadsarchief Gent (SAG)

Schepenen van de Gedele, Jaarregisters, series 330, nos. 1, 1[1], and 2.

Schepenen van de Keure, Jaarregisters, series 301, no. 1.

Printed Sources

Blockmans, F. *Het Gentsche stadspatriciaat tot omstreeks 1302.* Rijksuniversiteit te Gent werken uitgegeven door de faculteit van de wijsbegeerte en letteren, 85. Antwerp: De Sikkel, 1938.

Blockmans, W.P. and A. Janse, eds. *Showing Status: Representation of Social Positions in the Late Middle Ages.* Medieval Texts and Cultures of Northern Europe, 2. Turnhout: Brepols, 1999.

Boone, Marc. *Gent en de Bourgondische hertogen ca. 1384–ca. 1453. Een sociaal-politieke studie van een staatsvormingproces.* Verhandelingen van de koninklijke academie voor wetenschappen, letteren en schone kunsten van België, no. 133. Brussels: Paleis der Academiën, 1990.

Buylaert, Frederik. "Eeuwen van ambitie: Edelen, steden en sociale mobiliteit in laatmiddeleeuws Vlaanderen." Ph.D. diss., Ghent University, 2008.

Carlier, Myriam, and Tim Soens, eds. *The Household in Late Medieval Cities: Italy and Northwestern Europe Compared: Proceedings of the International Conference Ghent 21st-22nd January 2000.* Studies in Urban Social, Economic and Political History of the Medieval and Early Modern Low Countries, no. 12. Leuven-Apeldoorn: Garant, 2001.

Decavele, Johan. "Bestuursinstellingen van de stad Gent (einde 11de eeuw–1795)." In *De gewestelijke en lokale overheidsinstellingen in Vlaanderen tot 1795,* edited by Walter Prevenier and Beatrijs Augustyn. Algemeen Rijksarchief en Rijksarchief in de Provinciën, Studia 72. Brussels: Algemeen Rijksarchief, 1997, 277–321.

De Pauw, Napoléon, and Julius Vuylsteke, eds. *De Rekeningen der Stad Gent. Tijdvak van Jacob van Artevelde 1339–1349.* 3 vols. Ghent: Ad. Hoste, 1874–1885.

Duby, Georges. *Medieval Marriage: Two Models from Twelfth-Century France.* Translated by Elborg Forster. Baltimore: Johns Hopkins University Press, 1991.

_____. *La société aux XIe et XIIe siècles dans la région mâconnaise.* Paris: S.E.V.P.E.N., 1971.

Dumolyn, Jan. "Nobles, Patricians and Officers: The Making of a National Political Elite in Late Medieval Flanders." *Journal of Social History* 40 (2006): 431–452.

Evergates, Theodore, ed. *Aristocratic Women in Medieval France.* Philadelphia: University of Pennsylvania Press, 1999.

Gheldolf, A. E., A. Du Bois, and L. De Hondt, eds. *Coutume de la ville de Gand. Vols. 1 and 2 of Coutumes des pays et comté du Flandre. Quartier de Gand.* Commission royale pour la publication des anciennes lois et ordonnances de la Belgique. Brussels: G. Gobbaerts, 1868–1887.

Godding, Philippe. *Le Droit privé dans les Pays-Bas méridionaux du 12ᵉ au 18ᵉ siècle.* Académie Royale de Belgique, Mémoires de la classe des lettres, Collection in –4°, –2° série, vol. 14. Brussels: Palais des Académies, 1987.

Haemers, Jelle. *For the Common Good: State Power and Urban Revolts in the Reign of Mary of Burgundy (1477-1482).* Studies in European Urban History (1100–1800), no. 17. Turnhout: Brepols, 2009.

Heirbaut, Dirk. "Weduwen, erfgenamen en lenen: De evolutie van het feodale erf- en huwelijksvermogensrecht in Vlaanderen (1000–1300)." *Jaarboek voor Middeleeuwse Geschiedenis* 1 (1998): 7–26.

Herlihy, David. *Medieval Households.* Cambridge, MA: Harvard University Press, 1985.

Howell, Martha. "From Land to Love: Commerce and Marriage in Northern Europe during the Late Middle Ages." *Jaarboek voor Middeleeuwse Geschiedenis* 10 (2007): 216–253.

_____. *The Marriage Exchange: Property, Social Place, and Gender in Cities of the Low Countries, 1300-1550.* Chicago: University of Chicago Press, 1998.

Howell, Martha C., and Marc Boone. "Becoming Early Modern in the Late Medieval Low Countries." *Urban History* 23, pt. 3 (1996): 300–324.

Hutton, Shennan. "'On Herself and All Her Property': Women's Economic Activities in Late Medieval Ghent." *Continuity and Change* 20, no. 3 (2005): 325–349.

_____. *Women and Economic Activities in Late Medieval Ghent*. The New Middle Ages Series. New York: Palgrave Macmillan, 2011.

Kittell, Ellen E., and Mary A. Suydam, eds. *The Texture of Society: Medieval Women in the Southern Low Countries*. The New Middle Ages. New York: Palgrave MacMillan, 2005.

Kusman, David. "Jean de Mirabello dit van Haelen (ca. 1280–1333). Haute finance et Lombards en Brabant dans le premier tiers du XIVe siècle." *Revue belge de philologie et d'histoire/Belgisch tijdschrift voor filologie et geschiedenis* 77 (1999): 843–931.

LoPrete, Kimberly A. "Women, Gender and Lordship in France, c. 1050–1250." *History Compass* 5, no. 6 (2007): 1921–1941.

McNamara, Jo Ann, and Suzanne Wemple. "The Power of Women Through the Family in Medieval Europe, 500–1100." In *Gendering the Master Narrative: Women and Power in the Middle Ages*, edited by Mary Erler and Maryanne Kowaleski. Ithaca: Cornell University Press, 2003, 83–101.

Meijers, E. M. *Het Oost-Vlaamsche erfrecht*. Vol. 3 of *Het Ligurische erfrecht in de Nederlanden*. Haarlem: H. D. Tjeenk Willink & Zoon, 1936.

Murray, James. "Family, Marriage and Moneychanging in Medieval Bruges." *Journal of Medieval History* 14 (1988): 115–125.

Nicholas, David. *The Domestic Life of a Medieval City: Women, Children, and the Family in Fourteenth-Century Ghent*. Lincoln and London: University of Nebraska Press, 1985.

_____. *The Growth of the Medieval City: From Late Antiquity to the Early Fourteenth Century*. London and New York: Longman, 1997.

Prevenier, Walter. *Marriage and Social Mobility in the Late Middle Ages/ Mariage et mobilité sociale au bas moyen âge: Handelingen van het colloquium gehouden te Gent op 18 april 1988*. Studia Historica Gandensia, no. 274. Ghent: Rijksuniversiteit te Gent, 1989.

Prevenier, Walter, and Marc Boone. "The 'City-State' Dream: 1300–1500." In *Ghent: In Defence of a Rebellious City: History, Art, Culture*, edited by Johan Decavele. Antwerp: MercatorFonds, 1989, 81–105.

Rogghé, P. "Mirabello, Simon de." In *Nationaal Biografisch Woordenboek*. Brussels: Paleis der Academiën, 1964, vol. 1, columns 709–712.

Van Werveke, Alfons, ed. *Gentse Stads- en Baljuwsrekeningen (1351–1364)*. Brussels: Paleis der Academiën, 1970.

Unions of Interest: Florentine Marriage Ties and Business Networks in the Kingdom of Hungary during the Reign of Sigismund of Luxemburg

Katalin Prajda

In the late fourteenth and early fifteenth centuries, it was usual for Florentines to make marriage alliances within their own social strata, even in their own neighbourhood.[1] While several studies have drawn attention to endogamous marriage ties that existed among Florentine merchant families, little has been said about exogamous marriages with outsiders to the Florentine merchant society.[2] There has also been less analysis of the effects of the matrilineal extension of Florentine merchant families on the composition of business networks, which might explain why several Florentine merchant brothers formed endogamous marriages while others were sought to marry woman outside their social strata or business network. The importance of *parentado*, as an extension of the agnatic *consorteria*, is well-reflected in several cases of Florentine merchant families who found trustworthy allies in the families of their in-laws enhancing their business, social and political life.[3] The studies of Maria Elisa Soldani on the presence of Florentine and other Tuscan merchants in the territory of Kingdom of Aragon reveal the inseparable connections between marriage patterns and the social integration of those

---

[1] An early version of this paper was delivered at the Conference "To Have and Hold. Marriage in Premodern Europe 1400–1600" at the University of Toronto, Centre of Reformation and Renaissance Studies, in 2009. I would like to express my gratitude to the organizers for the invitation. The research benefited from the support of the Department of History and Civilization at the European University Institute. I am especially grateful to Jacqueline Murray and Konrad Eisenbichler for reviewing the manuscript and to Gábor Szatlóczki, and the two anonymous readers for their valuable comments.

[2] Klapisch, "Parenti, amici, vicini," 953–982; Herlihy, *Les Toscans*, 393–419; Molho, *Marriage Alliance*, 299–348.

[3] Kent, *The Rise of the Medici*, 49–61.

families who were engaged in long distance trade between Tuscany and the Crown of Aragon.[4] Similar to Florentines in the Kingdom of Aragon, Florentine merchants seeking to integrate into the local society of the Kingdom of Hungary probably used their marriages to obtain social advantages, such as a new *parentado*, local rights or citizenship.

This essay focuses on exogamous ties that developed between Florentines and subjects of the Hungarian crown and Florentine settlement in the Kingdom. It will also reconstruct the relationship between endogamous marriages patterns among Florentine merchant families and their participation in long distance trade with the Kingdom of Hungary during the reign of Sigismund of Luxemburg (1387–1437). The time with which this essay is concerned, the late fourteenth and early fifteenth centuries, coincides with the late republican period in Florence, dominated by the oligarchic regime, extending from the Ciompi Revolt until 1434, when Cosimo de' Medici returned to the city.

The principal hypothesis that emerges from this case study on Florentine merchant families and their business networks is that close cooperation between male relatives, in both the social and economic spheres, was crucial to a family's success and that commuting was integral to the life of international merchants. Therefore, it was essential for families interested in long distance trade that somebody from the *parentado* took on the role of mediator between the two regions where they engaged in business. In the case of families employed in the royal administration or in the import-export business of luxury goods and raw materials, thus was even more necessary, since they needed to work in close cooperation with local inhabitants. Thus Florentines who chose a subject of the Hungarian crown as a wife were able through their connections with the local society, to extend their business opportunities and obtain a certain social status in the kingdom. At the same time, other male members of the family kept their residence in Florence and cultivated their social and business connections in their home city. This kind of close cooperation among brothers and other male relatives can be observed within several Florentine merchant families who were operating outside of their homeland [5]

---

[4] Soldani, "A Firenze mercanti, cavalieri nella Signoria dei re d'Aragona," 583, 602; Soldani, "Da accettanti a setantì," 220, 226–229.

[5] See the example of the Strozzi brothers. Crabb, *The Strozzi of Florence*, 127.

This essay is organised in two parts. First, I will examine the social endogamy found among Florentine merchant families engaged in long distance trade with the Kingdom of Hungary. Second, I will analyse the exogamous ties that developed between Florentines and subjects of the Hungarian crown.

Many Florentines residing in the Kingdom of Hungary or commuting between the two lands, imported and exported both luxury goods and raw materials. Florentines, through their business channels, served to connect Buda and Florence. They were international merchant families, with generations of experience in long distance trade; their ancestors had been owners or employees of merchant banking companies in Florence. These included silk manufacturers and wool entrepreneurs who also, at the same time, were influential politicians in the Florentine Signoria. The majority operated, through their agents, in the Kingdom of Hungary, while a few others opened branches or independent companies in Buda. The agents of such merchant companies travelled continuously between the two states, for business purposes, while their primary residence and their families remained in Florence. There was, however, an even smaller group of merchants who obtained offices and settled permanently in the Kingdom of Hungary. The merchants who were primarily transient tended to form marriage alliances with other Florentine merchant families, whereas expatriate Florentine merchants chose to marry members of the Hungarian crown. It was not unusual, however, for both patterns of spousal selection to occur within the same nuclear family.

The example of Pippo called lo Spano and his family, the Scolari, reveals the difficulties in making generalisations about a collective family strategy, since the Scolari employed aspects of both endogamy and exogamy, despite the fact that both Pippo and his brother, Matteo, spent a considerable amount of time in the Hungary beginning in the early 1390s. One can hypothesise that this began when they were in their mid-twenties, as they started working for a number of different employers in the kingdom. Their father, Stefano, had died around 1390, about the time they reached adulthood.[6] Since they lacked considerable property in Florence, they remained in Hungary. In 1399, Pippo and Matteo entered the king's service and became officers at the royal gold mines, in Körmöcbánya.[7] That same year, Pippo (1368/69–1426) married into

---

[6] ASF, Estimo 209, fol. 124v.

[7] Körmöcbánya today belongs to Slovakia and is known as Kremnica.

a local family. His spouse, Borbála Ozorai (Barbara of Ozora), was from an estate neighbouring the castle where Pippo served as an officer. The Ozorai (*De Ozora* in Latin) family was not of baronial rank; however, Borbála's father, András (Andrew of Ozora), was a nobleman, with a considerable estate and without any male heirs. Pippo Scolari was fortunate to gain royal permission, along with his new wife, to inherit the estate at Ozora. From that time onwards, Pippo no longer known as *Pippo gallicus filius Stephani de Florentia* but, as early as in a document dated 1400, after the inheritance became legal, as *Pippo de Ozora*.[8] With this legal act, the Florentine foreigner joined the nobility of the Hungarian crown, obtaining both a noble estate and rank, probably through his marriage. His brother, Matteo (1370/71–1426), also remained on in the kingdom, following Pippo into the administration of gold mines. Given their fortune, we might expect that both the Scolari brothers were settled permanently in their new home. On the contrary: within a few years of his brother's marriage, Matteo chose to marry a Florentine woman from a magnate family with Ghibelline loyalties like the Scolari (fig. 7.1).

One explanation for the differences in social behaviour within the same merchant family could be that neither Pippo nor Matteo entirely abandoned their mercantile activity after becoming Sigismund's *familiares*.[9] Since Pippo chose a noblewoman for wife he was able, through his connection with the nobility, to establish economic ties with other Hungarian noblemen, as well as to serve the king as administrator of different mines. It was through the Scolari brothers' business connections that raw materials from these mines reached Italy. Matteo exchanged the raw materials for luxury goods such as exotic animals and high quality textiles and imported these into the kingdom. Therefore Matteo maintained his permanent residence in Florence in order to control the market, while Pippo did the same in Buda, and in other regions of the kingdom through their agents. This is one of many examples of Florentine brothers from merchant families that illustrate close cooperation among male relatives designed to promote the family's collective success.

Activities in the import-export business of luxury goods and raw materials no doubt accounted for the Scolari's new alliance with the Infangati, neighbours of the Scolari in Florence after 1405, when Matteo moved into the prestigious neighbourhood of Borgo degli Albizi and married one of the three daughters, Piera. The Infangati, in particular Matteo Scolari's father-in-

---

[8] ZSO, vol. II/I, doc. 406.

[9] On their mercantile activity see Prajda, "The Florentine Scolari Family".

law, Catellino di Baldinaccio, and his family were important local bankers in Florence, and Catellino's two sons, Antonio and Baldinaccio, cooperated closely with the Scolari, both in Florence and in Hungary.[10] With Matteo Scolari, now his brother-in-law, Baldinaccio invested in opening a workshop, in Via Vaccareccia, specializing in the wool trade and probably in silk. Baldinaccio himself also spent considerable amount of time in the kingdom and he frequently stayed in the court the bishop, Andrea Scolari, held at Várad. Baldinaccio remained there, even after the bishop's death, in 1426, not returning to Florence until at least 1433.[11] Probably due to his foreign sojourn which made him unable to recoup all the credits owed to his father, Baldinaccio refused to accept his inheritance from his father, in 1424.[12] His business affairs did not go smoothly, even in the kingdom after the deaths of the Scolari in 1426, since, shortly afterwards, he was imprisoned, probably on account of debts.[13] At the same time, the strong social as well as economic solidarity between Catellino di Baldinaccio Infangati's offspring and Matteo Scolari's family is demonstrated to by Matteo's donations, which provided a fair living for one of Catellino's three daughters, Caterina, who was a nun in the convent of San Francesco.[14]

Like Matteo Scolari's marriage with a Florentine woman, other merchants of Matteo's business network, with an interest in long distance trade with the Kingdom of Hungary, tended to form endogamous marriage ties with other elite Florentine merchant families. The endogamous marriage

---

[10] Giovanni and Baldinaccio di Catellino Infangati had a company together at the Arte del Cambio in 1359–1363. ASF, Cambio 14, fol. 37v. In 1366 Baldinaccio had already died, Giovanni di Catellino and his nephew, Catellino di Baldinaccio, continued the company. ASF, Cambio 14, fol. 53r. The matriculation of Baldinaccio di Catellino in 1353 is in ASF, Cambio 44, fol. 68r.

[11] Baldinaccio was present at the issue of Andrea Scolari's last will in 1426 in Várad. ASF, Corp. Rel. Sopp. 78.326, fol. 291r. Baldinaccio did not return back after Andrea Scolari's death in 1426, but remained in the Kingdom of Hungary at least until 1433. ASF, Catasto 478, fol. 463r. Várad today belongs to Romania and holds the name: Oradea.

[12] ASF, Repudie d'eredità 10, fol. 186v; ASF, Corp. Rel. Sopp. 78. 326, fol. 282r.

[13] Francesco di Vieri Guadagni's report in 1433 on the Infangati brothers' debts mentioned that one of the brothers, Antonio was a bad debtor, meanwhile Baldinaccio was sent to prison in Hungary. ASF, Catasto 478, fol.772v; ASF, Catasto 57, fol. 911r.

[14] ASF, Corp. Rel. Sopp. 78. 326, fol. 267v. See also: ASF, Notarile 5814, fol. 28v. However, it was not only important to focus on commercial affairs, but there was also necessary the issue of political alliances to consider: it was thus no coincidence that both families belonged to the magnates and were Ghibellines in Florence.

pattern is also well reflected by the case of the third of Catellino Infangati's daughters, who married to Piero di Bernardo della Rena (?–1432), an international merchant and also close neighbour to the Infangati in the Borgo degli Albizi. Catellino's daughter, however, died after only a few years of marriage, leaving behind four children, one of whom, Sandra, was adopted by Matteo Scolari and brought up by Matteo's wife, Piera di Catellino Infangati, in their palace.[15] The good social relations between the two families were certainly consolidated by additional business connections, since Piero also acted as a procurator on behalf of his brother-in-law.[16] The Della Rena family were silk and retail cloth merchants in Florence; Piero was once even nominated as consul in the Por Santa Maria guild.[17] One of his brothers, Gianozzo, set up a money exchange business; two other brothers, Bartolomeo and Baldinaccio, appeared several times with Piero as debtors of the Scolari with whom they shared certain economic interests.[18]

The trading company formed by Piero della Rena, as a junior partner with Matteo Scolari, Antonio di Geri Bardi and Tommaso di Domenico Borghini for the long distance trade between the Florentine Republic and the Kingdom of Hungary, was probably operating in close cooperation with one that ran under the name of Tommaso Borghini (c.1381–c.1428/30) and which specialized in silk processing.[19] Tommaso was a silk manufacturer, a member of the silk guild and, between 1410 and 1428, was elected several times as consul for the wool guild. It was probably Tommaso's brother, Jacopo, who started producing high quality textiles in the convent of San Martino.[20] Following his death, in 1401, the young Tommaso took over the business, running a warehouse-workshop (*fondaco*) in town. The company that Tommaso and Matteo Scolari formed was probably a good arrangement

---

[15] However Piero and his first wife had more children from their marriage, only Sandra lived continuously with her aunt. His father, Piero remarried, in the early 1420s, a new wife who was Piero di Corso Adimari's daughter, Caterina. ASF, Catasto 482, fol. 433r; Catasto 484, fol. 544r.

[16] ASF, Monte ser. II. 1806, fol. 144v.

[17] Bartolomeo's matriculation to the Por Santa Maria guild in 1414 see: ASF, Seta 7, fol. 162v; ASF, Lana 246, fol. 15r.

[18] ASF, Cambio 65, fol. 67r; ASF, Catasto 35, fols. 1064r, 1067r; Catasto 59, fols. 874v, 647r.

[19] ASF, Catasto 296, fol. 163v. One of Matteo Scolari's last wills refers to the partnership between the four Florentine merchants. ASF, Corp. Rel. 78. 326, fol. 270r.

[20] ASF, Lana 325, fol. 39v.

for both parties, especially for Tommaso who, after Matteo's death, in 1426, received the living provided by one of Matteo's estates, because he was Matteo's creditor.[21] The Borghini and the Scolari families continued their cooperation in business even after 1426. The cousins, Filippo, Lorenzo and Giambonino di Rinieri Scolari, Matteo's heirs were in daily contact with Tommaso Borghini's son, Domenico, through letters of business.[22] The three brothers and the young Borghini may also have shared an interest in a business in Venice that imported and exported precious metals with the mediation of Domenico's company co-founded in Venice with the Scolari's other important business partner, Agnolo di Zanobi Gaddi.[23] As Tommaso Borghini traded in goods in close cooperation with the Scolari, it is not surprising that he married the daughter of Giovanni Cavalcanti, Lena, another Florentine who was also engaged in long-distance trade in the territory of the Kingdom of Hungary (fig. 7.2).[24]

The Cavalcanti family, headed at this time by Giovanni di messer Amerigo Cavalcanti, were also closely linked to the Scolari family through the business networks of Giovanni's three sons. Two of them, Gianozzo and Simone, became Pippo Scolari's trusted men.[25] Gianozzo was an agent who travelled between Florence and Hungary, working in close cooperation for the Venetian branch of Cosimo de' Medici's company. He was also linked to Gianozzo's family through marriage.[26] From 1420 until at least until 1430, a junior partner of the Venetian branch was Gianozzo's other brother-in-law, Andrea di Lipaccio Bardi, who married Gianozzo's third sister, Cecca.[27]

---

[21] ASF, Corp. Rel. Sopp. 78.326, fol. 258r. According to the tax declaration of Pippo, Matteo and Andrea Scolari's heirs, in 1427, the living provided by the estate of Il fornello, located in Santo Stefano a Campi was given to Tommaso Borghini and company in payment for a debt of 900 florins. ASF, Catasto 59, fol. 871r.

[22] ASF, Corp. Rel. Sopp. 78.326, fol. 354v.

[23] ASF, Strozziane ser. V. n. 1760, fols. 101v –102r.

[24] He married around 1411. ASF, Monte ser. II. 3733, fol. 129r.

[25] He was a testimony for Pippo Scolari, in Buda. ASF, Strozziane ser. IV, fol. 635r.

[26] Pippo Scolari had business affairs with Cavalcanti and, with his mediation, with the Medici of Venice. ASF, Corp. Rel. Sopp. 78. 321, fols. 98r–99r. According to Filippo di Rinieri Scolari's tax declaration, in 1431, he had accounts to be closed with the Medici company, but, in reality, with Gianozzo Cavalcanti. ASF, Catasto 296, fol. 160r. Lorenzo de' Medici's wife was Giovanni Cavalcanti's other daughter, Ginevra.

[27] De Roover, *Medici Bank*, 393; ASF, Monte ser. II. 2416, fol. 207v; MAP, filza 153.2, fols. 4r–5r. For the marriage between Cecca and Andrea, see: ASF, Monte ser. II. 3733, fol.

Further evidence of overlapping marriage and economic ties can be seen in the marriage between a distant niece of Gianozzo, Caterina di Baldinaccio di messer Salice Cavalcanti and the factor of Andrea di Filippo Scolari, Jacopo di Geppo da Monterinaldi.[28] The Cavalcanti and Da Monterinaldi families worked in close cooperation with the Scolari and with other merchants operating in the kingdom since Jacopo and his brother, Bernardo, served Andrea Scolari as his factor in the city of Florence.[29]

Members of neither the Cavalcanti or the Borghini families had ever settled in Hungary nor took an active part in the royal administration, whereas other Florentine families appear to have been of double-rooted and developed further economic connections in the kingdom by reason of the offices held by the king's commission. Among the Cavalcanti, Gianozzo di Giovanni was bound by marriage ties also to another expatriate Florentine merchant family, the Buondelmonti; the mother of Giovanni di Andrea Buondelmonti was probably Gianozzo's aunt.[30] After Pippo Scolari's death, in 1426, Giovanni Buondelmonti, the archbishop of Kalocsa in the Kingdom of Hungary, became the most influential member of the Florentine community. He received his office thanks to the benevolence of Pippo, who was one of his kinsmen. We can thus infer that Giovanni Buondelmonti and his brothers Lorenzo and Simone, who occasionally sojourned in their brother's court, were the Scolari's trusted agents and active participants in the trading that saw goods move between the two states.

One of the brothers, Lorenzo di Andrea Buondelmonti, also married another Florentine, Cecca di Filippo del Bene, with whom he shared a

---

130v.

[28] They married around 1408. ASF, Monte ser. II. 3733, fol. 213v.

[29] Baldinaccio's name appears in Francesco di Vieri Guadagni's account that made for Matteo Scolari's heirs. ASF, MAP filza 150, doc. 17, fol.19r. Jacopo di Geppo da Monterinaldi was mentioned several time, in business letters addressed to Andrea Scolari, as the one who handled the bishop's business affairs in Florence. ASF, Corp. Rel. Sopp. 78.326, fols. 335r, 327r. Jacopo da Monterinaldi and his brother Bernardo as Andrea Scolari's factors in Florence entered into the possession of the living provided by Andrea Scolari's extensive estate when after the bishop's death in 1426, his heirs remained debtors of the brothers with a considerable amount of money. According to Jacopo da Monterinaldi's tax declaration, he took the estate of Vicchiomaggio. ASF, Catasto 81, fol. 495r.

[30] They were in Bács (Bač, Serbia) with the archbishop Buondelmonti who is a close relative to Gianozzo. "erano a Baccia chol arciveschovo de Buondelmonti che parente stretto di Gianozzo" ASF, Corp. Rel. Sopp. 78.321, fol. 98v.

common ancestry.[31] This branch of the prestigious international merchant family, the Del Bene, had already settled in the Kingdom of Hungary. Filippo di Giovanni del Bene was employed by Pippo Scolari, to administer the salt mines, and he also held offices in Florence.[32] His son, Jacopo, followed Filippo's path at the salt mines, cooperating in this capacity with lo Spano's heirs and nephews, Lorenzo and Filippo di Rinieri Scolari, while, at the same time, he followed the pattern of travelling back and forth between the two places.[33]

Like Filippo del Bene, many other Florentines who had been settled for years in the kingdom were employed directly by King Sigismund or Pippo Scolari in the administration of the mines and the mints. The number of Florentine merchants resident in Hungary, who received a certain interest in administration, collection and in import-export of precious metals, was as impressive in the case of Hungary as it was in the Iberian Peninsula, in Germany and in England during the same period.[34]

Similar to the Del Bene, members of the Zati family were also employed in the royal administration. The Zati were international merchants who maintained company branches in various places in the Italian Peninsula, including Florence and Venice.[35] The companies were owned by Amerigo Zati's sons, Giuliano, Simone, Niccolò and Uberto, who already had connections with Hungary through the business contacts of their maternal family, the Bardi.[36] The Zati company in Venice specialized in the import and export of wool, precious metals, precious stones, spices and other luxury goods. All of the companies founded by the Zati brothers played an

---

[31] ASF, Monte II. 3733, fol. 165r. Ghetta di Francesco del Bene and Banchello di messer Manente Buondelmonti were married in the 1330s. ASF, Del Bene 27, fol. 8v.

[32] He was also the papal legate in the Kingdom of Hungary, in 1412. ZsO, vol. III, doc. 2692.

[33] Lorenzo di Rinieri Scolari referred to the fact that he shared certain business interests with Jacopo del Bene, during King Sigismund's reign. ASF, MAP filza 16, fol. 35r.

[34] Soldani, "A Firenze mercanti, cavalieri nella Signoria dei re d'Aragona," 594; Weissen, "Florentines Kaufleute in Deutschland," Allen, "Italians in English Mints and Exchanges".

[35] There were two separate companies under the brothers' name: Uberto Zati and company, probably in Florence, and Giuliano and Niccolò Zati and brothers' company, in Venice. AOI, Estranei 188, fol. 128r.

[36] Amerigo Zati's wife was Margherita, the daughter of Giovanni di messer Bindo de Bardi, ASF, Catasto 452, fol. 620r.

intermediary role between Florentine merchants operating in Hungary and their fellow-citizens, who conducted their business at home.[37] The brothers also invested money with the company of Simone di Pagolo Carnesecchi and his brothers in Buda and they carried out business transactions with Giambonino di Rinieri Scolari, with the intermediation of Domenico Borghini.[38] In addition, they imported wool into the Kingdom of Hungary, sometimes through their business channels and sometimes directly through one of the brothers, Uberto, who accompanied their goods to Buda.[39] The Zati were directly bound by marriage ties to the Scolari, since a cousin of the four brothers: Andrea di Francesco di Giovanni Zati (c.1402) married Matteo Scolari's adopted child, Sandra di Piero della Rena (c.1418), around 1433.[40] Andrea was a merchant in the wool guild, as were his relatives.[41] Although his

---

[37] Among their business partners, in the 1420s, were Giovanni di maestro Niccolò Falcucci, who was a travelling agent in the kingdom to the Scolari, as well as to other Florentines and Giovanni di Fronte, another experienced merchant, in Hungarian territory, was the Scolari's business partner. For the cooperation between the Zati company and Giovanni Falcucci, see his declaration: ASF, Catasto 52, fol. 1096v. For Giovanni's work as a travelling agent, see his letters to Andrea Scolari, from Szeben, in Transylvania. ASF, Corp. Rel. Sopp. 78.326, fols. 277r, 328r, 388r. See Giovanni di Fronte's declaration, in 1427. ASF, Catasto 35, fol. 739r.

[38] ASF, Catasto 475, fol. 578v; Catasto 477, fol. 573r. The three Carnesecchi brothers had business with the Zati's company, in Venice. ASF, Catasto 55, fol. 791v. Evidence is provided in several letters written by Giambonino di Rinieri Scolari to his brother, Filippo. ASF, Corp. Rel. Sopp. 78. 326, fols. 354r–355v, 357r–v, 361r–v.

[39] There are references in the brothers', Uberto, Giuliano and Niccolò's, tax declaration, in 1433, to the fact that Uberto had brought silk and wool with him to the Kingdom of Hungary. ASF, Catasto 452, fol. 825r.

[40] In the tax declaration of Piero della Rena's offspring, in1433, Sandra was still unmarried at the age of fourteen. ASF, Catasto 480, fol. 307r. Even though they had a separate record in the catasto, Sandra lived in the household of Piera, Matteo Scolari's widow, since their father had already died and they were from the previous marriage of their father. ASF, Catasto 481, fol. 462v. In 1427 Francesco di Giovanni Zati lived in the same household with his sons, among whom Andrea and Antonio were in their twenties and unmarried. ASF, Catasto 36, fol. 372r; In 1446, Sandra and Andrea had already been married, probably in 1433, since their eldest child was around fifteen years old. ASF, Catasto 665, fol.264r. As for the relationship between the two Zati branches; according to the tax declaration of Amerigo Zati's wife, she kept the dowry deposit for Francesco Zati's daughter, Checca. ASF, Catasto 452, fol. 620r.

[41] ASF, Lana 25, fol. 2v. Uberto d'Amerigo and his brothers were retail cloth merchants. ASF, Lana 319, fol. 130r.

economic activities remain obscure, there is more information at our disposal regarding his brother, Antonio (c.1407). Antonio appeared in the kingdom for the first time, in 1427, as an international merchant acting as intermediary between Florentine merchants in Buda and Venice. Shortly afterwards, he received a royal commission to administer a salt mine and a mint, remaining there and serving the Hungarian kings in various offices.[42]

Matteo Scolari, probably acknowledging the importance of a marriage within his own social and economic circle, married his daughter, Caterina, to another Florentine merchant, close neighbour and family friend. Caterina, therefore, entered into an even more advantageous marriage than did Sandra, with Vieri di Vieri Guadagni's son Francesco, in 1419. The Guadagni had been members of the Cambio and the wool guilds for several generations.[43] Vieri di Vieri (c.1426) and his brother, Bernardo, owned several other companies in Florence, including a banking company that was subsequently run by the Cambini family. They opened branches in Florence and Rome and, as moneychangers, they also maintained a table at the Mercato Nuovo. In addition they also had a warehouse-workshop for their wool manufacturing company.[44] It was probably the Guadagni bank that provided financial support to Matteo Scolari, investing money in his trading activities and maintaining a constantly open account for the Scolari in their bank.[45]

---

[42] Draskóczy, "Olaszok," 126–127.

[43] Membership of the Guadagni in the Cambio guild: Bernardo and Vieri di Vieri, Francesco, Simone, Migliore and Malatesta di Vieri di Vieri. ASF, Cambio 12, fols. 74r, 79r, 95r–97r. Membership in the Wool guild: Bernardo di Vieri di Migliore, Filippo and Francesco di Vieri di Vieri. ASF, Lana 25, fols. 8r, 17r; Vieri di Vieri member of the Calimala guild. ASF, Calimala 6, fol. 8r.

[44] Vieri di Vieri Guadagni during his life founded several companies, a banking company with Andreuolo di Niccolò Sacchetti and Fruosino di Luca da Panzano in Florence. ASF, Catasto 29, vol. 1, fol. 8r; ASF, Guadagni 14.10, fol. 1r. For the *fondaco* see: ASF, Lana 318, fols. 45v, 76r, 52r; ASF, Catasto 478, fol. 280v.

[45] In 1427, an open account was kept, under the Scolari brothers' name: ASF, Corp. Rel. Sopp. 78.326, fol. 242r. There was also an account between Matteo Scolari's heirs and the heirs of Vieri di Vieri Guadagni, Niccolò Sacchetti and Giovanni del Bellaccio. ASF, Corp. Rel. Sopp. 78.326, fol. 259v. Francesco di Vieri di Vieri Guadagni was the one who kept a current account under Matteo Scolari's name, after his death, in 1426. ASF, MAP filza 150, fol.17r. Two deposits of considerable size, 2000 florins and 6038 florins, were made under the names of Matteo Scolari and Vieri di Vieri Guadagni. ASF, Monte ser. II. 1806, fol. 148r.

Vieri di Vieri and Matteo were not only business partners but also neighbours and friends, since they lived on the same street in Borgo degli Albizi.[46]

The examples of several Florentine merchants, operating in the kingdom, during Sigismund of Luxemburg's reign, reveal that international merchants tended to forge marriage alliances with each other in order to strengthen their economic relationships. The Scolari, Guadagni, Della Rena and Infangati families were not only neighbours and relatives through the female line, but they were also important business partners. Their unions provide evidence of the intergenerational cooperation that was prevalent among Florentine families operating in Hungary, on both the social and the economic level.

In spite of the fruitful cooperation between Florentine merchant families linked together by matrilineal ties, not all profitable unions were shaped by endogamous relationships between business partners. Other marriages were also arranged by men intending to settle in Hungary who sought to marry into local families who did not participate in long distance trade but rather owned a noble title or belonged to the restricted group of citizens, in towns close to the royal mines, mints or important market places. As Pippo Scolari's case demonstrates, a few of Florentine expatriate administrators were fortunate to arrange to marry into local families and these new familial ties influenced their economic success.

Similar to the Scolari, the Melanesi, one of the royal administrator families was a family of double roots, bound both to Florentine and Hungarian societies by their marriages. The Melanesi were originally from Prato, but they had obtained citizenship in Florence in the middle of the fourteenth century and took an active part in long distance trade.[47] The Melanesi brothers, Tommaso and Simone di Piero, appeared in the Kingdom of Hungary as Florentine merchants and opened an independent company in Buda.[48] There they engaged in the import-export business of textiles and copper between the Italian Peninsula and the Kingdom of Hungary, cooperating with several

---

[46] In 1423,Vieri di Vieri helped Matteo to recoup his stolen goods. ASF, MAP filza 98, fol. 29r.

[47] See the correspondence of Jacopo del Bene and Luigi Melanesi. ASF, Del Bene, 49, fol. 11r.

[48] Tommaso was a senior partner of a merchant company, the partners were all Florentine merchants interested in the trade of wool and silk: Tommaso and Simone Corsi, Tommaso Davizi and Lodovico di ser Viviano Viviani. ASF, Catasto 29. 654r; Catasto 447. 528r.

Florentine merchants residing in the region.[49] Similar to other male members of the family, who were matriculated members of one of the five major guilds of Florence, one of the brothers, Tommaso became a member of the silk guild as *setaiolo*.[50] Probably the economic ties had bound the family for decades to important families of the Florentine wool industry, led Tommaso to establish marriage ties with the Falcucci family. Tommaso's father-in-law was the merchant Luca di messer Niccolò, brother of Giovanni who acted for several years as Andrea Scolari's factor in the Kingdom of Hungary.[51] Giovanni through his business network imported precious metals, including gold and silver, to the Italian Peninsula. As factor, he probably received an interest in those precious metals which came from the mines under Pippo Scolari's control and from other mines administered by Pippo's trusted men, the Bardi family. At the same time, Giovanni Falcucci also dealt with precious metals which probably came from ecclesiastical revenues collected by the Bishop Andrea Scolari. Both of the in-law-families, the Melanesi and the Falcucci, probably worked for Pippo Scolari in Hungary, working in the administration of mines while simultaneously conducting their own businesses. Therefore, a marriage tie between the Melanesi and the Falcucci families consolidated not only their relationship among each other, but also their connections to the influential Scolari family. This strategy seems to have been successful since both of the Melanesi brothers acted several times as witnessed to notarial documents and executors of testaments by members of the Scolari family.[52] Furthermore, after Andrea Scolari's death, in 1426, Tommaso's and Simone's third brother, Giovanni, was made bishop of Várad, an elevation largely attributed to Pippo Scolari's influence.[53] In order to accumulate further economic advantages from their foreign sojourn, Simone married into a local family in Buda (fig. 7.3). This act was probably part of a strategy to obtain a citizenship in the city of Buda.[54] In consequence, Simone received citizenship in 1427 and rented a house in the so-called *Platea Italica*,

---

[49] See the correspondence of the Scolari family: ASF, Corp. Rel. Sopp. 78. 326, fol. 348r; 354r; 355r; 361r; 366r.

[50] ASF, Seta 7, fol. 188r.

[51] Petriboni, Di Borgo Rinaldi, *Priorista (1407–1459)*, 177.

[52] ASF, Corp. Rel. Sopp. 78.326, fol. 291v–292r.

[53] ASF, Strozziane I. 229, fol. 56r.

[54] ASF, Catasto 46, fol. 655v. Simone's marriage was also discussed earlier from the point of view of citizenship by Krisztina Arany. Arany, "Siker és kudarc", 949.

which was populated mainly by other merchants of Italian origins. The Menalesi's businesses both, in Buda and in Florence, were flourishing during the years when the three elder Scolari were alive. Later on, when all of the Scolari disappeared — Andrea and Matteo probably died in an epidemic in Várad and Pippo had suffered from gout for a long time — in the same year, 1426, precipitating an economic crisis that resulted in the Melanesi falling into bankruptcy in Florence. It was probably due, not only to the deaths of the Scolari, but also to the fact that two of the three brothers also died in the subsequent years; Giovanni within a few months after his nomination and Simone sometime between 1429 and 1430.[55] As a result of this economic crisis in the family, Tommaso and his uncle, Filippo di Filippo were forced to sell everything they owned in the cities of Florence and Prato and, for the outstanding debt, the elderly Filippo was even sent to prison in Prato.[56] Contributing to this crisis to a considerable extent, the Hungarian king had also confiscated a large amount of cash from the brothers in 1429.[57] In the same time, contradicting this image of misfortune, is the economic situation of the Melanesi. In the 1430s Tommaso had still been working in the king's service and when he died he was major royal administrator (*comes*) of copper mines.[58] It is probable that both Simone and Tommaso obtained citizenship in Buda as a result of Simone's marriage. Tommaso was able to remain in Buda and preserve his rights as a citizen, even after his brother's death. It is also highly likely that the same happened in the Scolari's case, given that the brothers not only held offices together and jointly owned property, but also Matteo had become a nobleman of the Hungarian crown by reason of Pippo's marriage and by royal donation.

The example of another administrative family, the Mannini, also reveals the close connections that could exist between settlement and marriage. The father, Salvestro di Giovanni, and his brothers were international merchants and members of the Calimala guild in Florence and they had forged connections in the Kingdom of Hungary by the 1420s, cooperating

---

[55] According to Baldassare di Luigi Melanesi, the heirs of Simone Melanesi and his brother Tommaso, they lost all of their substance in Hungary with the death of the bishop, they brother. "ànno perduto ongni loro sustanza in Ungheria per la morte del veschovo loro fratello" ASF, Catasto 380, fol. 269r.

[56] ASF, Catasto 466, fol. 394r; 445, fol. 82v.

[57] ASF, Corp. Rel. Sopp. 78.326, fol. 370r–v.

[58] Draskóczy , "Kamarai jövedelem és urbura a 15.század első felében," 152–153.

with Florentines who had already obtained a certain interest there in the long distance trade.[59] Salvestro's son Papi settled permanently in the Kingdom of Hungary, commissioned by Pippo Scolari to administer salt mines in the 1420s.[60] Papi's other male relatives, his brother or first cousin, Angelo, became an officer at the salt mines at Dés in Transylvania in the 1420s, and married into a local family (fig. 7.4).[61] Severally of the Mannini cousins — including the sons of Antonio and Salvestro di Giovanni — remained permanently in the Kingdom of Hungary, administering salt mines.[62] Giovanni di Antonio also worked in the royal administration, and he also settled in Transylvania in the 1440s, marrying a Hungarian noblewoman.[63] Later on, in the 1450s, members of the family residing in the Kingdom of Hungary received a noble title and their family name became Szentpéterszegi, which came from their most important estate.

Like the Mannini, members of the Baldi family also served as royal administrators, appearing in the Kingdom of Hungary even earlier than the reign of King Sigismund. According to Bonaccorso Pitti's diary, a certain Bartolomeo di Guido Baldi, administrator of the royal mint in Buda, provided him with hospitality in 1376.[64] It is likely that either his brother or his son (who was the Matteo in charge of the salt mines at Vízakna, in Transylvania) worked in Pippo Scolari's service, sometime before 1408.[65] As a citizen of Szeben, he settled in the Transylvanian town and married into a local family.[66]

---

[59] His brothers were Luigi and Antonio. ASF, Calimala 6, fols. 4r, 2v. Their fourth brother, Manno, was member of the Silk guild. ASF, Seta 7, fol. 126v. Salvestro made a pilgrimage, in 1411, to St. Patrick's Purgatory, where he met a Hungarian nobleman. "Purgatorio di San Patrizio," 57. For the business connections between the Zati brothers and the Mannini brothers see: ASF, Mercanzia 11778, fol. 14v.

[60] The bishop had left money for Papi in his last will, probably for his services. ASF, Corp. 78. 326, fol. 260v. , ASF, Catasto 80, fol. 599r.

[61] Draskóczy, "Olaszok," 129–131. Dés today belongs to Romania and holds the name: Dej.

[62] For the genealogy of the family see: ASF, Catasto 450, fol. 514r–515r.

[63] DL 55612. (1457)

[64] Bonaccorso Pitti, "Ricordi," 367.

[65] ZsO, vol. II/2, doc. 1613. Vízakna today is found in Romania and holds the name Oca Sibiului.

[66] ZsO, vol. II/2. doc. 6040, doc. 8080. Szeben today belongs to Romania and holds the name: Sibiu.

However difficult it is to find evidence for the phenomenon, it is highly likely that there were significant differences between expatriate and commuting Florentine merchants, which are manifest in patterns of household formation. Contradicting the traditional view, which describes Florentine households as patrilocal, in which brides moved to their in-laws' house after the wedding, expatriate Florentine merchants instead tended to live in the neighbourhood or even in the family house, of their in-laws.[67] We have already seen through the case of the Melanesi brothers and that of Pippo Scolari that grooms were the ones who moved into proximity with their in-law-families and not the brides. Lo Spano moved to Ozora, to his father-in-law's residence and also his heirs; Filippo and Lorenzo di Rinieri settled with their in-laws, after returning to Florence from a long foreign sojourn.[68] Also, Simone Melanesi, Matteo Baldi and the Mannini followed the same pattern of settlement, moving into their father-in-laws' neighbourhood. It is also probable that the pattern of household formation shown by the Scolari and Melanesi families, wherein one brother stayed in Florence while the other moved to their adopted home might explain not only the close connection between economic ties with social behaviour but also with practices of inheritance. Management of family properties and inheritance, in Florence, required the presence of an able male member of the family, who was able to recoup the debts owed to his late relative, pay off his own debts and deal with the family's overall financial affairs. Lacking such a family member, resident in Florence, could lead either repudiation or loss of family property, as in the case of Baldinaccio di Catellino Infangati.[69]

Since Hungarian sources regarding the lives and marriages of expatriate Florentine merchants resident in the Kingdom of Hungary are scarce, we might conclude that when Florentine merchants chose as wives subjects of the Hungarian crown, it was because they intended to settle there and integrate into the local community. In the medieval Kingdom of Hungary, marriage was practically the only way open to strangers who wished to integrate rapidly into the local society. Florentine merchants who

---

[67] Kent, *Household and Lineage*

[68] Filippo Scolari lived with Luigi di Giovanni Aldobrandini's family in the Piazza di Santa Maria Novella and Lorenzo Scolari lived in the parish of the San Jacopo sopr'Arno Church, in the house of Bernardo Sapiti.

[69] For practices of inheritance and repudiation see: Kuehn, *Heirs, Kin, and Creditors in Renaissance Florence.*

engaged in long-distance trade tended to form business and social networks among themselves. International merchants married their daughters to other international merchants. They also practiced endogamy in their living arrangements; in most cases, husbands and wives were not only of Florentine origin, but were also born in the same neighbourhood, or even on the same street. As we have seen, there were only a few cases when exogamic considerations influenced the selection of a spouse among the Florentine merchants in the kingdom. One possible explanation might be that the minority of these long-distance merchants saw, in their host country, the possibility to elevate their social rank and status. Among the majority, the Kingdom of Hungary was viewed as a source of income, a place they would leave behind once their business affairs were concluded.

European University Institute

Cited Works

Abbreviations

DL = *A középkori Magyarország levéltári forrásainak adatbázisa,* ed. Rácz György Arcanum: Budapest, 2003.

ZsO= *Zsigmond-kori oklevéltár,* 8 vols. (1387–1422) ed. Mályusz Elemér and Borsa Iván and C. Tóth Norbert, Arcanum: Budapest, 1951–2001.

Manuscript Sources

Florence. Archivio di Stato di Firenze (ASF)
    Arte del Cambio (Cambio), 12, 14, 44, 65.
    Arte della Lana (Lana), 25, 246, 318, 319, 325, 329, 543.
    Arte di Calimala (Calimala), 6.
    Arte di Por Santa Maria o della seta (Seta), 7.
    Carte Strozziane (Strozziane), ser. I. 229, ser. II.76, ser. IV. 635.
    Catasto 15, 29, 35, 36, 43, 46, 52, 55, 57, 59, 64, 75, 80–81, 296, 380, 437, 445, 447, 450, 452, 466, 475, 477–482, 484, 665.

Corporazioni religiose soppresse dal governo francese (Corp. Rel.
　　Sopp.) 78. Badia Fiorentina 321, 326.
Del Bene, 27, 49.
Estimo, 209.
Guadagni, 14.
Mediceo avanti il Principato (MAP), filze XVI, XCVIII, CL, CLIII.
Mercanzia, 11775, 11778.
Monte comune (Monte), ser. 2. 1806, 2416, 3730, 3733.
Notarile antecosimiano (Notarile), 5814.
Repudie d'eredità (Repudie), 10, 12.
Signori
Legazioni e comissarie 7.

Florence. Archivio dell'Ospedale degli Innocenti (AOI)
　　Estranei, 188.

Printed Sources

Albizzi, Rinaldo degli. *Commissioni di Rinaldo degli Albizzi per il Comune di Firenze dal 1399 al 1433*, ed. Cesare Guasti, vol. 2. Florence: Tipi di M. Cellini, 1869.

Allen, Martin. "Italians in English Mints and Exchanges." In *Fourteenth Century England II*, ed. Chris Given-Wilson, The Boydell: Woodbridge, 2002, 53–62.

Arany, Krisztina. "Siker és kudarc. Két firenzei kereskedőcsalád, a Melanesi-k és a Corsini-k Budán Luxemburgi Zsigmond uralkodása (1387–1437) alatt." *Századok* 143 (2009): 943–966.

Crabb, Ann. *The Strozzi of Florence: Widowhood and Family Solidarity in the Renaissance*. University of Michigan Press, 2000.

De Roover, Raymond. *The Rise and Decline of the Medici Bank, 1397–1494.* Cambridge MS: Harvard University Press, 1963.

Draskóczy István. "Olaszok a 15.századi Erdélyben." In *Scripta manent: Ünnepi tanulmányok a 60. életévét betöltött Gerics József professzor tiszteletére*, ed. Draskóczy István, Budapest: ELTE Középkori és Koraújkori Történeti Tanszéke, 1994, 125–135.

_____. "Kamarai jövedelem és urbura a 15.század első felében." In *Gazdaságtörténet, Könyvtártörténet: Emlékkönyv Berlász Jenő 90.*

születésnapjára, ed. János Buza, Budapest: Argumentum, 2001, 147–167.

Herlihy, David and Klapisch-Zuber, Christiane. *Les Toscans et leur familles: une étude du catasto florentin de 1427*. Paris: Presses de la fondation nationale des science politiques, 1978.

Kent, Dale. *The Rise of the Medici: Faction in Florence 1426–1434*. Oxford: Oxford University Press, 1978.

Klapisch-Zuber, Christiane. "Parenti, amici e vicini: Il territorio urbano di una famiglia mercantile del XV secolo." *Quaderni storici* 33. (1976): 953–982.

Kuehn, Thomas. *Heirs, Kin, and Creditors in Renaissance Florence*. Cambridge, UK: Cambridge University Press, 2008.

Molho, Anthony. *Marriage Alliance in Late Medieval Florence*. London: Harvard University Press, 1994.

Petriboni, Pagolo di Matteo and Di Borgo Rinaldi, Matteo. *Priorista (1407–1459). With Two Appendices (1282–1406)*, ed. Jacqueline A. Gutwirth, transcribed Gabriella Battista and Jacqueline A. Gutwirth, Rome: Istituto Nazionale di Studi sul Rinascimento, 2001.

Pitti, Bonaccorso. "Ricordi." In *Mercanti scrittori: Ricordi nella Firenze tra Medioevo e Rinascimento*. ed. Vittore Branca, Milan: Rusconi, 1986, 343–498.

Prajda, Katalin. "The Florentine Scolari Family at the Court of Sigismund of Luxemburg in Buda." *Journal of Early Modern History* 14 (2010): 514–533.

Soldani, Maria Elisa. "A Firenze mercanti, cavalieri nella Signoria dei re d'Aragona: I Tacchini-Taqui tra XIV e XV secolo." *Anuario de Estudios Medievales* 39. 2 (2009): 575–604.

_____. "Da accettanti a setantì: il processo di integrazione di una famiglia lucchese nella società barcellonese del quattrocento." In *Per Marco Tangheroni: Studi su Pisa e sul Mediterraneo medievale offerti dai suoi ultimi allievi*, ed. C. Iannella. ETS: Pisa, 2005, 209–233.

Weissen, Kurt. "Florentiner Kaufleute in Deutschland bis zum Ende des 14. Jahrhunderts." In *Zwischen Maas und Rhein: Beziehungen, Begegnungen und Konflikte in einem europäischen Kernraum von der Spätantike bis zum 19. Jahrhunert*, ed. Franz Irsigler, Trier: Kliomedia, 2006, 363–401.

OUR DAUGHTERS AND OUR FUTURE: ELITE GRECO-VENETIAN MARRIAGES 1520–1610

ERSIE BURKE[1]

The Venetian patriciate maintained its position through a series of laws that established and protected its political, economic and social dominance. These measures sought to define and clarify its duties and responsibilities politically and socially. One of the patriciate's concerns was the regulation of its members' lives as a way of ensuring its continuation. The institution that protected the exclusivity and lineage of the class was marriage, the legal union of a patrician man and a patrician woman and the production of (legitimate) patrician children, especially sons. Exogamy, that is marriage to non-patricians (local or foreign) was permitted but only after a thorough examination of the prospective partner and his or her family for any whiff of scandal or inappropriate behaviour. Marriage laws, enacted to protect the purity of the ruling class and keep out those who would taint it, were regularly reviewed to keep out "undesirables."[2] The list of those who might do damage included non-patrician partners of unknown or questionable lineage and patricians who brought shame or infamy to their families and by extension their class. Most people married within their class, but a substantial minority married outside it. The latter chose, or had chosen for them, elite women and men from Venice, its land empire, the *Terraferma*, and its sea empire, the *Stato da Mar*. Many of these non-patrician partners were Greek men and women whose families had immigrated to Venice. This essay focuses on Greek women and their marriages into the ruling class. Though subjects of the *Serenis-*

---

[1] This article is a revised version of a paper I gave at the annual conference of the Centre for Reformation and Renaissance Studies, University of Toronto, "To Have and To Hold: Marriage in Premodern Europe 1200–1700" from 16–17 October 2009. I take the opportunity to thank Jacqueline Murray and Konrad Eisenbichler for their assistance with the early drafts of this paper.

[2] Cowan, *Marriage, Manners and Mobility*, 13. For the history of Venetian marriage legislation see Chojnacki, *Women and Men*, 53–75 and Cowan, 86–90. There is a summary of the marriage laws at the end of this article.

sima, the women and their families were different from Venetians culturally, ethnically, linguistically and, in many instances, religiously. For this reason, cross-cultural marriages raised issues which were not evident in Venetian-to-Venetian or Venetian-to-Italian unions. Even though such unions did not occur often, the importance of safeguarding the purity of the ruling class caused the authorities to review the marriage laws on a regular basis to "exclude undesirable women." Exogamy was truly a complex affair for Venetian and non-Venetian elites.

There has been a substantial body of research devoted to patrician marriage, but very little on foreign marriages in general, and Greco-Venetian ones in particular. Sally McKee has examined Veneto-Cretan unions and their impact on the political and social world of medieval Crete. In the early years of Venetian rule, intermarriage between Venetian patrician families and Cretan nobility was discouraged, but over time the rules were relaxed and, as McKee shows, there emerged a class with its own unique Veneto-Cretan identity.[3] Benjamin Arbel has focused on Cypriot nobility, especially the Synglitico and Podacataro families, and the way they used marriage to patricians to realize their ambitions and secure their future.[4] The study of prominent families in the Venetian *Terraferma* and their marriage alliances to local and Venetian elites has been the focus of James Grubb's research.[5] Stanley Chojnacki's great body of work analyzed and dissected the background, intricacies and consequences of patrician unions, the marriage laws and the socio-political concerns governing them.[6] Alexander Cowan has looked at the period between the late 1500s through the 1600s when the burden of proof of suitability and eligibility fell on the non-patrician bride-to-be and her entire

---

[3] McKee, "Greek Women in Latin Households"; "Women Under Venetian Colonial Rule in the Early Renaissance"; "Households in Fourteenth Century Venetian Crete"; *Uncommon Dominion*.

[4] Arbel, "Greek Magnates in Venetian Cyprus: The Case of the Synglitico Family"; "The Cypriot Nobility from the Fourteenth to the Sixteenth Century: A New Interpretation."

[5] Grubb, *Provincial Families of the Renaissance*; "Memory and Identity: Why Venetians Didn't Keep Ricordanze."

[6] Chojnacki, "Dowries and Kinsmen in Early Renaissance Venice"; "Social Identity in Renaissance Venice: The Second Serrata"; "Identity and Ideology in Renaissance Venice: The Third Serrata"; "In Search of the Venetian Patriciate: Families and Factions in the Fourteenth Century"; *Women and Men in Renaissance Venice: Twelve Essays on Patrician Society*. Cowan, *Marriage, Manners and Mobility*.

family. The scholarship has included close scrutiny of the many marriage laws, the definition of what constituted an acceptable spouse, the clarification of the status of illegitimate children and the administrative procedures that patrician and non-patrician families had to go through in order to win the state's approval to marry.[7] Much of this work focused on the legalities, politics and the procedures which defined and governed patrician marriage. The research here looks at the women themselves, not the men who arranged their unions, questioned their suitability in processes that were often inquisitorial and wrote the laws that dictated marital terms and conditions. The women left a substantial body of evidence notably petitions, wills and other notarial documentation. These types of documents were written in set styles that employed stock phrases, and in truth most people adhered to the language and form of the documents as dictated by the scribes who composed them. Therefore, they are not the most accurate sources for gauging how women felt about their lives. Unfortunately, no personal documentation written by Greek women, such as letters and diaries, has been found to date. Fortunately, a good number of the women ventured beyond the accepted formulae that characterised notarial and other documentation and spoke openly about their circumstances, in this way providing an interesting and more intimate look into their lives. More importantly, the sources highlight two important issues about Greek out-marriage this essay will address: the advantages of a foreign spouse for both sides of the family and the effects of exogamy on women's identity, that is, whether foreignness survived exogamy.

Greeks made up the largest group of subject people to settle in Venice. Between 1470 and 1540, and then again in 1570 with the fall of Cyprus, the community, already old and well established, more than doubled in size. It had its own confraternity, the Scuola di San Niccolò dei Greci, established in 1498, and an Eastern rite church, San Giorgio dei Greci which was completed in 1573. Most Greeks (over ninety percent) were commoners: artisans and mariners, minor merchants, printers, publishers and soldiers. The community's elite — three privileged groups — consisted of a few prominent mercantile families, military commanders of the light horse (*capi dei stratioti*)

---

[7] Venetian elites were defined by law: the patricians who ruled and the original citizens (*cittadini originari*) who administered. Both classes derived and maintained their status with the birth and registration of legitimately born sons. Greek elite status was based on mercantile and other wealth, association with certain professions, and nobility conferred by Byzantine or other rulers, or a combination of these.

and landed nobility. Half the population were migrants from the territories that would remain, with the exception of Crete, part of the *Stato da Mar* until the fall of the Republic in 1797, while the other half were refugees who had fled the Ottoman takeover of their homelands. A by-product of these waves of immigration was an increase in the availability of women from well-to-do families and the subsequent rise in the number of Greco-Venetian unions. This was nothing new. In truth, Greeks and Venetians had been marrying each other for a very long time both in Venice and in the sea colonies.[8]

The three privileged groups were a very small percentage of the Greek population yet they dominated the community.[9] They were elite because of wealth, lineage, family history and large socio-economic networks. They regularly held elected offices in the Scuola di San Niccolò dei Greci, employed a significant number of their compatriots in their many enterprises, financially supported Greek commercial ventures such as printing presses and publishing houses, acted as sponsors and patrons for countless people and gave generously to the Greek church and its charities. Their wealth, acquired over many generations, was based on any or all of the following: landholdings, inheritance, rewards and gifts from local rulers and Venice in return for services. They were proud of their ancient family histories which were inexorably tied to their homelands. They had large social and political networks which they extended further through marriage to local and foreign elites. Just as important were the links between themselves and the Venetian presence in the *Stato da Mar*, particularly in areas like commerce, colonial administration and warfare. It was therefore logical that some of these relationships, forged over many years, eventually led to marriages between

---

[8] One of the earliest recorded marriages was that of Benvenuta Prothimo's to Niccolò Zorzi; there is no marriage date but their son was registered in the Book of Gold on 27 July 1441, ASV, Balla d' Oro II, fol. 28. The Prothimo were nobility from Negroponte and held high offices in the Venetian administration of the island. Between 1489–1511 four women from the Spandounes family married patricians. The family was from Constantinople and had escaped before the fall of the City to the Ottomans. The women were the sisters Regina, Chiara and Elena di Demetrio Spandounes and their cousin Regina di Matteo. ASV, AdiC Index 86/2, 364.

[9] There were no more than twenty-five elite families during the whole of the sixteenth century, each consisting of several branches. Some of these were extremely wealthy, others moderately so. The list of names is too long to include here, but some of the more prominent ones were the Paleologo, Clada, Rali, Mormori, Catticora, Lascari-Megaduca, Seguro, Vergi, Sofianò, Cavopenna, Samariari, de Nores, Podacataro, Spandounes, Nassin and Synglitico.

themselves and Venetians and the creation of new and powerful family, kin and friendship networks.

There is little evidence of close personal relationships between the three privileged groups, other than for the occasional commercial purpose. Mercantile elites lived and worked in the world of trade, industry and investments. Military men went where the state sent them, and many left their families in Venice rather than move them from city to city. The nobility maintained a few ties to the Greek community either through the scuola or the church, but on the whole they lived apart from the rest of the community. Not surprisingly, there were considerable tensions within each group. The Vergi and Cubli, important mercantile families, were bitter commercial rivals; the capi dei stratioti and their men often came to blows over territorial rights and past, unsettled feuds.[10] While they did not mix socially, all three groups shared the view that marriage was about preserving the uniqueness of the family and ensuring its continuity and prosperity. Good marriages meant the acquisition of useful and influential in-laws, and new relations and friends.[11] These common goals, however did not translate into marriages between the groups. Military families and the nobility preferred partners from within their own group, and then patricians. The mercantile elites were different. For a start, they were fabulously wealthy.[12] The most important families were the

---

[10] Sanuto described several of these arguments which often resulted in physical fights. In September 1500 he reported a quarrel between Theodoro Rali and Domenico Bosichio which degenerated into a fist fight. The argument was caused by unresolved and underlying tensions between Greek and Albanian soldiers and officers. "Item, per una altra letera, avisa il venir qui di Domenego Busichio, capo di stratioti, qual con Thodaro Rali a Udene sonno in parole, e ditto Domenego li dè un pugno a Thodaro, *adeo* messi nel governador, l'Alviano e capetanio di fantarie, hanno sententiato, e manda la copia di la sentenzia, che 'l ditto Domenego vadi da Thodaro a dir li dagi un altro pugno a lui; e voleva esso Thodaro prometesse nol ge dar; qual non volse prometer. Dice albanesi e greci sono per questo le compagnie divise." Sanuto, III: 813.

[11] These qualities were shared by all elites in the early modern period. Klapisch-Zuber, *Women, Family and Ritual*, 68–69.

[12] Two classic cases show how easily wealth and status could disappear. From 1520–1550, Andrea Curcumeli from Candia was the wealthiest man in the Greek community. A series of very poor investments and bad luck (the loss of some of his ships to storms and piracy) saw his wealth vanish. At the time of his death (27 October 1556), he owed investors 8,000 ducats which his brother Alessandro had to repay. The second person was Giacomo Samariari, the richest man in the community in the second half of the sixteenth century. He died with his massive wealth intact but most of his family had predeceased

Vergi, Seguro, Samariari and Cubli, yet no marriages ever took place between them for the whole of the sixteenth century. If the other two groups chose partners among their own, why not this one? Perhaps commercial rivalries made it difficult to do so; the Vergi and Cubli barely spoke and on several occasions their rivalry spilled over and affected the administration of the Greek confraternity and church.[13] More likely the families saw no financial or social advantages to such unions since they already had wealth, respect and authority within a Greek context and inter-marriage brought no further benefits. Out-marriage however, held the potential for greater gain, new markets and entry into the top echelons of society. For the three groups, the creation of new, broader marriage networks indicated a measure of confidence about their place in Venetian society, their acceptance by the Venetian upper classes and the return of the sort of status they enjoyed in their homelands

Achieving this integration into the upper levels of Venetian society did not come easily, nor cheaply. Non-patrician families were not subject to the dowry laws and in some cases Greek women's dowries were higher than the amount dictated by the state. This was the case with Cecilia Podacataro. At the time of her second marriage, in 1521, patrician dowries were set at 3,000 ducats; hers was 4,000.[14] By 1525, the upper limit of the dowry was 4,000

---

him. He distributed his possessions to a variety of charities, churches, monasteries and convents throughout the city and in his native Zante. His immediate heirs were two nieces. Samariari was the first and the last of his family to have any impact on the Greek and Venetian communities. After his death, the Samariari, like the Curcumeli, disappeared from both Venetian and Greek records. Curcumeli's commercial contracts are too many to list here; his favourite notaries were Agostino Pellestrina and Paolo di Grandi: ASV, Notarile Atti, bb. 10636–10644 for the years 1538–1557 (Pellestrina) and bb. 6486–6514 for the years 1551–1589 (di Grandi). A petition was submitted by Alessandro Curcumeli, Andrea's brother, seeking financial assistance from the authorities so he could pay off his late brother's debt. The petition is in ASV, Collegio, risposte di fuori, filza 312, fol. 219, 22 July 1557. Samariari also used di Grandi for many of his commercial transactions: ASV, Notarile Atti, bb. 6487, 6502, 6503; the inventory of his house is in di Grandi, b. 6511, fols. 64v–71r, 78v–83r, 31 August 1586.

[13] Mavroidi referred to the antagonism between the Cubli and the Vergi but the only examples she cited were their clashes over control of the committees and board of the Scuola di San Niccolò dei Greci. The scuola administered the community's charities and supervised the construction of the church. Those who sat on its many committees were the community's leaders, answerable to the membership and the Venetian authorities charged with supervising confraternities. Mavroidi, *Symvole*, 140; 143–144.

[14] ASV, Notarile Testamenti, b. 124, Francesco Bianco, 167, 16 October 1532.

ducats. The following year the Cypriot Zegno Synglitico, Count of Rochas concluded his granddaughter's marriage agreement in which he pledged a dowry of 21,000 ducats.[15] But as Alex Cowen has shown, the extent to which dowry size was an important factor in patrician out-marriage is debatable. Indeed, when Gratiosa Cubli married Pietro Manolesso, in 1584, her dowry was 5,000 ducats while the amount set by the state was 6,000.[16] Patricians chose foreign partners for many reasons, including access to greater wealth, but there were other factors in play. Some of the Greek families, like the Spandounes and Prothimo, were truly noble; for example, the Spandounes were related (in the loosest possible sense of the term) by marriage to the Cantacuzene imperial line. Others, especially the military families were fief-holders in the Morea, having acquired their properties from their Byzantine, Ottoman and later Venetian overlords. The Republic rewarded their bravery and loyalty with more gifts of land, initially in the Morea and later in Dalmatia, the *Terraferma*, Crete and the Ionian Islands. The mercantile elite had no claims to nobility; they were wealthy because they were commercially successful. The acquisition of property (not fiefs) was a consequence of their wealth, not its basis. These are some of the reasons Venetian elites were attracted to outsiders. A far more significant reason was their familiarity with the "other." Patrician and *cittadino* families had had close associations with Greeks for a very long time, especially in the sea colonies where they worked and held high office but relied on local notables for advice, service and companionship. One only need look through Marco Barbaro's family trees (with great care and a critical eye), or the marriage indices of the Avogaria di Comun to see that Venetian out-marriage was not uncommon.

No Greek elites arrived in Venice and then began to make their name and fortune. They already enjoyed wealth and status in their homelands because of a combination of some or all of these factors: lineage traced to the Byzantines or to the more recent Crusader or other western (Norman, Florentine, Genoese, Catalan) families; a history of long and distinguished service to the Venetian state (even better, to the Byzantine too), from which they obtained lands, titles and privileges; knowledge of and dealings with the Ottomans commercially, politically and diplomatically; mercantile know-how, including a range of family, Greek and non-Greek business partners,

---

[15] Arbel, "Greek Magnates in Venetian Cyprus," 331.

[16] The marriage contract between Gratiosa's father, Andronico Cubli, and her future husband, Pietro Manolesso is in AAIEV, b. 2, filza 2, fols 1v–2r.

already well established trade routes and markets, a keen sense of where and when to expand business networks, the ability to procure from the state the right to expand to new geographic areas and to secure state licences to trade in a variety of commodities and goods. The Cavopenna of Napoli di Romania are a good example of this multi-faceted road to success. Cavopenna wealth originally came from land ownership and commerce. One branch of the family were seigneurs of Pediada, an area of the Argolid (eastern Morea), while another were lords of the island of Aegina till 1451, after which the Venetians took it over and put it under the authority of the *rettor* of Napoli di Romania. After this various family members worked for successive *rettori* as interpreters and emissaries in their dealings with the Ottomans at nearby Argos.[17] After 1540, at least three Cavopenna branches settled in Venice where they pursued mercantile interests, held important positions in various magistracies, obtained *cittadini originarii* status and acquired Venetian in-laws. That they succeeded in doing so rather quickly is not surprising since the Cavopenna had been marrying out since the early fifteenth century. Even before they immigrated they counted among their in-laws Greek nobility (the Prothimo of Negroponte) and Venetian patricians from the Ferro, Molin and Lando families. Once in Venice, they continued the pattern of choosing partners from their Nafpliot compatriots and then local elites, so that by the middle of the 1550s the Cavopenna had acquired new sets of Venetian in-laws from the Michiel, Trevisan and Bollani families. From early times Cavopenna men and women attracted the attention of prominent partners because of who they were and what they did. Out-marriage was not restricted to the women of this family; in the early years in Aegina and the Argolid more Cavopenna men than women married out. The opposite occurred in Venice.

Ultimately, this study is about the women, so the question remains: how did their marriages to Venetians affect them? Preliminary investigations indicate many similarities in their stories. They displayed remarkable candour about the people with whom they lived and interacted, including husbands, birth families and in-laws. With minor exceptions, the majority of women maintained intimate ties with their own families throughout their marriages

---

[17] When the *rettor* of Napoli di Romania, Bartolomeo Minio was too ill to meet with the new Ottoman governor (*flamburar*) in March 1483, he sent Olivoto de Cavopenna in his place. Wright and Melville-Jones, *The Greek Correspondence*, 288–289. The origins of the Cavopenna are unclear, but they might have originally been part of the Catalan companies that overran Greece in the early fourteenth century.

and into widowhood. There is little evidence of pressure from in-laws and spouses to embrace Venetian customs and mores, for instance to become fluent in Italian or to adopt the Latin rite. The latter is consistent with all Greco-Venetian unions, regardless of class. Finally, most of these relationships reflected what elite marriage was meant to be: a sound transaction between two families which would produce heirs and other benefits for both sides. The women expressed feelings towards their partners that ranged from emotional indifference to affection and respect. Some couples displayed strong feelings while one woman was fairly indifferent to her husband and distrustful of her in-laws. Through their marriages, the women helped to promote, cement and strengthen their family's political, social and economic position in Venice. They bridged the gap between their family's ambitions and the needs of the patriciate. In doing so, they performed the function of all privileged women: to enter into a marriage that provided good kin, further cemented relationships and created new opportunities. How this affected them personally, and how each handled her new situation, is a familiar theme in the stories of immigrant women. The focus here is on women from three families and the way they handled their circumstances. Their families were the Cubli of Napoli di Romania, the Seguro of Zante and the Paleologo of the Morea. Each represented the highest levels of success in one or more of these areas: commerce, administration and the military. They also had large networks which included fellow Greeks, other subject people and Venetians of all classes. The men enjoyed a variety of experiences. The Seguro were active in the administration of their native Zante. The Cubli became one of the top commercially successful clans. The Paleologo were military men and served on diplomatic missions, accompanying ambassadors and other high officials to Constantinople as interpreters (*dragomani*) and minor officials. To a large extent, their daughters' marriages helped the families establish firmer footholds in Venice.

The Seguro

The Seguro were a noble Zachynthian clan with a long and distinguished history of service to their homeland and Venice.[18] In 1542, the *rettor* wrote of them, "They are the first [family] in this place, they have come together [are related to] through consanguinity with all the other citizens, they have half this island in their hand."[19] They held important posts in the civil administration of the island and sent regular reports to Venice about its affairs.[20] Isabella and Giacomo Seguro had eight children, three sons and five daughters. From 1521 onwards, they arranged marriages for their daughters and sons to Venetian and Greek elites. In this way, they acquired in-laws and kin from Crete, the Morea and Venice. Two daughters married notable Zachynthians, while the other three married patricians from the Pizzamano, Malipiero and Balbi families. For the next three generations, in every branch of this family, there were at least two, sometimes more, patrician marriages, so that by the middle of the seventeenth century, in addition to those already mentioned, the Seguro were related to the Loredan, Vitturi, Memmo, Zane, Pasqualigo and Lippomano as well. The integration of the family into the patriciate was almost complete, thanks to their daughters. There were Seguro households throughout Venice on both sides of the Grand Canal, but especially in the parishes of San Vio, Santi Apostoli, San Geremia and Santa Margarita.

Seguro women expressed feelings for their husbands ranging from affection to disdain. Most of the marriages could best be described as emotionally distant. The women reserved their affections for their children and their natal family, especially their siblings, nieces and nephews. Diana

---

[18] The family were originally Norman crusaders who settled in Zante in the thirteenth century. They integrated into the island's nobility through marriage. Venice annexed Zante in 1482 and the family continued to play an important part in the island's affairs. Seguro men held military and naval commissions and high administrative offices; they were scholars, landowners, merchants and the family produced the island's patron saint, St. Dionysius (born Trachanioti Seguro di Nufri). Ph. Bouboulidou, «Συμβολή εις την ιστορίαν της Ζακυνθιάς οικογενείας Συγούρου» ["The contribution to history of the Zachynthian family Seguro"], 84.

[19] "Sonno li primi in questo luoco, sonno conivuti in consanguinità con tutti li altri cittadini, hanno la mittà di questa Isola in sua mano," ASV, Capi del Consiglio dei Dieci. Lettere dei *rettori* e altre cariche, b. 296, fol. 1 unnumb., 25 August 1542.

[20] Sanuto, X: 58; XXIX: 463; XLII: 654–655; L: 497; LI: 352–353, 354, 411–413; LIV: 324.

Seguro barely mentioned her husband in her will, even though she was eight months pregnant with her first child when she made it in 1587.[21] She appointed her husband, Marco di Antonio Pasqualigo one of the three executors of her estate, and named one of her brothers, Zorzi, and her sister, Bettina, as the other two. According to the terms of her will, if she died before him, Marco would receive 400 ducats along with his portion of her dowry and the remainder of her estate would go to her children. Other beneficiaries, in addition to her brother and sister, included Seguro nieces and nephews, her parish church, the convent of Santi Rocco e Margherita, several charities and hospitals and the Greek church, San Giorgio dei Greci. She left nothing to any members of Pasqualigo's family. Diana's sister, Bettina, was more expansive with her bequests, partly out of affection and partly out of necessity, as she had to look after her own and Diana's children. She asked her executors, her son and a relation by marriage, to look after the estates of her nieces and nephews, the children of the now deceased Diana and Marco.[22] She distributed money, clothing and furniture to household servants and their children, a common practice at the time. But the focus of her will was to provide adequate care for her orphaned nieces and nephews and to settle her estate, which included property holdings in Venice and the *Terraferma*, on her daughter Chiaretta, a nun in Santa Marta. As well, she left fifty ducats each for two of her late husband's first cousins, who were nuns in the same convent. It is not clear whether she did this out of affection or to ensure the older cousins looked after Chiaretta. She left nothing to her son as he had already inherited from his father. Neither Diana nor Bettina expressed any feelings towards their husbands. This was not unusual, in fact it was most common. Their aunt Sofia, on the other hand, openly expressed her feelings. Sofia Seguro appointed her husband, Marco Balbi, her sole heir and executor. What set Sofia apart from her nieces were her feelings for Balbi. Every reference to him was preceded by terms of affection such as my "dear husband" (*mio caro marido*), "most loving husband" (*amatissimo marido*).

---

[21] ASV, Notarile Testamenti, b. 47, Bortolomeo Bressan, 188, 5 September 1587.

[22] ASV, Notarile Testamenti, b. 157, Antonio Brinis, 332, 18 October 1598. "Lasso et instituisco mei commissari il Clarissimo ser Stefano Ghixi mio parenti et Antonio Pasqualigo mio fiol il qual Clarissimo ser Steffano prego ad autar questa mia comissaria con ogni affetione per amor di mio fio: liquali mei commissari instituisco anche comissarii delli figlioli del q. Clarissimo ser Marco Pasqualico et della q. madonna Diana mia dilettissima sorella, con quella istessa autorità ch' Io havera, alli quali mei commissarii racomando essi figlioli et le cose sue con quel maggior affetto di spirito ch' Io ho reposso."

Again, these were stock phrases but most Greek elite women did not use them. In keeping with tradition, she left her estate to her children, but only if Marco remarried; otherwise, he was the heir, executor and beneficiary.[23] Sofia, Diana and Bettina's wills were in marked contrast to the 1606 will of Guglielma Seguro, the wife of Pietro Loredan. This one sounded like a rather difficult marriage. Guglielma composed a very long will in which she devised and addressed any and all possible circumstances to ensure that her children, not yet born or conceived, would be her sole heirs and beneficiaries. Her executors were her siblings. Should she die first, Loredan would receive his one-third share of the cash component of her dowry, as required by law. For one year after her death, he would also have access to all the income from her estate but only if he fulfilled the terms of her bequests and any other bequests the executors directed him to meet. Her siblings and their children were her principle heirs if none of her [future] children, survived. Guglielma was very precise about her estate should her children die young or childless:

> [...] and should my sons and daughters die before the above said age of twenty and twenty-five years without heirs, that is without sons and daughters, in that case I want that all that is mine should go to my brother and sister, but if the girls die after the age of twenty without children or else the boys die after the age of twenty-five without children, in that case, I want and ordain that [the executors and trustees] to freely dispose of my abovementioned property because I do not want my husband's relations to be beneficiaries.[24]

---

[23] ASV, Notarile Testamenti, b. 127, Francesco Bianco, 789, 28 May 1535. "Voio esser sepulta dove et cum quella spesa che parera al illustrissimo missier Marco mio amatissimo marido/ voio che sia mio commessario solo el magnifico misier Marco Balbi mio marido. Tutti li mei beni mobili et stabili presenti et la mia dota, lasso et voio che sia del magnifico misier Marco Balbi mio caro marido, liberamente El qual voio che sia mio herede de tutto el mio al qual racommando l'anema mia voio tamen che si marisse el dito misier Marco mio marido, che tutti li mei beni sia de mie fioli cosi mascoli come femene egualmente et si morisse tutti li mei fioli tutto venga in misier Marco mio marido suo padre."

[24] ASV, Notarile Testamenti, b. 1243, Giulio Ziliol, 302, 22 May 1606: "Et morendo li ditti miei figli et figlie avanti la sudetta etta d' anni vinti et 25 senza heredi cio senza filgi o filgie voglio in tal caso che tutti li miei beni vadino alli miei fratello, et sorella, ma morendo le femine doppo che haveranno fini a anni 20 senza figlii et cosi overo se morisse li mascoli doppo l' etta d'anni 25 senza figlii in tal caso voglio et ordino che possino disponer

There were affectionate unions, indifferent ones, and then there were unhappy ones such as Guglielma's. She did not explain her feelings towards her husband's family, but it is clear from her will that she had encountered difficulties in dealing with them. She and Pietro had married in 1598 when she was only fourteen, a fairly young age since at the time most elite women married in their late teens. Pietro was twenty-two, so there was not a large age difference between them. They remained childless until 1610. There might have been babies who did not survive, but the inability to produce children for twelve years may have weighed heavily on her and could have been a source of tension between her and her husband's family. She had recently lost her father when she made her will in May 1606. It could be that the loss, coupled with an unhappy marriage and no living children had taken its toll.

Zante remained the Seguro family's base throughout the sixteenth and seventeenth centuries. Generally Seguro men divided their time between the island and Venice. Their families however, stayed in Zante and only the women who married patricians moved to the city permanently. It is not surprising then that Venetian-based Seguro sisters, cousins, aunts and nieces relied on each other. The daughters of Isabella and Giacomo, that first generation to move to Venice, wed men who had dealings with their brothers and their father. The women were not part of that world, but through their close ties they comforted and supported each other, and in this way established a pattern repeated by subsequent Seguro women. Whether by design or accident, in every generation there were two or more women married to patricians and living in Venice. From their accounts, their world centered on their children and natal family. They had few contacts with the Greek community.[25] For Seguro women, exogamy meant more than moving house. It meant the physical separation of the women from their natal families and their homeland and its traditions. It is not surprising that they relied on each other for help, guidance and friendship. This dependence was unique among elite Greek women.

---

liberalmente delli miei beni accenttuate perche non voglio che siano beneficati li parenti del sudetto mio marito."

[25] Several Seguro joined the Scuola di San Niccolò dei Greci. The siblings Costantino, Zorzi and Nufri were members in the first half of the century and the names of their sons and nephews appear in the latter part of the century. Mavroidi, 201, 238 (Costantino, Zorzi and Nufri's entries) and AAIEV, reg. 134, fols 7r, 37v, 94v, 125r, 196r. Diana Seguro was the only member of the family who left a bequest to the Greek church.

The Cubli

The Cubli (or Cuvli) family differed from the Seguro. The men did not seek administrative and other postings. Indeed they had a very thin record of public service, and actually received more from a generous state than they put in.[26] They married out, but not as often as other elites, preferring partners from their native Napoli di Romania instead. They remained merchants, although towards the end of the century they began investing in property on the *Terraferma*. Unlike the Seguro, the Cubli successfully incorporated their Greek and Venetian halves and the result was a broad yet cohesive extended family. The catalysts of this blending were the daughters of Andronico and Agnese Cubli. The family and most of its branches immigrated to Venice in the 1530s. Andronico and Agnese's four children, Ludovica, Isabetta, Gratiosa and Lorenzo, were all born in Venice. The extended family lived in the *sestiere* of San Pietro di Castello, in the parishes of San Pietro di Castello, San Severo and Sant'Antonin, where they also owned substantial properties. The wills of Gratiosa, Isabetta and Ludovica Cubli illustrated not only the integration of this family into Venetian society, but also its unbroken links to its roots. The three sisters incorporated their own and each others' relations by marriage, and even *their* relations, into their world, a world which encompassed every layer of Venetian society. The family continued the pattern of Nafpliot and Venetian marriages into the seventeenth century.

Lorenzo and Isabetta di Andronico married people from Napoli di Romania while Ludovica and Gratiosa had Venetian spouses. These two were not the first to do so. Their uncle Niccolò, their father's brother, had married a woman named Cecilia Dolfin in the early 1550s.[27] The three sisters' husbands

---

[26] Because they came from Napoli di Romania the Cubli were entitled to awards the Senate gave out to Nafpliots and Monemvasians between 1541 and 1548. The awards were not based on poverty or real need but were seen both by the petitioner and the state as recompense for loss of income, home and belongings as a consequence of the Ottoman conquest of the two cities. The *paterfamilias* Canachi Cubli received hundreds of ducats a year from several concessions awarded to him and his sons. Andronico di Canachi had a salary from the Customs House (*Dogana da Mar*). In both cases, father and son were allowed to pass their concessions to their heirs, upon approval from the issuing authority. ASV, Senato da Mar, reg. 29, fols. 167v, 177v.

[27] There is no evidence that Cecilia came from the patrician Dolfin. Her name is not in the marriage records of the Avogaria di Comun or Barbaro's family trees. She may have been illegitimate. Dolfin was a common Venetian surname.

came from different backgrounds. Isabetta married Andrea Londano, a nobleman and scholar from her family's homeland; Ludovica's husband, Almoro Finetti (or Filetti), was from a *cittadino* family, and Gratiosa married the patrician, Pietro Manolesso. The Manolesso had strong ties to Crete and there is some speculation that Pietro was born there.[28] When Andronico Cubli and Manolesso negotiated the terms of the marriage contract, Cubli wanted assurances that his money did not end up in distant Crete. He provided Gratiosa with a generous dowry, on the condition that his son-in-law guarantee its value. Manolesso agreed to do so by selling property in Crete and promising to live only in Venice. If Gratiosa predeceased him, Manolesso was entitled to one-third of her dowry and the remaining two-thirds would return to the Cubli family. Finally, if Manolesso died before Gratiosa, and they had no legitimate children, his family was forbidden to make demands on her dowry.[29] In this way, Andronico Cubli ensured that Gratiosa's dowry — and his own hard earned money — stayed firmly in Cubli hands, in Venice. The Cubli, like the other mercantile elites, had no established tradition of out-marriage. In fact, all the families in this group first acquired elite in-laws after they moved to Venice. What had changed? The only way to greater social and economic prosperity was through exogamy. The Cubli had money, but now they needed the "trappings" that went with wealth, especially access to more markets and entry into Venetian society. Only marriage to patricians

---

[28] For the Manolesso family tree, including Pietro's marriage to Gratiosa see Marco Barbaro, IV: 20, 449.

[29] AAIEV, Testamenti, legati, commisarie e donazioni, no. 9b, fasc. 2, doc. 1, fol. 1r–v. "Cioè promette Il detto Magnifico m. Andronico padre in dotte […] ducatti cinque milla in questo modo, vz. in vestimenti, et mobelli per ducati tresento in quatrocento in circa. Il resto veramente […] della 1,000 ducati de contadi numero 600 per vestire della sopraditta sposa, et Il restante veramente, che sarano ducati 4,000 in contadi consegniarli immediate anche attenderano […]de ducatti 5,000 da esser posti in uno scrigno et il sopra ditto Magnifico m. Andronico tenira una chiave, et il Clarissimo sposo un altra fin che venira partitto, da poterli, investir, apiacer et, comodo d' una parte et d' altra, et, questo sia per asicuratione della ditta dotte. Il qual el Clarissimo sposo promette vender tutti li beni che s' atrova, havere nel Regno di Candia et investrili in queste parte, cioè li sopradetti duc. 4,000 […]et di piu, esso Clarissimo sposo, promette, habbitar, Luoco, et Fuoco in questa città per osservanza, di tutte le cosse di sopra […]Ma in caso di restitution di dotte, che Iddio non voglia, detto Clarissimo sposo, habbi per il suo terzo, ducati 1000/ et òccorendo, Il detto caso al Clarissimo sposo che Iddio non voglia mancando perhò senza figluoli, avanti la sposa, li suoi heredi non habino cosa alcuna li quali parti se sotto scrittura, di lor proprie mani […]"

and *cittadini originarii* could bring this about. Therefore, that Venetian elites sought ties with them now was not surprising given the women's assets, their family's extensive commercial holdings, the number of properties they owned, in other words, their wealth. The sisters had considerable investments which they personally managed; the sheer size and breadth of Isabetta and Gratiosa's bequests reflected this wealth.[30] The two did not have children, so a good portion of their estates went to their nephew, Alvise Finetti, and his family, and to their brother Lorenzo and his sons, Nicoletto and Andrea. But they also generously gave to their many employees, local shopkeepers, artisans and others who worked for them, as well as to the many religious houses, charities, hospitals and orphanages around the city.

It is difficult to know the nature of the relationship between the Cubli and their husbands, but it is possible to make some observations. Almoro Finetti died ten years before Ludovica, so she did not refer to him in her will (1595). Isabetta had been widowed a long time too, but she lost no opportunity to mention Londano's title, *cavaliere* (knight).[31] In fact, she appropriated the title for herself and was known to family and friends alike as *la cavalliera*. Gratiosa followed the accepted practice of the day and referred to her husband by his title, *Clarissimo nobile*. When it came to family, the sisters incorporated their relations by marriage into their natal family. Ludovica lived with Laura, a Finetti relation. This Laura's circle of women friends included

---

[30] Ludovica Cubli Finetti made few bequests because she left her estate to ehr only child, Alvise. Among her investments was a lease from the Scuola della Misericordia. Isabetta and Gratiosa held long term leases with the Commune of Feltre from which they derived an income. Isabetta owned a house in the parish of San Pietro di Castello as well as estates on the *Terraferma* at Farsinella and Carvello, a property in Padua, a lease on grain from the Commune of Este, and a lease on the capital of 400 ducats from the Commune of Feltre: "La mia parte delli campi della Farsinella che fano in tutto quindeci, et la mia cura da Carvello, et il mio livello de cavedal de ducati quatrocento che ho con la comunità de Feltre." She left her Paduan properties to Gratiosa: "mei campi da Padua in vita sua, et dapoi la sua morte vadi in el mio residuo." Gratiosa also held a lease from the Commune of Feltre, as well as a considerable amount of cash. The wills of the three sisters are in ASV, Notarile Testamenti, b. 382, Federico Figolin, 148, 20 January 1604 (Isabetta); 166, 29 February 1599 and 7 August 1607 (Gratiosa); 229, 6 January 1595 (Ludovica). Isabetta's first will is in b. 440, Giovanni Figolin, 296, 16 June 1593.

[31] Andrea Londano held a law degree from Padua University. He was a scholar and noted collector of, and dealer in rare books and antiquities.

Cecilia Dolfin, Isabetta and Gratiosa.[32] Isabetta remembered Londano nieces and gave precious gifts to her brother-in-law Pietro Manolesso. Gratiosa's list of beneficiaries included her own family, her in-laws and their relations.

Not surprisingly, Isabetta and Gratiosa were most generous to their natal family. Their overwhelming desire (perhaps because of their own childless state?) was to ensure the continuation of the Cubli family name, to hear the names of the deceased repeated in every generation. To this end, they gave gifts to young Cubli cousins, nieces and nephews and encouraged them to marry and have children. They were particularly solicitous of their nephew Alvise Finetti and his family, and more so to his daughter Ludovica, the granddaughter of their late sister. Much to everyone's distress, the little girl died in 1605, when she was eight years old. Gratiosa Cubli then urged her nephew and his wife to have another child, and if female to name her Ludovica, as well.[33]

The mix and range of friends, family and relations (natal and by marriage) reflected the women's shift from the predominately Greek world of their parents and grandparents to a Greco-Venetian one. In this and other ways, the Cubli women were different from the Seguro. For one, all three were born and raised in Venice, whereas the Seguro grew up on Zante. Each had married men from the neighbourhood, and with the exception of Finetti, men with ties to the Greek speaking world.[34] The Cubli women were surrounded by immediate and extended family, and lived near each other. This was not the case with the Seguro. Giacomo and Isabella Seguro remained on Zante. Their sons and grandsons divided their time between Venice and the island,

---

[32] The Cubli women lived near one another in San Severo parish. Isabetta, Cecilia and Ludovica were immediate next door neighbours in the Corte Malipiero; Gratiosa and Pietro lived nearby in the Calle Larga. ACPV, status animarum, b. 3, filza 9, unnumb.

[33] Several references to young Ludovica Finetti appear in Isabetta's and Gratiosa's wills. After the child's death, Gratiosa made the following stipulation in her last will (7 August 1607): "Voglio che siano investiti ducati 200 da esser dati alli fioli del sudetto ser Alvise Finetti, et che detto suo padre sii usufruttuario del pro di quelli in vita sua: ma se egli havesse per sorte una fiola che nomesse Lodovica, voglio che quelli ghe siano dati à lei al suo maritar overo monachar." The child's death appears in the death registers of the parish of San Severo, ACPV, registri dei morti, reg. 1 (1576–1627), San Severo, unnumb.

[34] Pietro Manolesso was a member of the Scuola di San Niccolò dei Greci in 1578 and again from 1599–1606. AAIEV, reg. 134, fols 167v, 347r. In 1607 he and Gratiosa went to Crete, to the city of Candia where Manolesso had been appointed to the island's treasury (*Camerlengo da Candia*). Gratiosa died on 11 October 1608 in Crete. Manolesso was her sole heir. He never remarried and died in Venice in 1616.

while daughters, nieces and granddaughters who had married patricians, lived in Venice. Not the Cubli: after moving to Venice they never returned to Napoli di Romania which was now under Ottoman control. The family became Venetians of Greek origin. It was natural then that Andronico and Agnese's children felt at home in both worlds, and their family, kin and social networks reflected this shift.

The Paleologo

The military class had a fixed approach to marriage. Sons, with very few exceptions, married daughters from other military families be they Greek, Dalmatian or Albanian. Ethnicity did not matter whereas preserving the exclusivity of the profession did. Where possible, endogamy remained the preferred option mainly for sons, to a lesser extent for daughters. Of the eighteen military families that settled in Venice only five, the Bua, Bocali, Clada, Rali and Paleologo, had in-laws who were not from the military class. Military commanders did not seek patrician in-laws for financial gain or prestige because they already had these. Instead, exogamy helped them establish powerful political networks that would otherwise have been difficult to create. The family that succeeded at this best was the Paleologo. In the sixteenth century, they concluded nine patrician marriages; in the same period the Bua, Bocali and Clada families recorded one out-marriage each, the Rali two.

There were at least five branches of Paleologo living in Venice, the Ionian islands, Crete and Cyprus. This section focuses on Teodoro Paleologo's branch because Teodoro was one of the most popular *capi dei stratioti* and his branch had the largest number of patrician marriages. The family remained close to their relations in the various parts of the Venetian sea empire, as well as those living in Ottoman Morea.[35] The Paleologo shared several features with the Seguro and Cubli. Like them, they tended to produce more

---

[35] Teodoro Paleologo's sister was married to a Turkish official and lived in the old Byzantine capital, Mistra. In February 1499 the governor (*provveditor*) at Zante wrote to the Signoria about information he had received from the abbot of a local monastery. The abbot was Teodoro's brother. He had recently visited his sister at Mistra where he learned (from his Turkish relations) about an armada the Ottomans were building that would be used against Puglia. Sanuto, II: 573. The Venetians had a strong military presence in Puglia because of its strategic importance as the entrance to the Adriatic Sea. If foreign fleets succeeded in penetrating the Adriatic they could wreck havoc along the Italian and Dalmatian coastlines and ultimately attack Venice itself.

daughters than sons, which partly explains the high number of exogamous unions. Paleologo women maintained close ties to siblings, cousins, aunts and uncles, kin and friends and blended their Venetian and Greek halves in much the same way as the Cubli. They lived near each other, in five parishes of San Pietro di Castello. From the start, Paleologo marriages illustrated the family's prominence and its lineage. In 1486, Teodoro Paleologo married Maria Cantacuzene, the daughter of Byzantine nobility. Paleologo was the surname of the last Byzantine dynasty, but whether Teodoro's family was related to them in any way is uncertain and highly unlikely.[36] His lineage must have been fairly pure however, to make him acceptable to the Cantacuzene. The couple had eight children, two boys and six girls. Initially they settled in Zante, where Teodoro and his younger brother Zorzi were responsible for the island's defences. Zorzi was killed in battle in 1497 and Maria died in an earthquake that struck the island in April 1513.[37] Soon after, Teodoro moved his and Zorzi's families to Venice. He carefully arranged suitable marriages for his own children, his nephews and nieces, as well the children of his eldest son Paolo, who died in action in 1525. Paleologo's daughters inherited from their mother's estate and that inheritance grew when their father received various concessions for them and his granddaughters from the Camera of Uderzo.[38] Had he lived a few more years — he died in 1532 at the age of 80 —

---

[36] Paleologo was also the surname of the despots of the Morea who, in the fifteenth century, were the children or siblings of the emperor at Constantinople. Consequently, there were many Paleologo cousins and other relations administering a large part of the peninsula; Teodoro's family might have come from one of these minor branches. His father, Paolo, was recruited by the Venetians, in Morea, in the middle of the fifteenth century. Teodoro and his younger brother Zorzi followed in their father's footsteps.

[37] A young daughter was injured (Sanuto used the word mangled) and a son, possibly the youngest boy, Demetri, escaped unharmed: "Di la terra è sta la moglie de missier Teodoro Paleologo e sa fia magagnata; el puto scapolò." Sanuto, XVI: 265.

[38] ASV, Consiglio dei Dieci, parti comuni, reg. 1, 9 July 1525, fols. 36r–37v. The Council of Ten awarded concessions for the dowries of Paleologo's daughters and granddaughters. "Che attente le cose narrate in la supplicatsione del fidelissimo et benemerito messer Domino Theodore Paleologo sia statuido per auctorità de questo conseio, che dapoi la morte sua la cancellararia de Oderzo (Uderzo) che lui ha al presente sii concessa a le fiole del dicto misser Teodoro et a le nepote sue, fiole del ser Paulo suo fiol, leqale dapoi la morte del dicto Domino Teodoro se troverano donzelle et nubile per el maridare de quelle per Doi Rezimenti per cadauna de esse." The concession was renewed in 1528 and again in 1534.

Teodoro Paleologo would have been able to count the Bembo, Balbi, Corner, Celsi, Minio and Trevisan among his Venetian family.[39]

At least two of Paleologo's daughters married patricians: Efrosina married Girolamo Bembo, in 1531, while another, Emilia, married Stai Balbi, in 1534. Little is known about the women, except through sources left by their cousin Elisabeta and Emilia's husband, Stai Balbi. Emilia was Balbi's third wife. He had no children from the first two marriages, at least no sons.[40] At the time of their marriage, Balbi would have been considerably older than Emilia. They had five children between 1535–1542: three sons, Zaccaria, Bernardo and Teodoro and two daughters, Marieta and Isabetta. The relationship between husband and wife was a tender one, at least on Balbi's part. A few weeks before he died, he appointed Emilia his heir, executor of his estate and returned her dowry, valued over at 3,000 ducats. He gave her complete control over his affairs and properties and did not name anyone else beneficiaries, trustees or executors. Emilia was to become the head of the household (*donna e madonna*) in his place because, as he said, he recognised her merits.[41] Balbi's was a short will, yet it conveyed a warm relationship between the couple and the close family bond they shared. Every reference to Emilia was preceded by terms such as *carissima* (dearest) and *dilettissima* (delightful, beloved). There is nothing extraordinary about these terms; they appeared in wills all the time. But it is worth noting that very few men, particularly patrician men, gave complete control over their affairs to wives the way Balbi did to Emilia. In this context these terms of endearment reflected the affection and trust he had for her.

Paolo Paleologo and his wife, another Emilia, had six daughters but alas, no sons. It is no wonder then, that Teodoro Paleologo petitioned for state assistance. He had to dower fourteen women (five daughters, six

---

[39] Demetri di Teodoro Paleologo was briefly married to Laura di Giacomo Seguro. She died in the early 1530s but not before Demetri faced an ecclesiastic court in Venice, charged with bigamy. The woman who brought the charges was Lucieta Martini whose father was the head (*proto*) of the shipwrights at the Arsenal. It appears that for a time Paleologo managed a wife on Zante (Laura), where he was stationed, and another in Venice (Lucieta), where he went regularly to report to officials administering the sea colonies. The court proceedings and annulment are in ACPV, Cause Matrimoniali, b. 33, 12 February 1533.

[40] Barbaro, I.2: 136.

[41] "Io ho ben cognosciuto la qualetta della detta mia consorte." ASV, Notarile Testamenti, b. 44, Avidio Branco, 359, 24 July 1555.

granddaughters and three nieces), a daunting prospect even for the richest of men. Three of Paolo and Emilia's children married patricians from the Celsi, Minio and Trevisan families. The eldest, Isabetta, married Zuanne Celsi in 1554. The Celsi were administrators of several important cities along the Dalmatian coast, including Spalato and Budua, an area where several Paleologo were stationed, so it is possible that this union came about through the military and administrative activities of the men. Isabetta was close to her natal family, especially her mother. She made Emilia an executor of her estate and looked after her sisters and their children. She did not forget her Celsi in-laws either. She was particularly fond of and generous to the siblings Gasparo, Baldissera, Hieronyma and Andrianna Celsi, her husband's first cousins. Gasparo became the other executor of her estate. As for Zuanne Celsi, Isabetta said little about him. She named him in her 1562 will but only to say that he was in Spalato on assignment; she mentioned him again in her 1569 will but only by way of identifying herself as his widow.[42] They had no children.

Paleologo men had well established ties to the Venetian patriciate going back several decades, and it was this, more than anything else that led to the high number of Greco-Venetian marriages in this family. They were brave and loyal fighters, but their activities were not restricted to fighting; in fact Teodoro Paleologo ceased going to war by the early 1520s, devoting himself instead to looking after his large family, tending his properties on Zante, and accompanying diplomatic missions to the Ottoman empire.[43] He spoke Turkish fluently and he and his nephew, Costantino da Zorzi, were two of the official interpreters (*dragomani*) who looked after Ottoman envoys in Venice. He knew the doge, Andrea Gritti well, having fought alongside him during the wars of the League of Cambrai.[44] When Paleologo died, on 3 September 1532, the entire Signoria attended his funeral in San Giorgio dei

---

[42] Isabetta's three wills are in ASV, Notarile Testamenti, b. 768, Agostino Pellestrina, 133, 29 January 1549 and b. 847, Francesco Renio, 260, 16 April 1562 and 1 May 1569.

[43] Teodoro Paleologo and his son Demetri (the chap charged with bigamy) were fortunate to die of old age. Most *capi dei stratioti* and their men were killed in battle.

[44] The League of Cambrai was an effort by the Papacy, the Holy Roman Empire and France to strip Venice of her possessions on the *Terraferma*. It did not succeed, but from 1508–1517 the Republic was constantly at war against the combined forces of the three. The person in charge of the *stratioti* at the time was Andrea Gritti, the future doge. Teodoro Paleologo saved Gritti's life during the Battle of La Motta in October 1513. Bugh, "Andrea Gritti and the Greek stradiots," 81–96.

Greci.[45] There is no doubt that the daughters, nieces and granddaughters of such an important person would have made suitable patrician brides. After Paleologo's death his sons-in-law, Stai Balbi and Francesco Corner, looked after the family since Demetri di Teodoro was stationed on Zante. Among other things, Balbi offered financial help to Emilia's first cousin, Elisabeta Paleologo Megaduca when she was preparing to move to Cyprus where her son, Alessandro, had taken up his late father's command.

Most of the men and women of this family had considerable contact with the wider Greek community. They were members of San Niccolò dei Greci. Teodoro was the only *capo dei stratioti* to sit on various scuola committees and to serve as chair (*gastaldo*) of the board. He led the delegation that petitioned the Council of Ten for permission to buy land to build a Greek rite church. He and his family represented the reality of Greek immigration: Venice was now home and nothing announced this more than the creation of permanent institutions, the establishment of new social networks through marriage and the incorporation of the Greek and the Venetian into one, new entity.

Conclusion

The marriages of the Seguro, Cubli and Paleologo illustrate that most women remained close to their natal family and their customs. They sought comfort from, and gave support to, siblings, kin and friends. Some had formal, almost passive, relationships with their spouses and in-laws, while others maintained warm relations with them. There was no obvious pressure to adopt the spouse's culture or even learn his language; Sofia Seguro dictated her will in Greek because she felt more comfortable in that language and another woman, Helena Rali never learned Italian even though she had two patrician husbands. None of the women who followed the Eastern rite were pressured to adopt the Latin one. Sixteenth-century Venetian society was fairly tolerant of difference and the issues that separated the two churches were not significant, at least to most people. The movement between rites was fluid and Greek women and men prayed and attended Latin churches as easily as they went to San Giorgio dei Greci.[46] Except for the Seguro, all the other women had

---

[45] Sanuto, LVI: 877–878.

[46] Greek men participated in the religious life of the guilds and scuole of which they were members. Both men and women were involved in parish life. Ersie Burke, "The

connections with the Greek community. The Paleologo and Cubli were members of the Scuola di San Niccolò dei Greci, attended mass at San Giorgio dei Greci and provided cash bequests to its charities and the dowry fund for poor Greek girls. The Cubli family tombs were in the church. The women (including the Seguro) had ties to Venetian institutions such as convents, hospitals, orphanages, charities and their parish churches. Some husbands, like Pietro Manolesso became involved in the Greek community. Sebastian Trevisan, the husband of Andrianna Paleologo attended the annual meeting of the Greek dowry fund to pay his wife's gift.[47] So exogamy for Greeks and Venetians did not impose severe restrictions on either partner in terms of language, faith, customs or choice of friends. The women were able to maintain their predominantly (though not exclusively) Greek social circles. Contrast this with the two Venetian women who married Greeks. Laura Bon's father was the patrician Fantin Bon; she was probably illegitimate because her name did not appear in any patrician marriage registers. She married Niccolò Cavopenna sometime in the early 1530s. Cecilia Dolfin's husband was Niccolò Cubli (her status has already been discussed). Among the elite of the community, only Cavopenna and Niccolò Cubli took Venetian wives. As we saw earlier, marriage to foreign elite women was very common among Cavopenna men in the fourteenth and fifteenth centuries; the Cubli, of course, had no history of out-marriage at that stage. By the 1500s, new measures regulating marriage had made patrician exogamy difficulty. There were new rules about suitability and a greater emphasis on patrician sons. If a patrician woman married out, any sons she might have could not be patricians. At the same time, circumstances had changed for Greek feudal elites. With the Ottoman takeover of their homelands, came the loss of their titles and their lands. A patrician daughter's marriage to a noble Greek now living in Venice, with no prospects of recovering his fiefs brought very few benefits. A patrician son's out-marriage, on the other hand, carried several benefits like the opportunity to cement well-established ties or create new ones. Despite the loss of their fiefs, the Cavopenna kept their titles and continued in the service of the state. The reasons behind the Cubli-Dolfin marriage are less clear. Certainly Niccolò was very well off. He mainly traded in grains and co-owned a boat with the patrician Niccolò Barozzi. He had excellent commercial networks with other patricians from the Contarini, Giustiniani and Dolfin families; whether the latter was related

Greek Neighbourhoods of Sixteenth Century Venice," 190–207; 224–231.

[47] AAIEV, b. 18, filza 234.

to Cecilia is unclear.[48] Bon had one child, a daughter named Arsenia, who married a man from her father's homeland, Napoli di Romania.[49] Dolfin had no children, but Niccolò Cubli had a natural son whom he recognized; Dolfin made no mention of this child in her will. Bon and Dolfin's social circles were almost completely Greek. Laura mentioned only one Venetian relation, Vicenzo Michiel, but she knew him because he was married to one of her Greek nieces. Cecilia Dolfin had a Venetian nephew and niece but they were the only blood relations she mentioned. She settled most of her estate on her Cubli in-laws. Both women retained their affiliation with the Latin church, as was the custom of the day. Their lives however, revolved around the Greek world of their in-laws. No women, from any class, who married out lived so completely in their husbands' worlds as Dolfin and Bon.

Regardless of the nature of the relationship, the fluency of language or religious rite, all the women lost some of their Greekness when they married out. In its place a new identity emerged, part Greek, part Venetian. This acknowledged a new homeland and retained many of the characteristics of the old identity, like language and rite. All the same, Greekness was further diluted with the marriage of the children of Greek women and Venetian men. All of them married patricians, just as Laura Bon's child married a noble Greek from her father's homeland. Did these elite children show any interest in their Greek (or Venetian) roots? Did they speak their mother's language or participate in the rites of her church? It is impossible to say at this point. What is certain is this: the elite were not the only ones to choose their children's partners from the father's world. The same thing happened among the popular classes: in most cases the child's partner came from the father's ethnic group, not the mother's.

In the end, one has to ask: did it matter if the Greek, that is language, customs and faith, was forgotten? Certainly the families who engineered these marriages did not give priority to preserving Greekness, otherwise they would have arranged only Greek marriages. Their aim was to secure

---

[48] Mavroidi, 141.

[49] Arsenia Cavopenna married a man named Francesco de' Atene de' Medici. Theirs was a complicated relationship. Arsenia wrote a will when she was pregnant with what must have been her first child. But she left everything, her estate, the settlement of her affairs, the care of her child, to a man named Zorzi Notara, a noble from Candia. She demanded that no one interfere with her wishes or bother Notara and she insisted that her husband defer to him. She gave no explanation as to the nature of her relationship with this man. ASV, Notarile Testamenti, b. 477, Paolo di Grandi, 21, 30 June 1560.

their future. Exogamy brought privileges and benefits to both sides. It was a well-established and familiar custom. So was endogamy which is why for every Venetian marriage there were several Greek ones. The patriciate worked on the same principle, which is why endogamy continued to be the norm. Greek identity survived because the strength of Greekness was its elasticity and openness. It was not a narrowly defined, restricted concept. It was constantly being redefined to incorporate new [Greek] arrivals and adjust to new circumstances. Did the women an in this study eventually become Greek speaking Venetians? To the extent that all immigrants adopt the attitudes and manners of their new homelands, yes. Did they (and the men) lose the customs, language and faith of the homeland? Not at all. The outward symbols of Greekness, the church and the scuola were (and still are) the physical proof of a community of Greco-Venetians. In any case, one has to wonder how seriously elites and *popolani* thought about identity in ethnic, linguistic or religious terms, if they thought about it at all. It is possible that in the early modern period class defined identity, more so than ethnicity, language and faith.

MONASH UNIVERSITY

Appendix
Venetian Marriage Laws 1376–1589[50]

1376 law
~ aim: to stop illegitimate sons of patrician men inheriting their fathers' status
~ at this stage there was no consensus that the purpose of patrician marriage was the continuation of the class in its pure form; that was the purpose of a later law, that of 1422.

1420 law
~ aim: to restrict the amount of the dowry as a result of ambitious families pushing its value to levels that many patricians could not afford. The ceiling proposed was 1,600 ducats of which 2/3 was dowry and 1/3 *corredo* (the husband's gift)
~ further aims: to make it difficult for fathers to waste wealth on the marriage of one daughter thereby consigning others to the convent or spinsterhood; to stop the demotion of the dowry while inflating the *corredo* as a means of attracting desirable sons-in-law

1422 law
~ aim: to deny noble status to sons (even legitimate ones) of noble fathers who had married non-noble women, to prevent "denigration" of the Great Council by "unworthy" members
~ the first of many laws where patrician status turned its focus from fathers to mothers
~ this law further cemented the move for more government supervision of marriage as a way of protecting the exclusivity of the patriciate

1425 and 1443 laws
~ the 1425 law directed state attorneys, the *Avogadori di Comun* to prosecute those who broke the law of 1422
~ the 1443 law ensured handicapped noble women the right to marry by increasing the value of their dowries

1449 law
~ aim: to require all notaries to submit a copy of dowry receipts to ensure that all property belonging to the wife remained in her name

---

[50] Chojnacki, *Women and Men*, 53–75; Cowan, *Marriage, Manners and Mobility*, 13–14.

1505 law
~ aim: to close the loopholes in the 1422 dowry law by setting a new limit of 3,000 ducats and requiring families to register their dowry contracts
~ decreed marriage a public event which required official approval to move beyond signing the contract

1506 law
~ aim: to set registers of male noble births
~ patrician fathers had to register births of legitimate sons with the *Avogadori di Comun*. Sons of low-born women were banned from registration, regardless of the father's status
~ the son's birth record included the father's family, but more importantly, the mother's (as well as her place of birth and family name) to ensure she met the criteria set down by the 1422 law

1526 law
~ aim: to register all patrician marriages with the *Avogaria di Comun* within one month of the nuptials and to protect the "purity" of the ruling class by registering births and marriages in the *Libro d' Oro* (Book of Gold)
~ marriage ceremony to require the presence of two near kin of the groom and two of the bride to swear that the union was legitimate and affirm the bride's status and the suitability of her father

1535 law
~ aim: to further restrain dowry size; set at 4,000 ducats in the hope that this would put an end to widespread cheating
~ this law stipulated the husband could not have more than one-third of the dowry (1,000 ducats) and a quarter of the *corredo* (previously one-third); as well, the husband was fined if the dowry was in excess of 4,000 ducats (his fine was half the excess)

1589 law
~ aim: to govern the marriages of nobles to non-noble women; the *prove di nobiltà* established with the onus shifting to the non-noble woman and her family, especially her mother and other female relations, to prove they lived "modestly and honourably"; at the same time, the state re-asserted the purpose of noble marriage as the means of "procreating legitimate sons who would ensure the continuity of the patriciate and of the Venetian political system by sitting as members of the Great Council."

Cited Works

Abbreviations

AAIEV = Archivio antico dell'Istituto Ellenico di Venezia
ACPV = Archivio della Curia Patriarcale di Venezia
ASV   = Archivio di Stato di Venezia
AdiC = Avogaria di Comun

Manuscript Sources

Venice. Archivio di Stato di Venezia (ASV)
    Arbori de' patritii veneti, Misc. codici, Istoria veneta, nn. 17–23, 1.2, 4
    Avogaria di Comun, Index 86/1–2
    Balla d' Oro, II
    Cancelleria inferiore, Privilegi dei Cavalieri di San Marco, 174
    Capi del Consiglio dei Dieci, 296
    Collegio, Risposte di fuori, 312
    Consiglio dei Dieci, Parti comuni, 1
    Miscellanea Gregolin, 21
    Notarile, Atti, 6486–6514, 6511, 10636–10644
    Notarile, Testamenti, 44, 47, 124–125, 127–128, 157, 382, 440, 477, 768, 847, 1243

Venice. Archivio antico dell'Istituto Ellenico di Venezia (AAIEV)
    Amministrazione, 1. Testamenti, legati, commisarie e donazioni, 2, 9b, 18
    Scuola di San Niccolò dei Greci, 134

Venice. Archivio della Curia Patriarcale di Venezia (ACPV)
    Cause Matrimoniali, 33
    San Severo, Registri dei morti, 1
    Status animarum, 3

Printed Sources

Arbel, Benjamin. "Greek Magnates in Venetian Cyprus: The Case of the Synglitico Family." *Dumbarton Oaks Papers* 49 (1995): 325–337.

_____. "The Cypriot Nobility from the Fourteenth to the Sixteenth Century: A New Interpretation." In *Latins and Greeks in the Eastern Mediterranean after 1204*, eds. Benjamin Arbel, Bernard Hamilton and David Jacoby eds. London and Totowa, NJ: Cass, 1995, 175–197.

Bouboulidou, Phaedon K. «Συμβολή εις την ιστορίαν της Ζακυνθιάς οικογενείας Σιγούρου επί Ενετοκρατίας.» ["The contribution to history of the Zachynthian family Seguro during Venetian times"]. *Επετιρίδος του Μεσαιωνικού Αρχείου Z* [*Yearbook of the medieval archive*, (vol) Z], (1958): 84–128.

Bugh, Glenn R. "Andrea Gritti and the Greek Stradiots of Venice in the Early 16th Century." *Thesaurismata* 32 (2002): 81–96.

Burke, Ersie C. "The Greek Neighbourhoods of Sixteenth Century Venice, 1498–1600: Daily Life of an Immigrant Community." Unpublished Ph.D dissertation. Melbourne, Monash University, 2005.

Chojnacki, Stanley. "Dowries and Kinsmen in Early Renaissance Venice." *Journal of Interdisciplinary History* 4, 1975, 571–600.

_____. "Identity and Ideology in Renaissance Venice: The Third *Serrata*." In *Venice Reconsidered: The History of an Italian City-State, 1297–1797*, eds. John Martin and Dennis Romano. Baltimore: Johns Hopkins University Press, 2000, 263–294.

_____. "In Search of the Venetian Patriciate: Families and Factions in the Fourteenth Century." In *Renaissance Venice*, ed. John Hale. London: Faber, 1973, 47–76.

_____. "Social Identity in Renaissance Venice: The Second Serrata." *Journal of Renaissance Studies* 8:4 (1994): 341–358.

_____. *Women and Men in Renaissance Venice: Twelve Essays on Patrician Society.* Baltimore: Johns Hopkins University Press, 2000.

Cowan, Alexander. *Marriage, Manners and Mobility in Early Modern Venice.* Aldershot, UK: Ashgate, 2007.

The Greek Correspondence of Bartolomeo Minio, eds. Diana G. Wright and John Melville-Jones. Padua: Unipress, 2008.

Grubb, James. *Provincial Families of the Renaissance: Private and Public Life in the Veneto.* Baltimore: Johns Hopkins University Press, 1996.

_____. "Memory and Identity: Why Venetians Didn't Keep Ricordanze, *Journal of Renaissance Studies* 8:4 (1994): 375–387.

Klapisch-Zuber, Christiane, *Women, Family and Ritual in Renaissance Italy*, trans. Lydia Cochrane. Chicago: University of Chicago Press, 1985.

McKee, Sally. "Greek Women in Latin Households of Fourteenth-Century Venetian Crete." *Journal of Medieval History* 19 (1993): 229–249.

_____. "Women Under Venetian Colonial Rule in the Early Renaissance: Observations on their Economic Activities." *Renaissance Quarterly* 51:1 (1998): 34–67.

_____. "Households in Fourteenth-Century Venetian Crete." *Speculum* 70 (1995): 27–67.

_____. *Uncommon Dominion: Venetian Crete and the Myth of Ethnic Purity*. Philadelphia: University of Philadelphia Press, 2000.

Maltezou, Chryssa. «Νέαι ειδήσεις περί Ευγενίου Συγκλιτικού εκ των κρατικών αρχείων της Βενετίας.» In *Πρακτικά του πρώτου διεθνούς Κυπρολογικού συνεδρίου* [Proceedings of the First International Conference on Cyprus], eds. T. Menelaou, T. Papadopoulos, M. Christodoulou. Nicosia: Etaireia Kypriakon Spoudon, 1973, 227–244.

Mavroidi, Fani. *Συμβολή στην ιστορία της Ελληνικής Αδελφότητας Βενετίας στο ΙΣΤ' αιώνα. Έκδοση του Β Μητρώου Εγγραφών 1533–1562* [The Contribution to History of the Greek Confraternity of Venice in the Sixteenth Century 1533–1562]. Athens: Noti Karavia, 1976.

Pardos, Antonios. «Αλφαβητικός κατάλογος των πρώτων μελών της Ελληνικής Αδελφότητας Βενετίας από το κατάστιχο 129 (1498–1530), Μέρως Α: Οι Άντρες.» [Alphabetical catalogue of the first members of the Greek confraternity of Venice from register 129, 1498–1530. Part A: The Men]. *Thesaurismata* 16 (1979): 294–386.

_____. «Αλφαβητικός κατάλογος των πρώτων μελών της Ελληνικής Αδελφότητας Βενετίας από το κατάστιχο 129 (1498–1530), Μέρως Β: Οι Γυναίκες.» [Alphabetical catalogue of the first members of the Greek confraternity of Venice from register 129, 1498–1530. Part B: The Women]. *Thesaurismata* 17 (1980): 149–205.

Sanuto, Marin. *I Diarii di Marin Sanuto 1496–1533*, eds. Rinaldo Fulin, Federico Stefani, Nicolò Barozzi, Guglielmo Berchet, Marco Allegri. Bologna: Forni, 1969–1979.

Wright, Diana. "Bartolomeo Minio and the *Stato da Mar*, 1479–1483." *Electronic Journal of Oriental Studies* 3: 5 (2001).

Vlassi, Despina. «Δύο διαθήκες των αρχών του 17° αιώνα.» *Thesaurismata* 31 (2001): 181–209.

Regional Intermarriage Among the Italian Nobility in the Sixteenth Century

P. Renée Baernstein

The rape of the Sabine women, a story which underscores marriage as an act of both violence and peacemaking, enjoyed great popularity in Renaissance Italy. It appeared on marriage chests (*cassoni*), in wedding orations celebrating the happy couple, in decorations adorning nuptial bedchambers, in public statuary, in commentaries on the institution of marriage itself.[1] One stunning example of the *spalliera*, or furniture-back genre, dating from about 1488, hangs in the Galleria Colonna in Rome and portrays both episodes of the story (figs. 1 and 2). On one panel, we see the moment of the Romans' duplicitous capture of the Sabine virgins, lured with their men folk to an athletic competition by their wife-starved Roman neighbours. Surrounded by Roman monuments, vigorous young Roman men seize the diaphanously draped women, chasing them over the walls of the Circus Maximus, wresting them onto horseback or embracing them on the spot; the older Sabine men protest helplessly. Romulus, mastermind of the plot, looks on from the foreground. On the second panel, we see the abduction's happy outcome: it is a few years later. The Sabine men attack Rome seeking revenge, but the newly Romanized women, now with a host of toddlers in tow, throw themselves between the warring tribes and beg their fathers and husbands to make peace.[2]

This protean story of wife-stealing encapsulated the complexities of Renaissance elite marriage, perhaps most sharply of all the classical tales of

---

[1] Baskins, *Cassone Painting*, 103–127; D'Elia, *The Renaissance of Marriage*, 86. Musacchio, "The Rape of the Sabine Women," links the rise of the Sabine theme on marriage chests in the later Quattrocento to a growing sense of demographic precariousness in the wake of repeated waves of plague, 75: "the procreative emphasis of the Sabine myth found a distinct counterpart in Renaissance society, since both were driven … to enlarge their population." The principal classical treatments were by Livy (the most detailed), Plutarch, and Ovid. See Brown, "Livy's Sabine Women," *passim*.

[2] The panels are attributed to Bartolommeo di Giovanni: Safarik, *Catalogo sommario*, 28.

heroism then current.[3] The Roman humanist, Marco Antonio Altieri, in his treatise on Roman marriage customs, written shortly after 1500 (*Li nuptiali*), repeatedly invoked the fate of the Sabine women as an inspiration for local marriage rituals: "every slightest act in the wedding can be reduced to the memory of the rape of the Sabines; thus, this taking [of the bride's hand] demonstrates doing violence against her." For Altieri, the story served to emphasize marriage's inherent violence. Continuing in this vein, he stressed the bride's similarity to war booty with another classical allusion, to the vestal virgins. "Taken from paternal power [*potesta paterna*] by the priest, [the virgins] belonged to him *as if they had been taken in war*."[4] Tellingly, however, the story is not completely apt for his purposes. Altieri's ostensible audience was his own class, the Roman civic nobility (*municipali*), whose fortunes had been declining in the face of growing papal power. Altieri urged the Roman nobles to marry their own kind; he particularly condemned marrying down for high dowries, a practice to which the civic nobility had been reduced, in his view, both because popes denied them their traditional monopoly on many church offices, and also because of Rome's propensity for attracting new wealthy families from outside and integrating them quickly into local power structures.[5] In marrying the Sabines, the ancient Romans were certainly not marrying their own; the ethnic mixing that legendarily characterized ancient Roman expansion had no proper place in Altieri's urgent cry for endogamy.

As Altieri's selective use of the story suggests, the legend of the Sabine women held attraction for Renaissance ears because it legitimated the implicit violence of marriages contracted between families primarily for economic or political reasons, without regard to personal choice of partners; and because it emphasized women's roles as property to be exchanged at the will of men, or to be taken by force if the men of the bride's family did not consent. But the story also vindicates the utility of marriage in making political alliances

---

[3] The intensity of current debates over its meaning speaks volumes about the story's opacity. See Musacchio, "The Rape of the Sabine Women," Baskins, *Cassone Painting*, 105–110, and Wolfthal, *Images of Rape*, 9–17.

[4] Altieri, *Li nuptiali*, 93. "per ogne minimo acto che in nelli sponzalitii se notino observarse, sence reduca alla memoria el rapto de Sabine; similemente in tal pigliare [taking the bride's hand] demostrase farle violentia. Et alguni vogliono esser retracto dalle vergine vestale: quale levandoli el pontefice dalla potesta paterna, tanto erano le soe, quanto se prese fussiro alla guerra; per lo quale acto se intitulassiro poi rapte." Emphasis added. See Klapisch-Zuber, "Ethnology of Marriage," 254–255.

[5] Kolsky, "Culture and Politics," 82.

between tribes or nations. In fact, a close reading of Livy's account, the most detailed textual source for the story, suggests that for him, the key non-consenting parties were the Sabine men, not the women. After the initial capture, Livy has Romulus and the other Roman men courting the foreign women, wooing them with promises of citizenship and children, apologizing for their wrong-doing and promising "love and passion." (To these latter attractions, Livy remarks in a dry aside, "women are much subject."[6]) This angle diminishes the element of rape in the modern sense, and highlights the element of *"raptus,"* that is, capture with intent to marry, in which the violated party is the woman's kinfolk, regardless of her consent or lack thereof. In the crucial second scene, not discussed by Altieri but appearing often in Renaissance visual representations, the women are transformed from passive victims to heroic actors, interposing themselves between armies of men. Read in this manner, the legend of the Sabine women becomes a story of exogamy creating alliances between nations, or perhaps legitimating the conquest of one people by another, as much as one of personal violence.

It is to this aspect of Renaissance Italian marriage that we turn here. Altieri's Rome was the site of many marriage negotiations, and not only of locals. Increasingly, in the century after he wrote, noble Italians who aspired to high position turned their gaze to Rome, seeking ecclesiastical offices and incomes, political influence and a presence at court. An essential part of this ascent involved marrying into the Roman nobility, both the "civic" nobility of Altieri and his peers — families like the Conti and the Albertoni — and the baronial or feudal nobility led by the Colonna and Orsini clans. Papal and curial nobilities, too, were marital prizes. While some of these aspiring families immigrated in full to the papal city, most had branches that remained fixed in home bases elsewhere. Since most Renaissance marriages were patrilocal, brides contracted in Rome travelled all over the peninsula to settle with new families. Predictably, these women stayed in contact with their natal families, corresponding regularly and helping to maintain the cognatic ties for which they had been chosen. Scholarship on the Roman elites has established their comparatively dynamic and open nature and their propensity to absorb newcomers rapidly.[7] But the impact of these alliances outside the papal city has not been measured in any synthetic way. Moreover, the widespread scholarly view that endogamy prevailed within most Italian

---

[6] Brown, "Livy's Sabine Women," 299.

[7] Visceglia, "Introduzione," *La nobiltà romana*, xiii–xix; Pellegrini, "Corte di Roma."

civic elites, based on urban studies of varying statistical weight, such as those for Florence, Venice and Bologna, may need to be contextualized somewhat in light of the Roman case and its ramifications elsewhere.[8] This article first discusses Roman noble, and especially baronial, exogamy in the Italian context. It then turns to the marriage strategies of one Roman baronial family, the Colonna (Paliano branch), in the sixteenth century. Subsequently, one exemplary cross-regional marriage allows insight into the nature of the "sabine" experience and suggests possible directions for further research.

Rome As Marriage Entrepot of Italy

Writing around 1640, the Flemish jurist and long-time Roman observer, Teodoro Ameyden, sorted Roman noble families according to how long they had been in town and claimed noble status. He divided the newest arrivals, those of the past century, into two groups: "those who by choice have left their own homes, although they were honourable and noble there, and taken up residence here without any particular business;" and those "many other new families… who have come from Florence or Genoa to conduct their banking business."[9] The distinction is an interesting one, but more important here is Ameyden's casual acceptance of the constant turnover in Roman elites. Ameyden himself was an immigrant, to be sure, but nonetheless highly sensitive to local Roman hierarchies: his nonchalance contrasts neatly with Altieri's unease at outsiders a century and a half earlier. More generally, acceptance of immigration grew with the papal court's expansion, begun after the papacy's return from Avignon in 1417 and accelerated after the Sack of Rome in 1527. As papacy and cardinalate became increasingly Italian-dominated,

---

[8] For endogamy: synthesis in Fabbri, "Trattatistica e pratica dell'allieanza matrimoniale," 102–103; on Florence, Molho, *Marriage Alliance*, chap. 7; on Bologna, Carboni, "La formazione," 18–20; on Naples, Visceglia, *Il bisogno*. The most extreme instance of patrician endogamy in a larger city would seem to be Venice, on which see Hunecke, *Der venezianische Adel*, but Burke, "Foreign Wives," notes some Venetian patricians married women from elites of the Stato da Mar. For smaller, provincial towns, see for example Benadusi, "Rethinking the State," 172 and Carrino, *La città aristocratica*, 71–120.

[9] BC, Ameyden, "Relazione," fol. 33v: "prima quelle che per elezione hanno lasciato le proprie patrie, benche fossero ivi onorevoli, o nobili, e posto quivi il domicilio senza occasione di negozio;" and fol. 34v, "molte altre … sono venute da Firenze, e Genova coll'occasione del Negozio di banco, e di fondaco." Ameyden also names other Italian and Flemish families, "venute a Roma con l'occasione del negozio di banco," fol. 36r.

Italian elites turned to Rome for patronage and advancement. Despite regular interventions by non-Italian powers, particularly Spain in the middle years of the sixteenth century, church politics and offices remained a largely Italian affair, drawing ambitious individuals from all classes to the papal city in search of the main chance. Rome's pull in the period bracketed by Altieri (1500) and Ameyden (1640) thus consisted not only in the wealth of its civil and ecclesiastical government, but also in its role as the center of a "system of relations" that linked the Roman court with those of all the other Italian states.[10] Immigrants, primarily male — permanent or temporary — helped to make Rome the most dynamic, varied and male-heavy urban setting in Italy.[11] Ameyden reiterated that Rome's approximately 100,000 souls were "mostly outsiders, of whom many settle for good, for it seems that sometimes Rome treats outsiders better than natives." He exaggerated, but when he concluded the thought with the Latin proverb, "Rome is a mother to guests, and a stepmother to her own,"[12] he surely echoed the perceptions of many that Rome was a city of newcomers.

For elites, the successful launching of a Roman presence required inserting themselves into local society, through marriage, patronage and conspicuous consumption. A family palace, a few well-placed charitable projects, a sponsored church and so forth were all part of the Romanizing strategy. Arrival had to be solidified through intermarriage with the local aristocracy. That group could be divided, as both Altieri and Ameyden remarked, into several layers. The *municipali*, Altieri's peers, held a traditional monopoly on city offices. They were entitled to call themselves "noble" but were generally without major extra-urban landholdings. The curial aristocracy included papal and cardinalate families of recent immigration to the city and frequently of great wealth, such as the Farnese of Parma. The barons, or feudal aristocracy, consisted of the eight medieval families whose wealth came not from ecclesiastical offices but from feudal lands in the Papal States and, for

---

[10] As Chittolini ably summarized: "Alcuni ragioni," 2. On the emergence of the papal city as Italian power center in the years prior to the sack of 1527, see this volume, *passim*; for the period after 1527, see Pellegrini, "Corte di Roma."

[11] Sonnino, "Roma," 793 posits a "Roman model" of marriage involving immigrant men and Roman women, extending across all social levels.

[12] Ameyden, "Relazione," fols. 15v–16r: "per lo più forestieri, de' quali però molti vi si annidono, parendo che tal volta [Roma] sia più benigna verso li forastieri, che verso li nativi, conforme il distico, hospitibus mater, natis urbs Roma noverca, plena dat externis, ubera sicca suis."

most of them, the Kingdom of Naples as well. Particularly when compared with the elites of Florence, Venice or Milan, the Roman ruling classes were unusually permeable, with new families marrying in regularly.[13]

Networks and power back home had also to be maintained. Among papal families, the Borghese and Chigi originated in Siena, the Farnese in Parma, the Boncompagni in Bologna; all made their way through intermarriage into the Roman nobility, while maintaining connections in their home cities, to a greater (Farnese) or lesser (Chigi) extent. Many more families started down that path without achieving the papal throne. Consider, for example, the case of the Salviati family, well studied by Hurtubise and Fosi. The Salviati arrived in Rome in the entourage of their relatives, the Medici, in the 1510s. In 1514, Lorenzo Salviati married Costanza Conti, a daughter of the civic aristocracy; his brother became the family's first cardinal. Another Salviati woman married an Orsini son. By the 1560s, they had abandoned mercantile efforts in favour of curial careers and feudal properties and titles.[14] The Sacchetti, Soderini and Ruspoli all followed similar paths.

That is not to say, of course, that all baronial marriages were to up-and-coming non-Romans. Endogamy within the baronial nobility was still an important means of mending fences and consolidating the group's power. Nor did newcomers exclusively marry Romans. Some families of the Florentine community in Rome exhibited a strong preference for marrying one another, thus replicating in Rome the high endogamy rates Molho found for Florence in the Quattrocento.[15] The Genoese, too, had many marriages within their own immigrant community. Those compact immigrant communities paired a continued cultural identity with strategic marriages into the Roman nobility. Cross-regional marriages could also by-pass Rome altogether, linking families from other regions, though often such matches

---

[13] Fosi and Visceglia, "Marriage and Politics;" Ago, *Carriera.*

[14] Fosi, "Archivi di famiglie toscane," 260; Hurtubise, *Une famille-témoin.* Ameyden, "Relazione," fol. 33v, names the Salviati among those Florentines who came for offices rather than banking. Feci, "Signore di curia," notes that papal matches were not always highly preferred, as the power of the pope was inevitably short-lived, 209–210. She also notes that most papal matches were to Italian nobles, both Romans and those from regions near the family's original power base. Catherine de' Medici was a notable exception, going to a cadet of the French ruling house; she had, in fact, been rejected by the d'Este family of Mantua as a prospective bride. See also Spagnoletti, *Le dinastie italiane,* 168.

[15] Molho, *Marriage Alliance,* chap. 1. Dandelet argues that the Spanish expatriate community in Rome, too, saw high rates of endogamy. *Spanish Rome,* 159.

were arranged in Rome by cardinal uncles representing the families.[16] The Cibo Malaspina family, dukes of Massa and Carrara on the Tyrrhenian coast, intermarried with Florentine and Genoese patriciates as part of a broader strategy that brought them, as Duke Alberico Cibo Malaspina wrote, in 1590, "under the shadow and protection" of the Medici.[17] At the highest dynastic levels, the Medici took spouses from mainly Italian noble ranks, reaching only occasionally abroad for a French or Spanish princess, while the Savoyard preference for French royal alliances reflected their "absolute dependence" on the French crown.[18]

Failures are as instructive as successes. Some families tried, and failed, to get a Roman foothold. An excellent example is the Sfondrati, a Milanese (originally Cremonese) family which rocketed from a single cardinalate, achieved in 1566, to winning the papacy, briefly, in 1590–91, without yet having established a regular presence in the papal city. The Sfondrati pope, Gregory XIV, set two of his nephews quickly into their proper roles — one as cardinal nephew, the other as general of the papal armies. Marriage strategy posed more of a problem. At the time of Gregory's surprise election, he was already negotiating a marriage for his only eligible nephew to a daughter of the afore-mentioned Cibo Malaspina family. Despite the many prestigious Roman brides eagerly pressed forward by their families, Gregory refused to scrap the Tuscan match and his nephew married Lucrezia Cibo Malaspina soon after his election. This may have been Gregory's fatal mistake: after his death, the Sfondrati family struggled to hold onto its presence in Rome and ultimately decamped. Among the many reasons for this, the family's failure to establish Roman networks through marriage was a significant factor in their decline and hasty retreat to Lombardy. In short, even being Pope was not enough: a family had to consolidate its position through marriage with the Roman elite.[19]

---

[16] On cardinal uncles as family representatives in marriage negotiations, see Ago, *Carriere*.

[17] He made this observation in the preliminary marriage agreement between his daughter and Ercole Sfondrati, published in Staffetti, *Donne e castelli*, 8. On the Cibo marriage strategies, see Solfaroli Camillocci, "La memoria del principe," 230–238.

[18] Spagnoletti, *Le dinastie italiane*, 182. On a regional level, urban families often intermarried with families from rural areas where they owned property: see for example Carboni, "La formazione," and Carrino, *La città aristocratica*, 100–120.

[19] Baernstein, *A Convent Tale*, chap. 5; Solfaroli Camillocci, "La memoria del principe," 237; Reinhard, "Papal power and family strategy," 339; see also Fosi and Visceglia,

This peninsular reach of the upper echelons of the marriage market had numerous consequences, some of them perhaps unintended. Marriage negotiations had to be undertaken long-distance, often through a family's Roman representatives, strengthening cardinalate hands in internal family dynamics. Further, the varied marriage laws of the Italian states had to be brought into dialogue, or at least compared, as families negotiated which state's laws would apply. At least one Roman father of the bride grumbled that Milanese law was "very disadvantageous for women" compared to Roman law, affirming the split in dotal regimes between north-central and southern Italy noted by Sperling and Wray.[20] Betrothal portraits of the bride became more important when a girl's looks could not be inspected first-hand. A whole set of rituals evolved to govern the bride's transfer to her new home.[21] And finally, whether or not absence made the heart grow fonder, it certainly required a written form of communication. For this reason, historians may be forever grateful that noble Italian wives were expected to stay in close touch with their distant natal families. Largely because of the expectation that wives could conduct business by letter, by the sixteenth century, nearly all noblewomen were literate and comfortable with the basic forms of epistolary convention. Their letters home, amassed by the thousands in family archives, reflect a near-daily practice of long-distance network building that had women at its heart.[22] We now turn to one such archive, that of the Colonna family, to consider the context and consequences for one long-distance match, that of Costanza Colonna.

"Marriage and Politics," 219.

[20] Marcantonio Colonna to Carlo Borromeo, 9.1567, BAM F. 110 inf. fol. 53, describing marital negotiations for his daughter with the cardinal cousin of his prospective son-in-law: "col Card. Sforza si è pratticato sempre il matrimonio del marchese di Caravagio con Costanza mia figlia tanto che semo d'accordo. Non resta altra difficultà che lo statuto di questo stato che certo a me par molto desavantagioso per le donne." See Sperling and Wray, *Across the Religious Divide*, 5–7.

[21] Klapisch, *Viaggi di nozze*, 372–373.

[22] On Renaissance epistolarity, the literature is vast; for an overview on women's letters, see Zarri, *Per lettera*, ix–xxix, and Nico Ottaviani, *"Me son missa a scriver,"* 3–7.

"The Girl Is All Alone:" Costanza Colonna's Marriage

The Colonnas of Paliano, one of the Rome's oldest baronial families, for all its prominence, suffered the same precarious conditions in the mid-sixteenth century as did many struggling minor princes. Mounting papal and royal power encroached on the family's sovereignty in its feudal lands, both in the Papal States and the Kingdom of Naples. After a humiliating defeat at the hands of Pope Paul III, in the Salt War of 1541 — the "final scene" of true baronial independence in the lands of St. Peter[23] — the family faced a process of domestication undergone by other barons, too, but forced, in their case, to a heightened crisis by Ascanio Colonna's quixotic rebellion against papal taxation. The task of extricating the Colonnas from exile fell to Ascanio's estranged wife, Giovanna d'Aragona, on behalf of her youngest and only surviving son, Marcantonio. No longer able to play the independent *condottiere* his uncle Fabrizio had most famously represented, Marcantonio and his mother established a firmer link to the Spanish crown, holding his father, Ascanio, at arm's length until the older man's death in 1557.[24] After a triumphant return to Rome from exile in 1560, the mother-son team re-acquired most of the family properties and titles that had been confiscated by Paul III. The newly domesticated barons would have to adapt if they were to remain relevant in a world of more highly centralized states.

At the same time, and perhaps in compensation for diminished feudal authority and military independence, the Colonnas deployed marriage alliances to extend their reach as widely as possible across the peninsula's nobility. As one of the most valued of marital prizes, the family had no trouble finding potential matches, but choices were difficult and complex given the relatively small market of eligible partners at this rank, and the family's restricted finances.[25] A series of marriages with Romans solidified local contacts: Marcantonio married Felice Orsini in 1552, helping to bridge the two families' traditional rivalry, though the Colonnas' continued alienation from papal favour meant he had to settle for a dowry of only 20,000 scudi.[26] In

---

[23] Prodi, *Il Sovrano pontefice*, 105.

[24] On the transition from Ascanio's to Marcantonio's stewardship, see Baernstein, "Reprobates and Courtiers."

[25] Raimondo,"La rete creditizia;" Bazzano, *Marco Antonio Colonna*, 50–51, 112–113. For Colonna strategy in an earlier period, see Serio, *Una gloriosa sconfitta, passim.*

[26] Bazzano, *Marco Antonio Colonna*, 51.

1558, Marcantonio's sister, Agnese, married Onorato Caetani, heir of another important Roman baronial family.[27] The family's long-standing ties to the Kingdom of Naples were strengthened with three matches: Marcantonio's sister, Vittoria, took a grand dowry of 50,000 scudi to Garcia de Toledo, son of the viceroy of Naples. Another sister, Geronima, married Camillo Pignatelli, the Duke of Monteleone, while Marcantonio's daughter, Giovanna, married Antonio Carafa, Duke of Mondragone. Both women joined their aunt in Naples. Family marital policy looked northward with the betrothal of Marcantonio's daughter, Costanza, in 1567, to Francesco Sforza, the Marquis of Caravaggio, and that of her younger brother, Fabrizio, betrothed in 1562 to Anna Borromeo, sister of the Milanese aristocrat Carlo Borromeo and niece of Pope Pius IV (Medici). These northern connections replaced an earlier tie to the Gonzaga of Mantua, through the 1549 marriage of Marcantonio's older brother, Fabrizio, to Ippolita Gonzaga, which had come to naught when Fabrizio died without heirs.[28] A final match reached beyond Italy to the important Spanish realm: Marcantonio's youngest daughter, Vittoria Colonna, wed a Spanish grandee in 1586.[29]

A simple list of marriages can give the impression that all of these connections worked out unproblematically. But a long-distance, high-stakes marriage faced a multitude of challenges. Costanza Colonna's marriage to the Marquis of Caravaggio provides one well-documented example of Colonna exogamy, its complications and its long-term consequences for inter-regional connections.[30] In 1568, aged barely twelve, Costanza traveled from Rome to Caravaggio, via Genoa and Milan, accompanied by a number of servants and her trousseau. The marriage contract, agreed to in Rome a year earlier by her father and the groom's cousin, Cardinal Alessandro Sforza, promised a moderate dowry of 30,000 scudi, to be paid in cash instalments over several years.[31] Costanza was slightly less well placed than her brother Fabrizio, possibly due to her father's relatively tight financial straits. The Sforza of Caravaggio were of lesser rank and wealth, and much newer title than the Borromeo. Nonetheless, the match extended the Colonna's connections in

---

[27] Betrothal agreement, AC III BB cart. 2 n. 48; the dowry was 33,000 scudi.

[28] Betrothal agreement at AC III BB cart. 2 n. 46. Ippolita was the daughter of Ferrante Gonzaga, governor of Milan at the time of the marriage.

[29] Cabibbo, "Percorsi del potere," 429–435.

[30] Berra, *Il giovane Caravaggio*, chap. 2, gives a generously documented account.

[31] Dowry agreement of 13.VI.1567 at ASM, Arch. Triv. di Milano, vol. 308 n. 78.

the State of Milan, one of the two poles of Spanish power in Italy, and helped to consolidate the bond with the Borromeo-Medici power axis. The groom was the legitimate grandson of an illegitimate son of the Duke of Milan, Ludovico Sforza. For his family, marriage to a Colonna woman brought an old name and prestige, as well as a Roman connection that might, if successfully cultivated, bring the family greater power and presence in the papal capital.

Costanza's father was not insensible to the emotional costs of the journey for one so young; he wrote to his kinsman, Archbishop Carlo Borromeo, "Lady Costanza my daughter is coming to her husband. Certainly I feel her distance very deeply, for she is so young; but your presence in Milan consoles me, for I know you'll look out for her there and protect her."[32] But for Costanza, things did not go well at the start despite Borromeo's oversight. Her new husband, age seventeen, was the titular family head, but he still relied heavily on his grandmother, Violante Bentivoglio Sforza, to conduct his business. It was apparently she who managed the household. Compelled by her in-laws to write pious notes home declaring her happiness, Costanza reported she was well; but slipped inside one letter was a hastily scrawled note: "The letter in my hand that you received, the chaplain made me copy, and everything is just the opposite, and please do not abandon me, father, for the love of Christ."[33] In further secret letters Costanza complained of misery and mistreatment. Marcantonio, frustrated at his inability to exert pressure at such a distance, asked the archbishop to intervene. Borromeo expressed his hope to Marcantonio that Violante's departure for Milan would improve the situation,[34] but this was not to happen.

Nearly a year after the wedding, with Costanza still not pregnant, the Colonna family raised the possibility of an annulment. Costanza had managed to intimate that the marriage might not have been consummated, and made no secret of her desire to flee the "inferno" of married life in Caravaggio. The Colonnas, meanwhile, were expanding their goals and horizons; Pope Pius V elevated the family's title to Prince of Paliano, in 1569, and Marcantonio

---

[32] BAM F 114 inf. fol. 196, 21.X.1568, "Donna Costanza mia figlia se ne viene à marito, et certo sento infinitamente questa sua lontananza, per esser così giovinetta, pur mi vo consolando la presentia di Vostra Signoria Illustrissima in Milano, dove so che mirerà per lei et ne terrà protettione."

[33] AC MAC 50 let. 1160, 14.II.1569, insert: "La lettera che ve ne pasata de mano mia l'ano fatta copiare al cappellano, et e pasata è tutto lo contrario et non me abandonate, S.r padre mia, per amore de la pasione de Christo. Costanza Colonna."

[34] AC PI BY cam. 18, 16.II.1569.

was about to be promoted to General of the Church's armies, in which role he would go on to claim victory over the Turks at the Battle of Lepanto in 1571. From Madrid, where he spent much of the year solidifying his connection to King Philip and his advisors, Marcantonio very likely thought he could place Costanza better if he had her marriage card to play again. The groom, equally eager to be released from an evidently unpleasant situation, freely confessed his own impotence to Cardinals Cesare Gonzaga and Alessandro Sforza, called in by the Pope to investigate prior to a formal annulment hearing in Rome. "I affirm that I could never do what I was supposed to do with my lady Costanza," he repeated in a letter to Borromeo in September, urging a speedy "liberation and separation of this marriage."[35] Resistance now seemed mainly to come from Borromeo, whose implacable insistence on physical proof of impotence the Colonnas sought to override. Letters flew through the summer and fall of 1569 concerning the legal options.

Costanza's aunt, Geronima, by now well established in her adopted city of Naples, bubbled over with concern for her niece: "On the matter of my Lady Costanza," she opined in August to Marcantonio's agent in Rome, "I'm greatly anxious, seeing things move so slowly, whether because of Borromeo's coolness or his bad intentions. I wonder it doesn't lead that lady to desperation, knowing as I do her nature, and how spontaneous and impatient she is."[36] A month later, with Borromeo still foot-dragging on a solution, Geronima exploded in fury at the Milanese cardinal. She wrote to her brother's agent in Rome: "I am dead, troubled, lost, desperate at seeing my lady Costanza in this dire state. The least bad course seems to be the convent, but I would see her not only a nun but even dead rather than in the hands of those cruel people [the Sforza] … There is no one there, the girl is all alone, without anyone of authority or advice…. Oh how cursed is that Borromeo. Christianity without mercy, governance without prudence, religious without charity!"[37] Geronima's

---

[35] BAM F 117 inf. f. 148, 23.IX.1569. "affermo che mai ho puotutto far quello che mi conveneva con l'Ill.ma S.ra Donna Costanza … atio che si puoscia venir alla liberatione et separatione di questo matrimonio."

[36] AC PI AB cam. 1 let. 6. To Cesare Gallo in Rome, 27.VIII.1569. "Delle cose della sig.a d. Costanza mia passo antia grandissima veggendole caminare si lentamente per caggione, o della freddezza, o della mala intentione di Borromeo, che mi fare dubitare non induchino quella signora a disperatione sapendo ben io il suo naturale, e quanto ella sia subitanea, e poco patiente in cose sue."

[37] AC PI AB cam. 5 let. 2 to Cesare Gallo in Rome, 9.X.1569. "io sto morta aflitta persa desperata de veder donna Costanza mia in questa necessità che il manco male saria

intense identification with her niece's distress — and her scathing mockery of Archbishop Borromeo's claims to Christian governance in the age of Tridentine bishops — reflect the seriousness of the perils involved in high-stakes alliances. With so much money and political force applied to the personal relationship of two teenagers, the enterprise was bound to falter from time to time. Not every bride could rise to the challenge in the Sabine manner, nor did hard feelings between clans always evaporate once a bride was transferred. The tense negotiations among the Sforzas, the Colonnas, and Borromeo suggest how quickly alliances could break down under such pressure.

Costanza and Francesco thus might have gotten their annulment, but for the inconvenient fact of Costanza's pregnancy. After several months in a Milanese convent, she delivered a still-born child in November. This unforeseen event compelled all the parties to reconsider. By January, Costanza was back in the Caravaggio household with a whole battery of Roman attendants, sent to shore up her spirits and remind the Sforza of her family's clout. The Marquis pronounced himself eager to try to meet her needs.[38] The couple patched up their differences and lived together for fourteen years. When Francesco died in 1583, Costanza became sole tutrix of their six surviving minor children.

As a wife and a widow, Costanza's duties and conflicts mingled her powerful Roman connections with her new ties, both familial and religious. Deeply loyal to the Angelic nuns of Milan, with whom she had passed the summer of 1569, she read their favourite spiritual books, attended sermons at their convent church of San Paolo Converso and considered their priests, the Barnabites, to be her most important spiritual advisors. Several attempts at becoming a nun herself came to naught, though she did succeed in placing two of her three daughters in other Milanese convents, in a pattern more resembling Milanese than Roman marriage practices.[39] Her sons led more cosmopolitan lives than their sisters; Costanza sent them to Rome, to the care of her brother, Cardinal Ascanio Colonna, for proper education at court

---

il monacato, gia che non solo monaca ma morta la voria prima che saper che fusse in mano de quelli signori crudeli … La non cie nisciuno, la figliola e' solissima, senza persona ne de autorità ne de consiglio … O che maledetto Borromeo e questo. Cristianesimo senza pieta governo senza prudentia relicioso senza carita."

[38] Borromeo to Marcantonio Colonna, AC PI BY 29, 25.XI.1569. Colonna's reply at BAM F 117 inf. fol. 555, 21.XII.1569.

[39] On the widespread monachization of noble daughters in Milan, see Zanetti, *La demografia.*

and the obligatory Spanish sojourn. Nearly as often as she proposed taking religious vows, Costanza proposed returning to Rome herself, and she did so for several tours during her widowhood, most notably in 1601–06, when she acted as family head while Cardinal Ascanio traveled to Spain. During the long years in Caravaggio — the "inferno" she always detested — her contacts with Rome and Milan kept her gaze outward and her pen busy. As she wrote to her parents soon after her arrival, "Write to me, so that for all that I'm far away from you, and settled (*casata*), you keep me always in your presence."[40]

Nor did the Roman link evaporate in the next generation. The centrifugal pull of the *urbs* kept her first-born son, Muzio, there, improbably for a Milanese title-holder and, in 1595, he married Felice Orsini Peretti, the young widow of his cousin Marcantonio Colonna III, agreeing to live in Rome with her for at least three years. This match suited Colonna strategy very well, as it kept the Peretti dowry in the family and allowed the widow to remain with her infant son, the prospective heir to the Colonna estate, but it did little for the Sforzas' presence in the state of Milan. Nor did the transfer from Caravaggio to Rome seem to displease Muzio, for a few years later he asked King Philip III for permission to exchange his title of Marquis of Caravaggio for another title, in the Kingdom of Naples.[41] Although his request was not granted, it speaks volumes for the strong cross-regional pulls created by Costanza's multifaceted match.

Conclusion

If the movements and actions of Italian elite women formed a crucial component of inter-regional relations, then we should be looking for cultural as well as political consequences. Recent work on the Medici women as cultural mediators is an excellent example of this sort of transmission at the level of sovereigns;[42] but there may also be a multiplier effect at a slightly lower level, where many families of means sent brides far afield. Here, the single case of Costanza Colonna's cultural work must suffice. The painter, Michelangelo

---

[40] AC MAC 50 n. 1159, 7.II.1569: "mi scrivete ancora che con tutto che vi stia lontano, et casata, me tenete sempre nella presentia."

[41] Berra, *Il giovane Caravaggio*, 293–333.

[42] Tomas, *Medici Women*; Conference "Artful Allies: Medici Women as Cultural Mediators, 1533–1743," Harvard Center for Renaissance Studies - Villa I Tatti, Florence, October, 2008.

Merisi, known as Caravaggio, owed many of his career choices, patrons and even his move to Rome to Costanza's lifelong patronage. As Giacomo Berra has shown in an extensively documented work, Colonna used her Roman and Neapolitan connections, as well as her presence in those cities after 1591, to arrange commissions and other favours for the artist.[43] Thus, Rome's role as artistic center, too, functioned in part as a consequence of cross-regional ties fostered by intermarriage.

To look, perhaps Whiggishly, into the future, it is worth asking whether the process of inter-regional marriage described here, with its central node in Rome, contributed to building a peninsular ruling class that provided some semblance of elite identity when the new Italian nation emerged in the nineteenth century.[44] In the light of recent trends in Risorgimento scholarship, seeking the roots of a national culture in the Renaissance may be more viable than it has hitherto seemed. In a provocative and ground-breaking study, historian Alberto Banti describes Italian nationalism of the 1860s as the heir of long-standing uniquely Italian cultural characteristics, specifically: kinship, holiness and honour.[45] In Banti's view, Italy's new nationhood did not spring solely from economic and social forces, nor from an imitative, modernizing impulse to catch up with the rest of Europe, but was rather a remodelled or updated version of pre-existing cultural features. Debates over Banti's paradigm have focused on his implication that we should see a tighter connection between the Risorgimento and Fascism; few have tested his insights by looking backward. If the Risorgimento drew on a significant earlier Italian identity, then much more must be done to trace the roots and nuances of that identity. The hypothesis seems most sustainable for Italy's ruling classes, linked by a shared written language, church institutions and marriage alliances. Seen in this light, the marriages of the early modern nobility, while less openly violent than the Roman capture of the Sabines they so admired, may echo the Roman nation-building project more closely than we, or the early moderns, thought.

MIAMI UNIVERSITY

---

[43] Berra, *Il Giovane Caravaggio*; similar conclusions in Calvesi, *La realtà di Caravaggio*.

[44] Prosperi, "Alle origini di una identità nazionale," 170, points out that the Roman Inquisition formed the first near-peninsular bureaucracy.

[45] Banti, *La nazione del Risorgimento*, xi.

CITED WORKS

Manuscript Sources

Milan. Archivio di Stato (ASM).
Archivio Trivulziano di Milano, 308.

Milan. Biblioteca Ambrosiana (BAM).
Epistolario San Carlo, F 110 inf., F 114 inf., F 117 inf.

Rome. Biblioteca Casanatense (BC).
Ms. 5001, fols. 1–65, Teodoro Ameyden, *Relazione della città di Roma Fatta dell'anno 1642*

Subiaco. Biblioteca Nazionale Monumentale di Santa Scolastica. Archivio Colonna (AC).
Carteggio dei Personaggi Illustri (PI), AB, BY.
Corrispondenza di Marco Antonio Colonna "Il Grande" (MAC), 50.
III BB cart. 2.

Printed Sources

Ago, Renata. *Carriera e clientela nella Roma barocca*. Bari: Laterza, 1990.

Altieri, Marco Antonio. *Li nuptiali*, ed. E. Narducci. Rome: Roma nel Rinascimento, 1995.

Baernstein, P. Renée. *A Convent Tale. A Century of Sisterhood in Spanish Milan*. New York: Routledge, 2002.

————. "Reprobates and Courtiers: Lay Masculinities in the Colonna Family, 1520–1584." In *Florence and Beyond: Culture, Society and Politics in Renaissance Italy*, ed. David S. Peterson with Daniel Bornstein. Toronto: Centre for Reformation and Renaissance Studies, 2008, 291–304.

Banti, Alberto. *La nazione del Risorgimento. Parentela, santità e onore alle origini dell'Italia unita*. Turin: Einaudi, 2000.

Baskins, Cristelle. *Cassone Painting, Humanism, and Gender in Early Modern Italy*. Cambridge, UK: Cambridge University Press, 1998.

Bazzano, Nicoletta. *Marcantonio Colonna*. Rome: Salerno, 2003.

Benadusi, Giovanna. "Rethinking the State: Family Strategies in Early Modern Tuscany." *Social History* 20 (1995): 157–178.

Berra, Giacomo. *Il giovane Caravaggio in Lombardia*. Rome: Fondazione Roberto Longo, 2005.

Brown, Robert. "Livy's Sabine Women and the Ideal of Concordia." *Transactions of the American Philological Association* 125 (1995): 291–319.

Burke, Ersie C. "Our Daughters and Our Future: Elite Greco-Venetian Marriages, 1520–1610." In *Marriage in Premodern Europe*, ed. Jacqueline Murray. Toronto: Centre for Reformation and Renaissance Studies, 2012, pp. 169–199.

Cabibbo, Sara. "Percorsi del potere femminile fra Italia e Spagna: Il caso di Vittoria Colonna Enriquez (1558–1633)." In *Donne di potere nel Rinascimento*, eds. Letizia Arcangeli and Susanna Peyronel. Rome: Viella, 2008, 417–443.

Calvesi, Maurizio. *La realtà del Caravaggio*. Turin: Einaudi, 1990.

Carboni, Mauro. "La formazione di una élite di governo: Le alleanze matrimoniali dei senatori bolognesi (1506–1796)." *Studi storici Luigi Simeoni* 52 (2002): 9–27.

Carrino, Annastella. *La città aristocratica: linguaggi e pratiche della politica a Monopoli fra Cinque e Seicento*. Bari: Edipuglia, 2000.

Chittolini, Giorgio. "Alcune ragioni per un convegno." In *Roma capitale (1447–1527)*, ed. Sergio Gensini. Pubblicazioni degli Archivi di Stato, Saggi, 29. Rome: Ministero per i Beni Culturali e Ambientali, 1994, 1–14.

Dandelet, T.J. *Spanish Rome, 1500–1700*. New Haven: Yale University Press, 2001.

D'Elia, Anthony F. *The Renaissance of Marriage in Fifteenth-Century Italy*. Cambridge, MA, and London: Harvard University Press, 2004.

Fabbri, Lorenzo. "Trattatistica e pratica dell'alleanza matrimoniale." In *Storia del matrimonio*, eds. Michele de Giorgio and Christiane Klapisch-Zuber. Bari: Laterza, 1996, 91–117.

Feci, Simona. "Signore di curia. Rapporti di potere ed esperienze di governo nella Roma papale (metà XV–metà XVI secolo)." In *Donne di potere nel Rinascimento*, eds. Letizia Arcangeli and Susanna Peyronel. Rome: Viella, 2008, 195–222.

Fosi, Irene, and Maria Antonietta Visceglia. "Marriage and Politics at the Papal Court in the Sixteenth and Seventeenth Centuries." In *Marriage in Italy, 1300–1650*, eds. Trevor Dean and K.J.P. Lowe. Cambridge, UK: Cambridge University Press, 1998, 197–224.

Fosi, Irene. "Archivi di famiglie toscane nella Roma del Cinque e Seicento: Problemi e prospettive di ricerca." In *Archivi nobiliari e domestici. Conservazione, metodologie di riordino e prospettive di ricerca storica*, eds. Laura Casella and Roberto Navarrini. Udine: Forum, 2000, 255–275.

Hurtubise, Pierre. *Une famille-témoin, Les Salviati*. Vatican City: Biblioteca Apostolica Vaticana, 1985.

Klapisch-Zuber, Christiane. "Viaggi di nozze nel Quattrocento." In *Altrove. Viaggi di donne dall'antichità al Novecento*, ed. Dinora Corsi. Rome: Viella, 1999, 365–376.

_____. "An Ethnology of Marriage in the Age of Humanism." In *Women, Family, and Ritual in Renaissance Italy*. Chicago: University of Chicago Press, 1985, 247–260.

Kolsky, Stephen. "Culture and Politics in Renaissance Rome: Marco Antonio Altieri's Roman Weddings." *Renaissance Quarterly* 40:1 (1987): 49–90.

Molho, Anthony. *Marriage Alliance in Late Medieval Florence*. Cambridge, MA: Harvard University Press, 1994.

Musacchio, Jacqueline. "The Rape of the Sabine Women on Quattrocento Marriage-panels." In *Marriage in Italy, 1300–1650*, eds. Trevor Dean and K.J.P. Lowe. Cambridge: Cambridge University Press, 1998, 66–82.

Nico Ottaviani, Maria Grazia. *"Me son missa a scriver questa letera..." Lettere e altre scritture femminili tra Umbria, Toscana e Marche nei secoli XV–XVI*. Naples: Liguori, 2006.

Pellegrini, Marco. "Corte di Roma e aristocrazie italiane. Per una lettura storico-sociale della curia romana." *Rivista di storia e letteratura religiosa* 30 (1994): 543–602.

Prodi, Paolo. *Il sovrano pontefice: Un corpo e due anime: la monarchia papale nella prima età moderna*. Bologna: Il Mulino, 1992.

Prosperi, Adriano. "Alle origini di una identità nazionale. L'Italia fra l'antico e i "barbari" nella storiografia dell'Umanesimo e della Controriforma." In *Le sentiment national dans l'Europe méridionale aux XVIe et XVIIe siècles (France, Espagne, Italie)*, ed. Alain Tallon. Madrid: Casa de Velazquez, 2007, 169–188.

Raimondo, Sergio. "La rete creditizia dei Colonna di Paliano tra XVI e XVII secolo." In *La nobiltà romana in età moderna. Profili istituzionali e pratiche sociali*, ed. Maria Antonietta Visceglia. Rome: Carocci, 2001, 225–253.

Reinhard, Wolfgang. "Papal Power and Family Strategy in the Sixteenth and Seventeenth Centuries." In *Princes, Patronage and Nobility. the Court at the Beginning of the Modern Age*, ed. R.G. Asch and A.M. Birke. Oxford: Oxford University Press, 1991, 329–356.

Safarik, E. *Catalogo sommario della Galleria Colonna in Roma: Dipinti.* Bramante: Busto Arsizio, 1981.

Serio, Alessandro. *Una gloriosa sconfitta. I Colonna tra papato e impero nella prima età moderna.* Rome: Viella, 2008.

Solfaroli Camillocci, Daniela. "La memoria del principe. Il libro di famiglia di Alberico Cibo Malaspina." In *Alberico I Cybo Malaspina. Il Principe, la Casa, lo Stato (1553–1623)*. Modena: Aedes Muratoriana, 1995, 227–242.

Sonnino, Eugenio. "Roma, secolo XVII: Popolazione e famiglie nella "città maschile." in *La popolazione italiana nel Seicento*. Turin: CLUEB, 1999, 777–796.

Spagnoletti, Angelantonio. *Le dinastie italiane nella prima età moderna.* Bologna: Il Mulino, 2003.

Sperling, Jutta and Shona Kelly Wray, eds. *Across the Religious Divide. Women, Property, and Law in the Wider Mediterranean (ca. 1300–1800).* New York: Routledge, 2010.

Staffetti, L. *Donne e castelli di Lunigiana.* Vol. 1. *Un sposa principesca del '500.* Massa: Medici, 1902.

Visceglia, Maria Antonietta. *Il bisogno di eternità: i comportamenti aristocratici a Napoli in età moderna.* Naples: Guida, 1988.

Wolfthal, Diane. *Images of Rape: The "Heroic" Tradition and Its Alternatives.* Cambridge: Cambridge University Press, 1999.

Zanetti, Dante. *La demografia del patriziato milanese nei secoli XVII, XVII, XIX.* Pavia: Università di Pavia, 1972.

Zarri, Gabriella ed. *Per Lettera. La scrittura epistolare femminile tra archivio e tipografia secoli XVI–XVII.* Rome: Viella, 2000.

The Management of Marriage in Reformation-Era Scotland: The Carnegie Family

Heather Parker

In the mid-sixteenth century, the Carnegies of Kinnaird were lairds in eastern Scotland who held moderate estates and influence with the local landholders. By 1633, the laird of Kinnaird had been raised to the Earldom of Southesk and his younger brother to the Earldom of Northesk. The rise of this family to the peerage was the result of a combination of political savvy, economic know-how and careful marital arrangements. The Carnegie patriarchs assisted family members both with money and legal expertise to allow them to marry well. The marriages of this family both reflected an increase in status and contributed to the rise in power of a series of these Carnegie lairds and their children through the Scottish Reformation, even throughout the upheaval and uncertainty of the civil war.

Marriages from sixteenth-century Scotland are often examined for their power to influence major political changes. The marriages of Mary Queen of Scots, for example, are often understood to have been central to her downfall, especially in contrast to the drastically different approach taken by Elizabeth I of England to her nuptials. Marriages among the Scottish nobility could have dramatic political outcomes, but Scottish historians rarely examine the nature of marriage negotiations and arrangements on a local scale. Certain middling families could climb the social ladder by marrying into increasingly powerful families; however, the Carnegies took a different route to power. They formed a series of local marriages, with families of varying position in society, using contracts to protect their arrangements. Patriarchs Robert and David Carnegie used their legal training to negotiate advantageous pre-nuptial agreements for their family. These carefully arranged marriages enabled them to consolidate power on a local scale. The wishes of the brides and grooms were considered, but generally this meant that they accepted marriages that supported their families' goals. The Carnegies pursued a strategy of local unions, even when they were presented with the opportunity to marry up on national level, using the royal court to find eligible spouses. This is in contrast to much of the historical literature, which focuses on how families made use of every advantage they had to increase their national standing.

Local unions could be effective to buttress a family's estates and social status, by bringing in new lands to estates that were sometimes depleted by marriage dowries. They could also significantly boost a family's local standing, if they consistently married into other wealthy families. The Carnegies were very good at this and the careers of Robert and David Carnegie as matchmakers, in the second half of the sixteenth century, demonstrate the utility of marriage, as well as the pragmatism of families, to ensure ideal matches and land deals for their children and kin. It is not clear whether the Carnegies' local marriages were part of a conscious overarching strategy, but it is clear that marriages with neighbours and kin enabled the Carnegies to secure their power.

The decision to look for marriage partners locally had some drawbacks. Families were confined to a certain area of the country and, therefore, to a limited number of opportunities for marriage. For some Scottish kin groups, marriages across a wide geographical area were crucial to their social advancement. A strategy of marrying outside the existing kin group and often across geographical distance, could substantially increase the territory under a family's control, but the strain of distance could also result in their power being diluted over too great an area. The evidence for such a marriage strategy consists primarily of the legal documentation surrounding marital unions, namely, written pre-nuptial contracts. Although such marriage contracts were rare for anyone but members of the royal family in Scotland before the mid-fourteenth century, these became increasingly popular and increasingly complex during the fifteenth and sixteenth centuries, to the point that they became standard among noble families and lairds such as the Carnegies.

Geography, politics and religion were all important for how the Carnegies managed their lands. Their family seat was in Brechin, in Angus, Scotland. One of their centres was Kinnaird Castle, acquired from Mariota of Kinnaird between 1401 and 1409, by Duthac of Carnegie. This remains a Carnegie seat to this day and is where most of the family documents are still housed in the family's charter chest.[1] Robert Carnegie was the laird of Kinnaird and the patriarch of the Carnegies until his death, in 1565, and he

---

[1] Fraser, *History of the Carnegies*, 1:xxx.

spent much of his adult life on legal and diplomatic assignments for King James V. Despite his frequent absences from Kinnaird, Robert was actively involved in arranging marriages for his children. His son and heir, John, who was eventually overshadowed by his younger brother, David, succeeded him. John died, in 1595, with no living children, leaving David, the father of ten, as laird and head of the family. David worked to buttress the kin group's power, especially on the local level. This strategy proved effective and, in 1633 and 1647, during major expansions of Scottish peerages, David's sons, David and John, were made the Earls of Southesk and Northesk, respectively.

The dramatic changes in circumstances of many powerful families during the Reformation provided the Carnegies with opportunities for advancement in both the Protestant and Catholic camps. During the Reformation, the Carnegies were predominantly part of the Catholic faction.[2] Certainly, in political matters, the Carnegies associated closely with the Gordon Earls of Huntly, who were some of the most stubbornly Catholic magnates in Scotland. The Carnegies were also part of the famous reformation-era "Queen's Party," the allied families and clans who supported Mary, Queen of Scots after she was deposed, in 1567. Immediately before the Reformation, some of the Carnegies were active in the established Church. For example, Robert the younger was preceptor of the chapel and hospital of Maison Dieu at Brechin, by 1549.[3] The family, however, soon became known for their Protestant leanings, but managed to straddle both factions in the Reformation, with no obvious religious schisms among family members. This ability to balance both sides of the Reformation must have been quite common at the time, but it is often hard to determine precisely where families stood. It could have been the result of a desire to maintain property or political power, but it is also clear that the Carnegies participated in both Catholic traditions and the Protestant reforms.

This period is traditionally portrayed as a time of sudden change in Scotland and the Carnegies' approach towards the formation of marriage displayed carefully planned continuity. The only major change to marriage law in Scotland was a 1567 act that allowed first-cousin marriage where previously even third cousins had been forbidden to marry.[4] The Carnegie

[2] Fraser, *History of the Carnegies*, 1:35.

[3] Fraser, *History of the Carnegies*, 1:39 and Jervise, *Memorials of Angus and the Mearns*, 121.

[4] *The Records of the Parliaments of Scotland* to 1707, A1567/12/15.

family engaged in a series of marital unions among their kin and a handful of local landowning families both before and after the marriage reform. For the most part, Scottish families repeatedly intermarried and there were many couples where the bride and groom were already closely related through the marriages of their siblings or cousins. This made for confusing webs of consanguinity and affinity. These endogamous marital bonds resulted in an increase in the family's lands and in the strengthening of local relationships. This pattern continued throughout the Reformation, even as the Carnegies shifted their loyalties. Their method of arranging marriages stayed consistent and did not reflect changes in power structures or the religious doctrine affecting marriage.

By the mid-sixteenth century, the Carnegie's clear pattern of marrying locally was implemented through the use of marriage contracts. A written record of the arrangements surrounding a marriage allowed Scottish families to be specific in their negotiations since they had the expectation that the contracts would be upheld in court. This was a new legal process for the Carnegie family who, although they had been exposed to marriage by their peers, did not use them until at least a generation later than some of their neighbours had adopted them. In fact, the first record of the Carnegies using pre-nuptial contracts was in a marriage with a neighbouring family that had used contracts as early as 1509. Margaret Lundy and David Ramsay were contracted to marry on 2 February 1509.[5] The Lundys were neighbours of the Carnegies and, indeed, the next contract in the Carnegie collection is for a Lundy-Carnegie marriage.

In 1549, Helen Carnegie, the eldest daughter of Robert Carnegie of Kinnaird, was contracted to marry William Lundy. The decision to use a written contract for the marriage is not surprising. The Lundys had already begun to use marriage contracts in their negotiations and Helen's father, Robert, was a lawyer at court and so exposed to a wide range of marriage negotiations and pre-nuptial contracts. By 1548, he was in charge of an embassy to England, involving, among other things, marriage discussions with Queen Elizabeth concerning Lord Darnley.[6] When he returned home

---

[5] Kinnaird Castle, NRAS792/5/1, no. 66 (1509/1510), "Marriage Contract."

[6] Fraser, *History of the Carnegies*, 27.

to arrange the marriage of his daughter, Helen, he would have been up-to-date on the marriage arrangements already in vogue at both the English and Scottish courts.

Robert arranged for Helen to marry William Lundy, using a marriage contract.[7] The contract was formally drawn up by Helen's father and William's mother, Margaret Scrymgeour, and is extremely unusual because it also includes a side note that the groom's sister, Margaret, should be married to George Lumby of Durcany, with no "tocher" (a Scots "dowry") and at "any dait," a formula unseen in any other surviving contract of the time. This double marriage provides a glimpse of a common marital arrangement of the sort that was hardly ever recorded in legal documents because of its simplicity. Perhaps preparing the contract for Helen and William provided the Lundys with the opportunity to resolve outstanding issues pertaining to their son. Although not an immediate relative of either the bride or groom in the Lumby/Lundy marriage, Robert Carnegie was directly involved in this match when he was put in charge of seeking out a dispensation for Margaret Lundy and George Lumby. If Robert was not successful, he was required to pay Margaret's mother 510 merks, perhaps to provide a tocher for the bride for another marriage. Whatever the cause, it is clear that the negotiation of a marriage included many facets beyond the traditional monetary and territorial arrangements of tocher, terce (dower) and conjunct fees (shared property). There were other ways in which the new kin bonds were useful and participation in further marriages was one way to share money and power.

Requests for a dispensation to marry were common in pre-Reformation Scotland. One reason was that the Scottish aristocracy was so small that the members were nearly all related by consanguinity or affinity, in the fourth degree, a degree of relationship that, according to the Church in Rome, prohibited marriage. In 1554, the Archbishop of St Andrews wrote a petition to the pope asking for leniency in the granting of dispensations. Within the social structure, at certain levels of society, nearly every eligible man or woman was within the prohibited degree of relationship, making a valid marriage impossible.[8] Failure to obtain a dispensation could result in the subsequent annulment of the marriage. Kin groups could use the possibility of annulment strategically and so careful families needed to establish when and at whose cost, a dispensation would be sought.

---

[7] Kinnaird Castle, NRAS792/7/7 (8 September 1549), "Marriage Contract."

[8] Brown, *An Introductory Survey of the Sources and Literature of Scots Law*, 1:136.

There is, however, evidence that these prohibitions based on consanguinity were not always followed. In fact, some evidence points to the manipulation of the system of dispensations by couples seeking separation.[9] Given how lightly dispensations could be treated in Scotland, questions arise concerning piety, social ambition and the effects of the Reformation on the formation of marriage. It is clear from the pre- and post-Reformation Carnegie contracts that similar marriage strategies were employed before and after 1560.

The last pre-Reformation contract was that of Christian Carnegie and David Strachan of Carmyle, dated 25 May 1559, in which the bride and groom were instructed to marry "in gudlie haste."[10] Robert Carnegie and Thomas Strachan, the fathers of the bride and groom, arranged the contract just as the Reformation crisis was beginning. Although there is no indication in the contract of local instability, it was written while men from the area were assembling and rioting in Dundee and Perth. The Strachans lived in Forfar, south of Angus and were closely associated with the Maules of Panmure, friends and neighbours of the Carnegies.[11] The contract between Christian and David was in accord with the pattern of local matches that Robert arranged for his children. The tocher amount had less to do with the status of the Strachans than with Robert's attitude towards his daughter, Christian and the amount that was owed to her as an inheritance and a guard against future poverty. In his last will and testament of 1557, just as he was leaving on a diplomatic mission to England, Robert wrote that should he die, Christian should receive 400 merks money and 400 merks worth of his goods, which together would have almost equalled her tocher of 900 merks.[12]

It is possible, too, that there were other factors involved in the formation of this marriage, since it may have been one of two marriages between these families. Christian's sister, Mary, is listed in modern genealogies as having married an "unknown Carmyle of Strachan," while Christian's

---

[9] For instance, see the marriage contract of George, Master of Huntly and Elizabeth, Countess of Murray (1455) in *Spalding Club Miscellany*, 128–131.

[10] National Archives of Scotland (NAS), GD45/16/682 "Marriage Contract."

[11] See Alexander Strachan of Carmyle's bond of manrent, dated 8 February 1508 in Rogers, *Memorials of the Scottish Families of Strachan and Wise*, 13.

[12] Fraser, *History of the Carnegies*, 1:50.

marriage arrangements have always been listed as unknown.[13] There may initially have been a marriage arrangement for Mary that was transferred to Christian, but it is certainly clear that Christian and David's marriage did proceed, because they were later named in a marriage contract for their daughter, Margaret.

~

The post-Reformation marriage arrangements of the Carnegies continued along the same path, despite changes in their political status, including the brief seizure of their castle, when they were named as rebels in 1568.[14] The thirteen contracts, from the years 1568 to 1599, show a continuation of the pre-Reformation marriage strategy among the family members. Fathers and occasionally uncles and brothers, formally drew up the contract for the bride and groom. The matches were arranged both for the wishes of the couple and the wealth of the families. The marriages were consistently local, so many of the couples were already related to each other. Consequently, it is most likely that the bride and groom knew their future spouse before marriage.

The first extant post-Reformation contract is that between David and his second wife, Euphame.[15] Euphame's dowry of 2000 merks was relatively high for a bride marrying a younger son, who had children from a previous marriage. David, however, did have some lands from his first marriage and would eventually inherit his brother's lands of Kinnaird.

The first of David's children to marry were two daughters from his first marriage, who were heiresses to their mother's lands in Leuchars. In the case of Elizabeth Carnegie, whose contract is not extant, there is an indication that she was able to have a role in the selection of her husband. The most recent historian of the Carnegies has argued that notes on the family's charters indicate that Elizabeth was allowed to select her own husband, John Inglis, in 1579, a luxury not available to many of her contemporaries.[16] Elizabeth, the eldest, appears to have married a man of her own choice, a younger son of a local family, after insisting that she would marry neither

[13] For instance, Fraser, *History of the Carnegies*, 1:44. and Mosley, *Burke's Peerage*, 1:1427.

[14] Fraser, *History of the Carnegies*, 1:53.

[15] Kinnaird Castle, NRAS792/5/1, no. 137 (3 October 1568) "Marriage Contract."

[16] Fraser, *History of the Carnegies*, 1:61.

Ramsay men who had been suggested as suitable husbands. These men were most likely relatives, since her mother was also a Ramsay. Elizabeth's father provided her with a very high tocher of 6000 merks and the contract was dated 15 November 1579, the day after she turned fourteen.[17] Her father's large contribution was related to her resignation of her inheritance to him. When David arranged for the marriage of Elizabeth's sister, Margaret, to William Dundas, in 1584, he once again allowed for a tocher of 6000 merks, which was identical to that of her sister. Like her sister, Margaret already had given her inherited lands to her father and he reciprocated by providing a substantial tocher thus ensuring that both girls would marry and live well.

That same year, 1584, David's eldest brother, John Carnegie, who had inherited their father's lands, arranged the marriage of their niece, Katherine, daughter of their deceased brother George.[18] As the eldest brother and the richest landowner, it was John's responsibility to arrange the marriages of his nieces and nephews. John provided Katherine with a reasonable dowry and a reasonable match. He also used his money and his negotiation skills, to help arrange marriages for local families in need. In his testament, dated 5 January 1565, Robert listed debts owed to him, including 500 merks "awen to hyme for the mariag of Thomas Fresar of Brackie" and 1100 merks "awen to hym be the arschebischop of Sanctandros to pay his dochther" her tocher.[19] David assumed the role of avuncular oversight after his brother's death, in 1595 and he was involved in the marriage of his niece, Margaret, providing her with a substantial tocher of 3000 merks.[20] It was very common for uncles to be involved in marriage arrangements in this way, especially when the uncles were more prominent landowners than the parents of the bride or groom.

Despite the prominent role of family patriarchs in managing the relationships of their kin, the only evidence that remains of John Carnegie, Laird of Kinnaird's involvement in arranging marriages for his own sons and daughters was in the case of his eldest son and heir.[21] This agreement, between John Carnegie, on behalf of his son Robert and Patrick Ogilvy of Inchmartin, on behalf of his daughter, Margaret, was of special significance for the Carnegies. The contract is, surprisingly, in Latin rather than in Scots.

---

[17] Fraser, *History of the Carnegies*, 1:61.

[18] Kinnaird Castle, NRAS792/6/3 (9 June 1585) "Aquittance."

[19] Fraser, *History of the Carnegies*, 1:51.

[20] Kinnaird Castle, NRAS792/6/5 (26 May 1599), "Marriage Contract."

[21] Kinnaird Castle, NRAS792/6/3 (26 March 1589), "Marriage Contract."

The use of Latin may reflect the fact that this was the most significant marriage among the contemporary Carnegie contracts and was, therefore, more formal. The pre-nuptial contract of James VI and Anne of Denmark is the only extant marriage contract from that period, written in Latin presumably because neither Anne nor her advisors spoke Scots.[22] Not even the contract between Mary Queen of Scots and James Bothwell was written in Latin.[23] John placed an emphasis on this contract, even though the people involved were not particularly notable. John Carnegie died with no surviving children and David, John's brother and heir, became responsible for the family's marital negotiations.

David kept in close contact with his kin, even when he was in Edinburgh on business and he participated in the legal arrangements for land moving in and out of his holdings. David's opinion on the management of land and money was valued and his brother-in-law, the laird of Wemyss, consulted him about the financial arrangements he was making for his children, David's nieces and nephews. David's response, in a letter dated 11 March 1588, supported Wemyss' decision to parcel out bits of land to all his children in order to provide for them.[24] He wrote that he would follow up with Wemyss in person and sent greetings to his sister: "I purpes, God willing, to se yow on Fryday or Setterday at the farrest [...] eftir my hartly commendationis to the Lady, your bedfallow, I commit yow to the protectione of God."[25] It is clear from this correspondence that David was not only actively involved in counselling his family members on how best to manage their estates but he was also physically present during many negotiations.

David's skill in arranging marriages for his children can be seen in a number of unique agreements in which he was involved. 25 April 1590 was a particularly significant date, on which two Carnegie sisters were contracted to marry.[26] Jane Carnegie was betrothed to James Carmichael and Katherine was bound to marry John Aytoun. The two marriages reveal similar strategies and goals and the two contracts are almost identical, with a few small exceptions. Unlike the bulk of the family's contracts, which were written in Brechin or

---

[22] NAS, SP8/7, "Marriage Contract."

[23] NAS, GD26/7/392, "Marriage Contract."

[24] Fraser, *History of the Carnegies*, 1:59.

[25] Fraser, *History of the Carnegies*, 1:59.

[26] Kinnaird Castle, NRAS792/6/3, no. 162 (25 April 1590) "Marriage Contract" and NRAS792/6/3, no. 163 (25 April 1590) "Marriage Contract."

Kinnaird, these were written in Leuchars, the lands ceded to David by his daughters, Elizabeth and Margaret, half sisters of Jane and Katherine. The reason for this may have been that each sister already possessed a quarter of the lands of Kynninmonth, lying in St Andrews, quite close to Leuchars. Now that they had received their inheritance, in the form of their tochers and were able to provide for themselves, the girls ceded their lands to their siblings. Katherine's quarter of the lands went to her sister, Euphame and Jane's quarter went to her second-eldest brother, John. David Carnegie was generally quite careful to ensure his daughters had access to income-generating land lest their husbands fail to provide for them, and did so in these marriage negotiations, as well. The two pre-nuptial contracts are similar, written on the same day, in the same hand, yet each document reflects each woman's individual circumstances.

Both unions were advantageous for the Carnegies and were the result of both serendipity and careful planning. James Carmichael's wardship, a gift to the Carnegies from Dame Jane Lyon, Countess of Angus, brought moderate lands to his marriage with Jane.[27] In the case of John Aytoun, although he did not have significant lands when David obtained his wardship, David was confident that his daughter and son-in-law would eventually inherit. The marriage contract between Katherine and John Aytoun contain a clause, stating that when John's relative, Robert, who "is ideot", died, John would inherit his lands, which were immediately north of John's property.[28] Thus, David secured even greater status for his daughter and son-in-law by ensuring them an even greater inheritance, without paying for an expensive wardship. David had inherited John and James' wardships from his father through his brother, John.[29] It is also interesting that David Carnegie provided lands to both couples in conjunct fee, an equal form of land tenure, which would provide his daughters with greater lands in their widowhood than if he had relied on the terce. Both women also received an equal tocher of 1500 merks, far less than their elder half-sisters received, but, in this case, the two grooms did not have much leverage in the negotiations. David arranged these marriages shrewdly and saved himself thousands of merks compared to what he normally would have provided as tocher. He also arranged for a series of

---

[27] Kinnaird Castle, NRAS792/6/3, no. 163 (25 April 1590) "Marriage Contract" and Fraser, *History of the Carnegies*, 1:64.

[28] Kinnaird Castle, NRAS792/6/3, no. 162 (25 April 1590) "Marriage Contract."

[29] Fraser, *History of the Carnegies*, 1:50.

linked land transactions that allowed him to minimize his losses to valuable properties near at hand.

Marriages were often arranged in pairs or groups in order to maximise the benefits received from the land deals and kinship links. Multiple marriage arrangements conducted on the same day for the same purpose, however, were unusual. More commonly, families arranged for a series of unions with specific kin groups, in order to reinforce existing economic, political and kinship bonds. Jane Carnegie was part of this type of double marriage. After the death of her first husband, four years into their marriage, Jane then married Archibald Dundas, her half-sister Margaret's husband's brother. The Dundases of Fingask were nearby lairds from Perthshire and, by 1579, were probably heavily involved with King James VI, rather than Queen Mary. Despite this political difference, it is clear that the two families wished to be kin. William and Margaret were contracted to marry and to hold their land in conjunct fee, although Margaret's inherited lands were resigned to her father, with William's consent.[30] In August 1588, William succeeded his father to the lordship and died less than a year later.[31] David Carnegie quickly arranged for his newly widowed daughter, Jane, to marry the second Dundas son and heir to the lairdship of Fingask.

David arranged a similar double marriage when he paid for the tocher of his niece, Margaret, daughter of James. Both Margaret and her cousin, Agnes, married Falconer brothers. The Falconers of Halkerton were a middling landholding family from Angus. The Falconers had originally been the keepers of the king's falcons and hawks and both their surnames and their locale derive from this position.[32] The earliest record of the Falconers was from a small village on the River North Esk, which, by the sixteenth century, was well within the Carnegie circle of influence.[33] As late as 1594, the Carnegies continued to require the traditional marriage *in facie ecclesiae*, or "in face of halie kirk," in their marriage contracts, unlike some reformed families, who had begun to stipulate marriage "in face of Christis congregatione."[34] Agnes was contracted to marry Alexander Falconer on 18 November 1594, "in face

---

[30] *Register of the Great Seal of Scotland*, 5, no. 502, 16 and 1577.

[31] Fraser, *History of the Carnegies*, 1:62.

[32] Jervise, *Memorials of Angus and the Mearns*, 360.

[33] Jervise, *Memorials of Angus and the Mearns*, 360.

[34] Kinnaird Castle, NRAS792/6/4 (18 November 1594). "Marriage Contract" and GD8/352 "Marriage Contract."

of halykirk," and they were married by the following January.[35] Agnes received a much higher tocher of 8800 merks, compared to Margaret's tocher of 3000 merks, to marry the eldest brother, in 1594, but both sums were substantial, even when compared to the dowries of other siblings. The rationale for this lower tocher might have been because Margaret married a younger son or because she was David's niece, rather than his daughter. Margaret married after David's death, but his last will and testament included this 3000-merk payment, provided Margaret listen to the advice of David, the younger, new laird and the counsel of his friends.[36]

These double marriages demonstrate that the Reformation-era unions in the Carnegie family were primarily endogamous and based around the acquisition of specific lands and strengthening of specific local kinship bonds. They were not politically-driven marriages, centred on the Edinburgh court, a strategy which might have enabled David to maximize his ties to other royal advisors. David Carnegie and his father, Robert, both had successful public careers in Edinburgh. They would have had many opportunities to arrange marriages with their colleagues' families, in order to promote their own careers. Instead, the Carnegie's focus was consistently local, concentrating on providing sound marriages for their family members.

After the death of his brother, John, David inherited Kinnaird and with it the responsibility for the family's well being. When David married Jonet Henrison, his third wife, in 1594, the marriage contract was carefully laid out, lest there be negative consequences for David's children.[37] This contract, in particular, shows that David was consistently strategic in his approach to managing his family and property. He agreed to provide Jonet Henrison, already a widow, with a living if he predeceased her. This allowance included land for annual rents and an annual allowance of food and beer. The contract stipulated that in lieu of her guaranteed terce, a third of David's wealth, Jonet would receive 500 merks upon his death. Jonet agreed to these terms, as her signature on the brief pre-nuptial contract makes clear. What is startling is that Jonet would sign away her rights to such substantial wealth, given that David's estate was much wealthier than the allowance of 500 merks would suggest; an inventory of his moveable goods, alone, amounted to 21

---

[35] *Register of the Great Seal of Scotland*, vol. 6, no. 208 and NRAS792/6/5 (26 May 1599). "Marriage Contract."

[36] Fraser, *History of the Carnegies*, 1:69.

[37] Kinnaird Castle, NRAS792/6/4, no. 171 (26 April 1594), "Marriage Contract."

760 merks upon his death, a few years later.[38] The arrangements probably reflect Jonet's poor background and the fact that she had little leverage in the negotiations, which occurred in her hometown of Edinburgh. There was little likelihood that Jonet and David would have children given that Jonet's children, from her first marriage, were already adults and so the challenge to the inheritance rights of David's older children was minimal.

It was not until after this third marriage that David Carnegie's eldest son, David, was contracted to marry, in 1595.[39] The marriage of the younger David was of much greater status than those of his siblings. He married Margaret Lindsay, daughter of Sir David Lindsay of Edzell, who was a Lord of Session, a wealthy local entrepreneur and the son of the Earl of Crawford. The contract drawn up by the fathers of the bride and groom, who were two of the country's leading law experts, was, not surprisingly, the most detailed of all surviving contracts. The marriage contract was made with the consent of John Carnegie, the elder David's brother. This was a shift from the practice followed in the recent marriages of David's children, which had been overseen by David alone. At this point, John must have realised that his brother and nephew would be heirs to Kinnaird Castle and so he oversaw marriage negotiations. It would have been normal for John to have been involved in the marriage of his nieces and nephews all along, since he was the eldest uncle and the laird of Kinnaird, but his brother, David, had gained substantial landholdings in both Angus and Fife and so had taken full charge of his family's legal arrangements.

David continued his negotiations with nearby lairds, including the negotiation of contracts by correspondence. On 6 September 1597, David wrote to his neighbour, Patrick Maule of Panmure, to negotiate a reversion.[40] He wrote that there was an error in the contracts that was repeated not once but four times and so he was unable to amend it himself. He would have had his secretary rewrite the contract, but he was away. Instead, he sent the contract back to be revised. Although there was some delay, while they waited for Patrick's uncle to return to resolve some outstanding debts, Patrick and David remained collegial throughout their negotiations. David's postscript read, "my corn is almaist schorn, therfor ye may cum est ye pleis and chais

---

[38] Fraser, *History of the Carnegies*, 1:68.

[39] Kinnaird Castle, NRAS792/6/4 (8 October 1595). "Marriage Contract."

[40] Fraser, *History of the Carnegies*, 1:60.

pertikis [partridges] and ye sail get yowr reversione than and silver."[41] The Carnegies used their legal expertise to consolidate lands at home and to increase their influence as advisors. Their use of marriages to rearrange properties within their family allowed them to extend their influence on the east coast of Scotland, becoming one of the premier families and, eventually, earls.

In Reformation-era Scotland, other families were behaving very differently in their marriage arrangements. For instance, the Campbells of Glenorchy, a family of relatively equal status to the Carnegies, executed an explicit strategy of local marriage for their younger children but sought progressively higher-status marriages, with distant but powerful families, for the elder children.[42] The Campbell marriages were, for the most part, arranged by their mother and sealed by their father, as revealed in the personal letters of Kathryn Ruthven, the wife of the Sir Colin Campbell of Glenorchy. There is clear evidence in her letters that Kathryn was the primary contact for other families negotiating marriages with the Campbells and that, although Colin was involved in finalising details about money and land transfers, much of the negotiations were conducted by Kathryn herself.[43] The Campbells used a strategy of endogamous marriages for their younger children and exogamous unions for their elder children. This allowed them to maximise their power, both at home in Argyll, as well as across Scotland.

There is no evidence that the Carnegie family practiced a similar strategy. Two letters remain from the very end of the sixteenth century, both related to land reversions. One was written by an Angus neighbour, Maule of Panmure and the other was part of the correspondence between the younger David Carnegie and his brother-in-law. These letters show that David played the primary role in the negotiations, even within his nuclear family and there is no evidence that the mothers of the Carnegies took a major role in marriage negotiations.

The Campbells of Glenorchy serve as ideal comparators for the Carnegies because of their status and their moderate landholdings. Neither

---

[41] Fraser, *History of the Carnegies*, 1:60.

[42] Dawson, *Campbell Letters 1559–1583*, 28–34.

[43] Dawson, *Campbell Letters 1559–1583*, 29.

laird was a peer during the sixteenth century, but both rose to earldoms during the seventeenth century. The earldoms of Southesk and Northesk were created for the Carnegies and the earldoms of Breadalbane and Holland were created for John Campbell of Glenorchy. These lordships were geographically removed from court in Edinburgh, but were close enough that the lairds could visit when necessary. The Campbells were located in Breadalbane, in Argyll, near the west coast of Scotland. The Carnegies were in Angus, on the east coast. Both lordships were nearly equidistant from Edinburgh and the royal court. Finlarig Castle, a Campbell centre near Killin, on the southern shore of Loch Tay, is about 115 kilometres from Edinburgh Castle while Brechin is about 130 kilometres north of Edinburgh.

The two kin groups were also aligned politically throughout the religious troubles of the 1560s and 1570s, despite major factors that might have pulled each family into the opposing camp. Both families were members of the Protestant Party of the Revolution, in 1559–60, that supported the Reformation. This was partly due to religious leanings and partly due to pressure from powerful Protestant magnates, such as the Earl of Argyll.[44] By 1565, however, both the Campbells of Glenorchy and the Carnegies of Kinnaird had defected from the Protestant-led rebel group to join the Queen's Party, supporting Mary Queen of Scots, remaining loyal even though they were under pressure to defect. Both Robert Carnegie and his son John continued to show Protestant inclinations, but they fought under the powerful Catholic Gordon earls of Huntly.[45] Moreover, the Campbells of Glenorchy, a minor branch of the Campbells of Argyll, were under substantial pressure from Archibald Campbell, the Earl of Argyll, to defect to the Protestant rebels.[46] There were many different factors that could dictate loyalties during the Reformation including religious conviction, kinship and geography. Adherents of Queen Mary were far flung and generally associated through close ties of kinship.[47] Despite similarities in religion, power and politics, the Carnegie marriage negotiations differed from those of the Campbells. The Carnegies pursued a singular strategy of close-knit marriages with neighbours and kin that allowed them to become powerful figures on the east coast of Scotland in both Angus and the Mearns.

---

[44] Donaldson, *All the Queen's Men*, 41, 161 and 64.

[45] Donaldson, *All the Queen's Men*, 70 and 110.

[46] Dawson, *Campbell Letters*, 6 and 50 and 128.

[47] Donaldson, *All the Queen's Men*, 3.

Even when contacts were agreed between the Carnegies and Scottish magnates, were not to arrange marriages. The Campbells of Glenorchy sought out marriages for their eldest children far afield from their land base in order to develop and extend the political strength of their kin group. The Carnegies, in contrast, repeatedly married into the same local families and thus built a power base in Angus, that eventually stretched into the Mearns to the north, Forfar and Fife to the south and Perthshire to the west. The Carnegies' power at court did not lie in their extensive web of powerful kin, but instead in their skill as lawyers who were assigned important local and international diplomatic tasks for the monarchy. As their local power grew, so too did their role at court, until they were promoted to the rank of peers.

The Carnegie marriage strategy resulted in the family's rise in Scotland's social hierarchy. This, combined with David's rise as a legal advisor at court, resulted in the elevation of David junior, to the Earldom of Southesk, in 1633. This increase in status helped the family's marriage prospects in the long run and the family's marriage strategy later became focused on wide-ranging aristocratic matches. This promotion to the aristocracy was not, however, the result of careful social climbing, facilitated by marrying into the most powerful and influential noble families. Instead, in the sixteenth century, the focus was on endogamous marriages that were advantageous locally, those that gained the family vast swathes of land and prominence within Angus, itself. This was a different route to gain power at court.

The Reformation was not a catalyst for change in the Carnegie marriage strategy. Instead, it was the younger David's promotion to earl that altered how the family operated and substantially extended their marriage network. The Carnegie family is representative of an understudied segment of society that held status at court but did *not* use the royal court as a hunting ground for marriages for their children.

University of Guelph

Cited Works

Manuscript Sources

Edinburgh. National Archives of Scotland (NAS)
GD45/16/682 "Marriage Contract."
SP8/7 "Marriage Contract."
GD26/7/392 "Marriage Contract."
GD8/352 "Marriage Contract."

Kinnaird Castle, Brechin. Southesk Charter Collection.
NRAS792/5/1, no. 66 (1509/1510), "Marriage Contract."
NRAS792/5/1, no. 137 (1568, October 3), "Marriage Contract."
NRAS792/6/3 (9 June 1585), "Aquittance."
NRAS792/6/3 (26 March 1589), "Marriage Contract."
NRAS792/6/3, no. 162 (25 April 1590), "Marriage Contract."
NRAS792/6/3, no. 163 (25 April 1590), "Marriage Contract."
NRAS792/6/4 (18 November 1594), "Marriage Contract."
NRAS792/6/4, no. 171 (26 April 1594), "Marriage Contract"
NRAS792/6/4 (8 October 1595), "Marriage Contract."
NRAS792/6/5 (26 May 1599), "Marriage Contract."
NRAS792/7/7 (8 September 1549), "Marriage Contract"

Printed Sources

Brown, James Cowie. *An Introductory Survey of the Sources and Literature of Scots Law.* Vol. 1. Edinburgh Stair Society, 1936.
Dawson, Jane E.A. and Scottish History Society. *Campbell Letters 1559–1583.* Series 5, vol 10. Edinburgh: Lothian Print, for the Scottish History Society, 1997.
Donaldson, Gordon. *All the Queen's Men: Power and Politics in Mary Stewart's Scotland.* London: Batsford Academic and Educational, 1983.
Fraser, William. *History of the Carnegies, Earls of Southesk and of Their Kindred.* 2 vols. Edinburgh: T. and A. Constable, 1867.
Jervise, Andrew. *Memorials of Angus and the Mearns.* Edinburgh: Adam and Charles Black, 1861.

Mosley, Charles. *Burke's Peerage, Baronetage & Knightage, Clan Chiefs, Scottish Feudal Barons*. Ed. Charles Mosley. Stokesley: Burke's Peerage & Gentry, 2003. 107th ed.

The Records of the Parliaments of Scotland to 1707. Eds. K.M. Brown, et al. St Andrews, 2007–2010. http://www.rps.ac.uk/trans/A1567/12/15. no. A1567/12/15.

Registrum Magni Sigilli Regum Scotorum. The Register of the Great Seal of Scotland, 1306–1668. Eds. J. Maitland Thomson, J.H. Stevenson and James Balfour Paul. 11 vols. Edinburgh: General Register House, 1882–1914.

Rogers, Charles. *Memorials of the Scottish Families of Strachan and Wise*. Edinburgh: MacFarlane and Erskine, 1877.

Spalding Club Miscellany. Ed. John Stuart. Aberdeen: William Bennett, 1809.

Marriage Strategies and Oligarchy in Early Modern Bologna

Mauro Carboni

The intricate meshing of family and government in Italian cities is best captured by Berengo's brilliant observation that the family was the real protagonist of early modern Italian urban history.[1] Recent literature has highlighted the "reciprocal dynamic of state and family," the constant interplay between public and private, the uncertain boundaries and the tensions between family strategies and government policies, at the local and central level. Strategies of consolidation favoured a twin evolution, leading to both a concentration of power in the hands of oligarchical groups, and to greater social and political stability. As their grip on power solidified, patrician families displayed remarkable ingenuity in devising strategies to maintain their political and social primacy. Ties of kinship shaped ruling groups, supporting the political and social pre-eminence of élite families through lineage and marriage, which were organizing principles in both politics and society. Lineage served as a primary means to preserve political power over generations, while matrimonial alliances underlay personal as well as political relationships, renewed through the constant circulation of women and dowries. Together they were able to protect family interests, to preserve family wealth and to guard family representation in office.[2]

In exploring the politics of marriage in early modern Bologna, it will be argued that patrician families made their strategies conform to the new oligarchical power structure, adopting a twin civic and class endogamy. In the main, nuptial bonds were designed to protect status and keep wealth within a closed circle of families, renewing or reinforcing, generation after generation, inter-family cooperation and alliances. Yet, the high level of endogamy was moderated through a prudent opening to outsiders, which suited the ambitions and agnatic interests of individual families.

---

[1] Berengo, "Il Cinquecento," 493.

[2] Romano, *Patricians and Popolani*, 152–158 ; Chittolini, "Il 'privato', il 'pubblico', lo Stato," 553–589; Molho, *Marriage Alliance*, 1–18; Benadusi, "Rethinking the State," 157–178; Chojnacki, "Daughters and Oligarchs," 63–86.

Sixteenth-century Bologna can be aptly regarded as a success story in replacing the last late medieval factional *Signoria*, under the Bentivoglio, with a stable and closely-knit oligarchical regime: the Bolognese so called *governo misto* — mixed government — established a system of collaboration between the papal overlord, represented by a residing Cardinal Legate, and the city *Reggimento* or Senate, staffed by councillors, named by the pontiff, but, in fact, chosen from a small pool of élite families. In the absence of a Venetian style *serrata*, shutting the access to newcomers, the Bolognese patriciate was not defined clearly in law, but came, nonetheless, to be a recognisable social group, defined by a *de facto* monopoly of the city's political representation.[3]

Despite internal competition and endemic vendettas, a largely hereditary ruling class of officeholders consolidated its ranks and assumed a recognisable aspect which it conserved unchanged till the waning of the eighteenth century. The collective pre-eminence and magnificence projected by these families was graven in stone within and without the city walls, in the senatorial palaces and villas. A sumptuous urban residence and a suburban villa became the required "architectural outfit" in order to belong to, or to be admitted to, the patrician élite. The diffusion and the monumental character of these mansions not only displayed the patriciate's opulence and power, but betrayed a collective desire of eternity, tenaciously pursued and shared.

The papal conquest of 1506 restored Rome's lordship and expelled the ruling Bentivoglio family, which found shelter under the wings of the Este's eagle in nearby Ferrara, but the positions and privileges of families associated to the doomed regime were, in the main, respected. Successive popes aimed to strengthen their grip by relocating authority and favoured the formation of an aristocratic élite as exclusive agents in Bolognese administration. From the outset the composition of the new Senate, summoned by Pope Julius II, reveals a remarkable effort at civic reconciliation: of the thirty-four families whose members had staffed the office of the *Riformatori*, between 1466 and 1506, twenty-three managed to retain their post, while an additional four saw their standing restored shortly afterwards. To these twenty-seven houses confirmed in their political capacity, others, previously sidelined or exiled, were added. In the main they were political opponents rather than newcomers. As a matter of fact, *case* such as the Pepoli, the Isolani and the Bolognini were equal in antiquity, wealth and influence to houses associated to the ousted *Signoria*.

---

[3] De Benedictis, *Repubblica per contratto*, 107–136.

Julius II and his successors were careful not to replace one faction with another. The new Senate — doubled in size, from twenty-one to forty members, and then further expanded to fifty — aimed at ending factional strife by reducing fierce clan competition and by promoting the collective power of an oligarchy of aristocratic families. Even the norms that regulated attire and behaviour aimed at projecting the image of an impersonal magistracy of wise men through the prohibition of any sign of individual distinction, the prescription of uniforms and the respect of rigid ceremonial rules of precedence based on seniority of service. Contrary to the traditional reading given by local historiography, the Senate's expansion, from 40 to 50 members, introduced by Pope Sixtus V in 1590, can be regarded as an update of, rather than a deviation from, Julius II's strategy. Renewed papal intervention supported and directed rather than obstructed oligarchy consolidation. As a matter of fact, increasing the number of senatorial posts had no adverse impact on the Senate's authority and made it easier for patrician lineages to retain, or to reclaim, their ancestral seat, reducing tensions and easing inter-family competition, which had dangerously flared up again in the age of Pope Gregory XIII (1572–1585), with the Pepoli and the Malvezzi acting as ringleaders.

For all practical purposes, it was a further step in the direction of making senatorial appointments *de facto*, if not *de iure*, hereditary. Indeed among the ten new senators picked in 1590 only one, the marquis Girolamo Boschetti, belonged to a *casa* which had not been awarded a senatorial post in the past. Of more immediate concern, the new nominees helped to restore the fragile internal political balance of the *Reggimento*: during the reign of Gregory XIII, representation of older lineages, in power during the Bentivoglio's regime, had dropped to a low of 14 (out of 40) — 35% — from a high of 23, in 1513 — 57.5%. The lion's share of new seats (7) went precisely to representatives of these older families, bringing their share to a reassuring 42% (21 out of 50).[4]

The closure of Bologna's highest magistracy was achieved informally. When seats became vacant upon the death of a councillor, they passed to the next of kin. In the absence of suitable candidates from the patriline, either lateral relatives or members of families already represented in the Senate, were routinely preferred. As a result, 590 office-holders, belonging to just ninety-three houses, were selected during the *governo misto* two-hundred-

---

[4] Carboni, "La formazione di una élite di governo," 14–16.

and-ninety-year history. In addition, Senate participation grew even more elitist over time. If, in the sixteenth century, the mobility ratio — that is to say, the likelihood of seat turn over — was a moderate 41.2%. In the subsequent eighty-five years, despite an increase in available seats, the senatorial mobility ratio more than halved, dropping to just 19.4%. In other words, from the mid-sixteenth century to the late seventeenth century, a senatorial family's chances to retain its seat increased from slightly less than 60% to over 80%.

Disciplining Marriage

Spousal strategies and connections, established through marriage, mirrored the evolution of the political power structure. The stormy political life of late medieval Bologna had induced families to seek a measure of protection in intense matrimonial exchanges. A wide demographic base, and the establishment of a wide web of cognatic ties, were crucial to protect a family's political fortunes. The risk of this was the fragmentation of patrimony. As factional politics gave way to oligarchy, an opposite strategy of marriage set in: the horizontal bonds of *parentado* lost ground to the vertical bonds of the *casato*. A stricter patrilineal structure called for endogamy and marriage limitations. A carefully disciplined network of closely-knit matrimonial relations guaranteed cohesion and helped to consolidate social standing and political monopoly. No less important, endogamy held the promise of reciprocity over time: generation after generation it ensured that wealth circulated within the same close network of families, protecting the patriciate's collective patrimony. Marriage limitations compounded endogamy. Contrary to earlier patterns, in which élite families sought to marry the most children, Bolognese aristocratic families began to introduce severe restrictions on marriage, to preserve family fortunes from dispersal.[5]

The heavy demands of tradition, status and patrimony provided the moral compass that guided marriage strategies and dictated men's and women's fate. Intent upon shoring up family fortunes, most patriarchs resorted to *fideicommissum* (entails) in order to consolidate property, and to place strict limits on ever rising dowry payments, in order to prevent the alienation of patrimonial assets.[6] The heightened sense of lineage, evidenced

---

[5] Pomata, "Family and Gender," 71–72.

[6] For a fresh and thorough discussion of this topic, see Colonaci, *Dietro lo scudo incantato*, 19–58.

by these provisions, had the serious drawback of placing marriage beyond the reach of most children. For instance, the Gozzadini, Magnani, Malvezzi and Ranuzzi recorded forty-nine marriages, between 1525 and 1550. The number of marriages declined to thirty-three in the last quarter of the sixteenth century, and dropped to just sixteen in the last quarter of the seventeenth century. Whereas about four out of five adults, belonging to the generations born in the first half of the sixteenth century, married, successive cohorts saw their matrimonial chances diminish progressively. In the second half of the seventeenth century, just two out of five patricians, who reached adulthood, could expect to marry.

The exclusionary forces of the marriage market discriminated heavily against cadets and women.[7] Since children could marry only if they received adequate property, impartible inheritance practices favoured one son over all others. Only the untimely death of a designated son, or his inability to produce a male heir, could change the celibate destiny of younger sons. If anything, daughters were worse off because the burden of marital payment fell squarely on the bride's family. For women, one of the fundamental steps in arranging a marriage was the constitution of a dowry, which indicated the bride worth and was the main signifier of the family's standing in society. In addition, the scarcity of suitable grooms drove up the size of dowries, generating the inflationary pressure well known to historians of Renaissance Florence and Venice, where oligarchical practices had already set in in the fifteenth century.[8]

Mirroring the relatively late consolidation of an oligarchical regime, dowry inflation had little impact in Bologna before the middle of the sixteenth century. The rise was sharp afterwards: the cost of dowering a young patrician woman increased, from around 4,000 lire in the 1550s to between 10,000 and 12,000 lire in the 1590s, to more than 50,000 lire by the middle of the seventeenth century. As dowries soared, becoming a major financial investment, patriarchs scrutinized ever more carefully the potential

---

[7] Entails provisions and drastic marriage limitations affected both daughters and younger sons, whose destinies show remarkable similarities. Chojnacki, "Dowries and Kinsmen," 571–600; Pomata, "Family and Gender," 78–81.

[8] Molho, *Marriage Alliance*, 310; Chojnacki, "Gender and Oligarchs," 75–84; Sperling, *Convents and the Body Politic*, 1–17. A significant rise in dowries has been also documented in sixteenth-century Castile: Casey, *The History of the Family*, 82–83; Casey, *Family and Community*, 103–106.

advantages of matrimonial alliances and limited the number of marriages, consigning most daughters to a religious profession.

This novel approach is best illustrated by the painstakingly elaborate will, drafted in 1604, by senator Lorenzo Magnani. Protection of the patrimony and elevation of the lineage were Lorenzo's priorities. Strict guidelines determined the order of succession, under all possible eventualities, and precise *fideicommissum* provisions locked the family wealth, placing patrimonial assets beyond the whims of future generations. In addition, Lorenzo left detailed instructions to his heir, Ludovico, on how to meet patriarchal responsibilities and obligations towards women in the family. Upon the birth of a daughter, Lorenzo recommended his successor to begin to set aside and to invest a fixed amount from the annual income from the family's estates, for ten consecutive years, and to use the accumulated sum as a dowry. However, Lorenzo was careful to point out that dotal saving should be proportionate to annual available income, and he was explicit in forbidding the alienation of the family patrimony, which was intended to serve the lineage. Payments to daughters could not come at the expense of the assets destined to future generations of male heirs.[9]

Conflicting Imperatives

Marriage limitation was accompanied by an increase in the number of upper class women who renounced the world and took the veil. Nunneries were turned into aristocratic sanctuaries. The phenomenon of high monachization rates among aristocratic women was commonplace in sixteenth-century Italian cities. Equally high ratios have been documented in Florence and in Venice, where up to three-fourths of all nuns came from the ranks of the patriciate. If anything, the rise of convent population there was more precocious.[10]

Although a surge in female spiritual calling and religiosity, in the decades following the Council of Trent, should not be ruled out, the steep rise in monachization rates among upper class women was driven principally by worldly concerns. Soaring dowry prices induced most aristocratic fathers to limit the damage by concentrating dowry expenditures on one

---

[9] AMG, Instrumenti Magnani, 17, n. 35.

[10] Brown, "Monache a Firenze," 126–131; Sperling, *Convents and the Body Politic*, 26–29; Laven, *Virgins of Venice*, 22–42; Chojnacki, *Daughters and Oligarchs*, 71; Strocchia, *Nuns and Nunneries*, 28–38.

or two daughters, dispatching the others to the convent. The economic motivations propelling the rise of "vocations" were widely acknowledged by contemporaries, who justified this development by pointing to the distress of patrician families, torn between the Scylla of dowry inflation and the Charybdis of female misalliances. In Bologna, the use of convents as sanctuaries for unmarried noblewomen was a choice upheld defiantly, in the early 1560s, by a prominent member of the patriciate itself, Giovanni Boccadiferro. In an essay addressed to the city bishop, Giovanni Campeggi, Boccadiferro defined local cloisters as the precinct of those who could not be married off ("il ridotto di quelle che maritar non puonsi") and called for greater civic involvement in their administration because of their eminent social and political functions.[11]

Since, for élite families, the spiritual dowries required to enter a convent represented a significant savings, almost 90% compared to matrimonial ones, the religious profession provided tempting and convenient relief to families anxious to place their women honourably. The response of the brothers, Alessandro and Giulio Cesare Amorini, to the problem of placing their thirteen daughters was exemplary: between 1580 and 1600, they arranged the marriage of four — Erminia, Olimpia, Laura and Lodovica — providing each one with a dowry of 9,000 lire, but they then placed the remaining nine daughters in six Bolognese convents, at less than one fourth of the cost, only 2,000 lire.[12] Between 1490 and 1633, the number of nunneries in Bologna rose from 20 to 29 and the overall population of convents more than doubled. Just between 1574 and 1631, the number of women placed in cloisters increased 50%, growing from 1,758 to 2,624. The proportion of nuns in the population of Bolognese women rose from approximately 5.4%, in 1570, to almost 10.5%, in 1631, but among these the proportion of patrician women was much higher. According to Gabriella Zarri, in 1574, there were 5.5 coriste (choir nun) for each conversa (servant nun), indicating that nuns from upper class families made up over 80% of the female monastic population.[13]

---

[11] Fanti, introduction to Abiti e lavori, 20–31.

[12] ASB, Salina-Amorini, Strumenti e scritture, 115. Bona and Alenia joined the monastery of St. Lodovico and Elena, Ottavia and Antonia entered the nunnery of St. Vitale and Agricola and Pantasilea took the veil in St. Bernardino, Albinea professed in St. Agostino, Caterina entered St. Margherita, Lucilla and Florinda joined the community of St. Naborre and Felice.

[13] Bellettini, La popolazione di Bologna, 47, 61; Beloch, Storia della popolazione, 244–247; Zarri, Recinti, 130–137. My own estimates, based on available convent records, listing

Despite the burden of sacrifice imposed upon them for the welfare of their families, remarkably few women joined Arcangela Tarabotti in denouncing paternal tyranny.[14] Women's silent obedience conformed to the submissiveness prescribed by patriarchal ideology and was, in itself, a clear indication of the patriarchs' ability to impose strict discipline. It signalled, also, the daughters' acceptance of their obligations to the family, and of the ancillary role assigned to their gender.

Strategies aimed to preserve wealth and status were good for the dynastic family, but had an adverse impact on the demographics of the patriciate. With the notable exception of the Gozzadini, who have left a wealth of family memoirs, Bolognese patricians did not write extensively about themselves, and demographic data are insufficient. Genealogies, however, allow us to gauge important facts about family life. Following the genealogies compiled by the local chroniclers, Dolfi and Carrati, it is possible to gather basic information about 68 patrician families.[15] Calculations based on their data indicate a 40% drop in the population of patrician houses in roughly less than a century. Between the third quarter of the sixteenth century and the third quarter of the seventeenth century, the demographic strength of these families declined from roughly 2,600 adult members to less than 1,600. By the end of the seventeenth century, about one senatorial family out of five (20 out of 93) faced the grim prospect of either the disappearance of the senatorial lineage or the extinction of the whole house.

The agnatic obsession of transmitting name, patrimony and rank through the male line had to be reconciled with the need to renew or extend the ties of cognation and affinity, through marriage alliances and the exchange of women and dowries. As the oligarchy solidified and horizontal ties became fewer and dearer, patriarchs strove to strike a careful balance between the conflicting imperatives of protecting the assets of the lineage and of participating in the web of nuptial alliances. Failure to protect family wealth would spell disaster through social demotion, while a shrinking demographic base could lead to dynastic extinction. Both outcomes were dreaded but the

---

nuns with their family names, confirm the high level of aristocratization reached by Bolognese nunneries: in St. Agnese (1576), 86% of nuns were from noble families, in St. Mattia (1581), 85%, in St. Vitale (1624 and 1648), 70%, in St. Agnese (1634), 70%, in St. Elena (1647), 44%, in Jesus and Mary (1648), 87%.See Carboni, *Le doti della povertà*, 55–56.

[14] Sperling, *Convents and the Body Politic*, 31–35.

[15] BCAB, ms 698/2, Carrati, *Alberi genealogici delle famiglie di Bologna*; Dolfi, *Cronologia delle famiglie bolognesi*.

preservation of wealth and honour took precedence. In other words, status and honour were dearer than life itself.

Cronos' Syndrome

Civic loyalty, exchanges and solidarities among peers were the cornerstone on which both the power of the urban patriciate and the autonomy of the city rested. One mirrored and sustained the other. Senators' matrimonial choices reveal how civic and group identity found expression in the preference for marriages within the city walls and alliances with peers. Of the 428 senators who held office between 1506 and 1700, 380 contracted at least one marriage: over two thirds married within their ranks and when they did not, their local orientation stood out. In over four fifths of documented unions, senators married local women.

Tab. 1 Senators and their spouses[16]

	Number of senators	Number of repre- sented *Case*	Number of new *Case*	Patrician spouses	Other Bolognese spouses	Number of Bolognese spouses	% Bolognese spouses	Foreign spouses	% Foreign spouses
1506–49	118	53		90	19	109	86.5	17	13.5
1550–89	77	50	15	53	14	67	84.8	12	15.2
1590–1645	136	61	11	84	22	106	76.8	32	23.2
1646–1700	97	59	7	65	14	79	80.6	19	19.4
Totals	428			292	69	361	81.8	80	18.2

Overall, the matrimonial choices of Bolognese senators, summarized in Table 1, show a remarkably high degree of civic (81.8%), and social (68.2%), endogamy with the latter placed significantly in between the endogamy found by Anthony Molho in Renaissance Florence (55%), and that documented

---

[16] Guidicini, *I Riformatori dello Stato di Libertà*; Carboni, "La formazione di una élite di governo."

by Volker Hunecke and Jutta Sperling, in early modern Venice (75–80%).[17] Despite the incorporation of the city into the wider structure of the Papal States, the matrimonial market remained municipal and rarely crossed the medieval city walls. As in other Italian urban contexts, endogamy was part of a larger strategy, designed to preserve political and social primacy, by perpetuating a municipal body politic: it favoured cohesion and it strengthened group identity. Moreover, it worked to protect the economic wellbeing of the élite, consolidating and maintaining patrimonies within the circuit of the patrician houses.

Few lineages privileged exogamous matrimonial alliances, and such choices indicated fundamental shifts in political strategy. Indeed, the frequency of external bonds was often a signal of progressive estrangement from Bolognese affairs. After the pontificate of Gregory XIII, the Boncompagni leaned progressively towards Rome, although they held on to their senatorial seat. Marriages reflected a strategy which, by mid-seventeenth century, would lead to the family's political relocation. A similar route was followed by the Ludovisi, who, in 1672, renounced their senatorial post: of the seven marriages contracted by Ludovisi's senators, between 1506 and 1672, only the first three were with local noblewomen.[18]

The families that formed the patriciate constituted an exclusive, but far from monolithic, universe. Lineages of different origins and wealth coexisted. Average behaviours are, therefore, likely to conceal different strategies and approaches among families which shared public responsibilities. Most established families went to great lengths to protect their wealth. In order to prevent fragmentation and dispersal of assets, patriarchs imposed severe marriage limitations on their children. Pursued over several generations, this strategy made the implosion of the demographically more fragile lineages a statistical certainty. Ironically, the Poeti, the Rossi and the Campeggi died out before 1700, in the desperate attempt to keep their agnatic patrimony intact.

Admission to the senatorial élite was rare, required long-term family planning, recognition and acceptance by established families and uncommon cunning in order to take advantage of favourable circumstances. "Fortune" and "virtue," qualities almost obsessively celebrated by the aristocratic ideology of the age, were the prerequisites of every success story. They were

---

[17] Molho, *Marriage Alliance*, 14; Hunecke, "Matrimonio e demografia," 269–319; Sperling, *Convents and the Body Politic*, 19.

[18] Carboni, "La formazione di una élite di governo," 24–25.

needed to seize the right opportunity, as well as to turn it into a permanent gain. Vibrant emerging families made the most effective use of horizontal connections to enhance their status through the acquisition of influential in-laws.

The ascent of the Malvasia, in the sixteenth century, and the spectacular rise of the Spada and of the Davia, in the seventeenth, offer paradigmatic examples of the skills needed to introduce a new family into the patrician consortium. In 1554, Pope Julius III appointed Cornelio Malvasia, a prominent banker, to the senatorial seat left vacant by the death (without male heirs) of Filippo Guastavillani. The Malvasia were a rising family, wealthy and already well connected, but these qualifications would have hardly sufficed without papal favour. The seat was awarded by Julius III to Cornelio, in recognition of the generous financial backing he had received from the banker, at the end of his tenure as legate in Bologna. The opportunity seized by Cornelio Malvasia was the loss to another local money dealer, Matteo Amorini, whose decision to deny a personal loan to the future Pope proved disastrously short sighted. In spite of the family's standing and connections the Amorini, they lost their chance to enter the patriciate. If admission to the Senate was the result of a fortunate combination of exceptional events, the Malvasia wasted no time to consolidate their gains, monopolizing, for almost 150 years, their assigned seat. Careful matrimonial alliances firmly tied the Malvasia to some of the main patrician lineages: Cornelio's brother, Costanzo, married Paola Campeggi, his son, Giulio, married Isabella Castelli, while Cornelio's daughter, Isabella, became the spouse of senator, Giovanni Girolamo Grati.[19]

Natives of the town of Brisighella, in the Romagna, and recipients of lucrative appointments in the Papal administration, the Spada experienced a dramatic rise in Bologna, thanks to Cardinal Legate Bernardino Spada (1627–1631). Bernardino's skilful manoeuvring laid the groundwork for his brother's, Giacomo Filippo, aggregation to the Bolognese patriciate and Bernardino's close friendship with Pope Urban VIII won a senatorial seat for Giacomo Filippo's son, Gregorio, in 1638. Bernardino's hand was instrumental in planning a suitably magnificent and lavish matrimonial campaign, designed to provide the Spada with connections adequate for their long-term social and political ambitions. Gregorio married Camilla Fantuzzi, while Gregorio's three sisters and two cousins, equipped with dowries in

---

[19] Fornasari, "Credito e banca," 29–42.

excess of 50,000 lire, linked the Spada to four prestigious senatorial lineages: Francesca married the senator, Camillo Bargellini, Teresa and Laura wed Giovanni and Ugo Giuseppe Pepoli, while the daughters of Gregorio's uncle, Francesco, Daria and Aurelia, married respectively count Paride Maria Grassi and senator Andrea Ghisilardi.[20]

The ascent of the Davia was even more remarkable, and required greater ingenuity and financial depth. Pietro Antonio Davia, a rare example of a seventeenth-century self-made-man, capped his spectacular economic success story by plotting the family's inclusion into the Bolognese aristocracy. The means was a matrimonial campaign adequate to his daring social and political ambitions. In 1648, Pietro's son, Giovanni Battista, married Porzia Ghisilieri, a woman from a most prestigious lineage. In order to establish ties with the Ghisilieri, Pietro Antonio was not only willing to accept a moderate dowry of just 16,000 lire, but even to add a personal gift of 28,000 lire to the prospective daughter-in-law. Pietro's campaign to connect the Davia with established élite families was completed by the unions he managed to secure for his daughters. Margherita married count Alessandro Fava (with a dowry of 50,000 lire) while Silveria, in 1660, married senator Bartolomeo Manzoli, with a top-dowry of 100,000 lire. Pietro's ambitious quest was fulfilled, in 1672, with his nephew's, Virgilio, aggregation to the Senate. To this felicitous outcome contributed Virgilio's uncle, Giovanni Antonio, recent recipient of a cardinal's hat.[21]

The nearly prohibitive cost for emerging families to forge lasting ties with ancient élite families, provided the latter with a protective shield that could be pierced only through a massive infusion of new wealth, which went to strengthen the older lineages. Endogamy did not just consolidate social cohesion, it worked to capture new wealth and to keep the patrimony of families that were dying, within the circle of the oligarchy. Dominant families stood to gain the most from the practice, and were careful to nurture both a city-wide network of spousal relations and a prudent opening to outsiders. It was the ancient families, active in Bolognese politics at least since the thirteenth century, that proved remarkably able to dominate both the oligarchical marriage market and the political arena. In addition to the Malvezzi, dominant roles were, in fact, played out by the Bentivoglio, the

---

[20] Evangelisti, "Bernardino Spada legato," 132–134; Casanova, "Per uno studio della nobiltà pontificia," 43–60; Casanova, *Gentilhuomini ecclesiastici*, 173–203.

[21] Miretti, *I Davia*.

Pepoli, the Orsi, the Fantuzzi and the Gozzadini. Perhaps their past of factional ringleaders induced the patriarchs of these houses to be more cautious in downsizing their families and in reducing the reach of their connections. In addition, greater demographic strength and deeper pockets allowed these houses to play an ambitious power game, casting a city-wide web of connections that placed them in a position to benefit from the demographic and financial difficulties that beset weaker lineages. By the mid-eighteenth century, the Malvezzi had annexed the name and patrimony of eight families, the Bentivoglio and the Pepoli incorporated three, the Fantuzzi and the Orsi two each.

It is useful to examine more closely the marriage strategies of the Malvezzi, one of the largest and most powerful patrician houses in Bologna. The matrimonial policy pursued by the Malvezzi was designed to cast a vast web of nuptial ties that proved remarkably effective at both projecting the house's leadership and at expanding the house's patrimony. On the one hand, competition for prestige involved in the exchange of women was used skilfully by the Malvezzi, who exploited hypergamic tendencies to come out ahead in the constant giving and taking of dowries: in the second quarter of the seventeenth century, Anna Maria Malvezzi brought to senator Girolamo Albergati a relatively moderate dowry of 20,000 lire, while her cousin Virgilio Malvezzi netted a dowry of 75,000 lire from his wife, countess Caterina Roverelli.[22] On the other hand, Malvezzi men were able to take advantage of the pending extinction of a number of prominent male lines by contracting unions with women who were heiresses of their families' patrimony: from the mid-seventeenth to mid-eighteenth centuries, the Malvezzi succeeded in annexing the coats of arms and ancestral assets of three distinguished civic families: the Locatelli, Lombardi and Leoni, and in absorbing five patrician lineages: the Campeggi, Angelelli, Bonfioli, Lupari and Ranuzzi. By 1750, the Malvezzi had also managed to win over the senatorial posts of Angelelli and Bonfioli, adding them to their ancestral seat.

A perfect example is provided by the marriage, in 1676, of Matteo Malvezzi (1646–1737) to Maria Francesca, daughter and last descendant of senator Tommaso Campeggi. The vast assets of the Campeggi, the splendid family mansion, the fief of Dozza, together with the obligation and the privilege to bear the Campeggi coat of arms, went to Emilio Malvezzi (1688–1767), the couple's second born, while Malvezzi's patrimonial assets were passed to

---

[22] ASB, Malvezzi-Lupari, *Carte d'amministrazione*, 314; Albergati, *Miscellanea*, 1.

the eldest brother, Antonio (1686–1712) and his offspring. The marriage of Ippolito Malvezzi to Lucrezia, sole daughter of Agostino Locatelli, paved the way for Malvezzi's acquisition of the name and the properties of the Locatelli. In 1662, Galeazzo Malvezzi claimed the name and ancestral patrimony of his mother, Ginevra Lombardi Barbieri. In the early decades of the eighteenth century, Giuseppe Ercole Malvezzi received the coat of arms and assets of his mother, Maria Caterina Leoni, and his uncle, Vincenzo Leoni. To be sure, the Malvezzi had plenty of competition in their quest for advantageous matches that held the promise of attracting into the orbit of the patriciate the assets of notable *cittadino* families. At times, this resulted in long and costly inter-family litigations: after the death without male issue of Filippo Ballatini, four senatorial houses, the Cospi, Fantuzzi, Legnani and Marsili, laid conflicting claims to Filippo's considerable patrimony.[23]

Participating in two lineages, and having obligations to both, could place married women in an ambiguous position of conflicting loyalties. Yet, in the main, Malvezzi women were disciplined agents in the Malvezzi agnatic power-game. Dorotea Malvezzi (1622–1691) provides an excellent example of loyalty to her lineage: married, in 1645, to senator Angelo Maria Angelelli, she became a widow in 1689. In the absence of male issue, she piloted the name and patrimony of her acquired family, the Angelelli, into the hands of her nephew, Nerio, son of Dorotea's brother, Lucio.

Women could be precious internal re-connectors, whenever a line of the lineage risked extinction and the patrimony was in danger of dispersal. Matches of this nature, where one might marry a first, second or third degree cousin, were often within the prohibited degrees. However, the Church regularly granted dispensation and patrician families frequently used this provision. By taking such measures, lineages on the brink of extinction could be revived and assets carefully preserved within the house. To keep the patrimonial integrity of the Ca' Granda branch, in 1516, the only daughter of Piriteo Malvezzi, Livia, married her third degree cousin, Ercole. In 1640, it was the turn of the surviving daughter of senator Francesco Pirro, Maria Violante, to marry count Sigismondo Malvezzi, a fourth degree cousin. The match restored the unity of the Ca' Granda branch, blunted hostile litigations and prevented patrimonial losses. A century later, a double marriage strengthened the intra-family ties between the Ca' Granda and Portico Buio lineages. As a matter of course, the Malvezzi were not alone in resorting

---

[23] ASB, Marsili, *Strumenti e scritture*, 175.

to intra-family marriages to protect agnatic assets. Odoardo Pepoli twice married first-degree cousins, Maria and Vittoria, in order to prevent the dispersal of family assets. In a double marriage spectacularly celebrated by the brush of Lavinia Fontana, Camillo and Annibale Gozzadini married their third degree cousins, Laudomia and Ginevra, daughters of senator Ulisse Gozzadini, who had died without a male heir.[24]

As elsewhere in early modern Italy, the politics of marriage among the Bolognese élite was affected by a twin Cronos' syndrome. On the one hand, patriarchs protected status and wealth by sacrificing their children, and by wasting their family's demographic potential; on the other hand, the oligarchical system tended both to stifle mobility and draw wealth upwards, restricting the circulation of brides to a limited pool of grooms of similar status. This facilitated the accumulation of wealth, honour and reproductive capacity at the very upper echelons of the élite, with the result of rendering the entire structure both stable and, yet, increasingly fragile. Conservatism was a mixed blessing: the main wealth preserving practices — *fideicommissum* (entail) and severe marriage restrictions — ignited a process of aristocratic implosion that would undermine the very foundations of the edifice they were intended to protect.

UNIVERSITÀ DI BOLOGNA

---

[24] Malvezzi; Murphy, "Lavinia Fontana," 111–138.

Cited Works

Manuscript Sources

Bologna. Biblioteca Comunale dell'Archiginnasio (BCAB)
MS. 698/2. Carrati, Baldassarre. Alberi genealogici delle famiglie di Bologna.

Bologna. Archivio della Fondazione Magnani Guidotti (AMG)
Instrumenti, Magnani, 17, 35.

Bologna. Archivio di Stato di Bologna (ASB)
Albergati, Miscellanea, 1.
Malvezzi-Lupari, Carte d'amministrazione, 314.
Marsili, Strumenti e scritture, 175.
Salina-Amorini, Strumenti e scritture, 115.

Printed Sources

Bellettini, Athos. *La popolazione di Bologna dal XV secolo all'unificazione italiana*. Bologna: Zanichelli, 1961.

Beloch, Karl Julius. *Storia della popolazione d'Italia*. Florence: Le Lettere, 1994

Benadusi, Giovanna. "Rethinking the State: Family Strategies in Early Modern Tuscany." *Social History* 20 (1995): 157–178.

Berengo, Marino. "Il Cinquecento" in *La storiografia italiana degli ultimi vent'anni*. Milan: Rizzoli, 1970, pp. 483–518.

Brown, Judith C. "Monache a Firenze all'inizio dell'età moderna. Un'analisi demografica." *Quaderni Storici* 85 (1994): 117–152.

Carboni, Mauro. *Le doti della povertà. Famiglia, risparmio, previdenza: il Monte del Matrimonio di Bologna (1583–1796)*. Bologna: Il Mulino, 1999.

————. "La formazione di una élite di governo: le alleanze matrimoniali dei senatori bolognesi (1506–1796)." *Studi Storici Luigi Simeoni* 52 (2002): 9–46.

Casanova, Cesarina. "Per uno studio della nobiltà pontificia. Le origini degli Spada." *Romagna Arte e Storia* 6 (1986), 43–60.

_____. *Gentilhuomini ecclesiastici. Ceti e mobilità sociale nelle Legazioni pontificie (secc. XVI–XVIII)*. Bologna: Clueb, 1999.

Casey, James. *The History of the Family*. Oxford: Blackwell, 1989.

_____. *Family and Community in Early Modern Spain. The Citizens of Granada, 1570–1739*. Cambridge: Cambridge University Press, 2007.

Chittolini, Giorgio. "'Il' privato', il 'pubblico', lo Stato" In *Origini dello Stato. Processi di formazione statale in Italia fra medioevo ed età moderna*, eds. G. Chittolini, A. Molho and P. Schiera. Bologna: Il Mulino, 1994, pp. 553–589.

Chojnacki, Stanley. "Dowries and Kinsmen in Early Renaissance Venice." *Journal of Interdisciplinary History* 5 (1975): 571–600.

_____. "Daughters and Oligarchs: Gender and the Early Renaissance State." pp. 63–86 in *Gender and Society in Renaissance Italy*, eds. Judith C. Brown and Robert C. Davis. London and New York: Longman, 1998, pp. 63–86.

Colonaci, Stefano. *Dietro lo scudo incantato. I fedecommessi di famiglia e il trionfo della borghesia fiorentina (1400 ca–1750)*. Florence: Le Monnier, 2005.

De Benedictis, Angela. *Repubblica per contratto. Bologna una città europea nello Stato della Chiesa*. Bologna: Il Mulino, 1995.

Dolfi, Pompeo Scipione. *Cronologia delle famiglie nobili bolognesi con le loro insegne, e nel fine i cimieri*. Bologna: Gio. Battista Ferroni, 1670; rpt. Forni Editore, 1990.

Evangelisti, Gino. "Bernardino Spada legato (e collegato) di Bologna (1627–1631)." *Strenna Storica Bolognese* 33 (1983): 117–138.

Fanti, Mario. *Abiti e lavori delle monache di Bologna in una serie di disegni del secolo XVIII*. Bologna: Tamari Editori, 1972.

Fornasari, Massimo. "Credito e banca nella prima età moderna. Matteo Bolognini *campsor bononiensis.*" *Studi Storici Luigi Simeoni* 51 (2001): 29–42.

Guidicini, Giuseppe. *I Riformatori dello Stato di Libertà della Città di Bologna dal 1394 al 1797*. Bologna: Regia Tipografia, 1876.

Hunecke, Volker. "Matrimonio e demografia del patriziato veneziano (secc. XVII–XVIII)" *Studi Veneziani* 21 (1991): 269–319.

Laven, Mary. *Virgins of Venice*. London: Penguin Books, 2003.

Malvezzi. *Storia genealogia e iconografia*, ed. Giuliano Malvezzi Campeggi. Bologna: Costa Editore, 1996.

Miretti, Monica. *I Davia. Profilo di una famiglia senatoria bolognese fra XVII e XIX secolo.* Florence: Le Monnier, 2007.

Molho, Anthony. *Marriage Alliance in Late Medieval Florence.* Cambridge, MA: Harvard University Press, 1994.

Murphy, Caroline P. "Lavinia Fontana and Female Life Cycle Experience in Late Sixteenth Century Bologna." In *Picturing Women in Renaissance and Baroque Italy,* eds. Geraldine A. Johnson and Sara F. Matthews Grieco. Cambridge: Cambridge University Press, 1997, pp. 111–138.

Pomata, Gianna. "Family and Gender." In *Early Modern Italy,* ed. John A. Marino. Oxford: Oxford University Press, 2002, pp. 69–86.

Romano, Dennis. *Patricians and Popolani. The Social Foundations of the Venetian Renaissance State,* Baltimore: Johns Hopkins University Press, 1987.

Sperling, Jutta Gisela. *Convents and the Body Politic in Late Renaissance Venice.* Chicago: University of Chicago Press, 1999.

Strocchia, Sharon T. *Nuns and Nunneries in Renaissance Florence.* Baltimore: Johns Hopkins University Press, 2009.

Zarri, Gabriella. Recinti. *Donne, clausura e matrimonio nella prima età moderna.* Bologna: Il Mulino, 2000.

Old Wives and Art
in Early Modern Bologna

Erin J. Campbell

Bartolommeo Passerotti's engaging *Family Portrait* in the Gemäldegalerie in Dresden has long puzzled scholars (Fig. 12.1).[1] Despite the efforts of Corinna Höper to substantiate the tradition that the portrait represents the artist and his family, there has not been universal acceptance of this identification. [2] Moreover, there is little agreement on the date of execution, with some placing it as early as 1555–1560, and others dating it as late as the end of the 1580s.[3] In the painting, we see three generations of a family gathered together in a closely-knit grouping, including an older man and woman, a younger man and woman, and a child. The active pose of the older man, who gestures as if to show the viewer a small object,[4] draws us into the intimate gathering. However, the most commanding portrait image within the painting is the

---

[1] Bartolomeo Passerotti (1529–1592) was a painter, draughtsman, engraver and collector in Bologna. For a recent study of the artist see Ghirardi, *Bartolomeo Passerotti*. The artist's last name is also transcribed as "Passarotti." I wish to thank Andreas Henning, Curator, Gemäldegalerie Alte Meister, for allowing me to view the painting while in storage, and Angela Ghirardi for sharing her thoughts on the image. The travel necessary to complete the research for this essay was funded by the Social Sciences and Humanities Research Council. I also wish to acknowledge the Centre for the Study of Religion and Society at the University of Victoria, which provided me with an office in the Centre and a stimulating intellectual community during the writing of this essay. As well, I am grateful to Catherine Harding, Catherine Nutting, and the two anonymous reviewers for their useful comments and insight.

[2] Höper, *Bartolomeo Passarotti*, 1:48; 2:78–79, cat. entry G 84. For a summary of the scholarship on the image and the controversy over the identity of the sitters see Ghirardi, *Bartolomeo Passerotti*, 197–198.

[3] Höper dates the portrait to the end of the 1580s; Angela Ghirardi dates it to the middle of the 1570s; other suggested dates include 1555–1560. For a summary of suggested dates see Ghirardi, *Bartolomeo Passerotti*, 197–198.

[4] Ghirardi refers to this object as "a sort of pyx on a circular base." Ghirardi, *Bartolomeo Passerotti*, 37, 198.

older woman.[5] Dominating the centre foreground of the picture field, and wearing a striking snowy white head covering, this figure is the focal point of the painting.[6]

Passerotti's compelling rendition of this old woman is just one of a number of portraits of older women — portrayed both alone and in families — that were fashioned for the homes of the well-off bourgeois and elite classes in post-Tridentine Bologna, when, under the impact of religious and social reform, women's lives came under increasing scrutiny.[7] Given that the patronage, date and identity of the sitters remain unknown, how do we begin to understand what Passerotti's old woman meant to viewers? What kind of historical understanding does this portrait provide about family life and especially the role of older women within the family in post-Tridentine Bologna?

To begin to answer these questions, the present essay explores how portraits of old women, like the woman in Passerotti's *Family Portrait*, operated as mediating objects for the life stages within the Bolognese domestic interior. Recent studies of the early modern Italian domestic interior have established the importance of a wide array of domestic objects to the life stages of young women, including betrothal, marriage, childbirth and childrearing. Furniture, birth trays, toys, jewellery, ceramics, sculptures, textiles, prints, paintings and other objects have been shown to operate as tools for the socialization of brides and mothers,[8] as talismanic objects for

---

[5] Regarding my use of the designation "older woman": Silvana Seidel Menchi, based on her research into literary, visual and legal sources, as well as the correspondence of women, suggests that "women internalized the three-stage calendar, marked by watersheds at ages twelve and forty." The three stages are childhood, maturity and old age, in which twelve marks the young girl's entry into adulthood and becomes marriageable, while forty marks the transition into old age. Menchi, "The Girl and the Hourglass," 41–74, quotation at 70. See also Baernstein, "'Sposa, figlia, sorella, e vecchia matre,'" 213–234, who concludes that women could be considered old by forty.

[6] Others have remarked on the prominence of this figure. As Angela Ghirardi writes: "At the center, the imposing figure of the elderly woman, leaning her hand on a book, dominates the scene." Ghirardi, *Bartolomeo Passerotti*, 198.

[7] For a detailed study of a number of such portraits, see Campbell, "Prophets, Saints, and Matriarchs," 807–849. Passerotti's patrons were from the aristocracy and the middle-classes, and tended to be well-educated and closely linked to the university. Ghirardi, *Bartolomeo Passerotti*, 14.

[8] Matthews-Grieco, "Pedagogical Prints," 61–87; Matthews-Grieco, "Models of Female Sanctity," 159–175; Matthews-Grieco, "Persuasive Pictures," 285–314; Johnson,

conception and childbirth,[9] and as pedagogical aids for raising children.[10] Yet, within the growing body of scholarship on domestic objects and the stages of life, objects and imagery related to the later stages of women's lives have received little attention.[11]

My approach to portraits of old women in Bologna builds on Caroline Murphy's research, which has shown how portraits and devotional paintings mediated the stages of women's lives in Bolognese households. [12] However, in this study Murphy analyzes portraits of widows without considering the age of the sitter. Instead, I argue that old age deserves to be examined as a distinct life stage for wives and widows. Gabriella Zarri has shown that literature on the guidance of the family and the education of children flourished in Italy during the sixteenth century.[13] As she notes, religious reform subjected the roles of wife and mother to increased examination and accelerated the need to establish models of behaviour, which were taught to women through writings on the stages of life as well as through the examples of the lives of the saints.[14] Along with the focus on providing models of behaviour for the different stages of life — virginity, marriage and widowhood — I contend that there was also a new interest in distinguishing the role of the later life stages and in offering specific advice not just for virgins, young wives or young widows, but also for older wives, older widows and for husbands of older wives. For example, the Spanish humanist Juan Luis Vives (1492–1540), in his widely circulated book, *On the Education of the Christian Woman* (1523), which appeared in Italian translation under the title *De l'istitutione de la femina christiana, vergine, maritata, ò vedova* (Venice, 1546), provides

---

"Family Values," 215–233; Klapisch-Zuber, "Holy Dolls," 310–329.

[9] Musacchio, *The Art and Ritual of Childbirth*; Musacchio, "Lambs, Coral, Teeth," 139–56; Johnson, "Beautiful Brides and Model Mothers," 135–161.

[10] Ajmar, "Toys for Girls," 75–89; Fulton, "The Boy Stripped Bare by his Elders," 31–40; Coonin, "Portrait Busts of Children in Quattrocento Florence," 61–71.

[11] Portraits of widows have been studied, and Andrea Bayer includes a portrait of an older widow, *Leandro Bassano's Portrait of a Widow at Her Devotions* (c. 1590–1600; Private Collection), discussed below, in the recent exhibition *Art and Love in Renaissance Italy*; however, widowhood is not synonymous with old age. On widows in art see Levy, *Widowhood and Visual Culture*; see also Bayer, *Art and Love*, 285–286.

[12] Murphy, "Lavinia Fontana and Female Life Cycle Experience," 111–138.

[13] Zarri, "Christian good manners," 83. On prescriptive writings for women see Zarri, *Donna, disciplina, creanza cristiana dal XV al XVII secolo*.

[14] Zarri, "Christian good manners," 77.

a separate chapter in his advice to married women, entitled "On the mother of the family who is of advanced years."[15] In his text addressed to husbands, *De l' ufficio del marito*, which also appears in the 1546 Venetian edition, Vives includes a chapter of advice for men who are married to older wives, entitled "On the wife who is of advanced years."[16] Vives also notes that old women and married women past middle-age are preferred for public dealings such as buying and selling.[17] Cesare Vecellio's (ca. 1521–1601) costume book, *Habiti antichi et moderni* (Venice, 1590), reflects the concerns of prescriptive writers to articulate the specific characteristics of the older wife. In his discussion of dress for "donne attempate" (women of mature age) and "dismesse" (women single by choice), Vecellio tells his readers: "Married women who have reached a certain age usually wear this clothing, very far indeed from fancy dress."[18] Prescriptive texts for widows also make a distinction between young widows who may potentially re-marry, and older widows for whom the likelihood of remarriage is rare. For example, Agostino Valier (1531–1606), in his text entitled *Institutione d'ogni stato lodevole delle donne christiane* (Venice: 1575), which was published while he was bishop of Verona, distinguishes between young widows and old widows.[19]

Such advice for older wives and widows circulated in the household alongside various kinds of material objects, including portraits, devotional paintings and prints, all of which served to articulate the meaning of the later life stages for women. Specifically, this article explores how portraits of old women responded to, shaped and complicated social constructs of matriarchy — a stage of life shared by older wives and older widows with children. Although scholars have argued that, across Europe during the second half of the sixteenth century, matriarchal imagery was displaced by images that stressed the patriarchal family,[20] I contend that in post-Tridentine Bologna at least, portraits of old women, devotional paintings, prints, and altarpieces provided culturally shared matriarchal symbols that allowed individuals to

---

[15] Vives, *De l'istitutione de la femina christiana*, 183.

[16] Vives, *De l' ufficio del marito*, 62–64.

[17] Vives, *De institutione feminae christianae*, 121.

[18] Vecellio, *Clothing of the Renaissance World*, 136.

[19] Valier, *Institutione d'ogni stato lodevole delle donne christiane*, 110. See also Cabei, *Ornamenti della donna vedova*, 20–21, 25.

[20] Matthews-Grieco, "Models of Female Sanctity," 161–162; Brandenbarg, "St. Anne and her Family," 124.

negotiate the tensions arising from pressures on familial roles, at all levels of society, during a critical period in Bologna's history.

Leandro Bassano's *Portrait of a Widow at her Devotions* (ca. 1590–1600) allows us to begin to unravel the complex interplay of representations of matriarchy that circulated within the home (Fig. 12.2).[21] While not a Bolognese work,[22] Bassano's juxtaposition within the painting of the figure of the aging widow with a devotional image points us towards possible interpretive frameworks for understanding how viewers responded to portraits of old women in Bologna. In Bassano's painting, the pious widow is represented dressed sombrely in black, with her head covered, and she is shown holding a prominently displayed handkerchief that alludes to her grief.[23] She is represented in the midst of her devotions at home, at an *inginocchiatoio*, or kneeling stool. Her prayers are aided by a rosary, a book of hours and a devotional image depicting the Birth of the Virgin[24] that evokes the type of small paintings, often on copper, that were given as bridal gifts.[25]

---

[21] Leandro Bassano (1557–1622) was trained in the Dal Ponte family workshop in Bassano del Grappa and then established his own workshop in Venice in 1588. For recent scholarship on the image see Bayer, *Art and Love*, 285–286; Humfrey, *The Age of Titian*, 2004, 199. On the Dal Ponte workshop, see Aikema, *Jacopo Bassano*, 82–84; Brown and Marini, *Jacopo Bassano*, clxii–clxiii.

[22] There were many points of artistic contact between Bolognese artists and the Dal Ponte workshop. On influence of Jacopo Bassano on Passerotti's genre scenes see Ghirardi, "Bartolomeo Passerotti," 2:549; Ghirardi, *Bartolomeo Passerotti*, 80.

[23] Handkerchiefs played a significant role in the gift-giving rituals of courtship, and could signify conjugal connections when represented in portraits of women. See Musacchio, *Art, Marriage, & Family*, 4, 8, 30–32, 84, 127. On the association of handkerchiefs with grief in portraits of older women in seventeenth-century Dutch art, see Dickey, "'Met een wenende ziel,'" 332–367.

[24] Certain aspects of the scene suggest this is a depiction of the birth of the Virgin. For example, neither the grown-up Mary nor Zechariah recording the name of St. John are present in the scene, which one could expect in a scene of the birth of St. John, and the figure in the bed is dressed in a rose coloured dress symbolic of St. Anne.

[25] On domestic devotional practice and the use of devotional images within the home see Morse, "Creating Sacred Spaces," 151–184; Kasl, "Holy Households," 59–89; Lydecker, "The Domestic Setting of the Arts," 175–183. On small religious paintings that were given as bride gifts see Murphy, *Lavinia Fontana*, 166–171. See also the small oil on copper painting by Leandro Bassano (55 x 44.5 cm), *The Presentation of Christ in the Temple* (private collection), which provides a good comparison for the small painting represented in *Portrait of a Widow at Her Devotions*. The painting is reproduced in: Humfrey, et al., *The Age of Titian*, 198. Armenini, in *De' veri precetti della pittura* (1587), relates that in Rome

Such devotions could take place in the widow's rooms, or if she were wealthy enough, in her private chapel.[26] We can imagine that this painting might have been commissioned to hang in the sitter's own room or apartments within the family home, which, while private, would have been accessible to other members of the family, both male and female.[27]

---

and Tuscany men will not marry unless the gifts include a beautiful painting in addition to the dowry. He notes that, particularly in Lombardy, devotional works by Titian, Correggio and Giulio Romano were owned by married women, and that the matrons cried when they were uncovered. Armenini, 188–189. Prayer beads such as paternosters or rosaries and devotional books were typically included in the bride's dowry, at least in Florence, and so might also allude to the widow's marriage. See Musacchio, *Art, Marriage, & Family*, 4, 130, 162, 175, 255. For a discussion of paternosters or rosaries in particular see Musacchio, *Art, Marriage, & Family*, 175. For a discussion of paternosters and rosaries in Venetian homes see Morse, "Creating Sacred Spaces," 163–166.

[26] Lydecker notes that kneeling benches imply private worship in a chamber rather than communal worship in a chapel, for in the Florentine inventories he surveys they are normally listed in the chambers or antechambers of the Florentine house. Lydecker points out that this type of furniture becomes "commonplace" during the sixteenth century with the increase in importance of private devotional practices. Lydecker, "The Domestic Setting of the Arts," 59. On domestic altars and chapels in Venice see Morse, "Creating Sacred Spaces," 170–176. On women's private chapels and altars, as well as devotional objects, see McIver, *Women, Art, and Architecture*, 180–184. Vives outlines the devotional process for married women: "The virtuous woman, when she is free of domestic cares, will choose for herself daily, if possible, but if not, on feast days, a secluded part of the house, apart from the noise and bustling. There, laying aside for a while the worries of the house and recollecting her thoughts, she will meditate on the contempt of these worldly things, since they are frivolous and unstable, insubstantial and quick to perish, and on how the brevity of our lives goes by with such speed that it seems not to pass but to be carried along, not to go by, but to flee. Then with the help of some divine reading she will raise herself to the thoughts and contemplation of divine things. Finally, having confessed her sins to God, she will suppliantly beg for pardon and peace from Him and will pray first for herself, then having found more favour with God, for her husband, her children and finally her whole household, so that the Lord Jesus will inspire a better mind in all of them." Vives, *De institutione feminae christianae*, 147.

[27] Armenini describes the gendering of domestic spaces: "Ma nelle camere poi dove si riposano le Matrone, & le Donne maritate, vi si fingono poi essempi d'Istorie di Donne Illustri, cosi Greche, come Latine, & il medesimo si dè fare in quelle dove habitano le Fanciulle, col fingervi le più famose per castità, per grandezza d'animo, & per fede." Armenini, *De' veri precetti della pittura*, 187–188. See also Thornton, *The Italian Renaissance Interior*, 288, 291, 295; and McIver, *Women, Art, and Architecture*, 116–117, who notes that "Even in a household where only a few male family members were present, the women clearly had separate spaces not just for sleeping and eating." However, see Alison Smith's

For viewers versed in the prescriptive writings aimed at women, husbands and families, at first glance, the pious widow evokes, through her dress and comportment, the ideals of withdrawal from the world and entry into the spiritual life prescribed for both old wives and widows, a stage of life that Vives calls "her most holy life" ("la sua vita santissima.)"[28] For example, Cesare Vecellio tells us that married women of "a certain age" have "distanced themselves from the vanities of the world, dedicating themselves instead to the life of the spirit, and accordingly they wear this simple, pious dress."[29] For Vives and other moralizing writers, the older wife should cultivate chastity, abstinence, spirituality, wisdom and virile authority.[30] As Vives writes concerning the older wife: "But when she arrives at this age, with her children all married, freed from earthly cares, turning the eyes of her body to the earth which she must render her body, and with the eyes of her soul looking to heaven, where she is to go to take up residence, she will raise all her senses, her mind and soul to the Lord, and girding herself for that departure, she will meditate on nothing that is not suited to that impending journey."[31] The standard of piety is magnified for the older widow, who is still a wife,

---

study of gender and domestic space in Verona, which argues on the basis of evidence from Veronese inventories "that gender did not have an explicit effect on the use of domestic space" and therefore "the recommendations of the normative literature were not carried out in practice." Smith, "Gender, Ownership and Domestic Space, 383.

[28] Vives, *De l'istitutione de la femina christiana*, 183.

[29] Vecellio, *Clothing of the Renaissance World*, 136. On the standards of dress for widows, which would include old widows, see Dolce, *Dialogo della institution delle donne*, p. 74; Cabei, *Ornamenti della donna vedova*, 37–38.

[30] Vives recommends chastity and more frequent prayer in old age. Although he notes that old women may fast "less often," clearly some fasting is expected. Vives, *De institutione feminae christianae*, 197: "And since the soul still retains more vigor than the body, let her omit physical labors and increase those of the soul. She will pray more frequently and with more attention. She will think more often and with more fervor of God. She will fast less often and will tire herself less in visiting churches." Giulio Cabei notes that old widows who do not remarry and remain chaste can act as exemplars of chastity for virgins: Cabei, *Ornamenti della donna vedova*, 20. On virile authority, Vives argues that if an old woman achieves a state of holiness "[t]hen the truly good woman through obedience to her husband will hold sway and she who always lived in obedience to her husband will command great authority over him." Vives, *De institutione feminae christianae*, 195. Vives asserts that old age affords women wisdom: they become an equal and a source of advice, an advocate or protector ("patrona"). Vives, *De l'ufficio del marito*, 63..

[31] Vives, *De institutione feminae christianae*, 197.

but is now married to Christ: "the widow should pray more frequently and with greater devotion, fast longer, attend mass and sacred functions, read more diligently, and turn her thoughts to those things that improve life and morals." While the advice is seemingly directed at widows young and old, Vives's exemplar for such behaviour is an old widow, the prophetess Anna, who was a widow for 84 years and spent that time in prayer in the temple.[32]

In Bassano's *Portrait of a Widow at her Devotions*, if, in light of the prescriptive writings on widowhood as a stage of sanctity, the figure of the widow evokes the contemplative life of the spirit and withdrawal from the world, the matriarchal imagery of the birth scene depicted within the painting locates the widow's piety firmly within the biological and social life of the family. Indeed, the painting establishes a close connection between the old widow and the religious narrative, by coordinating the setting and costumes of the sacred domestic interior with the domestic interior of the sitter. Both scenes are set in domestic spaces, and the architecture and colour of the birth scene make it appear to be an extension of the sitter's room. At the same time, the black curtains draping the bed of St. Anne echo the black drapery of the sitter, and the costumes on the women in the birth scene are in the same style as the dress of the sitter. Indeed, one of the foreground women, engaged in washing the baby Mary, wears exactly the same costume as the woman of the portrait, although without the heavy head covering. The similarity of dress, in particular, closely identifies the sitter with the narrative of the devotional image.

Such a folding together of past and present seems to recreate the process of praying, which promotes a mental universe merging the heavenly and the earthly, allowing the widow to transport herself mystically into the holy narrative as handmaiden of the saint.[33] However, I suggest that Leandro

---

[32] Vives, *De institutione feminae christianae*, 221.

[33] For an example of spiritual meditation leading to entry into a sacred narrative, see the writings of the English mystic Margery Kempe (b. 1373): "Another day, this creature gave herself up to meditation as she had been commanded before, and she lay still, not knowing what she might best think of. Then she said to our Lord Jesus Christ, 'Jesus, what shall I think about?' Our Lord Jesus answered in her mind, 'Daughter, think of my mother, for she is the cause of all the grace you have.' And then at once she saw St. Anne, great with child, and then she prayed St. Anne to let her be her maid and her servant. And presently our Lady was born, and then she busied herself to take the child to herself and look after her until she was twelve years of age, with good food and drink, with fair white clothing and white kerchiefs." This translation into modern English appears in Nixon, *Mary's*

Bassano's juxtaposition of the aging widow and an image of the Birth of the Virgin points us towards possible interpretive frameworks, not only for this portrait but also for other portraits of old women who, on the model of the holy matriarchs St. Anne and St. Elizabeth, fostered kinship and family continuity.

With respect to prints of holy births, Sara Matthews-Grieco has argued that such images were maternal mediators — visual aids that would assist expectant mothers — which she notes could function as a type of "prenatal insurance" for a safe delivery.[34] However, as Bassano's portrait clearly shows, such imagery continued to be of value to women long past the age of child bearing. Andrea Bayer has interpreted the birth scene as deepening the commemorative role of the painting, and contributing to the mood of *memento mori*, for she notes that the women in the birth scene represent the female life course from birth through to old age.[35] However, such birth imagery is also matriarchal imagery and forms part of the iconography of the holy matriarchs St. Anne and St. Elizabeth, whose identity within matriarchal imagery seems to be interchangeable: both saints are part of the same lineage; both appear in images of the Holy Family; both are represented in almost identical birth scenes[36] and their identities within images were confused by contemporaries.[37]

Mother, 103–104. For the original passage see Kempe, *The Book of Margery Kempe*, 75. For a discussion of this form of affective engagement, in which the devout starts with a representation of a sacred narrative, see Aikema, *Jacopo Bassano*, 124–125. Aikema discusses this meditative tradition in the context of post-Tridentine devotional practices and the art of Jacopo Bassano, Leandro's father and teacher. For an excellent exploration of the role of the visual image within spiritual practices see Falkenburg, *Image and Imagination*.

[34] Matthews-Grieco, "Persuasive Pictures," 292.

[35] The women in St. Anne's confinement room suggest "the stages of a woman's life, from infancy, maidenhood, and marriage, to widowhood and old age — a fitting subject for reflections on mortality." Bayer, *Art and Love*, 286.

[36] For example, Leandro Bassano's representation of the Birth of the Virgin is inspired by Albrecht Dürer's woodcut *The Birth of the Virgin* and Diana Mantuana's engraving *The Birth of St. John*. Bayer, *Art and Love*, 286.

[37] Matthews-Grieco suggests that the saints are interchangeable. Matthews-Grieco, "Models of Female Sanctity," 161. Giovanni Pietro Bellori (1613–1696), the author of *Le vite de' pittori, scultori et architetti moderni* (Rome: 1672), identifies St. Elizabeth as St. Anne in Annibale Carracci's etching and engraving *Madonna of the Bowl*. See Benati and Riccòmini, *Annibale Carracci*, 418.

Research on St. Anne as a matriarchal symbol has established that, as a role model for old women, St. Anne, as mother of the Virgin, grandmother of Jesus, three times wife and three times widow, was the ideal aging spouse, mother and pious widow.[38] Moreover, as Ashley and Sheingorn argue in their study of the saint, in addition to being the ideal "spouse, mother, widow," St. Anne is associated with concepts of lineage. As both mother and grandmother, as founder of the Holy Kinship (Christ's maternal family tree)[39] and as a symbol of fertility, St. Anne symbolized generational continuity. More than any other saint, Anne served as both concrete example and potent metaphor for ideas of kinship, connection and relationship. Indeed, Ashley and Sheingorn identify her symbolic role as that of: "connector, mediator, mother, kin."[40]

The identification of the widow with the symbolic functions of St. Anne as matriarch recalls the advice in the conduct literature that directly addresses the older woman, either married or widowed, who is engaged with family — who has children, or daughters-in-law. Although neither St. Anne nor St. Elizabeth seems to be explicitly mentioned as a role model for such women, nevertheless, out of these writings emerges the concept of older women who, like St. Anne and St. Elizabeth, perform a vital bridging role between generations, and who foster continuity, connection and kinship within the context of the family. Agostino Valier implies such a bridging role in his text on "the true and perfect widow." He devotes several chapters to the utility of widows who do not re-marry, emphasizing not only their role as models to virgins and married women, and as sources of consolation and advice, but also as vital support within extended family networks and brokers of concord and peace not only at home but also "in the neighbourhood."[41] Valier points to the widow Naomi, and her relationship with her widowed daughters-in-law, in the Hebrew scripture, as evidence of the importance

---

[38] Ashley and Sheingorn, *Interpreting Cultural Symbols*, p. 53. On St. Anne as a "widow saint" in Florentine art see Lawless, "'Widowhood was the time of her greatest perfection,'" 26. Lawless notes that in Florentine art no reference is made to St. Anne's three marriages, and that she is most often depicted in the role of mother rather than widow. See also Lawless, "'A widow of God?'" 15–42. Regarding Bologna, Caroline Murphy notes that "Saint Anne's feast day acknowledged her role as widow." Murphy, *Lavinia Fontana*, 147.

[39] On the Holy Kinship and its members, see Orth, "Madame Sainte Anne," 202–203.

[40] Ashley and Sheingorn, *Interpreting Cultural Symbols*, 53.

[41] Valier, *Institutione d'ogni stato lodevole delle donne christiane*, 132, 139–141. Quotation at 141.

of widows within family networks.[42] Christiane Klapisch-Zuber has argued that during the fifteenth century, in Florence, there existed the concept of the "good mother" who, in the event of the death of her husband, became, in the words of the Florentine Giovanni Rucellai, both "a father and mother for her children." This is the mother who stayed with her children after the death of her husband, hence ensuring the transmission of material goods and the continuance of the patrimony. As Klapisch-Zuber notes, "The virtues of an exceptional mother are from this point of view all manly virtues." In the case of widowhood, as Klapisch-Zuber argues, "the 'good mother' was an acceptable substitute for the father."[43] P. Renée Baernstein contends that "old" widowed mothers — widows past the age to remarry, who stay within the paternal household to become the head of the family if the male children are under age, play a vital bridging role for the younger generation of males as they make the transition from children to adulthood.[44]

To return to Bologna and Passerotti's Dresden *Family Portrait*, I want to suggest, based on the evidence of the Bassano portrait, that at least some of the portraits of old women produced by artists for Bolognese families similarly allowed individuals and families to grapple with both the social and religious meanings of matriarchy within the patrilineal family. Although Passerotti's Dresden portrait and other portraits of old women by Bolognese artists do not contain within the same frame the holy birth imagery which we see in Bassano's portrait, images of the holy matriarchs were in circulation

[42] Valier, *Institutione d'ogni stato lodevole delle donne christiane*, 139–140; Naomi is also mentioned by Dolce, *Dialogo della institution delle donne*, 66.

[43] Klapisch-Zuber, "The 'Cruel Mother,'" 128–129.

[44] Baernstein, "'Sposa, figlia, sorella, e vecchia matre,'" 226. David Herlihy also discusses the bridging role of mothers within the family, arguing that because the mother was typically younger than her spouse, she was closer in age to her children and was therefore "ideally placed to serve as intermediary between the often conflicting male generations." While Herlihy connects this function in an interesting way to the Virgin's role as intercessor, I would underscore that St. Anne and St. Elizabeth combine this intercessory role with concepts of kin and lineage. Herlihy, *Medieval Households*, 120–130; quotation at 121. See also Laura Smoller's study of holy women that were identified as "holy mothers" and how this concept was transformed in a post-reform context into a designation for older women in Protestant jurisdictions. She notes that old women in New England villages were called "mother", and she concludes that Puritan women in New England operated like the holy mothers of late medieval piety, and "often took on a nurturing role towards the whole community, a role that included a concern for the personal piety of others." Smoller, "Holy Mothers," 200.

in Bologna. In particular, Bassano's painting-within-the-painting evokes the *quadri da letto* that were placed beside the bed in the bedchamber. Such paintings were often made expressly for women, were given as gifts to brides and novices and could be included in the bride's *corredo* or trousseau.[45] Many artists participated in this market in Bologna, including Denys Calvaert, Francesco Albani, Lavinia Fontana and later on, Elisabetta Sirani, as well as a host of unidentified artists, judging from the ubiquity of small devotional works by anonymous artists recorded in Bolognese inventories. Although the seventeenth-century Bolognese inventories studied by Raffaella Morselli are later than our study, nevertheless, they confirm the enduring popularity of such devotional pictures in Bolognese homes.[46] Among the many subjects documented by Morselli, that are relevant to women's life stages and domesticity, there are a number of subjects that relate specifically to themes of matriarchy, including the Madonna and Child with John the Baptist and St. Elizabeth (p. 519), the Holy Family, and the Holy Family with Christ Sleeping which could include either St. Elizabeth or St. Anne (pp. 515, 609), St. Anne on her own (p. 534), as well as the Holy Family with John the Baptist and St. Anne, or both St. Anne and St. Elizabeth (p. 610), the Birth of the Virgin (p. 604), the Birth of St. John (p. 603), Anna teaching the Virgin to Read (p. 604) and Anna Selbdritt (pp. 603–604). In addition to devotional paintings, prints of the holy matriarchs were also in wide circulation and increased in popularity over the course of the sixteenth century, as Matthews-Grieco has shown.[47] Bolognese artists also produced prints of holy births and holy families that included the holy matriarchs.[48] Beyond the home, monumental images of the holy matriarchs St. Anne and St. Elizabeth appeared above the altars of local churches and reinforced the messages of domestic matriarchal imagery.[49]

---

[45] Murphy, *Lavinia Fontana*, 166–171.

[46] For the many devotional works that were in Bolognese homes between 1640–1707 see Raffaella Morselli's list of the subjects and sizes of paintings recorded in seventeenth-century Bolognese inventories in Morselli, *Collezioni e quadrerie*, 507–543; 599–618.

[47] Matthews-Grieco, "Persuasive Pictures," 292.

[48] Agostino Carracci, *Birth of the Virgin* (1560–75) (engraving after Andrea Del Sarto; Strauss, *Illustrated Bartsch*, vol. 39); Annibale Carracci *Madonna of the Bowl* (etching and engraving, 127 x 164 mm; 1606), which contains a striking image of St. Elizabeth (Benati and Riccòmini, *Annibale Carracci*, 418–419).

[49] Altarpieces include *The Birth of St. John the Baptist* of 1602–03, by Ludovico Carracci, now in the Pinacoteca Nazionale in Bologna, which graced the high altar of San

Given the wide range of images of the holy matriarchs in Bologna, how might matriarchal imagery contribute to our understanding of the historical reception of the older woman in Bartolomeo Passerotti's Dresden *Family Portrait*, whose commanding depiction has created much speculation about her role within the family? Scholars have identified her variously as grandmother, sister and nun.[50] I suggest that the confusion of modern viewers mirrors contemporaries' own search for meaning in the image. While part of the significance of this portrait could involve the viewer's own knowledge of the sitters and their lives, and would be informed by the commemorative and moral functions invested in portraits by Renaissance art theory and other writings on art,[51] I maintain that such portraits also acted as cultural symbols that activated or triggered social understandings of the roles of older wives and widows within the patrilineal family.[52] Although there is not a birth scene within the image, such representations were part of the material culture of the family home and community, and provided the network of associations within which this portrait resonated. Thus, the snowy white headdress, which some have identified as a nun's habit, ties Passerotti's old woman to the contemplative ideal for older wives and widows fashioned by Vives and others. Reinforcing the impression of piety is the book supporting her left hand. At the same time, her placement at the centre of three generations evokes the matriarchal imagery of St. Anne and St. Elizabeth, and conveys,

---

Giovanni Battista, begun in 1597 (Emiliani, *Ludovico Carracci*, 123–124); *The Birth of the Virgin* by Lavinia Fontana, in Santissima Trinita, and dated to around 1590 (Fortunati Pietrantonio, *Pittura Bolognese*, 2:764); as well as Bartolomeo Cesi's *Incarnazione della Vergine in Sant'Anna come Immacolata concezione* (1593/95) in the Pinacoteca in Bologna, originally in the Chiesa di S. Francesco, and the fresco *The Birth of the Virgin*, now destroyed, which was in the Archiginnasio, Cappella di S. Maria dei Bulgari (after 1591) (Fortunati Pietrantonio, *Pittura bolognese*, 2:822). Antonio Masini records in his history of Bologna, *Bologna perlustrata* (1666), that the Orations had some relics of St. Anne that were exposed in the church of Galliera during the feast day of the saint on July 26. Cited in Modesti, *Elisabetta Sirani*, 100, n. 107.

[50] Ghirardi, *Bartolomeo Passerotti*, 198. Roberto Zappieri identifies her as a nun and therefore the sister of the older man. Zappieri, *Annibale Carracci*, 107.

[51] For a good summary of these traditions see Wright, "The Memory of Faces," 86–113.

[52] As Kathleen Ashley argues regarding St. Anne: "we should avoid thinking of Anne's image as *containing* a variety of meanings. Rather, her potency as cultural symbol in the late Middle Ages was a function of her usefulness in *triggering* or activating ideological formations." Ashley, "Image and Ideology," 125.

on the one hand, abstract concepts of lineage, continuity and kinship, while simultaneously making concrete her role in the biological and social processes of the family. She is both figuratively and literally the bridging figure within the family, providing the link between the patriarchal figure on her right, and the younger generations on her left.

Although we cannot know the intentions of the artist, patron and sitter, we can ask what wider cultural role such matriarchal imagery played at this particular moment in the history of the Bolognese family. Research on St. Anne as a matriarchal symbol has shown that while such cultural symbols have a finite range of significations, nevertheless, they can speak to a broad constituency, and can mean different things to different groups, at different times.[53] Indeed, it seems the viability of a cultural symbol, based on this research, has to do with its ability to be polyvalent, making it useful to a variety of people in a range of circumstances. Deeply tied to social life, and also constitutive of the social, such cultural symbols, as Kathleen Ashley has argued, "enabled social understandings to be formed and social dilemmas to be confronted and even, on occasion, resolved." [54]

In Bologna, and indeed across Italy, matriarchal imagery helped people negotiate the harsh realities and social dilemmas that directly confronted the early modern family. Over the course of the sixteenth century, Bologna's population fluctuated due to recurrent bouts of the plague and famine. In 1527–1528 a devastating plague swept through the city, and in 1558 and 1561 famine killed approximately 10,000 city dwellers and 30,000 in the countryside.[55] A succession of crop shortages and failures in northern Italy, between 1587 and 1596, reduced the Bolognese population from 72,000 to 59,000. [56] Indeed, it was in response to these crises that the Bolognese developed a network of charitable homes to care for orphaned and abandoned children.[57] At the same time, Mauro Carboni's research on dotal strategies in post-Tridentine Bologna has revealed that, in the second half of the sixteenth century, Bolognese families were confronted with a dramatic social crisis due

---

[53] Ashley and Sheingorn, *Interpreting Cultural Symbols*, 1–68; Brandenbarg, "St. Anne and her Family, 101–127.

[54] Ashley, "Image and Ideology," 126.

[55] Terpstra, *Lay Confraternities*, 179.

[56] Carboni, "The Economics of Marriage," 381–382. See also Carboni's book-length study, *Le doti della povertà*.

57 Terpstra, *Abandoned Children*, 33–45.

to dowry inflation. The rising costs of dowries affected families across the social spectrum, and for elite families, in particular, this resulted in fewer marriages and increased monachization rates.[58] Consequently, for the wealthy families who were most likely to be the patrons of matriarchal imagery, the chances of the daughters of these families actually becoming mothers was less possible, as was the extension of the patrilineal family through the marriage of sons. Thus, while the actual size of families, both rich and poor, was subject to fluctuation over the course of the sixteenth century, as a result of famine, plague or marriage strategies, I would argue that visual images of actual and holy matriarchs continued to find an audience because such imagery was useful for families and individuals.

Research on the history of the family suggests that a type of family formation may constitute the ideal type in the cultural imaginary even if it is rare in actual practice.[59] Typically, within urban centres, wealthy families were larger and family size decreased as one went down the social scale.[60] For both well-off and poorer families, images of matriarchy allowed family members to imagine longevity, kinship and connection, which would be especially comforting at times of duress. While the ideal for an extended family might at least be attainable for the wealthy, in times of crisis it may even for the wealthy have remained less achievable;[61] for the poorer urban

---

[58] Carboni, "The Economics of Marriage," 375–376.

[59] Wheaton, "Family and Kinship," 611; Grubb, *Provincial Families*, 866.

[60] Marzio Barbagli's study of the Italian family has shown that family structures across Italy between 1400–1800 were highly variable, and were affected by geographic locale, social status, wealth, occupation, whether one lived in the country or the city and the incidence of plague, famine or other disasters. Barbagli, *Sotto lo stesso tetto*, 139–262. The evidence from Quattrocento Florence suggests that the proportion of extended families living together was low amongst the poor, rose slightly for those in the middle, and was highest amongst the wealthiest families. Barbagli, *Sotto lo stesso tetto*, 144. James Grubb argues that in the Veneto among the prosperous families he studies, domestic structures were "often complex, filiolocal, and fraternal"; Grubb, *Provincial Families of the Renaissance*, 86. On the occurrence of larger and complex families in other Italian cities see Grubb, *Provincial Families of the Renaissance*, 87–88. See also Barbagli's table of types of family structures in Verona in 1545 organized according to *estimo*, in which the number of nuclear families decreases and the number of complex family structures increases proportionately as *estimo* rises. Barbagli, *Sotto lo stesso tetto*, 169, Tab. IV.7.

[61] Barbagli's research on the impact on the family structure of what he calls "le crisi di mortalità" and, in particular, on the effects of the plague of 1630 on the structure of the Veronese family, shows a contraction of the family size and a simplification of the

families, extended family life could be construed as something to be aspired to as a mark of social prestige, if not actually attainable.[62] Significantly, despite the popular conception that Renaissance cities were filled with old women, data from the Veneto suggests that the majority of the elderly were in fact men, making the occurrence of matriarchs more rare than we might think.[63] Thus, matriarchal imagery provided families with an idealized image of the older woman as "connector, mediator, mother, kin," even if such women were relatively rare. While matriarchal imagery provided families with the necessary symbolic means to navigate social crises, for individual women, the matriarchal imagery that circulated in portraits, devotional images and prints, allowed individuals to engage in a dialogue concerning their roles within the family and the wider community. As Margaret Miles has argued, "The first task of any culture is to formulate and make available to its members effective symbols ... for comprehending and taking an attitude towards bodily experience: birth, growth, maturation, kinship, sex, life cycle, pain, death.... . The secondary task of culture is the articulation of the role and significance of particular individuals within the culture."[64] Images of matriarchy offered the symbolic means for older women to grapple with the social and psychological meaning of their own maturation within the structure of the family, to reflect on, complicate or reject the ideals of the contemplative or active life offered by prescriptive writings, portraits and devotional imagery and to articulate, and even defend, the significance of that maturing process to others.

To conclude with Passerotti's Dresden Family Portrait, Angela Ghirardi characterizes the painting as expressing "a quiet, somewhat mono-tonous domestic privacy." According to her, the image is "a 'bourgeois' tale flowing without fuss."[65] I hope to have established that, given the tenuous nature of life in Bologna over the course of the sixteenth century, such

---

structure. Barbagli, *Sotto lo stesso tetto*, 146–151. He also shows that when cities were in a state of expansion, as was the case with Verona in the middle of the sixteenth century, then complex family structures became more prevalent. Barbagli, *Sotto lo stesso tetto*, 151–157.

[62] Wheaton, " Family and Kinship," 610–611.

[63] Figures from the Veneto, which Grubb argues compare well with those of other cities, show that "[n]early half of men lived to the age of forty (48.7 percent), compared with little more than a third of women (36.2 percent). Among the old, those who survived to age sixty, the preponderance of males is also pronounced (34.2 percent versus 22.4 percent)." Grubb, *Provincial Families of the Renaissance*, 59.

[64] Miles, *Image as Insight*, 82.

[65] Ghirardi, *Bartolomeo Passerotti*, 198.

bourgeois tales were exactly the kind of stories people needed because, as figurations of a matriarchal ideal, they offered families across the social classes the symbolic reassurance that *come what may*, piety, kin and lineage would ensure that the social, economic and religious functions of the family were secure and enduring.

UNIVERSITY OF VICTORIA

CITED WORKS

Aikema, Bernard. *Jacopo Bassano and His Public: Moralizing Pictures in an Age of Reform ca. 1535–1600*. Trans. Andrew P. McCormick. Princeton, NJ: Princeton University Press, 1996.

Ajmar, Marta. "Toys for Girls: Objects, Women and Memory in the Renaissance Household." In *Material Memories*, ed. Marius Kwint et. al. Oxford: Legenda, European Humanities Research Centre, 1999, 75–89.

Armenini, Giovanni Battista. *De' veri precetti della pittura*. Ravenna: Francesco Tebaldini, 1587; rpt. Hildesheim: Georg Olms Verlag, 1971.

Ashley, Kathleen, "Image and Ideology: Saint Anne in Late Medieval Drama and Narrative." In *Interpreting Cultural Symbols: Saint Anne in Late Medieval Society*, eds. Kathleen Ashley and Pamela Sheingorn. Athens, Georgia and London: University of Georgia Press, 1990, 111–130.

Ashley, Kathleen and Pamela Sheingorn, eds. *Interpreting Cultural Symbols: Saint Anne in Late Medieval Society*. Athens, GA: University of Georgia Press, 1990.

Baernstein, P. Renée, "'Sposa, figlia, sorella, e vecchia matre': Invecchiare donne in età moderna." *Storia delle donne* 2 (2006): 213–234.

Barbagli, Marzio. *Sotto lo stesso tetto: mutamenti della famiglia in Italia dal XV al XX secolo*. Bologna: Mulino, 1984.

Bayer, Andrea, ed. *Art and Love in Renaissance Italy*. New Haven and London: Yale University Press, 2008.

Benati, Daniele and Eugenio Riccòmini, eds. *Annibale Carracci*. Milan: Mondadori Electa, 2006.

Brandenbarg, Ton. "St. Anne and her Family." In *Saints and She-Devils: Images of Women in the 15ᵗʰ and 16ᵗʰ Centuries*, ed. Lène Dresen-Coenders. London: The Rubicon Press, 1987, 101–127.

Brown, Beverly Louise, and Paola Marini, eds., *Jacopo Bassano c. 1510–1592*. Bologna: Nuova Alfa Editore, 1992.

Cabei, Giulio Cesare. *Ornamenti della donna vedova*. Venice: Cristoforo Zanetti, 1574.

Campbell, Erin J. "Prophets, Saints, and Matriarchs: Portraits of Old Women in Early Modern Italy." *Renaissance Quarterly* 63.3 (Fall 2010): 807–849.

Carboni, Mauro. *Le doti della povertà: famiglia, risparmio, previdenza: il Monte del Matrimonio di Bologna (1583–1796)*. Bologna: Società Editrice il Mulino, 1999.

_____. "The Economics of Marriage: Dotal Strategies in Bologna in the Age of Catholic Reform." *Sixteenth Century Journal* 39:2 (2008): 371–387.

Coonin, Victor, "Portrait Busts of Children in Quattrocento Florence." *Metropolitan Museum Journal* 30 (1995): 61–71.

Dickey, Stephanie. "'Met een wenende ziel...dock droge ogen': Women Holding Handkerchiefs in Seventeenth-Century Dutch Portraits." *Nederlands Kunsthistorisch Jaarboek* 46 (1995): 332–367.

Dolce, Lodovico. *Dialogo della institution delle donne di messer Lodovico Dolce*. Venice: Gabriele Giolito de Ferrari, 1547.

Emiliani, Andrea, ed. *Ludovico Carracci*. Essay and catalogue by Gail Feigenbaum. Milan and New York: Electa Abbevillle / Fort Worth: Kimbell Art Museum, 1994.

Falkenburg, Reindert, Walter S. Melion, and Todd M. Richardson, eds. *Image and Imagination of the Religious Self in Late Medieval and Early Modern Europe*. Turnhout: Brepols Publishers, 2007.

Fortunati Pietrantonio, Vera, ed. *Pittura Bolognese del' 500*. 2 vols. Bologna: Grafis Edizioni, 1986.

Fulton, Christopher. "The Boy Stripped Bare by his Elders: Art and Adolescence in Renaissance Florence." *Art Journal* 56.2 (1997): 31–40.

Ghirardi, Angela. *Bartolomeo Passerotti: Pittore (1529–1592)*. Rimini: Luisè Editore, 1990.

_____. "Bartolomeo Passerotti." In *Pittura Bolognese del '500*, ed. Vera Fortunati Pietrantonio. Bologna: Grafis Edizioni, 1986, 2: 543–594.

Grubb, James S. *Provincial Families of the Renaissance: Private and Public Life in the Veneto.* Baltimore: The Johns Hopkins University Press, 1996.

Herlihy, David. *Medieval Households.* Cambridge, MA: Harvard University Press, 1985.

Höper, Corinna. *Bartolomeo Passarotti.* Worms: Wernersche Verlagsgesellschaft, 1987.

Humfrey, Peter, Timothy Clifford, Aidan Weston-Lewis, and Michael Bury, eds. *The Age of Titian: Venetian Renaissance Art From Scottish Collections.* Edinburgh: National Galleries of Scotland, 2004.

Johnson, Geraldine A. "Beautiful Brides and Model Mothers: The Devotional and Talismanic Functions of Early Modern Marian Reliefs." In *The Material Culture of Sex, Procreation and Marriage in Premodern Europe,* eds. Anne L. McClanan and Karen Rosoff Encarnación. New York; Basingstoke / Hants: Palgrave, 2002, 135–161.

————. " Family Values: Sculpture and the Family in Fifteenth-Century Florence." In *Art, Memory, and Family in Renaissance Florence,* eds. Giovanni Ciappelli and Patricia Lee Rubin. Cambridge: Cambridge University Press, 2000, 215–233.

Kasl, Ronda. "Holy Households: Art and Devotion in Renaissance Venice." In *Giovanni Bellini and the Art of Devotion,* ed. Ronda Kasl. Indianapolis, Ind.: Indianapolis Museum of Art, 2004, 59–89.

Kempe, Margery. *The Book of Margery Kempe.* Trans. B.A. Windeatt. London: Penguin, 1985.

Klapisch-Zuber, Christiane. *Women, Family and Ritual in Renaissance Italy.* Trans. Lydia Cochrane. Chicago: University of Chicago Press, 1985.

————. "Holy Dolls: Play and Piety in Florence in the Quattrocento." In Christiane Klapisch-Zuber, *Women, Family and Ritual in Renaissance Italy.* Trans. Lydia Cochrane. Chicago: University of Chicago Press, 1985, 310–329.

————. "The 'Cruel Mother.'" In Christiane Klapisch-Zuber, *Women, Family and Ritual in Renaissance Italy.* Trans. Lydia Cochrane. Chicago: University of Chicago Press, 1985, 117–131.

Lawless, Catherine. "'A widow of God?' St. Anne and Representations of Widowhood in Fifteenth-Century Florence." In *Women in Renaissance and Early Modern Europe,* ed. Christine Meeks. Dublin: Four Courts Press, 2000, 15–42.

_____. "'Widowhood was the time of her greatest perfection': Ideals of Widowhood and Sanctity in Florentine Art." In *Widowhood and Visual Culture in Early Modern Europe*, ed. Allison Levy, Aldershot, UK: Ashgate Publishing, 2003, 19–38.

Levy, Allison, ed. *Widowhood and Visual Culture in Early Modern Europe*. Aldershot, UK: Ashgate, 2003.

Lydecker, J.K. "The Domestic Setting of the Arts in Renaissance Florence." Unpublished PhD diss., The John Hopkins University, 1987.

Matthews-Grieco, Sara. "Pedagogical Prints: Moralizing Broadsheets and Wayward Women in Counter-Reformation Italy." In *Picturing Women in Renaissance and Baroque Italy*, eds. Geraldine A. Johnson and Sara F. Matthews-Grieco. Cambridge and New York: Cambridge University Press, 1997, 61–87.

_____. "Models of Female Sanctity in Renaissance and Counter-Reformation Italy." In *Women and Faith: Catholic Religious Life in Italy from Late Antiquity to the Present*, eds. Lucetta Scaraffia and Gabriella Zarri. Cambridge, MA: Harvard University Press, 1999, 159–175.

_____. "Persuasive Pictures: Didactic Prints and the Construction of Social Identity of Women in Sixteenth-Century Italy." In *Women in Italian Renaissance Culture and Society*, ed. Letizia Panizza. Oxford: Legenda, European Humanities Research Centre, 2000, 285–314.

McIver, Katherine. *Women, Art, and Architecture in Northern Italy, 1520–1580: Negotiating Power*. Aldershot, UK: Ashgate, 2006.

Menchi, Silvana Seidel. "The Girl and the Hourglass: Periodization of Women's Lives in Western Preindustrial Society." In *Time, Space, & Women's Lives in Early Modern Europe*, eds. Anne Jacobson Schutte, Thomas Kuehn, and Silvana Seidel Menchi. Kirksville, MO: Truman State University Press, 2001, 41–74.

Miles, Margaret R. *Image as Insight: Visual Understanding in Western Christianity and Secular Culture*. Boston: Beacon Press, 1985.

Modesti, Adelina. *Elisabetta Sirani: una virtuosa del Seicento bolognese*. Bologna: Editrice Compositori, 2004.

Morse, Margaret. "Creating Sacred Spaces: the Religious Visual Culture of the Renaissance Venetian Casa." *Renaissance Studies* 21.2 (2007): 151–184.

Morselli, Raffaella. *Collezioni e quadrerie nella Bologna del Seicento: Inventari 1640–1707*. Los Angeles: The J. Paul Getty Trust, 1998.

Murphy, Caroline. "Lavinia Fontana and Female Life Cycle Experience in Late Sixteenth-Century Bologna." In *Picturing Women in Renaissance and Baroque Italy*, eds. Geraldine A. Johnson and Sara F. Matthews-Grieco. Cambridge and New York: Cambridge University Press, 1997, 111–138.

_____. *Lavinia Fontana: A Painter and her Patrons in Sixteenth-century Bologna*. New Haven and London, 2003.

Musacchio, Jacqueline M. *The Art and Ritual of Childbirth in Renaissance Italy*. New Haven and London: Yale University Press, 1999.

_____. "Lambs, Coral, Teeth, and the Intimate Intersection of Religion and Magic in Renaissance Italy." In *Images, Relics, and Devotional Practices in Medieval and Renaissance Italy*, eds. Sally J. Cornelison and Scott B. Montgomery. Tempe, AZ: Arizona Center for Medieval and Renaissance Studies, 2005, 139–56.

_____. *Art, Marriage, & Family in the Florentine Renaissance Palace*. New Haven: Yale University Press, 2008.

Nixon, Virginia. *Mary's Mother: Saint Anne in Late Medieval Europe*. University Park, PA: Pennsylvania State University Press, 2004.

Orth, Myra D. "Madame Sainte Anne: The Holy Kinship, the Royal Trinity, and Louise of Savoy." In *Interpreting Cultural Symbols*, eds. Kathleen Ashley and Pamela Sheingorn. Athens, Georgia and London: University of Georgia Press, 1990, 199–227.

Smith, Alison. "Gender, Ownership and Domestic Space: Inventories and Family Archives in Renaissance Verona." *Renaissance Studies* 12.3 (1998): 375–391.

Smoller, Laura A. "Holy Mothers: the History of a Designation of Spiritual Status." In *Piety and Family in Early Modern Europe: Essays in Honour of Stephen Ozment*, eds. Marc R. Forster and Benjamin J. Kaplan. Aldershot, UK: Ashgate, 2005, 178–200.

Strauss, Walter L. and Adam von Bartsch. *The Illustrated Bartsch*. Arabis Books: New York, 1978–.

Terpstra, Nicholas. *Abandoned Children of the Italian Renaissance: Orphan Care in Florence and Bologna*. Baltimore: The Johns Hopkins University Press, 2005.

_____. *Lay Confraternities and Civic Religion in Renaissance Bologna*. Cambridge: Cambridge University Press, 1995.

Thornton, Peter. *The Italian Renaissance Interior, 1400–1600.* New York: Harry N. Abrams, 1991.

Valier, Agostino. *Institutione d'ogni stato lodevole delle donne christiane.* Venice: Bolognino Zaltieri, 1575.

Vecellio, Cesare. *The Clothing of the Renaissance World: Europe, Asia, Africa, the Americas: Cesare Vecellio's Habiti Antichi et Moderni.* Essay and translation by Margaret F. Rosenthal and Ann Rosalind Jones. London and New York: Thames and Hudson, 2008.

Vives, Juan Luis. *De institutione feminae christianae: liber secundus & liber tertius,* eds. C. Fantazzi and C. Matheeussen. Trans. C. Fantazzi. Leiden: E.J. Brill, 1998.

_____. *De l'ufficio del marito, come si debba portare verso la moglie. De l'institutione de la femina christiana, vergine, maritata, ò vedova. De lo ammaestrare i fanciulli ne le arti liberali.* Venice: Vincenzo Valgrisi, 1546.

Wheaton, Robert, "Family and Kinship in Western Europe: The Problem of the Joint Family Household." *Journal of Interdisciplinary History* 5.4 (1975): 601–628.

Wright, Alison, "The Memory of Faces: Representational Choices in Fifteenth-Century Florentine Portraiture." In *Art, Memory, and Family in Renaissance Florence,* eds. Giovanni Ciappelli and Patricia Lee Rubin. Cambridge: Cambridge University Press, 2000, 86–113.

Zappieri, Roberto. *Annibale Carracci: ritratto di artista da giovane.* Turin: Giulio Einaudi, 1989.

Zarri, Gabriella. "Christian Good Manners: Spiritual and Monastic Rules in the Quattro- and Cinquecento." In *Women in Italian Renaissance Culture and Society,* ed. Letizia Panizza. Oxford: Legenda, European Humanities Research Centre, 2000, 76–91.

_____, ed. *Donna, disciplina, creanza Cristiana dal XV al XVII secolo: studi e testi a stampa.* Rome: Edizioni di storia e letteratura, 1996.

Poetry and Society in Aragonese Naples: Giovanni Pontano's Elegies of Married Love

Matteo Soranzo

On 1 February 1461, the King of Naples, Ferrante of Aragon (1423–1494), authorized his trusted assistant Giovanni Pontano (1429–1503) to marry the Neapolitan noble lady, Adriana Sassone (1444–1490), during a short break in the war between the Neapolitans and Venetians in Romagna.[1] This event was carefully planned and was at the centre of a complex sociopolitical context. The union of a state bureaucrat from Umbria with a lady of the local nobility was consistent with Ferrante's attempts to strengthen his principality by reinforcing the role of Italian and Neapolitan individuals in the administration of state institutions.[2] The connection with a rich and noble family provided the young state bureaucrat with the means to meet the prerequisites of Neapolitan nobility, that is, the acquisition of important relatives and the construction of lavish residences in the city and its outskirts.[3] The event, therefore, was the first step toward Giovanni Pontano's affirmation as a respected and influential citizen of Naples and as the King's personal secretary, two statuses that he managed to acquire in 1471 and 1486 respectively.[4]

---

[1] Monti Sabia, "Prolusione," 14–15. Monti Sabia has identified the date and location of Ferrante's campaign in Romagna, which biographers had mistakenly identified with the war of Ferrara in 1482–84; Monti Sabia, "Un canzoniere per una moglie," 27–29; see also her "Vicende belliche e sentimenti coniugali," 437–438 and her "Tra realtà e poesia: per una nuova cronologia di alcuni carmi del *De Amore Coniugali*," 353–356.

[2] Abulafia, "Ferrante of Naples. The Statecraft of a Renaissance Prince," 20; Vitale, "Sul segretario regio al servizio degli Aragonesi di Napoli," 300–301; and her *Modelli culturali nobiliari nella Napoli aragonese*, 9. Bentley has examined the intellectual ramifications of this pattern; Bentley, *Politica e cultura*, 263–264.

[3] Vitale, *Elite burocratica e famiglia*, 109, 116, 139–143.

[4] Monti Sabia, "Prolusione," 10, 18. Kidwell, *Pontano: Poet and Prime Minister*, 77, 103–104.

On 24 February 1495, King Charles VIII (1470–98) invaded Naples initiating the downfall of the Aragonese Kingdom.[5] Giovanni Pontano retired to private life and began to revise a considerable amount of writings which were only partially finished and printed during his busy life as a state administrator. In response to the humanist revival of the theme of marriage, Pontano finalized *De Amore Coniugali* (written 1461–90; first printed 1505), a collection of Latin poems in elegiac couplets, about his union with Adriana Sassone.[6] This project was in tune with the intellectual context of fifteenth-century Italy. As Anthony D'Elia has masterfully argued, Quattrocento Italian writers of nuptial orations, dialogues and epithalamia contributed to the rediscovery of the joys of married life, while at the same time setting the stage for the way in which this experience was rethought in Europe during the Reformation.[7] In addition, Mauro De Nichilo has demonstrated how the rediscovery of Greek rhetorical treatises on nuptial oratory stimulated a rebirth of nuptial writing in fifteenth-century Italian courts.[8] Married life, and the celebration of weddings, became the object of, and the setting for, public speeches that voiced the new, secular ideology that characterized Quattrocento elite culture. Differently from his contemporaries, however, Pontano's book explored the theme of married life from an unusually subjective angle not found among nuptial orations written for Renaissance princes or in other treatises *de re uxoria*.

This article argues that Pontano's *De Amore Coniugali* presents an ideal portrait of a married lover in order to adjust the culture of the state bureaucracy to the values of the Neapolitan nobility. Also, this collection criticizes aristocratic attitudes toward warfare, still found among Neapolitan nobles. I will start with an examination of Pontano's own marriage in relation to the elite society of Quattrocento Naples, and relate his book to the revival of Latin erotic elegy among intellectuals affiliated with the Neapolitan state bureaucracy. I will then situate Pontano's idea of love and marriage in the context of Neapolitan manuals of behaviour and advice books. From a theoretical point of view, the assumption that *De Amore Coniugali* half-consciously refracts the conflicting values of the several spheres that

---

[5] Abulafia, "Introduction: From Ferrante I to Charles VIII," 21–25.

[6] Parenti, *Poeta Proteus alter*, 80–91; Monti Sabia, "Un canzoniere per una moglie," 38.

[7] D'Elia, *The Renaissance of Marriage*, 9.

[8] De Nichilo, *Oratio nuptialis*, 15–34; and his *Retorica e Magnificenza*, 39–52.

intersected in Pontano's career presents a dilemma. On the one hand, this text may be reduced to the status of a document, and thus taken as a reflection of how marriages actually took place in Quattrocento Italy. On the other hand, the text may be approached as a specimen of literature addressed to a timeless culture and free from historical constraints. Both these approaches may be usefully overcome by adopting Pierre Bourdieu's theory of cultural production.[9] Bourdieu's models suits the condition of Renaissance writers like Pontano, who lived in a period of rapid social change needed in their works, to carefully craft their authorial personae to meet the expectations of critical and highly competitive audiences. From this perspective, Renaissance texts do not simply reflect social patterns, but rather *refract* the way in which these social patterns occurred in a field of multiple agents writing on a given subject.[10] Cultural products like Pontano's text, therefore, were not composed in a vacuum but were invested with a determinate quantity of prestige, or capital, by which authors designed a trajectory in relation to, and in competition with, other agents active in their field.[11]

Pontano's Marriage and Neapolitan Society

Pontano decided to write and publish *De Amore Coniugali* in order to turn a private moment of his life into a public event charged with political meaning, thus following a common pattern in Neapolitan elite society.[12] Differently from Quattrocento institutions such as the Florentine *Signoria*, in which members of the Chancellery conducted lives that were clearly distinguished between public commitments and private interests, the Aragonese administration was a work in progress and its agents' status was in the process of being defined. Since he had come to power as an illegitimate successor of the Angevin rulers of Naples, Alphonse the Magnanimous had gathered a group of loyal ministers from outside of Naples to protect his fragile authority from

---

[9] Bourdieu, *The Field of Cultural Production*, 13–14, 177–182.

[10] Bourdieu, *The Field of Cultural Production*, 14, 182.

[11] Bourdieu, *The Field of Cultural Production*, 50–51.

[12] By elite society, I mean a social group that is similar to the one identified in seventeenth-century Spain by Maravall, *Poder, honor y élites in el siglo XVII*. Giuliana Vitale has persuasively applied Maravall's notion to the case of Aragonese Naples; Vitale, *Elite burocratica e famiglia*, 72.

internal and external dissent.[13] Following in his father's footsteps, Ferrante further reinforced this institution by investing the figure of the secretary with an indefinite amount of political capital, while strengthening his agents' role in a way that was often perceived as outrageous by Neapolitan nobility.[14] This policy encouraged members of the state administration to display publicly their private wealth by adopting aristocratic behaviours such as the construction of buildings in strategic areas of the city, as well as the purchase of land in the surrounding territories.[15] Following this pattern, Pontano was himself an important patron of a richly decorated family chapel and lavishly adorned palaces.[16] Likewise, literary texts such as *De Amore Coniugali* responded to this widespread need for self-fashioning that blurred the boundaries between private and public sphere.

This pattern responded to the moment of exceptional change and redefinition of roles that marked Ferrante's kingdom and reconfigured the elite society of Naples under the Aragonese domination. In the Kingdom of Naples, aristocratic society was traditionally divided into two main groups. One group was the urban nobility, which comprised families organized into five town halls called *seggi* or *sedili* residing within the city walls.[17] The other group was the feudal nobility, which included ancient and powerful families of landowners scattered around the Kingdom's territory.[18] In inheriting this state of affairs from their Angevin predecessors, the Aragonese kings developed two different attitudes toward these groups and imposed their bureaucrats as a third group in the local elite society.[19] More specifically, Ferrante progressively involved the local nobility (*nobiltà di seggio*) in the administration of the Kingdom, by accepting its members into the royal bureaucracy and by starting a court.[20] Alphonse and Ferrante, however, used

---

[13] Abulafia, "Ferrante of Naples," 20.

[14] Vitale, "Sul segretario regio al servizio degli Aragonesi di Napoli," 315–6.

[15] Vitale, *Elite burocratica e famiglia*, 79–81; De Divitiis, *Architettura e committenza*, 11, 34–9.

[16] De Divitiis, "Giovanni Pontano and his Idea of Patronage," 124–125.

[17] Vitale, "La nobiltà di Seggio a Napoli," 151–169. Vitale has revised this article and framed it in a broader history of Neapolitan elite society; Vitale, *Elite burocratica e famiglia*, 83–133.

[18] Gothein, *Il Rinascimento nell'Italia meridionale*, 31–62.

[19] Sakellariou, "Institutional and Social Continuities in Naples," 336–339.

[20] Vitale, *Modelli culturali nobiliari*, 9; and her *Elite burocratica e famiglia*, 71–79.

an iron fist against the feudal aristocracy that lived outside of Naples; more than once the so-called barons conspired against the king and were violently defeated.[21] The cases of Antonello Petrucci (1420–1487) and Diomede Carafa (1406–1487), respectively a commoner who ended up involved in a conspiracy of barons, and a noble who became one of Ferrante's courtiers, are two extreme instances of the social changes at work in Neapolitan elite society.

Pontano's marriage with Adriana Sassone and the publication of *De Amore Coniugali* were means by which Pontano constructed his public image in front of the members of Neapolitan elite society. The Sassone family was enlisted in the prestigious *seggio* of Portanuova and, therefore, belonged to the city nobility, which was becoming increasingly inclined to approve unions between its members and the agents involved in the prestigious bureaucratic elite.[22] Not only did Pontano and his contemporaries intermarry, invest in the construction of worthy residences and accumulate precious house wares, but they also asserted their social status and defined their identities by writing and publishing idealized portraits, in the form of manuals of behaviour. Pontano, for example, devoted his treatises *De Magnificentia* and *De Splendore* to the definition of the perfect state bureaucrat.[23] In the meantime, members of the Neapolitan aristocracy, such as Tristano Caracciolo (1437–1528), discussed the features of the perfect noble citizen in his *Opusculum ad Marchionem Atellae* and *De Concordia et de Ineundo Coniugio*.[24] Marriage was a common theme in this body of literature. Therefore, I would suggest that *De Amore Coniugali* is a text that encodes Pontano's self-fashioning as a perfect state bureaucrat progressively involved in the life of urban aristocracy.

It would be an oversimplification, however, to approach Pontano's nuptial poems as if they were simply an outgrowth of the society of Naples in the second half of the Quattrocento. As Dominick LaCapra has proposed, this misleading use of the intellectual and historical context, as an explanatory matrix, is a form of determinism, which does not take into sufficient account the ambiguity of a text and, in particular, its relationship with other works produced in the same place and period. This methodological pitfall can

---

[21] Abulafia, "Ferrante of Naples," 22; Abulafia, "Introduction: From Ferrante I to Charles VIII," 6–9.

[22] Vitale, *Elite burocratica e famiglia*, 96.

[23] Welch, "Public Magnificence and Private Display," 216–219.

[24] Vitale, *Modelli culturali nobiliari*, 60–87, 162–164.

be fruitfully bypassed by looking at what role these contexts play within a text, and how the text inscribes different discourses within itself.[25] Applied to Pontano's text, this methodology permits an examination of how this text is engaged in a dialogue with, and is often critical of, similar writings on marriage that were produced by other members of the elite of Naples. In particular, since *De Amore Coniugali* comprises a selection of poems that belong to the genre of Latin love elegy, the first issue to be addressed is how this text is engaged in a dialogue with this genre, as it was practiced and diffused in Quattrocento Naples.

De amore coniugali *and Humanistic Elegy*

In its final version, *De Amore Coniugali* consists of three books of poems in elegiac couplets, organized chronologically. In the first book, the poet writes about his engagement, the wedding ceremony and the birth of his first son, Lucio, against the background of the war in Romagna (1467–8). In the second book, the poet deals with the purchase of his villa in Antignano, and his family life in the outskirts of Naples during the years of the War in Tuscany (1478–1480). The third and last book closes the cycle by collecting poems about the marriages of the poet's daughters, against the backdrop of the War against Ferrara (1482–4).[26] Apparently detached from this general design, but lyrically connected to the text as a whole, is a series of lullabies found at the end of the second book, which constitute the sentimental climax of the story told by *De Amore Coniugali*, that is, the birth of the poet's son.[27]

The choice of Latin elegy as a genre, and married love as the collection's exclusive theme, situates Pontano's project in the ambit of the intellectual community led by Antonio Beccadelli (1394–1471).[28] In Quattrocento Italy, writers of love poetry were becoming increasingly prone to imitate the model of Petrarch's *Rerum Vulgarium Fragmenta* and progressively inclined

---

[25] LaCapra, *Rethinking Intellectual History*, 84–117, 99.

[26] Monti Sabia, "Un canzoniere per una moglie," 25–34; and her "Vicende belliche e sentimenti nel *De Amore Coniugali*," 437–438; and "Tra realtà e poesia," 351–370.

[27] Monti Sabia, "Un canzoniere per una moglie," 31–32.

[28] Antonio Beccadelli, also known as Panormita, had established himself as Alphonse's ambassador during the 1450s, and he had quickly become the most influential member of the State bureaucracy. Like Pontano, Beccadelli reinforced his status by marrying a noble Neapolitan lady and investing his wealth in architectural projects; Beccadelli, *Hermaphroditus*, 13–15.

to choose the Tuscan vernacular as their literary language.[29] In Naples, the presence of Florentine bankers, the circulation of books in the Tuscan vernacular and, eventually, the close diplomatic relationship between King Ferrante and Lorenzo de Medici, contributed to create a receptive audience for Petrarch's book in the vernacular, as can be inferred from the composition of Francesco Patrizi's commentary on Petrarch, or Benit Gareth's collection of love poems, entitled *Endymion*.[30] In addition, books modeled upon Petrarch's *Rerum Vulgarium Fragmenta* endorsed its theme of unrequited love and told stories that alluded, with changing nuances, to Petrarch's longing for Laura and the psychological and religious torments caused by amorous passion. By choosing Latin, Beccadelli and his followers provocatively placed their work in opposition to the Neapolitan version of this widespread adoption of the Tuscan vernacular as the literary language.[31]

If the adoption of Latin entailed an antagonistic attitude toward the diffusion of Petrarchan poetry in the vernacular, the choice of writing elegies on married love was problematic. In its Roman origin, the elegy was a genre characterized by a critical attitude toward the traditional values imposed by Augustus, a series of commonplaces about the adventures and troubles that mark a young man's love life and the unforgettable portraits of cruel and playful mistresses, such as Propertius' Cynthia or Tibullus' Delia.[32] Written in the distinctive form of the elegiac couplet, a sequence of verses that resulted from the combination of one hexameter, the verse of epic poetry, with a hexameter deprived of one foot, elegy was traditionally practiced as an understated genre appropriate to an apparently lesser theme.[33] Elegiac poets presented themselves as living on the fringes of Roman society, devoted solely to the pursuit of poetry and love. The love of elegists, in particular, was constructed as free from official commitments and often was adulterous. Although Propertius wrote about a married couple, in a poem found in the fourth book of his elegiac corpus, married love was not compatible with elegy.

---

[29] Santagata, *La lirica aragonese.*

[30] Villani, "L'Umanesimo napoletano," 739–743; Paolino, "Per l'edizione del commento di Francesco Patrizi da Siena," 153–311; Parenti, *Benet Garret detto il Cariteo*, 34–45.

[31] Villani, "L'umanesimo napoletano," 709–712; De Blasi, *Profilo linguistico della Campania*, 122–124.

[32] Luck, "Love Elegy," 109–123; Keith, *Propertius. Poet of Love and Leisure*, 141–165; Miller, *Subjecting Verses*, 16–30, 107–117, 143–159.

[33] Luck, "Love Elegy," 109.

Unaware of Augustan elegists, medieval theorists and poets, writing in vernacular, failed to codify, and hesitated to embrace, the model of Latin love elegy, well into the fifteenth century. Dante, for example, positioned elegy between tragedy and comedy but loosely defined this genre as a generic way of uttering laments appropriate to miserable individuals.[34] Dante's position was consistent with medieval rhetorical treatises, which generally identified elegy with a mourning theme, separated its content from its form and proposed Boethius' *Consolation of Philosophy* as a model.[35] This position was destined to condition poets writing in Italian vernaculars for a long time to come. A group of vernacular poets, who were active in Aragonese Naples, for example, used the word elegy to label a collection of mourning poems.[36] The situation was different, if not reversed, among the growing influential intellectual communities, trained in Latin and Greek language and prone to use Latin as their literary language.

In fifteenth-century Italy, Latin love elegy constituted a complex alternative to the growing linguistic and thematic influence of Petrarch's *Rerum Vulgarium Fragmenta*. The humanistic rediscovery and imitation of the ancient Roman poets Tibullus (ca. 54–19 BC) and Propertius (ca. 50–15 BC) had given direct access to the world of Roman love elegy.[37] More specifically, love elegy was revived in Ferrara and Siena, during the first half of the fifteenth century, by authors such as Tito Vespasiano Strozzi (1424–1505) and the aforementioned Antonio Beccadelli. Strozzi, who tried to reconcile the fragmentary features of elegiac love stories with the solid structure of Petrarch's book, had a direct impact on Pontano's poetry, with his famous *Erotica* (written *ca.* 1459; first printed 1513), a collection of Latin elegies that was found in an elegant dedication copy at the Aragonese Library.[38] Beccadelli, who revived Latin elegy and epigram in his *Hermaphroditus* (written 1425–50; first printed 1790), influenced a group of elegists based in

---

[34] Curtius, *European Literature*, 357; Mengaldo, "L'elegia umile," 200–222.

[35] Carrai, "Appunti sulla preistoria dell'elegia volgare," 4, 8–9.

[36] Santagata, *La lirica aragonese*, 262; Vecchi Galli, "Percorsi dell'elegia quattrocentesca in volgare," 41.

[37] Parenti, "*Contaminatio* di modelli e di generi nel *Liber Parthenopeus*," 50–51.

[38] Tissoni Benvenuti, "Boiardo elegiaco e Tito Vespasiano Strozzi," 85.

Siena, before settling down in Naples, where he became Pontano's political and literary mentor.[39]

In line with their Roman predecessors, Quattrocento elegists wrote sexually explicit verses about their love affairs with outgoing women, whose features were modeled on the heartbreaker and reckless *puellae* of Latin elegy. Analogous with their ancient models, the women found in humanistic elegy were generally constructed as ambiguous figures of married ladies or courtesans, who divided their lives between parties and multiple love affairs, while provoking their suitors' jealousy and reinforcing their friendship.[40] In a way that drastically differs from Petrarch's unrequited love for Laura, around 1450 Beccadelli wrote and eventually collected in his *Hermaphroditus*, a poem that was meant to encourage his young pupil Pontano to enjoy the favours of a married young woman named Polla. In doing so, Beccadelli consciously adjusted a commonplace, found in Propertius and Tibullus, to gain the complicity of, and engage in a dialogue with, his young friend and pupil, while encouraging him to pursue his erotic ambitions:

> [...] and even if you sing sweetly, may your voice seem / even sweeter, and may she believe there's nothing sweeter, / and may this heat increase day by day, and he love her / more intensely, she more intensely her man, / and may the wonderful nymph seem to you / a Helen, and you to her a Paris./ May her hairy husband breathe his last immediately, / if he's not the god of gardens (*i.e. Priapus*) you think he is. / But whether he's a god or not, let her pretend / that you're her husband, and dream that she's sleeping with you. / And may it befall you at last to enclose her tongue / between your lips and feel the weight of your mistress's / pussy.[41]

Written under the influence of a mentor like Beccadelli, Pontano's first attempts in the elegiac genre were aligned with the joyful and light-hearted values of Roman erotic elegy and its Quattrocento revival. In his

---

[39] Viti, "L'umanesimo toscano nel primo Quattrocento," 281–286; Panormita, *Hermaphroditus*, 13–15.

[40] Miller, *Subjecting Verses*, 60–94.

[41] Beccadelli, *The Hermaphrodite*, 1: 28, 13–24. Beccadelli's verses are quoted in Parker's translation.

sophisticated book *Parthenopeus* (written 1455–8, first printed 1505), Pontano had used his perfect knowledge of Latin and love elegy to recount the amorous escapades that used to take place at the spa of Baia, on the outskirts of Naples, or his more or less romantic affairs with courtesans, such as the Neapolitan lady Fannia. In a poem, phrased according to the elegiac commonplace of the *paraklausytiron*, a love song set in front of the lover's door, Pontano celebrated Fannia with language that is reminiscent of Propertius' pathos and Beccadelli's sensuality:

> Open the door, Fannia. My Fannia, Fannia, I beg you: open the door, open the door. And on your warm breast, my sweet friend, you will warm up one, who is frozen by the wind and the rain. I am not asking that much: love and the winter season demand mutually joyful embraces.[42]

Although very different from Petrarch's unconsummated and unrequited love, elegiac love, as defined, and perhaps experienced, by its Roman inventors and Quattrocento practitioners never contemplated marriage as a feasible option. The young age of Propertius and Tibullus, as well as their common model Catullus, partially explains their critical attitude toward a social practice, which was also charged with important ideological meaning, in Caesar Augustus' restoration of tradition and discipline in first-century BCE Rome.[43] Although marriage and traditional religious worship were at the center of Augustus' program of social reform, and reintroduced in Rome through *ad hoc* laws, elegiac poets always fashioned themselves as marginal individuals, who never entertained the prospect of a legitimate union with their generally married mistresses. Along with their contempt for legitimate unions, elegiac poets like Tibullus also presented themselves as critical of warfare and political engagement, while fashioning their authorial personae as disengaged individuals dedicated to poetry and love alone.

I would suggest that the ideology of Latin love elegy was particularly suitable for a group of intellectuals who, like Beccadelli, were the members

---

[42] Pontano, *Parthenopeus*, 1, 3, vv. 17–22: "Fannia, solve fores, mea Fannia, Fannia, / quaeso / Solve fores, quaeso, Fannia, solve fores, / Et me, quem gelidus Boreas contraxit et himber, / In tepido foveas, dulcis amica, sinu. / Quod rogo, nec magnum est; et amor sibi mutua poscit, / Mutuaque amplexus gaudia poscit hiems." My translations.

[43] Pinotti, *L'elegia latina*, 156–158.

of an elite group of male foreigners, whose attitude toward marriage was generally irreverent. Beccadelli's death in 1471, Ferrante's policy to involve local citizens in his bureaucracy and Pontano's newly acquired intellectual leadership helped set the scene for the revised view of love implied in *De Amore Coniugali*. While working on his experimental nuptial elegy, Pontano, himself, tried to hedge Antonio Beccadelli's irreverent view of marriage in his *De Obedientia* (written 1470; first printed 1490), a philosophical treatise the third book of which is entirely devoted to an explanation of the philosophical and political virtues of marriage. Dedicated to Roberto Sanseverino, a member of the feudal aristocracy who had recently become the King of Salerno, Pontano's *De Obedientia* is both an advice book and a manifesto for the new direction taken by Pontano's intellectual community, after Beccadelli's death.

> Having been asked what he thought was most appropriate for a tranquil married life, I once heard Antonio Beccadelli replying that there could not be quiet and prosperous marriages unless the husband were deaf, or the wife blind.[44]

Consistent with Pontano's argumentative style, the third book of *De Obedientia* consistently grounds its propositions with quotations taken from *De Amore Coniugali*, so that the treatise turns Pontano's poetic celebration of his relationship into an exemplar of married love. In response to his contemporaries, who were increasingly inclined to endorse Petrarchan love in their collections of poetry, and in tune with the political agenda of Ferrante's statecraft, Pontano's *De Obedientia* creates a solid link between love and social order, by presenting obedience as the pillar of civic life.[45] The form

---

[44] Pontano, *De Obedientia*, 3, fol. 21v: "Antonium Panormita, cum ab eo quaereretur quibus maxime opus esse iudicaret ad connubij tranquillitatem, respondentem audiui, Nullas nec quietas, nec felices satis nuptias esse posse, praeterquam si uir surdus esset, uxor vero caeca." As professor Barbara Bowen has commented on an early draft of this article, this joke is a quotation from Beccadelli's *De Dictis et Factis Alphonsi Regis Aragonorum*, which can be read in English translation in *One Hundred Renaissance Jokes*, 11. Interestingly enough, Beccadelli originally attributed the joke to King Alphonse himself.

[45] Pontano, *De Obedientia*, 3, fols. 21v –22r: "Quanquam autem in hac coniunctione, quae prima quidem societas est, magnam esse amoris vim fatentur omnes, facile tamen amor vertetur in odium, ubi obedientia vireis suas amiserit." [Although everyone agrees that love has a major strength in this union, which is the first form of society, love easily turns into hatred when obedience loses its hold].

of love praised in *De Amore Coniugali*, therefore, is presented as the perfect result of love and obedience:

> A wife is not chosen to share exclusively domestic things, so that she can live without those concerns and dangers of which no life is lacking: she, who is married to procreate, is meant to endure concerns as well as pleasures. This is why, legitimately perhaps, I could praise my Adriana when I said: "You willingly come to share my concerns, and with legitimate art you support the household and the kids."[46]

Consistent with Pierre Bourdieu's theory of cultural production, the composition of a work of art is an act by which an historical agent takes position within an intellectual field and displays a taste that is analogous with, or different from, other options available at the time. Applied to the study of literature, this notion of taste translates into, for example, the adoption of specific languages, genres and stylistic features.[47] Therefore, according to this model, the choice of a genre (elegy), a language (Latin) and a theme (marriage) helps to situate Pontano in the ambit of the Latin intellectual community, originally formed around Antonio Beccadelli. This community had found, in the Latin love elegy, a suitable protocol, and an appropriate authorial persona, for sharing intimate episodes of its members' amorous life. Also, the choice of Latin elegy provided the members of this community with the means to distinguish themselves from their contemporaries, whose taste was defined by the adoption of a specific language, the Tuscan vernacular, and a particular ideology of love, Petrarchan unrequited love. By adjusting the Latin love elegy to the theme of marriage, Pontano was thus trying to distinguish himself from his mentor's legacy and from a growing Petrarchan trend in the Neapolitan intellectual field. The technical features of the ideological program inscribed in *De Amore Coniugali* is further understood

---

[46] Pontano, *De Obedientia*, 3, fol. 21v : "Neque enim in sociam domesticarum rerum lecta est uxor, ut laboris, ac periculi, sine quibus nullum esse vitae genus potest, expers vivat, cum ad labores non minus quam ad voluptates ducta videatur quae prolis causa ducta est. Quamobrem et nos recte fortasse laudasse Adrianam nostram videri possumus, cum diximus: "In partemque venis nostrorum sponte laborum / Remque domi et natos qua licet arte iuvas"." The quotation corresponds to Pontano, *De Amore Coniugali*, 1, 6, vv. 55–56.

[47] Bourdieu, *The Rules of Art*, 232–233.

by examining what role Renaissance wedding discourses played within the text, and how the text translates the words of weddings into the language of the love elegy.

Rewriting Renaissance Wedding

In refuting the ideas on love and marriage that marked Beccadelli's legacy, Pontano innovatively translated documents, ceremonial phrases and Renaissance wedding rituals into the language of the Latin love elegy. Before the Council of Trent (1545–1565), weddings were for the most part agreements between families, staged in front of a notary and the civic community. [48] Renaissance weddings were distributed over a long period of time and consisted of four distinct stages, marked by specific actions, actors, locations and language. [49] In Renaissance Florence, for example, these stages included the *impalmamento* (a private promise sealed by a handshake), the *sponsalitium* (a formal promise pronounced in front of male witnesses from the two families), the *matrimonium* (an oath pronounced by the groom and the bride in front of notary and their families) and the *ductio* (the public conveyance of the bride at her husband's house). [50] Moreover, Renaissance weddings were also linguistic events, made of carefully chosen spoken and written words. Each stage was characterized by the writing of official documents, which the notary phrased in different tenses. In particular, the notary sealed the *sponsalitium* by writing a document called the *istrumento delli futuri sponsalitii*, in which the groom promised, in the future tense (*in verba de futuro*), to wed the bride within the established time frame. [51] During the *matrimonium*, the notary invited the groom to place the ring on the bride's finger, while the couple exchanged vows in the present tense (*in verba de praesenti*), recorded in the *instrumentum matrimonii*. [52]

The four elegies that open the first book of *De Amore Coniugali* transform the stages of the wedding ritual, and its characteristic language, into

---

[48] Reynolds, "Marrying and Its Documentation," 17; Klapisch-Zuber, "Zacharias, or the Ousted Father," 193.

[49] Reynolds, "Marrying and Its Documentation," 5–7.

[50] Kuehn, "Contracting Marriage in Renaissance Florence," 390–401; Brucker, *Giovanni and Lusanna*, 82–83.

[51] Kuehn, "Contracting Marriage in Renaissance Florence," 392–306.

[52] Kuehn, "Contracting Marriage in Renaissance Florence," 396–398.

a carefully crafted narrative. The mechanism of Pontano's fiction consists in using the rhetorical trope of personification, and in rewriting the *instrumenta* according to the ancient genres of *Hymaneios* (the poem sung during the bride's procession to her husband's house) and *Epithalamium* (the poem for the bride on her way to the marital chamber). In Renaissance weddings, grooms and brides were not allowed to communicate directly before the *sponsalia* and the groom had to communicate his intentions through a third party.[53] Likewise, in the opening poem of his book, Pontano personifies Elegy and casts her in the role of a *sensale*, who directly interacts with the poet and persuades his future bride to accept him as her spouse. In this way, the text refracts the moment of *sponsalia* into a twofold literary event, that is, the affirmation of the poet's authorship as the new elegiac poet of marriage and the fictional translation of the *istrumento delli futuri sposalitii*. The first facet of this literary event insists on Pontano's characterization, as a man from Umbria who writes poetry in Naples, a motif that situates the poet in a literary genealogy whose founder is Propertius, the poet from Umbria who wrote elegies in Rome. In verses phrased as a persuasive speech, the poet seeks to convince Elegy to embrace the unusual theme by recalling her love for Propertius. This memory should induce her to accept Pontano's proposal:

> And so come close and embrace, goddess, the lyre but move its strings with a soft quill and a sweet sound. Your father is Mercury, your mother the attentive Eurymie: they gave you the knowledge of singing and the lyre. Moreover, if I am not wrong, you are an expert of new loves and approve those sweet traps hidden in the grass. They narrate that one day, while travelling among the paternal Umbrians, you rested by the clear waters of the river Clitumnus. Here, they say, you saw and ardently fancied a young boy swimming, and you desired to have him in your arms.[54]

---

[53] Kuehn, "Contracting Marriage in Renaissance Florence," 393.

[54] Pontano, *De Amore Coniugali*, 1, 1, vv. 23–32: "Ergo ades et cape, diva, lyram, sed pectine molli, / Sed moveas dulci lenia fila sono; / Nam tibi Mercurius pater est, tibi sedula mater / Eurymie cantus nosse lyramque dedit. / Quin etiam tu, experta novos (ni fallor) amores / Dulcia supposito gramine furta probas: / Nanque ferunt patrios vectam quandoque per Umbros / Clitunni liquidis accubuisse vadis, / Hic iuvenem vidisse, atque incaluisse natantem, / et cupiisse ulnas inter habere tuas."

As a result of the poet's request, and analogous to the third party's referral of the groom's intention to the bride, Elegy eventually addresses the young woman and persuades her to accept the poet as her spouse. In agreement with the protocol of the *istrumento delli futuri sposalitii*, Elegy phrases the poet's promise in the future tense. Moreover, in line with the traditional characterization of the elegiac poet, Elegy invites the future bride to neglect her suitor's modest financial situation in light of his poetic achievements, while urging her to accept him, regardless of his public commitments. In reporting the poet's promises, Elegy also makes reference to the conjugal bond as the highest form of friendship, a commonplace found in humanistic nuptial oratory:[55]

> Don't compare wealth with sacred poetry, and stop trying to sell your beauty for a price; I will not praise you, refined girl, if you will end up pursuing the money of a rich man after ditching a poet. Beauty is a celestial gift, which gold cannot buy.[56] [...] Don't you want a poet as your spouse, one who is divinely assisted, crowned with a laurel tree and in whose mouth poetry resounds? May he not refuse to be yours. Don't you want a suitor? May he be your everlasting suitor. And in the attempt to please you, may he not avoid facing dangerous battles and the shores of the Scythian sea; may the cold stars of Bootae not delay him, and neither the sun-burned fields of Libya; he will keep his marital faith until his old years, he will be fond of you and once an old man, he will live with caring love.[57]

---

[55] D'Elia, *The Renaissance of Marriage*, 109–110.

[56] Pontano, *De Amore Coniugali*, 1, 1, vv. 57–62: "Desine divitias versu conferre beato, / Et faciem pretio vendere velle tuam; / Non ego laudarim, cupias si, vate relicto, / Divitis argentum, culta puella, sequi. / Forma bonum coeleste, auro quam vendere non est."

[57] Pontano, *De Amore Coniugali*, 1, 1, vv. 97–106: "At vates, cui numen adest, cui delphica serpit / Laurus et arguto carmen in ore sonat, / Illi tibi coniuxne velis? Non esse recuset; / Anne comes? lateri sit comes usque tuo. / Dumque tibi placuisse velit, non horrida vitet / Praelia, non scythici litora adire maris; / Non illum gelidi remorentur signa Bootae, / Non usta assiduo sole libystis humus; / Coniugiique fidem seros perducet ad annos, / Tecum amet, et socio vivet amore senex."

Consistent with the Quattrocento revival of nuptial oratory and the diffusion of an explicit approach to sexuality diffused in Renaissance elite culture, Pontano's nuptial elegies adjust the erotic language used in the poems written at the time of Beccadelli to the theme of marriage. Renaissance weddings culminated with the *matrimonium*, when the spouses exchanged their vows and their rings in front of a notary or, occasionally, a priest. Similar to this ceremony, and according to the classical genre of the *hymenios*, the second poem of *De Amore Coniugali*, casts the Greek god Hymen in the role of the notary. Hymen, the Greek God of nuptial ceremonies, is described as a teacher in the kind of love praised by Quattrocento orators, who emphasized the mutuality and rightness of sexual pleasure in a married couple:[58]

> He (Hymen) taught how to embrace necks with hesitating arms, and how to bind limbs around a naked breast. He taught how to accept fights together with peace, and kisses given either when the mouth is closed, or when the lips are joined together. He taught how to speak with a trembling voice, while breath and sounds exhale from the humid throat and querulous mouth.[59]

In the literary equivalent of an *instrumentum matrimonii*, Hymen eventually addresses the newly married couple, and invites them to exchange the ring, while alluding to the mutual enjoyment that will soon follow. Phrased entirely in the present tense, as required by the ceremony (*verba de praesenti*), these verses transpose the language of a Renaissance wedding into the words of Roman love elegy:

> I now unite these hands with a prosperous vow; and you, young boy, and you, beautiful girl, say "so be it." And here it is: now receive your love, young boy, and may you not deny, maid, to give your first kisses. It is agreed: he gave, and she received. And this is honest. But why does your face blush,

---

[58] D'Elia, *The Renaissance of Marriage*, 97–106.

[59] Pontano, *De Amore Coniugali*, 1, 2, vv. 11–16: "Hic docuit lentis innectere colla lacertis / Atque renudato iungere membra sinu, / Hic rixas pacemque simul, nunc ore recluso, / Et nunc consertis oscula ferre labris, / Hic lingua titubante loqui, dum spiritus hudo / Gutture, dum querulo ducitur ore sonus."

wise girl? It is now right to uncover your soul with your eyes and your mouth. So, don't hide your joy in your silent chest. The night, Love, the bed and I will teach you the rest; now safely accept this symbol of certain faith. How beautifully this gold shines in these fingers; this ring will give you what both of you know. And now go as spouses, and with the same feelings for the vows of youth, give back what is due to the concord marital bed. May Love unite those whom Hymen and the nuptial torches have united, and may you take the same reciprocal care when you grow old.[60]

The Muse of love poetry, Erato, the personification of Elegy and an erotically charged language are all used to interpret poetically the stage of *ductio*, which corresponds to the consummation of marriage and the completion of the wedding process. In the third elegy of the collection, Pontano fashions himself as a groom, who leads his newly married bride to his house, in front of a festive crowd of young men and women. Structured as an ancient epithalamion, the poem turns the last stage of a Renaissance wedding into a literary and existential event by presenting the muse Erato and Elegy welcoming Ariadne into the poet's residence. In tune with the commonplaces of nuptial oratory, Erato and Elegy exhort the young bride to lose her virginity in the intimate encounter that seals the wedding process. At a literary level, the consummation of the marriage approved by Elegy and the muse Erato also celebrates the poet's investiture as the first nuptial elegist:

Here comes the Nymph. The god himself (*i.e. Hymen*) and the Thespian crowd of her nine Idalian sisters precede her. And they certainly look at the familiar residence and customary doorsteps, their poet's sedulous occupation. Look at how they

---

[60] Pontano, *De Amore Coniugali*, 1, 2, vv. 33–48: "Has ego felici iungo nunc omine dextras; / Dic, iuvenis, dic tu, bella puella: Placet. / En placet: ore tuos, iuvenis, nunc excipe amores, / Oscula neu, virgo, prima dedisse neges. / Convenit: dedit hic, accepit et illa. Pudicum / Hoc est. Quid vultus, scita puella, rubes? / Atque oculis animum fas est atque ore fateri, / Gaudia neu tacito, virgo, reconde sinu. / Caetera nox et nos et Amor lectusque docebunt; / Haec tu nunc fidei pignora certa cape. / Quam bene, quod digitis aurum perlucet in istis; / Anulus hic vobis, quod scit uterque, dabit. / Ite pares, paribusque animis in vota iuventae, / Et sua concordi reddite iura toro, / Iungat Amor, quos iunxit Hymen tedaeque iugales: / Quae iuvenes, teneat haec quoque cura senes."

walk with suitable steps, and how this prosperous procession applauds with its praising lyre. And while the goddesses dance and strike their Bacchic quills, for three times say "Io, Hymen, Io!" Here she comes, restrain your sounds; be silent, flute. The new bride hesitates on the unusual entrance door, and while she slows down her steps and blushes, Erato exhorts her with these words by moving her sweet mouth: "Don't be afraid, my dear, move on and cross the threshold, propitious to your husband and offspring. You will have a prosperous home, inviolate Penates, and an initially white peaceful nuptial bed, and also a husband. For him it is a treasure worthy of Croesus: may the rich river Hermus stain the bed with its red waters."[61]

So far, this article has argued that Pontano's intermarriage, and his invention of nuptial elegy, are correlated with the author's reorganization of the Neapolitan state bureaucracy after Antonio Beccadelli's death. Also, it has been shown how the text inscribes this project by rewriting the stages of a wedding ceremony into the language of Roman love elegy. The remainder of this article will examine how Pontano's intermarriage and treatment of the nuptial theme are related to the local nobility's marriage patterns and ideas. This final issue poses a methodological dilemma. Pontano's self-portrait as a married lover may be read as a reflection of the author's attempts to embrace the local nobility's culture, and thus be reduced to a pattern commonly found among members of the state bureaucracy. Moreover, *De Amore Coniugali* may be read as a literary experiment, achieved for aesthetic purposes, thus dismissing its relationship with its social context. Both these perspectives, however, can be overcome by adopting an extended notion of intertextuality.

---

[61] Pontano, *De Amore Coniugali*, 1, 3, vv. 27–44: "Nympha venit; praeit ipse deus, praeeuntque sorores / Idaliae, atque novem thespia turba deae, / Scilicet assuetasque do-mos assuetaque visunt / Limina, et est vatis sedula cura sui. / Cernite, ut apposito moveant vestigia gressu, / Et plaudat felix agmen, ovante lyra. / Dum choreas, dum plectra movent euantia divae, / Dicite: "Io -ter -io, o Hymenaee, io". / Iam venit, cohibete modos; iam, ty-bia, siste; / Haesitat ad primas iam nova nupta fores, / Atque hanc cunctantemque gradus atque ora rubentem / Admonet his Erato, dulciaque ora movet: / "Nec dubita, sustolle pedem, felixque marito / Et felix natis, o mea, limen adi. / Fortunata domus tibi erit sanc-tique penates, / Candidus imprimis et sine lite torus, / Isque etiam coniux, cui prae te et munera Croesi / Et dives rutilis sordeat Hermus aquis'."

Married Love in the Field of Naples

In literary scholarship, intertextuality is generally approached as a form of allusive art that appeals to the reader's ability to recognize classical sources.[62] Although useful and consistent with the humanistic practice of imitation, this view of intertextuality underpins a post-romantic understanding of texts as autonomous works of art, detached from the social context in which they were composed. In Quattrocento Naples, however, writers used artistic patronage and texts as tools to define their social status and to construct their public image against the background of the social changes resulting from Aragonese domination. The rapport between *De Amore Coniugali* and these practices, therefore, is better examined within Pierre Bourdieu's notion of intertextuality, by which he means the relationships among texts with the structure of the field in which they were produced, as well as with the agents involved in the field.[63] In this perspective, Pontano's *De Amore Coniugali* can be interpreted as the author's act of position-taking in a field populated by writers of manuals of behaviour and advice books concerned with the theme of marriage.

Whereas Beccadelli and his followers had a proverbially critical attitude toward marriage, Neapolitan nobles not only praised marriage but also criticized this group's irreverent outlook. Tristano Caracciolo was a Neapolitan noble and a prolific writer of advice books and manuals of behaviour. Among other things, Caracciolo wrote a treatise entitled *De Concordia et de Ineundo Coniugio* (*On Concord and on Getting Married*), which is an apology of married life, addressed to an old man who did not want to get married.[64] Caracciolo's treatise voiced the grave and positive view of marriage that characterized advice books written by, and addressed to, members of the local nobility, such as Diomede Carafa, who also outlined a severe model of a perfect wife, inspired by ideals of frugality and austerity.[65] In his biography of Pontano, Caracciolo commented on the poet's changed view of marriage, in a way that is at once ironic and critical of the mentality that characterized state bureaucrats before Beccadelli's death:

---

[62] For an excellent critique of this approach, see Giunta, *Versi a un destinatario*, 30–36.

[63] Pierre Bourdieu, *The Field of Cultural Production*, 182.

[64] Vitale, *Modelli culturali nobiliari*, 162.

[65] Vitale, *Modelli culturali nobilitari*, 164–182.

> While considering these problems, he (*i.e. Pontano*) decided
> to get married, a choice which he had always abhorred. And
> to his companions, who were asking him why he had all of
> sudden made this decision, he replied that by doing so he
> would not become ill again, under the care of Giovanni (who
> was a lad whom he was keeping). And so he married Adriana
> Sassone, who excelled in beauty and honesty.[66]

When compared with the descriptions of ideal marriages and spouses, produced in Naples, moreover, *De Amore Coniugali* was a provocative and sub-
versive text. In tune with nuptial orations and epithalamia addressed to the
members of Italian elite culture, Pontano adapts the values of this culture of
sex and marriage to celebrate his own married life. In his *Memoriale*, written
for Beatrice d'Aragona, on the contrary, Diomede Carafa advised the newly
married woman to modify her behaviour to her husband's wishes, in a way
that sharply contrasts with the praise of reciprocal love found in contemporary nuptial oratory and Pontano's poetry.[67] In his *De Concordia et de Ineundo Coniugio*, moreover, Tristano Caracciolo criticized the cult of beauty and
condemned the pursuit of pleasure (*voluptas*) in the context of married life.[68]
In his *De Educatione*, Antonio de Ferrariis (1444–1517) provided young nobles with a curriculum that combined this class' characteristic ideals of moral
severity and frugality with a canon of recommended texts that condemned
love elegy as a lascivious and harmful genre.[69]

Pontano's nuptial elegies and ideology of married love betray the
author's attempt to distinguish himself and his fellows from local nobles
and their culture. In its final version, *De Amore Coniugali* follows a rigorous
chronological order and a linear plot, whose basic unit is the separation
and reunion of the married couple in times of war.[70] The second book, for

---

[66] Monti Sabia, *Un profilo moderno e due* vitae *antiche*, 47 : "Haec meditans, uxorem
ducere in animum induxit, a quo hactenus abhorruerat, poscentibus amicis cur, quod diu
obstinate abnuerat, nunc tam repente aggrederetur, respondit ne iterum sub cura Ioannis
(puer is erat quem alebat) aegrotaret. Duxit autem Ariadnam Saxonem, forma et honestate
egregiam."

[67] Vitale, *Modelli culturali nobiliari*, 169.

[68] Vitale, *Modelli culturali nobiliari*, 169–170.

[69] Vitale, *Modelli culturali nobiliari*, 44.

[70] Parenti, *Poeta Proteus alter*, 93–94.

example, comprises poems set on the backdrop of the War of Tuscany (1478–80) and contrasts the moments of peace spent at the poet's country estate in Antignano with the labours suffered on the battlefield. In line with the poet's translation of wedding ceremonies into the language of elegy, real-life experiences, such as the poet's return home, are filtered through elegiac commonplaces, such as the *epibaterion* (speech of the arriver), which Roman elegists Tibullus and Propertius had widely employed in their works.[71] In reviving this literary *topos*, Pontano insists on the elegiac core of his book, that is, the contrast between love and war:

> Hail, fields, and hail to you, farmers! And goodbye, martial arms of the Tyrrhenian Siena; drop your lance, Gradivus (*i.e. Mars*), and calmly cast war off. Lazy winter and love require times of leisure. Venus is waiting for you in the nuptial bed, winter gives you never ending nights and labour himself asks for some rest. Are these my home and my estates? I can see my farm: o day born under propitious stars! Pour me a glass, boy; and may this Cretan lamp shine; pour me another one and may the fireplace shine of a big fire. May the fireplace be filled with fire, and the table covered with generous Lyaeus (*i.e. wine*), while a balm of shady mirth cover my grey hair. Away from me, Tyrrhenian labours! Peaceful Bacchus loves garrulous leisure.[72]

Pontano's praise of an idealized life of peace and love, spent in the dreamlike tranquility of his country estate, is not a simple echo of Tibullus, but is a criticism of the culture of the Neapolitan nobility. Aristocrats considered the ownership of a wealthy country estate and an acquaintance with agricultural techniques, to be necessary status symbols. In his advice books,

---

[71] Cairns, *Sextus Propertius, the Augustan Elegist*, 210–211.

[72] Pontano, *De Amore Coniugali*, 2, 2, vv. 1–14: "Rura, iterum salvete, iterum salvete, coloni, / Tyrrhenae valeant martiaque arma Senae; / Pone hastam, Gradive, quietus et exue bellum, / Ocia segnis hiems, ocia quaerit amor, / Te Venus expectat thalamo, tibi bruma perennes / Dat noctes, requiem poscit et ipse labor. / Hine lares fundusque meus? Mea praedia cerno: / O mihi tam fausto sidere nata dies. / Funde, puer, calices; lux haec cretensis agatur; / Funde iterum et multo splendeat igne focus, / Igne focus, madeat generoso mensa lyaeo, / Impediat canas myrtus opaca comas. / Tyrrheni, procul hinc, procul hinc estote, labores; / Ocia securus garrula Bacchus amat."

Disceptatio and *Praecepta*, Tristano Caracciolo outlined the ideal portrait of a noble man, who shares with his family living in the city, the situation of his country estates, in a way that demonstrates a thorough knowledge of agriculture. In his *De Concordia et de Ineundo Coniugio*, moreover, Caracciolo retells the story of a man who devotes himself to his country estates, after a life spent as a merchant and a courtier.[73] Belisario Acquaviva (1464–1528), a member of the feudal aristocracy, also praised agriculture and a life spent in his country estates in the preface to his paraphrases of Aristotle's *Economics*.[74] Neither Caracciolo nor Acquaviva, however, endorsed Pontano's praise of love and leisure, but on the contrary, they advised young nobles to devote their lives to the pursuit of physical vigour and the practice of arms, two values that needed to be combined with the study of edifying classical texts.[75] The values of love elegy, as well Pontano's revival of them, were not suitable for Neapolitan nobles.

Conclusions

According to Philip L. Reynolds, marriage entails a threefold change in the life of the two people, change which affects their core relationship, their economic status and family ties.[76] The case of Giovanni Pontano and Adriana Sassone reflects these three changes, which this article has examined in relation to the sociopolitical context of Naples at the time of King Ferrante. For a foreigner deprived of patents of nobility, the union with a member of a noble Neapolitan family represented an important step toward assimilation into the local society, which was finalized by the acquisition of the citizenship and made visible through an ambitious architectural program. For a lady from the urban aristocracy, moreover, a union with a prominent political figure represented a chance to solidify her family's economic status and political affiliations. These benefits, along with those accruing to a woman with a rich dowry, were in line with Ferrante's attempt to consolidate the ties between state and local aristocracy, and the consequent redefinition of Neapolitan elite society during the period of Aragonese domination.

---

[73] Vitale, *Modelli culturali nobiliari*, 125–126.

[74] Vitale, *Modelli culturali nobiliari*, 28–29.

[75] Vitale, *Modelli culturali nobiliari*, 32–39.

[76] Reynolds, "Marriage and its Documentation," 1–3.

When a writer is involved in contracting marriage, however, the reader must deal with a fourth change, one not contemplated by Reynolds. Pontano's invention of nuptial elegy, as this article has demonstrated, was not a reflection of a social pattern, but rather the result of a complex intellectual manoeuvre related to the Quattrocento rehabilitation of marriage, the humanistic revival of Augustan love elegy and the production of advice books in Naples. In modifying love elegy to the theme of marriage, Pontano distinguished himself from his predecessors, while at the same time he subtly criticized the surviving aristocratic values that marked the social group he was embracing. Consistent with Pierre Bourdieu's model, this article has, therefore, situated the writer's intellectual production in a field formed by multiple agents, contrasting voices, linguistic choices and literary tastes. If related to these social and intellectual contexts, Pontano's marriage and *De Amore Coniugali* can be understood as two closely intertwined facets of a complex act of position-taking that contribute to understanding the writer, while at the same time asking us to rethink the relationship between literature and society.

McGILL UNIVERSITY

I would like to thank my assistant Michael Solda and my colleagues Dario Brancato, Cristiana Furlan, Gilberto D'Escoubet and Barbara Bowen for their suggestions and advice on early drafts of this work.

CITED WORKS

Abulafia, David. "Ferrante of Naples. The Statecraft of a Renaissance Prince." *History Today.* 45:2 (1995): 19–25.

_____. "Introduction: From Ferrante I to Charles VIII." In *The French Descent into Renaissance Italy: 1494–5, Antecedents and Effects,* ed. David Abulafia. Aldershot, UK: Variorum, 1995, 1–25.

Beccadelli, Antonio (called Panormita). *Hermaphroditus,* trans. with an introduction and notes by Eugene O'Connor. Lanham, MY: Lexington Books, 2001.

_____. *The Hermaphrodite,* ed. and trans. Holt Parker. Cambridge, MA: Harvard University Press, 2010.

Bentley, Jerry H. *Politica e cultura nella Napoli rinascimentale,* trans. Cosima Campagnolo and with an introduction by Giuseppe Galasso. Naples: Guida, 1995.

Bourdieu, Pierre. *The Field of Cultural Production. Essays on Art and Literature,* ed. Randal Johnson. New York: Columbia University Press, 1993.

_____. *The Rules of Art: Genesis and Structure of the Literary Field,* trans. Susan Emanuel. Stanford: Stanford University Press, 1995.

Bowen, Barbara (ed.). *One Hundred Renaissance Jokes.* Birmingham: Summa, 1988.

Brucker, Gene A. *Giovanni and Lusanna. Love and Marriage in Renaissance Florence.* Berkeley and Los Angeles: University of California Press, 1986.

Cairns, Francis. *Sextus Propertius, the Augustan Elegist.* Cambridge, UK: Cambridge University Press, 2006.

Carrai, Stefano. "Appunti sulla preistoria dell'elegia volgare." In *L'elegia nella tradizione poetica italiana,* eds. Andrea Comboni and Alessandra di Ricco, with a foreword by Stefano Carrai. Trento: Dipartimento di Scienze filologiche e storiche, 2003, 1–15.

Curtius, Ernst R. *European Literature and the Latin Middle Ages,* trans. Willard R. Trask. Princeton, NJ: Princeton University Press, 1990.

D'Elia, Anthony F. *The Renaissance of Marriage in Fifteenth-Century Italy.* Cambridge, MA: Cambridge University Press, 2004.

De Divitiis, Bianca. "Giovanni Pontano and his Idea of Patronage." In *Research and Reflection: Studi di storia dell'architettura in onore di Howard*

Burns, eds. Maria Beltramini and Caroline Elam. Pisa: Edizioni della Normale, 2009, 121–145.

————. *Architettura e committenza nella Napoli del Quattrocento*. Venice: Marsilio, 2007.

De Nichilo, Mauro. *Oratio Nuptialis. Per una storia dell'oratoria nuziale umanistica*. Bari: Università di Bari, 1994.

————. *Retorica e magnificenza nella Napoli aragonese*. Bari: Palomar, 2000.

De Blasi, Nicola. *Profilo linguistico della Campania*. Bari: Laterza, 2003.

Giunta, Claudio. *Versi a un destinatario. Saggio sulla poesia italiana del Medioevo*. Bologna: Il Mulino, 2002.

Gothein, Eberhard. *Il Rinascimento nell'Italia meridionale*, trans. Tommaso Persico, with an introduction by Franco Cardini. Florence: Le Lettere, 1985.

Keith, Alison. *Propertius. Poet of Love and Leisure*. London: Duckworth, 2008.

Kidwell, Carol. *Pontano: Poet and Prime Minister*. London: Duckworth, 1991.

Klapisch-Zuber, Christiane. "Zacharias, or the Ousted Father: Nuptial Rites in Tuscany between Giotto and the Council of Trent." In *Women, Family, and Ritual in Renaissance Italy*, trans. L. G. Cochrane. Chicago: University of Chicago Press, 1985, 121–145.

Kuehn, Thomas. "Contracting Marriage in Renaissance Florence." In *To Have and to Hold. Marrying and its Documentation in Western Christendom, 400–1600*, eds. Philip L. Reynold and John Witte, Jr. Cambridge, UK: Cambridge University Press, 2007, 390–401.

LaCapra, Dominick. *Rethinking Intellectual History: Texts, Contexts, Language*. Ithaca: Cornell University Press, 1983.

Luck, Georg. "Love Elegy." In *Cambridge History of Classical Literature*, vol. 2 *Latin Literature*, part 3, *The Age of Augustus*, eds. E. J Kenney and W.V. Clausen. Cambridge, UK: Cambridge University Press, 1982, 390–401.

Maravall, Jose. *Poder, honor y élites en el siglo XVII*. Madrid: Siglo Ventiuno de España, 1979.

Mengaldo, Pier Vincenzo. "L'elegia 'umile' (*DVE* 2, 4, 5–6)." In *Linguistica e retorica di Dante*. Pisa: Nistri-Lischi, 1978, 200–222.

Miller, Paul A. *Subjecting Verses: Latin Erotic Elegy and the Emergence of the Real*. Princeton, NJ: Princeton University Press, 2004.

Monti Sabia, Liliana. "Prolusione." In *Atti della giornata di studi per il V centenario della morte di Giovanni Pontano*, ed. Antonio Garzya. Naples: Giannini, 2004, 7–27.

_____. "Tra realtà e poesia: per una nuova cronologia di alcuni carmi del *De amore coniugali* di Giovanni Pontano (I 5–8)." In *Classicità e Medioevo. Studi in onore di S. Monti*, ed. Giuseppe Germano. Naples: Dipartimento di filologia classica, 1996, 351–370.

_____. "Un canzoniere per una moglie. Realtà e poesia nel *De amore coniugali* di Giovanni Pontano." In *La poesia umanistica in distici elegiaci. Atti del Convegno Internazionale di Assisi (15–17 maggio 1998)*. Assisi: Accademia Properziana del Subasio, 1999, 23–65.

_____. "Vicende belliche e sentimenti coniugali nel *De amore coniugali* di Giovanni Pontano (per la cronologia del secondo e del terzo libro)." *Rendiconti dell'Accademia di archeologia, lettere e belle arti di Napoli* 67 (1997–98): 437–454.

_____. *Un profilo moderno e due* vitae *antiche di Giovanni Pontano*. Naples: Accademia Pontaniana, 1998.

One Hundred Renaissance Jokes. An Anthology, ed. Barbara Bowen. Birmingham, AL: Summa Publications, 1988.

Paolino, Laura. "Per l'edizione del commento di Francesco Patrizi da Siena al *Canzoniere* del Petrarca." *Nuova Rivista di Letteratura italiana* 2:1 (1999): 155–182.

Parenti, Giovanni. "*Contaminatio* di modelli e di generi nel "Liber Parthenopeus"." In *Intertestualità e smontaggi*, eds. R. Cardini e M. Regoliosi. Rome: Bulzoni, 1998, 47–75.

_____. *Benet Garret detto il Cariteo. Profilo di un poeta*. Florence: Olschki, 1993.

_____. *Poeta Proteus alter. Forma e storia di tre libri di Pontano*. Florence: Olschki, 1985.

Pontano, Giovanni. *De amore coniugali libri tres*, ed. J. Oeschger. Bari: Laterza, 1948.

_____. *De obedientia*, fols. 1r–48v in *Ioanni Ioviani Pontani opera omnia soluta oratione composita*. Venice: In Aedibus Aldi et Andreae Soceri, 1518.

_____. *Parthenopeus*, ed. J. Oeschger. Bari: Laterza, 1948.

Pinotti, Paola. *L'elegia latina. Storia di una forma poetica*. Rome: Bulzoni, 2002.

Reynolds, Philip L. "Marrying and Its Documentation in Pre-Modern Europe: Consent, Celebration and Property." In *To Have and to Hold. Marrying and its Documentation in Western Christendom, 400–1600*, eds. Philip L. Reynold and John Witte, Jr. Cambridge, UK: Cambridge University Press, 2007, 47–75.

Sakellariou, Eleni. "Institutional and Social Continuities in Kingdom of Naples between 1443 and 1528." In *The French Descent into Renaissance Italy: 1494–5. Antecedents and Effects*, ed. David Abulafia. Aldershot, UK: Variorum, 1995, 327–353.

Santagata, Marco. *La lirica aragonese. Studi sulla poesia italiana del secondo Quattrocento*. Padua: Antenore, 1979.

Storia della lingua a Napoli e in Campania, eds. Patricia Bianchi, Nicola De Blasi and Rita Librandi. Naples: Tullio Pironti, 1993.

Tissoni Benvenuti, Antonia. "Boiardo elegiaco e Tito Vespasiano Strozzi." In *L'elegia nella tradizione poetica italiana*, eds. Andrea Comboni and Alessandra di Ricco, with a foreword by Stefano Carrai. Trento: Dipartimento di Scienze filologiche e storiche, 2003, 81–102.

Vecchi Galli, Paola. "Percorsi dell'elegia quattrocentesca in volgare." In *L'elegia nella tradizione poetica italiana*, eds. A Comboni and A. Di Ricco. Trento: Dipartimento di Scienze Filologiche e Storiche, 2003, 38–79.

Villani, Gianni. "L'Umanesimo napoletano." In *Storia della letteratura italiana*, vol. 3, *Il Quattrocento*, ed. Enrico Malato. Rome: Salerno, 1996, 709–762.

Vitale, Giuliana. "La nobiltà di Seggio a Napoli." *Archivio storico per le province* 106 (1988): 151–169.

_____. "Sul segretario regio al servizio degli Aragonesi di Napoli." *Studi storici* 48 (2008): 293–321.

_____. *Elite burocratica e famiglia*. Naples: Liguori, 2003.

_____. *Modelli culturali nobiliari nella Napoli Aragonese*. Naples: Carlone, 2002.

Viti, Paolo. "L'umanesimo toscano nel primo Quattrocento." In *Storia della letteratura italiana*, vol. 3, *Il Quattrocento*, ed. Enrico Malato. Rome: Salerno, 1996, 211–294.

Welch, Evelyn. "Public Magnificence and Private Display." *Journal of Design History* 15:4 (2002): 211–221.

"Col Publicamento del Matrimonio Sgannar Ciascuno": Marriage and Betrothal in Bandello's Novelle

Reinier Leushuis[1]

Matteo Bandello (1485–1561) was both an active participant in Italian and French courtly circles and a Dominican cleric who occupied the important bishopric of Agen, France. He wrote a vast number of novelle that were collected in four volumes, of which three were published in 1554 and a fourth, posthumously, in 1573.[2] In these novelle, Bandello's views on how to contract the matrimonial bond were deeply influenced by the canonical doctrine of *consensus facit nuptias*, whereby the mutual consent of the partners alone ratified marriage and imbued it with its sacramental value.[3] None the less, in his novelle his obsessive insistence on designating the matrimonial bonds as *santo matrimonio*, strikes the reader as somewhat ironic, perhaps wilfully, given the ambiguous, and far from procedurally perfect, circumstances under which they were contracted. In many novelle that depict the conclusion of a marriage, a variety of conspicuous narrative details point to the chaotic pre-Tridentine crisis in matrimonial affairs, including confusion about the exact nature of the promises exchanged or the words of consent themselves — had

---

[1] I would like to thank the editor of the volume as well as the two anonymous assessors for their corrections and invaluable suggestions, which greatly improved the quality of this essay.

[2] For Bandello's life and work, see in particular Fiorato, *Bandello entre l'histoire et l'écriture; Matteo Bandello. Novelliere europeo;* and *Gli uomini, le città e i tempi di Matteo Bandello.*

[3] For the importance of consensualism in canon law, see in particular Gaudemet, *Le Mariage en Occident*, 151–193 and Esmein, *Le Mariage en droit canonique*, 1:95–202. For the most exhaustive treatment of the theological, doctrinal and canonical issues of matrimony, see the articles by L. Godefroy and G. Le Bras, "Mariage" in the *Dictionnaire de théologie catholique*, vol. 9, 2:2044–2371; see also Rasi, *La conclusione del matrimonio nella dottrina prima del concilio di Trento*, 99–131.

they been spoken in the future tense, so as to confirm a betrothal, or in the present tense, so as to seal a marriage? Moreover, ill-timed sexual intercourse, which ratified a preceding exchange of consent, either given in the present tense or the future tense, created an indissoluble marriage. Thus, generally, the marital bond was formed in successive stages, each characterized by a variety of rituals which crossed the boundaries between private and public and between sacred and profane.[4]

Silvana Seidel Menchi draws a vivid picture of the early sixteenth-century pre-Tridentine disorder in marital affairs that resulted from the Church's position that the simple consent of both partners sufficed for a valid, sacramental and indissoluble marriage.[5] While Church tribunals would recognize these marriages as clandestine, to varying degrees, reminding us that "clandestine" had multiple meanings, they decided, almost as a rule, in favour of the matrimonial bond and would refuse annulment, in particular if sexual intercourse had occurred. The confusion not only stemmed from the discrepancy between canon law's abstract definitions of betrothal, marriage and sacrament[6] and age-old social practices, but also from the linguistic ambiguities inherent in spoken words that are difficult to witness, confirm and recall, and that are open to misinterpretation and abuse. The latter point was of particular importance for the staging of the matrimonial crisis in literary texts, where rhetorical and linguistic tools allowed authors both to reflect, mimetically, on sociohistorical reality and to turn it, fruitfully, into literary art.[7] In this perspective, Bandello's novelle constitute a unique staging

---

[4] For an in-depth overview of the crisis in matrimonial affairs on the eve of the Council of Trent, see the series of case studies of Italian marriage trials by Seidel Menchi, Quaglioni and the team of Italian historians in *Matrimoni in dubbio: unioni controverse e nozze clandestine in Italia dal XIV al XVIII secolo*. For the French territory, see Flandrin, *Le sexe et l'Occident. Évolution des attitudes et des comportements*. For an in-depth study of the sociohistorical implications of pre-Tridentine canon law on marriage in Europe's late Middle Ages, see in particular Charles Donahue, *Law, Marriage, and Society in the Later Middle Ages. Arguments about Marriage in Five Courts* (in particular 14–45 and, for issues of words of consent in the Franco-Belgian region, 362–371 and 424–505).

[5] Seidel Menchi, *Matrimoni in dubbio*, 17–60.

[6] "Molte volte la distinzione tra *verba de præsenti* e *verba de futuro* doveva riuscire molto difficile non solo per l'uomo «della strada», o «dei campi», ma anche per il giudice o il giurista" (Rasi, *La conclusione del matrimonio*, 38).

[7] See also my *Le Mariage et l'«amitié courtoise» dans le dialogue et le récit bref de la Renaissance*.

ground from which to explore literature's questioning of slippery notions of marital clandestinity and secrecy on the eve of Trent. Bandello also reveals how the short narrative genre could exploit the precarious space between courtship and marriage, which, for lack of a more accurate term, I will refer to as betrothal.[8] Bandello's example is all the more pertinent since the author occupied a key position between the sacred and profane. A product of Lombardy's dogma-oriented Dominican orders,[9] and a seasoned courtier of noble stock with decades of life experience among Europe's courtly elites, he played a crucial role in the negotiation of several famous noble marriages.[10] Consequently, Bandello was acutely aware of the clash between ecclesiastical concerns to safeguard the ideal of the matrimonial sacrament and aristocratic interests of lineage and patrimony that required resolute family authority.[11]

In a series of novelle, the ambiguity of the spoken words that initiate or seal the matrimonial bond, or at least the characters' imagined version of such a bond, is the narrative starting point for a series of tragic events.[12] On the one hand, Bandello never fails to include some words of ritual sanction, exchanged by the partners, either a mutual promise or other words of consent. This emphasis on the moment of the exchange of consent reveals Bandello's

---

[8] Depending on legal jurisdictions and geographical spheres of influence, the pre-marital stages are variously indicated as *desponsatio, sponsalia de futuro, matrimonium initiatum* in Roman and canon law, *Verlobung, fiançailles, créantailles,* in local custom and customary law. The Italian derivatives *sponsali* or *spo[n]salizio* are ambiguous and could be understood as betrothal, in the sense of a promise (*promessa*) to marry in the future, or as contracting marriage, although in Bandello it is always considered to be separate from the larger and public *nozze.*

[9] See Fiorato, "L'image et la condition de la femme dans les *Nouvelles* de Bandello," 173–174.

[10] Still in the service of Aloisio Gonzaga, Bandello was in charge of the marriage negotiations between Costanza Rangone and Cesare Fregoso, his future employer (Fiorato, *Bandello entre l'histoire et l'écriture,* 369–371).

[11] See also Bellomo, "La donna, il matrimonio e la famiglia nel XVI secolo: Matteo Bandello."

[12] I have selected, for this essay, the following twelve novelle that I believe are most pertinent for the issues surrounding the formation of the matrimonial bond: I, 26 Antonio Bologna and the duchess of Malfi; I, 42 Didaco and Violante; I, 54 Boientis and Domenica; II, 5 Fabio and Emilia; II, 9 Romeo and Juliet; II, 27 Adelasia and Aleramo; II, 36 Nicuola and Lattanzio; II, 37 king Edward of England and Aelips; II, 41 Gerardo and Elena; III, 54 king John of Aragon and Maria; III, 60 Tomaso and the daughter of the Queen of Scotland; and IV, 5 Carlo Valdrio and the lady of Vergy.

belief that *consensus facit nuptias*. If the duke of Norfolk's powerful plea to King Henry VIII of England, in novella III, 60, to allow the secretly contracted marriage of two young subjects, reflects the author's view, this spoken consent holds even more importance than sexual consummation: "Matrimony is not created by a man and a woman's lying together and enjoying each other carnally, but what truly endorses marriage is reciprocal, free, and voluntary consent" ("Non fa il matrimonio il giacer insieme e godersi carnalmente un uomo e una donna, ma *il cambievole consentimento libero e volontario* è quello che rende il matrimonio vero" [2: 560]).[13]

Paradoxically, however, the formulations used to express this consent often remain vague with respect to the real intentions of the speakers, and in virtually all cases are quickly followed by sexual intercourse. The narrator thus seems equally anxious to keep the events in line with another dominating view in canon law — namely, to consider *copula carnalis* as the ultimate ratification of the matrimonial bond *de præsenti*, regardless of the exact nature of the words exchanged — as well as with lay social practices that always accorded great contractual value to consummation.[14] Indeed, Bandello employs the term *santo matrimonio* almost exclusively as the direct object of the verb *consumare*: "consumarono il santo matrimonio" is a stock phrase in his typical descriptions of lovers contracting clandestine or secret marriage. In one novella (II, 36), intercourse is explicitly proposed as the ultimate confirmation of the words of consent in the present tense that normally validate marriage. A certain maid, Pippa, who is the sole witness to the private marriage act between Lattanzio and Nicola, makes them sleep together to ratify their bond: "Monna Pippa, in order to confirm the marriage contracted by words in the present, had [Lattanzio] sleep in one room with Nicola and consummate holy matrimony" ("Monna Pippa per *più affermare* il contratto matrimonio per

---

[13] Bandello, *Tutte le opere*. All quotations from Bandello will be from this edition, with the volume and page number indicated in square brackets in the text. Please note that the volume numbers do not correspond with the four parts of Bandello's novelle. To identify separate novelle in the text, I use Roman numbers I to IV for the parts, followed by the number of the novella. All English translations are mine.

[14] For the varying importance attached to the *copula* in theology and canon law, see Rasi, *La conclusione del matrimonio*, 132–150; *Dictionnaire de théologie catholique*, vol. 9, 2:2044–2371. See also Esmein, *Le Mariage en droit canonique* and Gaudemet, *Le Mariage en Occident*, for meticulous discussions of the place of sexual intercourse in both church and lay views.

parole di presente [...] fece che in una camera [Lattanzio] si giacque con la Nicuola e *consumò il santo matrimonio*" [1: 1050]).

These private marital formulas are invariably the source of misunderstandings, ambiguity and secrecy, if not outright transgression and clandestinity, both in the sense of not abiding by the rituals specified by canon law, such as the presence of a priest and/or witnesses (even if these were not strictly compulsory before Trent), and in the more common sense of being secret and, therefore, transgressing society's requirement of parental or family consent. These evasive or offensive words, acts and behaviours subsequently become the driving forces of the narrative plot.

On the other hand, many of the narratives emphasize the need for the characters to disclose publicly their marital bond. This anxiety not only reflects the obvious social pressure to have their marriage embedded in, and approved by, the family and the larger community, but also suggests the need for a public religious presence, such as that provided by a priest, witnesses and a church ceremony, that removes the sacramental burden from the private exchange of promises or consent. Consequently, in Bandello's novelle we witness a fragile equilibrium, fraught with social and religious tension, between marrying, or promising to marry, by *privately* exchanged words of consent as opposed to *publicly* witnessed disclosure. These narrative situations anticipate the concern of post-Tridentine clerics. After the Church's regulation of marriage in *Tametsi* (1563), the focus moved to defining and enforcing the premarital bonds between partners as a private and less permanent stage of the future promise, free from intimacy and sexual intercourse, and more in line with Peter Lombard's original canonical position on betrothal (*desponsatio*) as an exchange of *verba de futuro*.[15]

The Renaissance novella, as presented by Bandello, can shed a revealing light on these issues, not only because the genre, as is often claimed, provides the perfect documentary snapshot of a sociohistorical reality, although Fiorato is definitely correct to remind us that the "pre- and pseudomarital situations" from this reality are, vice versa, fecund

---

[15] For this shift, see Lombardi, "Fidanzamenti e matrimoni dal concilio di Trento alle riforme settecentesche," Luperini, "La promessa sotto accusa (Pisa 1584)," and Flandrin, *Le sexe et l'Occident*, 61–82. For Peter Lombard's canonical position formulated in the *Sententiae*, see *Dictionnaire de théologie catholique*, vol. 9, 2:2151–2153 and Colish, *Peter Lombard*, 629, 650–655.

material for some excellent storytelling.[16] Rather, the narrative, rhetorical and metaphorical devices the novella employs in its specific literary realm bring to the surface deeper connections, hidden under matrimonial issues, between language, private and public life and sacred and profane thought in early modern culture.

A close reading of the stylistic rendering of the exchange of the spoken promise or words of consent, in the novelle that feature private or clandestine marriages, reveals the precarious status of spoken words in matrimonial bonding. Despite Bandello's emphasis on mutual consent, there is not a single example in which *verba de præsenti* are unambiguously formulated, in direct discourse, by the characters in question. While in many cases the characters exchange in direct discourse and in the *future* tense, their *promise* to marry, the actual exchange of consent, in the *present* tense, necessary for marriage, is always reported in the narrator's voice and in varying degrees of explicitness. The exact words, however, formulated in the grammatical present tense, such as '*I now take you* to be my wife/husband,' as prescribed by the Church, are never provided.[17] The story of Didaco and Violante, two young lovers from Valencia, is a case in point. Didaco falls in love with Violante and, after serious consideration, addresses her: "*if* it is your wish to be eternally mine, I, for as long as I *will live, will* always be yours taking you as my legitimate wife" ("quando voi vogliate perpetuamente esser mia, io, mentre che *viverò*, sempre *sarò* vostro prendendovi per mia legitima sposa" [1, 498]). Violante replies, "I will always be your loyal spouse and faithful servant" ("io vi *sarò* sempre leal consorte e fedelissima serva" [1, 498]). This mutual expression of intent in direct discourse and in the future tense is neatly set apart from the consent used to contract marriage a few days later: "Signor Didaco waited no more than two days before he came back, and, in the presence of the mother, the two brothers, and a servant [...] he solemnly *married with words in the present* his much desired Violante" ("Non stette il signor Didaco dui giorni che egli rivenne, e a la presenza de la madre, dei dui fratelli e d'un suo servidore

---

[16] Fiorato, "L'image et la condition de la femme dans les *Nouvelles* de Bandello", 205. See also Bellomo, "La donna, il matrimonio", 207–211.

[17] A good literary example of the wording to contract marriage, rendered in the characters' direct discourse, is the one spoken between Gualtieri and Griselda in the famous novella from Boccaccio's *Decameron* (X, 10): "«Signori, costei è colei la quale io intendo che mia moglie sia, dove ella me voglia per marito» ; e poi a lei rivolto [...] le disse: «Griselda, *vuoimi tu per tuo marito*?» A cui ella rispose: «Signor mio, sì.» E egli disse: «E io voglio te *per mia moglie*» ; e in presenza di tutti la sposò" (Boccaccio, *Tutte le opere*, 4:945).

[…] *sposò* solennemente *per parole di presente* la sua tanto desiata Violante" [1, 498]). But, in spite of this marked staging of mutual consent, which is moreover witnessed by a third party, albeit in a private setting, the reader does not hear the characters' voices contracting marriage in the present tense, as one would have when witnessing the ceremony, and so is forced to rely on the narrator's authority. In other cases, the narrator is even less explicit about the formulation of consent in the present tense, which is only suggested by vague references such as "those commonly spoken words" (II, 9; II, 41), or the exchange of consent is assumed to have taken place (I, 26).

The confusing use of verb tenses creates ambiguity about both the present and the future, and thus about intent and action in matrimonial contracts. A typical case is found in the novella concerning the opportunistic yet dim-witted Boientis (I, 54). He is depicted as a half-baked charlatan who stumbles by chance into the professions of notary and surgeon, for which he has not the slightest knowledge or training, but manages to play his part convincingly. Boientis falls in love with a certain Domenica and quickly realizes that the only way to possess her is through marriage: "He, who was *truly* in love, *considered* choosing her as his wife […] he *promised* her he *would take* her as his spouse […] Thus, a day later, Boientis […] in the presence of the mother, legitimately *married* his Domenica *both in words and in intention*" ("Egli che era *veramente* innamorato, si *deliberò* di prenderla per moglie […] gli *promise* che la *pigliarebbe* per sposa […] Andò adunque un giorno il Boientis […] ed in presenza de la madre *sposò* legitimamente, *quanto a le parole ed intenzione*, la sua Domenica" [1: 624]). Seemingly in accordance with procedures and customs, the narrator places the emphasis on future intent when rendering Boientis's discourse ("he *promised* he *would take* her as his spouse"), whereas, for the formation of marriage in the present tense, we must rely purely on the narrator's account. The ironic ambiguity of these lines is heightened, in retrospect, after we read the rest of the story. The swindler Boientis not only bullies everyone into keeping the marriage a secret, but also repudiates Domenica as soon as she is pregnant and he promises her mother twenty gold ducats if she will marry Domenica to another man, all the while maintaining the secret. After Domenica marries another man, Boientis suddenly feels an inexplicable need to confess. When the priest reminds him he has acted illegally, he tries to win back Domenica by force. The matter ends up in the ecclesiastical courts, which rule that Boientis's original marriage must be restored and validated. In light of these events, Boientis's so-called true love for Domenica, and his deliberations about marrying her, read as slippery and deeply ironic. This irony leaves us to guess what were the intentions behind the words with which he married Domenica, and which Bandello has so subtly hidden from the reader's sight at the very moment they were pronounced.

In another story (II, 5), a certain Fabio becomes intimate with his beloved Emilia, but when he seeks to "reach out to the parts that nature teaches us to hide" ("por le mani a le parti che la natura c'insegna celare" [1: 696]), Emilia tells him this can only happen in a bond that lasts for life. "I love you in order to be, if you wish, eternally yours. And if you [...] are of that mindset, give me your *promise* here, in the presence of my nursemaid, that you *will never take* another wife but me, seeing that I *do not intend* to have another husband" ("t'amo per esser, se tu vuoi, eternamente tua. Il perché se tu [...] sei di quest'animo, dammi la *fede* tua qui a la presenza de la mia nutrice, che mai altra moglie che me *non prenderai*, con ciò sia ch'io altro marito *non intenda* d'avere" [1: 696]). Consent is explicitly exchanged when Fabio makes his own unequivocal promise: "I bestow my faith upon you that *I will never take* another woman as wife, and for your peace of mind, if you like, *I will now marry you*" ("io t'impegno la fede mia che mai altra donna che te *prenderò* per moglie, e per più sicurezza tua, se ti piace, *adesso ti sposerò*" [1: 697]). Yet this consent to marry, rendered in direct discourse, is not only exchanged in the middle of sultry and climatic lovemaking — Fabio is "on fire with the burning flames of love" ("de l'ardenti fiamme amorose era acceso" [1: 697]) — but also is dominated by future verb tenses. These two elements are placed in sharp contrast to the short and dry comment, in the narrator's voice, that refers to the actual contracting of the marriage: "Since this pleased much to Emilia, *he married her*" ("Piacendo molto questo ad Emilia, *egli la sposò*" [1: 697]). Without giving us the slightest hint of what this marrying may have consisted (although later in the novella a ring is mentioned), the sentence continues on to describe, in hyperbolic style, the couple's sleepless night spent in lovemaking.

This sexual intercourse theoretically ratifies their bond as an indissoluble marriage, but that does not prevent Fabio from subsequently acceding to the wishes of his father, who is unaware of his secret bond to Emilia, to enter into a family-ordained marriage. His barely veiled intentions are revealed when he attempts to convince Emilia to accept the situation: she will not lose anything if Fabio continues to sleep with her, and later, after he hastens his father's departure from life with some poison, he *will marry* her again publicly ("and then I will marry you publicly" ["e te poi publicamente *sposerò*" [1: 698]). As expected, Emilia is not convinced. After Fabio marries the other woman, she seizes the first opportunity to plunge a knife into his heart when he is asleep. In these novelle, the pattern, created through a play of narrative and linguistic devices, is one of explicitly revealed future intent but subtly dissimulated words and actions in the narrative present. The unfortunate series of events that is triggered as a consequence of the murder leaves the reader with the strong sense that contracting marriage by spoken words of consent alone creates an opaque and ambiguous realm of doubt and uncertainty, for the partners themselves, as much as for their community.

Even in Bandello's version of the Romeo and Juliet story (II, 9), the characters' direct discourse remains conditional: "*If* it is your desire to be as much mine as I long eternally to be yours [...] you have to marry me as your legitimate wife. *If* you *will marry* me, I *shall be* ready to come with you wherever you want" ("*se* voi desiderate esser cosí mio come io eternamente bramo esser vostra [...] debbiate per moglie vostra legitima sposarmi. *Se* mi *sposarete*, io sempre *sarò* presta a venir in ogni parte ove piú a grado vi fia" [1: 736]). Romeo is quick to reciprocate his consent: "this was his entire desire and that whenever she wanted *he would marry her* in the way she requested" ("questo era tutto il suo disio e che ogni volta che le piacesse *la sposeria* in quel modo che ella ordinasse" [1: 736]). At least Juliet feels enough need for legitimacy to have their secret marriage ceremony conducted by a priest. Yet, it is only the latter's voice that we hear in direct discourse, asking the lovers if they are disposed to take each other as husband and wife, while the young couple's affirmative replies are again conspicuously relayed through the narrator: "The lovers answered that they *wished* nothing else. The friar, having heard the *wish* of both [...] said those words that according to Church procedures are commonly spoken in the *marriage ceremony*" ("Risposero gli amanti che altro non *desideravano*. Messer lo frate udita *la volontá* d'ambidue [...] dette quelle parole che si costumano secondo l'ordine de la Chiesa dir nei *sposalizii*" [1: 738]). Bandello steers clear of unambiguous language, spoken by the spouses, in the present tense. Strictly speaking, all the reader hears is the expression of a wish, reported by a third-party narrator. Even the words that the Church prescribed, which remind us of the ambiguous definition of *sponsalizi*, are spoken by the priest, not by the couple.

Finally, ambiguity in the expression of consent creeps into the secret ceremony that concludes the marriage between the lady of Vergy and a young vassal of the duke of Burgundy, in Bandello's version of the *Châtelaine de Vergy* (IV, 5). This was an old French courtly love poem that Marguerite de Navarre had already revamped into a Renaissance novella in her *Heptaméron*. When revealing his marriage to the duke, the young knight, Carlo, confesses: "the agreement between us, *sworn by holy oaths* […] was that it was never allowed to reveal to anyone our *inseparable tie*, if not with the *consent of both parties*" ("l'accordio tra noi, con *santissimi sagramenti giurato* […] fu che mai non fosse lecito manifestare a nessuno questo nostro *inseparabile nodo*, se non di *consenso di tutte due le parti*" [2: 667]) and "I *married her* as my wife, with the agreement I mentioned before not to make the marriage known unless she consented" ("per moglie *la sposai*, con quelle giurate convenzioni giá dette di non palesar questo matrimonio si ella nol consentiva" [2: 670]). While the terminology evokes the canonical conditions for a sacramental marriage by mutual consent,[18] in reality their agreement is only that they promise not to divulge their bond without each other's approval. Not only does consent of such nature fail to conclude matrimony, in spite of what the lovers think, but also, to the extent that this is a condition that the partners defined privately and mutually, and certainly was not one sanctioned by church law, it renders the union entirely in the private domain of *sponsalia per verba de futuro!*[19]

In the last two novelle, the tragic end of the young couples (the lady of Vergy and her knight, like Romeo and Juliet, commit suicide) can hardly be ascribed to the ambiguity and dissimulation of intent of the words of consent alone since, in both cases, larger family interests and socioeconomic forces are at work. Yet, the general opaqueness and the subtle levels of partial and relayed witnessing with which Bandello's literary art infuses the private and oral exchange of consent, draw a grey zone between present and future, intent and acts and private and public. These novelle do not just document and use to dramatic effect the underlying sociohistorical tensions generated by the difficulty in authenticating the marital bond. In the particular literary realm they delineate, which ultimately is distinct from historical reality and allows room for experimentation, these rhetorical and narrative devices also

---

[18] E.g. "oaths" (but *sagramento* can of course also mean "sacrament"), "inseparable tie", "consent of both parties".

[19] See A. Villien, "Fiançailles" in the *Dictionnaire de théologie catholique*, vol. 5, 2:2268–2276.

substantiate a deeper link between matrimonial issues and the role of spoken language in the shaping of social reality.

Further literary analysis permits more light to be shed on the slippery linguistic issues that surround the formulas, so easily spoken or performed, but with such serious consequences. The tragic potential harboured in clandestine betrothal or marriage bonds, perfectly fits the subgenre of Renaissance novella that Bandello developed and popularized: the *racconto tragico*, or in French *histoire tragique*, in which characters in the grip of uncontrollable depraved passion transgress a universal law and set in motion an ineluctable and violent course of events.[20] The textual staging of hyperbolic violence, another typical feature of the tragic subgenre, allows fiction to reflect back metaphorically on social reality, including matrimonial affairs. The symbolism of the tongue is a case in point, where Bandello exploits the flimsiness of spoken words in betrothal and marriage arrangements to unleash a violence that is hard to ignore as an authentic denunciation of this practice.

For instance, as if to fan the reader's suspicions regarding the *exact* words of consent exchanged between Violante and Didaco, Bandello tells us that the latter wants to keep their marriage a secret ("asking […] that […] they keep their marriage a secret until he would make it public" ["pregando […] che […] questo sposalizio fin che egli lo publicasse tenessero segreto" 1: 498]), but subsequently, in a narrative plot that recalls Fabio's scheming (II, 5), he publicly contracts marriage with another woman, supposedly to satisfy family interests. During a chance encounter, Didaco, not knowing that Violante is out for revenge, tries to cajole her into believing that he is still hers by making a speech filled with future tenses but conspicuously lacking any verb in the present tense ("you *will* never be abandoned by me […] and *in the future you will notice* that my love towards you has never failed" ["*sarete* mai da me abbandonata […] e *per l'avvenire v'accorgerete* che l'amor mio verso di voi non è punto mancato" [1: 501]). Like Fabio, he arranges a nightly meeting in the hopes of continuing his sexual relationship with Violante. Didaco having fallen sound asleep after their lovemaking, Violante, with the help of her maid, takes revenge by tying him naked and upside-down to a crossbeam

---

[20] See Sozzi, "Il racconto tragico in Francia nella seconda metà del Cinquecento," Wetzel, "Éléments socio-historiques d'un genre littéraire: l'histoire de la nouvelle jusqu'à Cervantès," Ferrari, "Histoire tragique et grande histoire: rencontre de deux genres." See also Francesco Flora's "Introduction" to Bandello, *Tutte le opere*, 1:xxiii–xxv.

in the ceiling and by cruelly slicing him up. In the horrendous spectacle that covers several pages, the tongue receives symbolic priority: squeezing it in a pair of pincers ("la lingua del tremante cavaliero intenagliò" [1: 503]), Violante laments: "Don't you remember, traitor, this place where you gave me the marital ring *with deceitful words* and with even *more fake talking* you took my virginity? [...] how many lies [...] this *false tongue* told me!" ("Non conosci, traditore, questo luogo ove *con simulate parole* il matrimoniale anello mi desti e con *piú falsi parlari* la mia verginitá mi rapisti? [...] quante bugie [...] *questa falsa lingua* m'ha detto!" [1: 503]), after which she takes a pair of scissors and cuts more than four inches from his tongue ("con un paio di forbici gli tagliò più di quattro dita di lingua" [1: 503]).

Likewise, it is no coincidence that Bandello chose the *Châtelaine de Vergy* story (IV, 5) to explore the drama of spoken promise or consent in matrimonial affairs. Originally a courtly love story that ends in bloodshed after its secret is divulged in a sequence of betrayals, Bandello's changes the two courtly lovers of the medieval version into a clandestinely married couple. This shift deliberately exploits this drama of speech, in which tragic events are triggered by speaking evil and betraying secrets, in order to question marriage by verbal consent.[21] In his final moments, the young knight, Carlo, stabs himself over the dead body of his spouse, who committed suicide as soon as she found out that their secret had been betrayed. He shouts at his duke: "Here you see to what end *my tongue and yours* have brought my beloved wife and me!" ("Eccovi a che termine *la mia lingua e la vostra*, la mia cara consorte e me hanno condotto" [2 : 682]).[22]

The hyperbolic violence that accompanies the metaphorical value of the tongue, in these two novelle, associates the deeply tragic outcomes of false or dissimulative speaking with the opaqueness and ambiguity that surrounds the promise or contracting of marriage by spoken words of consent, in a secretive context, hidden from broad public witness. This raises my next

---

[21] See also my "*La Châtelaine de Vergy* comme histoire tragique matrimoniale: de Marguerite de Navarre (1558) à Bandello (1573) et *Le sixiesme tome des histoires tragiques* (1582)."

[22] It is believed that Bandello encountered this story for the first time in a draft of Marguerite de Navarre's *Heptaméron* to which he had access only around 1550 (Bensi, "La *Chastelaine de Vergi* tra Margherita di Navarra e Matteo Bandello," and Fiorato, *Bandello entre l'histoire et l'écriture*, 524). The proximity in time of his rewriting of the *Heptaméron* story to the debates of the sacramental value of the exchange of *verba de præsenti*, at the Council of Trent, makes it all the more gripping.

point, that Bandello's novelle do not so much question the validity of the bond of matrimony in the context of the conflict between ecclesiastical and lay perspectives about what authenticates the marital union, but rather, they reframe the question in a more universal context of the relationship between private and secret acts.

Many narrative elements in the novelle suggest a shift away from the formulation of promise and consent, and even consummation, and the problems inherent in matrimonial clandestinity, toward a distinction between, on the one hand, an informal series of privately conducted, premarital stages that include some form of a non-binding exchange of consent between parties, and, on the other hand, marriage confirmed by disclosure in a public setting, often equated with *le nozze*, in the double sense of the contracting and the celebration of marriage. This change in perspective in Bandello's literary realm prefigures the post-Tridentine institutionalization of the distinction between marriage and betrothal.

The desire for an eventual *pubblicamento*, by at least one of the couple, usually the wife, is a pervasive leitmotiv in almost all of Bandello's fragile matrimonial narratives. Whatever actions and words, or objects such as the ring, that the couple performs or exchanges, or fails to perform or exchange, they are always set on an imaginary timeline with the ultimate goal of public disclosure. This moment retroactively bestows meaning on the preceding stages and is the ultimate authentication of marriage.

In novella I, 26, the widowed duchess of Malfi has concluded a risky secret marriage with her valet, Antonio Bologna, a husband she knows her two powerful brothers will not tolerate. Although Antonio is relatively wealthy, he is socially inferior and she would lose her noble title as a result of the marriage. The narrative plot hinges on the moment in which the duchess, after secretly giving birth to three children, finally decides to "take off the mask" ("cavarsi la maschera" [1: 327]) in front of a large assembly of nobles and members of the urban elite, in Antonio's palace in Ancona:

> Tempo è oggimai che io, gentiluomini miei e voi altri servidori, faccia *a tutto il mondo manifesto* quello che dinanzi a Dio è stato una volta fatto. A me essendo vedova parve di maritarmi e tal marito prendermi quale il mio giudicio s'aveva eletto. Il perché vi dico che sono giá alcuni anni passati che io sposai, a la presenza di mia cameriera *che è qui*, il signor

Antonio Bologna *che voi vedete,* ed egli è mio legitimo
marito, *e seco, perció che sua sono, intendo di rimanere* [...]
E per conchiudere, a me piú piace viver privatamente col
signor Antonio mio marito che restar duchessa. (1: 327–328)

(My dear gentlemen and you other servants, it is now
time that *I make known to everybody* that which was once
accomplished before God. Being a widow, I thought it would
befit me to marry and to take a husband chosen by my own
judgment. This is why I tell you that already some years ago
I married, in the presence of my chamber lady *who is here*,
lord Antonio Bologna, *whom you can see here*, and that he is
my legitimate husband, and that, *given that I belong to him,
I intend to remain so* [...] And to conclude, I much rather
live privately with my husband lord Antonio than to stay a
duchess).

This moment of public manifestation ("fare manifesto") and witnessing ("che
è qui", "che voi vedete") is the duchess's ultimate act to gain approval for her
marriage, by having the community witness her intentions spoken in the
present tense ("e seco, perció che sua sono, *intendo* di rimanere"). In fact,
the need for approval by witnesses had been, from the very beginning, part
of her deliberations about entering into a marriage with Bologna: "she was
deliberating [...] to become not Bologna's lover but his wife, and quietly enjoy
love with him *until she would be obliged to call* [literally: *manifest*] a wedding"
("deliberò [...] non amante del Bologna ma moglie divenire, e tacitamente
seco godersi del lor amore *fin a tanto ch'a manifestar le nozze fosse astretta*"
[1: 322]). Before they contract marriage privately, she informs Bologna of
her plan: "But to avoid the rumours of the people and moreover not to fall
into disgrace in the eyes of my family [...] I would like to keep the matter
hidden until an opportunity presents itself *to make it known* with less danger involved for me" ("Ma per schifar le mormorazioni del volgo ed altresí
per non cader in disgrazia dei signori miei parenti [...] vorrei tenere la cosa
celata fin che venisse occassione che si potesse con men mio pericolo *manifestare*" [1: 324]). To be sure, the duchess's fears centre mostly on her brothers'
strict sense of family honour and their thirst for revenge. Much of the story
recounts how the brothers capture and strangle their sister, together with her

three children, and find and assassinate Bologna. But what is striking here is the duchess's obstinate need for disclosure to the larger community, in spite of the dangers to her and her children, a risk she willingly takes. In other words, she distinguishes her need for general public disclosure from the need to comply with the patriarchal authority of her brothers, whom she knows she can never convince, and whose misplaced family honour Bandello unequivocally denounces in the *dedica* to this novella.[23]

The need to publicize also weighs on Didaco and Violante's bond. The reader's doubts are raised when Didaco asks for secrecy, until the moment of public disclosure: "asking [...] that they keep their marriage a secret *until he would make it public*" ("pregando [...] che [...] questo sposalizio *fin che egli lo publicasse* tenessero segreto" [1: 498]). However, Violante at first continues to put her faith in this moment: "hoping to shortly *undeceive* everybody with the *publication* of the marriage" ("sperando in breve col *publicamento* del matrimonio *sgannar* ciascuno" [1: 499]). She is encouraged, moreover, by the small circle of family intimates who are cognizant of their bond, and who "often urged her to press her husband into *publicizing* the marriage" ("quella sovente stimolavano che appresso al marito facesse instanzia che il matrimonio *si publicasse*" [1: 499]). However, whatever authenticity Violante or her family members may have ascribed to the bond, it is effectively obliterated by Didaco's second union, which, without much preceding ceremony, is presented as publicly contracted ("not long after [...] he *publicly* took the other one as his wife" ["non dopo molto [...] egli questa altra *publicamente* prese per moglie" 1: 499]) and instantly known in the entire city of Valencia. Likewise, we are reminded of how that other deceiver, Fabio, abuses Emilia's desire for, and confidence in, an eventual public confirmation

---

[23] Bandello condemns men's obsession to burden the woman with sole responsibility for the safeguarding of the family honour, while their own transgressions go unpunished: "it seems to me a great stupidity of men to think that their honour and that of their entire lineage would depend on the desire of one woman" ("grave sciocchezza quella degli uomini mi pare che vogliono che l'onor loro e di tutta la casata consista ne l'appetito d'una donna" [1: 320]). He is equally adamant in condemning the violence men employ to enforce family honour upon women: "we do not want that the poor women be able to do whatever they like, and whenever they do something that doesn't please us, we instantly reach for nooses, iron blades, and poison" ("non vogliamo che le povere donne possino far a lor voglia cosa che sia, e se fanno cosa alcuna che a noi non piaccia, subito si viene ai lacci, al ferro ed ai veleni" [1: 320]).

of their marriage ("and then I will marry you *publicly*" ["e te poi *publicamente* sposerò" 1: 698]).

A case similar to that of the duchess of Malfi, where the desire for the eventual publication of a secretly contracted marriage is shared by both partners, is that of Gerardo and Elena (II, 41). Their wish to "disclose" ("palesare") or "make manifest" ("manifestare") their marriage [2: 78; 2: 90] always remains vividly in the background of an intricate narrative that relates their attempts to avoid other, family-ordained, marital obligations. Another case is that of the two noble youths in the entourage of king Henry VIII of England (III, 60), who enter into a dangerous secret bond, but, in spite of the king's terrible reputation for cruel punishments ("he has become very terrible and cruel and he has shed human blood in great quantities; every day he has the heads of people left and right cut off" ["è divenuto molto terribile e crudele ed ha sparso grandissimo sangue umano, facendo ogni dí mozzar il capo a questi e a quelli" 2: 557–558]), decide to "wait for the opportune moment to make it public" ("aspettando il tempo oportuno di publicarlo" [2: 559]). While Bandello ironically reveals that in this case little other than a carnal confirmation of intent had preceded the marriage, the story grants the moral high ground to the lovers' firm and constant faithfulness, in contrast to the disproportionate punishment the king metes out after he is informed of their secret union. While convinced by the youth's uncle, the duke of Norfolk, to revoke his initial sentence of decapitation, the king nevertheless orders both spouses locked away for life. Imprisoned in two different towers but able to talk to each other through certain facing windows, they mutually declare eternal love and starve themselves to death. The story thus restores the universal moral legitimacy of their marriage and, consequently, of the spouses' original intent to validate it by a public announcement and celebration.

Further corroboration, that emphasizes the importance of public disclosure for the conclusion of marriage in Bandello's novelle while disassociating it from the age-old anxiety of marital partners to comply with familial and parental wishes, is provided by the cases in which the stages preceding a private contract are entirely devoid of clandestinity. In other words, even couples that do not have to worry about concrete or violent repercussions at the family level, and therefore do not act clandestinely by keeping their marriage a private affair, nevertheless, deem public disclosure to be the ultimate approval of their bond. In aristocratic circles, in particular, the private and public are more clearly distinguished as two separate moments of *sponsalizio* in the narrative, not because the couples seek to avoid social punishment, but because the ultimate approval and confirmation of their bond is linked to its public disclosure.

After king Edward of England has finally seduced countess Aelips, whose land and title fall into the king hands after her husband dies without heirs (II, 37), a series of ritual events takes place in private, such as the exchange of the common words ("le consuete parole che s'usano negli sposalizii" [1: 1107]), an exchange of rings, the presence of a few witnesses and sexual consummation. While the king, in this case too, orders the marriage to be kept secret until further notice ("indi ordinò che questo matrimonio senza sua licenza *non si divolgasse*" [1: 1107]), and their bond continues at the private level ("the king *privately* went to the count's house and stayed a couple of hours a day to enjoy his dearest wife" ["il re *privatamente* a casa del conte se n'andava ed una e due ore del giorno se ne stava in festa con la sua carissima moglie", 1: 1108]), it becomes clear that this is done only in order to increase the suspense for what is to come, namely a combined marriage and coronation ceremony of grandiose dimensions:

> Indi fatto l'apparecchio conveniente per le future nozze, il re fece divolgare il nuovo matrimonio ed invitar tutti i duchi, marchesi, conti, baroni ed altri signori suoi vassalli, che tutti a Londra a calende di luglio si trovassero a le nozze e coronazione de la reina [...] il re la matina onoratissimamente accompagnato, a casa del conte suo suocero se n'andò, e quivi trovata la lieta Aelips vestita da reina ed il palazzo pomposamente apparato, essendo ella da molte madame e signore accompagnata, andarono a la chiesa per udir la messa, la quale finita, *il re di nuovo publicamente la moglie risposò*. [1: 1108–1109]

> (After the upcoming wedding had been appropriately prepared, the king had the new marriage announced and invited all dukes, marquises, counts, barons, and other lords his vassals to attend the queen's wedding and coronation in London at the calends of July [...] In the morning the king went with a most honourable company to his father-in-law

the count's house and found a joyful Aelips dressed as a queen and the palace ceremoniously decorated. Aelips being accompanied by many ladies, they attended mass in church, after which *the king again publicly remarried his wife*).

The sumptuousness and pomp with which the marriage is not only announced but also conducted and witnessed by England's nobility, stands in stark contrast to the tales in which husbands attempt to avoid publication for malicious purposes. But the underlying idea is the same: only publicly witnessed disclosure validates marriage. This idea is most strikingly reflected in the last sentence that designates this occasion as one of marrying again ("di nuovo" and "*risposò*"), with the understanding that, whatever ceremonial activities had preceded, this is the real validation.

Similar vocabulary is found in III, 54, the strange tale of John, king of Aragon who, at the wedding of one of his subjects, the count of Prata, falls desperately in love with the bride, Maria, and sets his mind to marry her before it is too late. At one point, Bandello points to the custom of this country to marry in front of a large assembly and in a magnificently decorated room: "the custom of the country being such that all lords and important persons of the region, when taking a wife, held the first wedding celebration in this room where they *remarried their wife in person*" ("essendo così la costuma del paese, che tutti i signori e grandi personaggi de la contrada, quando conducevano moglie, che il primo convito de le nozze facessero in quella sala e quivi *di propria mano la moglie risposassero*" [2: 524]). This particular story further complicates matters because Bandello does not explain in what way this is "risposare," and also because the king manages to snatch the bride away and marry her himself (though not without papal dispensation) because the bond with the count had not yet been consummated. Nevertheless, the protracted inner struggle of the king of Aragon, pondering his course of action in an inner monologue that takes up almost a quarter of this short novella is set against the background of the unfolding wedding. It suggests that, in spite of the fact that the marriage and dowry contract with the count of Prata had already been signed, it is before the completion of all public aspects of the ceremony that he still has a chance to act; in this particular case, before the wedding participants accompany the bride to the count's house ("they formed a large group to accompany the spouse to the husband's residence" ["si misero tutti di brigata per accompagnar la sposa a l'albergo del marito" 2: 526]), a moment that effectively concludes the public side of the *nozze*.

One could object that the emphasis on *pubblicamento*, as staged in wedding ceremonies and, more importantly, as overriding private promises or consent exchanged previously between spouses, simply reflects the traditional tensions between the ecclesiastical matrimonial model, based on mutual consent of the spouses in whatever shape, time and place, and social practice that emphasized lineage, patrimony, family consent and, thus, endorsement by the community through the public witness of concrete acts, such as the *tocco della mano*, the exchange of rings and the transfer of the bride to the groom's house.[24] However, I would argue that the sense of finality vested by the characters of these novelle in the *pubblicamento* of their bond, whether simply imagined as a necessary step eventually, or indefinitely postponed for malicious purposes or, indeed, magnificently staged in front of large assemblies of people, underlines a mentality that considers *pubblicamento* a form of *sgannare*, of 'making true' in an anthropological sense, without which the matrimonial bond ultimately lacks universal authenticity. Consequently, these novelle point to a shift in the conception of marriage: not necessarily one from an ecclesiastical perspective, protecting the sacrament, toward an increasingly secularized view of marriage, favouring the socioeconomic community, but rather from private to public in the universal understanding of what contracts and validates matrimony.

That this shift, from private to public, concerns both the profane and the sacred, becomes clear in a number of novelle where the presence of recurring iconographical elements of sacrality, in the ritualistic setting of the marriage contracts, symbolically endorses the notion of public testimony in the context of a religious community as well. In II, 5, Fabio himself insists on speaking his flimsy promise not to take another wife in the future "in front of this image that *represents* the Virgin Mary and her son Jesus Christ" ("dinanzi a questa imagine che la Vergine Maria e il suo figliuolo Giesu Cristo ci *rappresenta*" [1: 697]). Likewise, the maid in II, 41 is adamant about conducting the private marriage ceremony between Gerardo and Elena in front of the picture of the Madonna with baby Jesus hanging over the bed: "Here at the head of this bed you see the image *representing* the glorious Queen of heaven with the figure of her little son our Saviour in her arm, to

---

[24] See for this issue also Klapisch-Zuber, *Women, Family, and Ritual in Renaissance Italy*, 178–212.

whom I pray, and you equally have to pray, that in this moment of marrying by words in the present they bestow you good fortune from beginning to end" ("Eccovi qui al capo di questo letto l'imagine *rappresentante* la gloriosa Reina del cielo con la figura del suo figliuolo nostro Salvatore in braccio, i quali io prego e voi altresí pregar devete che al matrimonio, che insieme sète per parole di presente per contraere, diano buon principio, meglio mezzo ed ottimo fine" [2: 77–78][25]). In the *Châtelaine de Vergy* story (IV, 5) Carlo emphasizes that his private marriage pact with the lady of Vergy had been sworn "in front of the images of the glorious image *representing* Lord Jesus Christ and the Queen of Heaven, the Virgin Mary, his mother" ("dinanzi a le imagini de la gloriosa imagine *rappresentante* il nostro signore Giesú Cristo e la reina del cielo Vergina Maria sua madre" [2: 667]).[26]

I have not encountered similar examples of conspicuous iconographical depictions of divine witness to the exchange of matrimonial promise or consent among the predecessors of Bandello's novelle, such as in Marguerite de Navarre's *Heptaméron* or Boccaccio's *Decameron*.[27] This insistence on sacred witnesses, represented iconographically — the word "rappresentante" figures prominently in these passages — suggests that the increased importance of the moment of *pubblicamento* extends to a perceived religious community. It is more than simply an image that substitutes for the priest, and thereby the conferral of the sacrament. It reveals a deeper need for a real and public presence of a sacred nature that removes the sacramental burden from the private promise or words of consent. This sacred presence, represented iconographically in these novelle, seeping both into the private rituals of contracting marriage, and into the characters' perceived need to

---

[25] It should be noted that here, too, in spite of the maid's reference to the words in the present tense, the reader does not witness the actual exchange of these words. In accordance with the narrative pattern discussed above, the maid's direct discourse is followed by the narrator's voice, from which it is clear that the spouses do not say anything at all: "*la buona balia disse le belle parole* che in simili sposalizii, secondo la lodata consuetudine de la catolica romana Chiesa, dir si sogliono communemente" (2: 78).

[26] It is not clear if the construction that doubles the word "image" ("le *imagini* de la gloriosa *imagine*") is intentional.

[27] With the exception of a less conspicuous detail in the Third Novella of the Second Day, in the private exchange of promises between Alessandro and the daughter of the king of England: "Essa allora, levatasi a sedere in su il letto, *davanti ad una tavoletta dove Nostro Signore era effigiato*, postogli in mano uno anello, gli si fece sposare" (Boccaccio, *Tutte le opere*, 4:115).

publicize their bond, anticipates post-Tridentine legislation and mentalities. After Trent, the clergy focused extensively on increasing divine and eccle-siastical witness of a more public nature at the marriage ceremony, not only through the central position of the priest, but also through the increased enforcement of already existing requirements, such as the publication of the banns in church on three successive Sundays, the conclusion of the marriage inside the church building and the registration of the marriage in the parochial registry. The insertion of sacred marriage iconography into these novelle further suggests a shift from marriage understood as an essentially private act towards marriage as an act requiring publicity to be valid, in both the sacred and profane contexts.

This fragile marital universe, narratively exploited by Bandello's novelle, to a certain extent anticipates the renewed interest in the issue of betrothal, or future promise, after the Council of Trent had safeguarded the sacrament of marriage in the 1563 *Tametsi* decree. In a move to institutionalize and regulate pre-marital promises and betrothal practices, post-Tridentine churchmen sought to impose and enforce the ecclesiastical perspective on *sponsali* as a private promise, between partners and between families, to contract a future marriage, according to the forms and requirements delineated in *Tametsi*, including publication, the reading of the banns and the presence of witnesses. Whichever words were spoken to this effect, the promise remained but a future engagement to marry: a non-sacrament-inducing family affair, to be defined, dictated, and broken if necessary (although often with great difficulty), by local conventions that could no longer infringe upon the sacrament of holy matrimony. This also meant that the Church stepped up its enforcement of the rule that the future promise does not allow the couple to engage in sexual intercourse or even intimacy, which was forbidden until the marriage was ratified according to the new rules.[28] The removal of the promise from the sacred realm surrounding the contracting of marriage is also reflected, as Jean-Louis Flandrin points out, in legal conflicts: the future promise to marry had to be of such a nature that

---

[28] See Lombardi, "Fidanzamenti e matrimoni," 221, 226, and Luperini, "La promessa sotto accusa," 381. See also Cavallo and Cerutti, "Female Honor and the Social Control of Reproduction in Piedmont between 1600 and 1800."

the church courts no longer had to worry about "what God had united, man cannot separate."[29]

Since in the early modern literary universe the genre of the novella can be considered the most suitable narrative form to experiment with verisimilitude and narrative dissimulation, as opposed to disclosure, it is not surprising that we find this shift in the private versus public conception of marriage most aptly performed in the novella's narrative poetics. On the one hand, Bandello plays with the private, inner, world of the characters, blurred by future intentions but little concerned with present realities. He artfully manipulates the reader's perception of this inner universe through the use of characters' direct and indirect discourse, and through the narrator's shifting game of dissimulation and revelation. On the other hand, he depicts an unambiguously realistic image of the public aspects of marriage that feature disclosure, unequivocal witness and mass celebrations, although these rarely occur in church. While the hyperbolic violence, typical for the *racconto tragico*, symbolically connotes the flimsiness of private and unwitnessed spoken words in these novelle, the necessity of an authenticating public disclosure constantly hovers over the narrative during the characters' complex and ambiguous dealings in the pre-marital stages. Finally, the recurring iconographical elements, symbolizing the representation of divine witnesses, suggest that the need for public and witnessed disclosure was a concern for both the profane and the sacred aspects of matrimony.

Bandello's novelle thus provide a unique literary perspective on the shifting understanding of betrothal and matrimony at the time of the Council of Trent. His literary and narrative art helps us to map the shifts and tensions between, on the one hand, the legitimacy bestowed on the marital bond by the conflicting models of ecclesiastical law and social custom, and, on the other hand, the legitimacy provided by the defining and ratifying moment

---

[29] "Quelle qu'ait été leur forme, il est, au reste, indubitable que les promesses de mariage ont perdu au XVIIe siècle, le caractère sacré qu'elles avaient aux XVe et XVIe siècles" (Flandrin, *Le sexe et l'Occident*, 74–75). This being said, the church tribunals would still get involved in conflicts involving the promise to marry and, to varying degrees, considered the promise to be binding from a religious point of view. Moreover, as is manifest in ecclesiastical cases from 1584, in Pisa, analyzed by Luperini, the distinction between promise, betrothal (*sponsali*) and contracted marriage was for a long time far from clear for the common folk, and the question of which words had been exchanged remained as thorny as ever ("Interrogato: *Che parole usò* quando li dette la fede e se li dette l'anello?" [Luperini, "La promessa sotto accusa," 375]).

of its public disclosure, perceived as the moment of truth, of *sgannare*, for all parties involved, including the partners themselves, and valid at both the sacred and profane levels.

Florida State University

Cited Works

Bandello, Matteo. *Tutte le opere di Matteo Bandello*, ed. Francesco Flora. 2 vols. Milan: Mondadori, 1952.

Bellomo, Saverio. "La donna, il matrimonio e la famiglia nel XVI secolo: Matteo Bandello." *La Cultura* 15.2–3 (1977): 205–221.

Bensi, Mario. "La *Chastelaine de Vergi* tra Margherita di Navarra e Matteo Bandello." In *Du Pô à la Garonne. Recherches sur les échanges culturels entre l'Italie et la France à la Renaissance. Actes du Colloque International d'Agen (26–28 septembre 1986)*, eds. Jean Cubelier de Beynac and Michel Simonin. Agen: Centre Matteo Bandello, 1990, 181–204.

Boccaccio, Giovanni. *Tutte le opere*, ed. Vittore Branca. Vol. 4, *Decameron*. Milan: Mondadori, 1976.

Cavallo, Sandra; Cerutti, Simona. "Female Honor and the Social Control of Reproduction in Piedmont between 1600 and 1800." In *Sex and Gender in Historical Perspective*, eds. Edward Muir and Guido Ruggiero, trans. Margaret Gallucci. Baltimore: Johns Hopkins University Press, 1990, 73–109.

Colish, Marcia. *Peter Lombard*. Leiden: Brill, 1994.

Dictionnaire de théologie catholique, eds. A. Vacant, E. Mangenot, E. Amann et al. 15 vols. Paris: Letouzey et Ané, 1923–1950.

Donahue, Charles. *Law, Marriage, and Society in the Later Middle Ages. Arguments About Marriage in Five Courts*. Cambridge, UK: Cambridge University Press, 2007.

Esmein, André. *Le Mariage en droit canonique*. 2 vols. New York: Burt Franklin, 1968.

Ferrari, Stéphan. "Histoire tragique et grande histoire: rencontre de deux genres." *Dalhousie French Studies* 65 (2003): 18–35.

Fiorato, Adelin Charles. *Bandello entre l'histoire et l'écriture. La vie, l'expérience sociale, l'évolution culturelle d'un conteur de la Renaissance*. Florence: Olschki, 1979.

_____. "L'image et la condition de la femme dans les *Nouvelles* de Bandello." In *Images de la femme dans la littérature italienne de la Renaissance. Préjugés misogynes et aspirations nouvelles. Castiglione, Piccolomini, Bandello*, eds. José Guidi, Marie-Françoise Piéjus, and Adelin Charles Fiorato. Paris: Université de la Sorbonne Nouvelle, 1980, 169–286.

Flandrin, Jean-Louis. *Le sexe et l'Occident. Évolution des attitudes et des comportements*. Paris: Seuil, 1981.

Flora, Francesco. "Introduction." In Bandello, *Tutte le opere*. 1:ix–xlix.

Gaudemet, Jean. *Le Mariage en Occident. Les mœurs et le droit*. Paris: Cerf, 1987.

Klapisch-Zuber, Christiane. *Women, Family, and Ritual in Renaissance Italy*, trans. Lydia Cochrane. Chicago: University of Chicago Press, 1985.

Leushuis, Reinier. *Le Mariage et l'«amitié courtoise» dans le dialogue et le récit bref de la Renaissance*. Florence: Olschki, 2003.

_____. "La *Châtelaine de Vergy* comme histoire tragique matrimoniale : de Marguerite de Navarre (1558) à Bandello (1573) et *Le sixiesme tome des histoires tragiques (1582)*." *Renaissance and Reformation / Renaissance et Réforme* 32.2 (2009): 5–31.

Lombardi, Daniela. "Fidanzamenti e matrimoni dal concilio di Trento alle riforme settecentesche." In *Storia del matrimonio*, eds. Michela De Giorgio and Christine Klapisch-Zuber. Bari: Laterza, 1996, 215–250.

Luperini, Sara. "La promessa sotto accusa (Pisa 1584)," In *Matrimoni in dubbio*, 363–394.

Matrimoni in dubbio: unioni controverse e nozze clandestine in Italia dal XIV al XVIII secolo, eds. Silvana Seidel Menchi and Diego Quaglioni. Bologna: Il Mulino, 2001.

Matteo Bandello. Novelliere europeo. Atti del convegno internazionale di studi, 7–9 novembre 1980, ed. Ugo Rozzo. Tortona: Centro studi Matteo Bandello e la cultura rinascimentale, 1982.

Rasi, Piero. *La conclusione del matrimonio nella dottrina prima del concilio di Trento*. Naples: Jovene, 1958.

Sozzi, Lionello. "Il racconto tragico in Francia nella seconda metà del Cinquecento." In *L'«Histoire tragique» nella seconda metà del Cinquecento francese*, ed. Lionello Sozzi. Turin: Genesi, 1991, 7–51.

Gli uomini, le città e i tempi di Matteo Bandello. II Convegno internazionale di studi Torino-Tortona-Alessandria-Castelnuovo Scrivia (8–11 novembre 1984), ed. Ugo Rozzo. Tortona: Centro studi Matteo Bandello e la cultura rinascimentale, 1985.

Wetzel, Hermann. "Éléments socio-historiques d'un genre littéraire: l'histoire de la nouvelle jusqu'à Cervantès." In *La Nouvelle française à la Renaissance*, ed. Lionello Sozzi and V.-L. Saulnier. Geneva and Paris: Slatkine, 1981, 41–78.

TO HAVE AND TO HOLD STILL: MARRIAGE AND MONUMENTALIZING IN EARLY MODERN ENGLISH DRAMA

LESLEY PETERSON

Recent scholarship in early modern English practices of memorialization characterizes the Protestant Reformation, in England, as a period of increasing suspicion or hostility towards the practice of reverencing corpses or body parts as relics, combined with, as J. Y Michel puts it, "an idealized vision" of tombs as "holy time-honoured buildings symbolizing an indestructible collective order."[1] Catholic theology and practice endowed the corpse with "magical powers," while the proliferation of memento mori emblems, which could include the corpse itself, helped to integrate "death into society by showing it as man's companion."[2] The emerging Protestant view of the corpse, by contrast, was as something dangerous that had to be contained: something capable of either physical or spiritual contamination.[3] "To Protestant Reformers," as Susan Zimmerman points out, "the Catholic preoccupation with the corporeal dangerously distorted the relationship between body and soul."[4] Furthermore, the deconsecration and destruction of tombs and other holy buildings during the English Reformation meant that the monument's function to reliably contain decay, and thereby to symbolize a stable social order, could no longer be taken for granted.[5]

---

[1] Michel, "Monuments," par. 5.

[2] Michel, "Monuments," par. 11–12.

[3] Compare Gittings's earlier observation that the Puritans' attitude of "disgust" towards the corpse "could be interpreted as a new development in attitudes towards death" (*Death, Burial and the Individual*, 47). This attitude could also express itself more mildly as a "sanitary concern" (Houlbrooke, *Death, Religion and the Family*, 349).

[4] Zimmerman, *Early Modern Corpse*, 8.

[5] Anxiety about this at the highest levels of Elizabethan society may be noted in Elizabeth I's 1560 proclamation forbidding "'the breaking or defacing' of any sort of funeral monument" (Houlbrooke, *Death, Religion and the Family*, 348).

These ideological shifts and tensions may help to explain why Christopher Marlowe, whose Protestant orthodoxy has long been questioned, makes the corpse of Tamburlaine's wife Zenocrate so necessary and central to the staging of *Tamburlaine the Great Part II*, written circa 1588; however, they explain less well the absence of either corpse or monument from two slightly later works that also dramatize a tyrannical ruler mourning the death of his wife. These are *The Tragedy of Mariam*, written circa 1604 by Elizabeth Cary, who was to convert to Catholicism later in life and who had been keenly interested in Catholicism since 1597 at least;[6] and Shakespeare's *Winter's Tale*, circa 1610, well known for its insistent troubling of the categories of corpse, monument and living wife. When Tamburlaine insists that his wife's body be embalmed and then wrapped in incorruptible gold, but not entombed, and that it follow him everywhere, he treats it both as something that can be domesticated (and thereby rendered familiar) and as something dangerous, to be contained (*Tam.*, 2:2.4.129–132). By contrast, although Cary presents Mariam as a martyr, she resolutely keeps her heroine's dead body off the stage, and in a way Shakespeare does the same. For while repeatedly inviting us to imagine a dead queen, he defers staging that particular spectacle, until finally he replaces both Hermione's supposed corpse and her supposed statue with their originary supplement—her living body. This significant difference between *Tamburlaine* and the later plays has, I would argue, less to do with the authors' theological positions on relics than with their attention to the impact on marriage of what Peter Stallybrass has termed the emerging "culture of surveillance."[7] Marlowe wrote at a time when the English audience's desire had not yet been aroused for the particular pleasure that single-point perspective provides: a fixed, authoritative point from which to view the framed object of his gaze.[8] Between the 1580s and the early decades of the seventeenth century, however, the advent of the proscenium stage combined with what Jonathan Sawday calls "the culture of dissection"[9] to strengthen the culture of surveillance and the associated monumentalizing impulse that Cary and Shakespeare both critique, in texts that dramatize,

---

[6] Peterson, "Source and Date," 257–260.

[7] Stallybrass, "Patriarchal," 126.

[8] See, for instance, Panofsky, *Perspective*, 60–61.

[9] Sawday, *Body*, 25.

as Marlowe's play does not, the devastating consequences that may result when a husband condemns what is changeable in his wife.

Although Elizabethan theatre was hardly short on spectacle (as *Tamburlaine* itself exemplifies), what it did not have was illusionistic scenic backdrops: these were used for the first time in England on the proscenium stage built for the masques of King James I at Whitehall. This new style of production depended heavily on the art of single-point perspective, and in doing so it privileged one seat in the house (the king's, of course) over all others.[10] As Albrecht Dürer's 1538 woodcut *An Artist Drawing a Recumbent Woman* illustrates so vividly (Fig. 15.1), both the early modern anatomist and the perspectival artist share with James's designer Inigo Jones a commitment to constructing the expert's position relative to the body viewed. Such practitioners, furthermore, strive to represent the body in such a way as to suggest that there is nothing the viewer has missed, nothing that has not been fully captured and known. Consequently, their work tends to deny any aspect of the female body that threatens this illusion, whether it be physical mobility, permeability or the fluidity of the unfixable body interior. This is not Tamburlaine's aesthetic: Marlowe depicts for Zenocrate, captured bride of a tyrant though she be, a marriage which not only accommodates mobility and flux, but also features a husband whose preferred method of representing his wife relies not on one perfect image but on a proliferation of incommensurate (and individually inadequate) representations. The marriage that Cary's Mariam finds herself in, by contrast, is one in which the husband expects his wife to fashion herself into a living monument to his invulnerability: a fiction that the wife's fixity is required to sustain, with terrible consequences to both parties.[11] Shakespeare's Hermione finds herself suddenly in a marriage like Mariam's, in which the undeniable changeability of her pregnant body shakes her husband's confidence in his ability to read her aright, an anxiety Shakespeare associates with a mistaken preference for marble over flesh. While all three dramatists affirm the

---

[10] Orgel and Strong, *Inigo Jones*, 1: 9.

[11] Because we cannot assign a precise date to the composition of *Mariam*, we cannot be entirely certain that Cary wrote it after Inigo Jones began to use perspectival scenery in the court masques. However, as Sawday among others makes clear, Jacobean masques were not the only expression of the demand for female fixity that was gathering strength by the end of the sixteenth century; consequently, we may safely assume that Cary was engaging with this important change in the dominant mode of representation at the turn of the seventeenth century.

importance of embracing change, then, Cary and Shakespeare differ from Marlowe in depicting husbands in whom heightened anxiety about personal and political stability and longevity generates heightened intolerance for wifely mobility or flux. Both of these Jacobean dramatists, furthermore, interrogate and critique the anatomizing gaze with scripts that acknowledge the particular pleasures offered by a fixed, authoritative perspective, but that deny these pleasures both to the viewers of the plays and to the husbands in the plays. Instead they valorize the very different pleasures that arise from celebrating the mysterious undecideability of the living human body, which no monument can hope to replicate.

Tamburlaine fights against it; Herod commands it; Leontes believes himself to have provoked it. However, no matter what his role in his wife's death, each man experiences it as, at least in part, a devastating loss of power that is, at once, a threat to his sense of integrity. Consequently, all three respond in similar ways. Tamburlaine tries to save Zenocrate, calling physicians to her in her final illness; when they fail, his rage prompts him to attack the very sources of mortality: he invites Techelles to "descend" with him "into th' infernal vaults / To hale the Fatal Sisters by the hair / And throw them in the triple moat of hell" (*Tam.*, 2:2.4.98–100). Herod, angry at Mariam's emotional withdrawal and tricked into believing her unfaithful, orders his queen executed in act 4. However, in act 5 the Nuntio brings Herod both the news of Mariam's death and the evidence of her innocence, and from that point on, this king reacts with a combination of denial and violent rage that is much like that of Tamburlaine. Herod, too, would argue with the Fates; he asks the Nuntio repeatedly, "But art thou sure there doth no life remain? / Is't possible my Mariam should be dead? / Is there no trick to make her breathe again?" One senses he would go on like this indefinitely, were it not that the Nuntio bluntly interrupts: "Her body is divided from her head" (*Mariam*, 5.87–90).

The scenario in *The Winter's Tale* is slightly different; this king, Leontes, does his railing against the Oracle before his queen collapses, rather than after. At the beginning of the trial scene he defies the Oracle's assertion of Hermione's innocence, asserting that "There is no truth at all i' th' Oracle" (*WT*, 3.2.138). However, from the moment Leontes hears of his son Mamillius' death, he ceases to argue with the Oracle, and when Paulina brings news of Hermione's supposed death, it is not Leontes but an attendant Lord who expresses resistance to the Fates: "The higher powers forbid!" (*WT*, 3.2.200).

Nevertheless, Leontes's response to news of his wife's changing physical state is quite different from his response to similar news of his son. When Leontes learns of Mamillius' death, he accepts his servant's word as unquestioningly as the Oracle's, not asking for visible proof. Yet he continues to argue about Hermione's physical state:

> LEONTES. Apollo's angry, and the heavens themselves
> > Do strike at my injustice. [*Hermione swoons.*] How now there!
> PAULINA. This news is mortal to the queen: look down
> > And see what death is doing.
> LEONTES.   Take her hence;
> Her heart is but o'ercharg'd; she will recover.   (*WT*, 3.2.144–148)

He began the scene insisting on his perfect ability to read his wife's living body as unchaste; to put it another way, he began insisting upon his power to realize Hermione's lack of chastity through a performative utterance. Now, in proclaiming that "she will recover," he attempts to realize her life in the same way. Much like Tamburlaine and Herod, then, Leontes continues throughout this scene to argue one key point: the limits to his power over his wife's body.

Furthermore, Leontes strongly resembles both Tamburlaine and Herod in his plans to commemorate his wife, for each king struggles to find a memorial rite adequate to his grief, and each king's grief ultimately finds its most coherent focus on his *own* body. Tamburlaine insists on keeping Zenocrate's embalmed body with him at all times, telling it that "till I die thou shalt not be interred" (*Tam.*, 2:2.4.132). He then proceeds to memorialize Zenocrate with a proliferation of objects and images, desperately inadequate supplements to her gold-wrapped corpse: he has a picture of her that he will "keep within the circle of" his "arms" (*Tam.*, 2:3.2.35); he plans a "stature [*sic*]" which he does not actually erect (*Tam.*, 2:2.4.140); instead his companions put up a "pillar," a "mournful streamer" *and* a "table" (*Tam.*, 2:3.2.15, 19, 23). These elaborate preparations may seem to announce a typical Elizabethan heraldic funeral; however, the subsequent proceedings are anything but typical.[12] Tamburlaine has in mind no solemn procession to church. As a backdrop to all of these memorials, he leaves a town burned to the ground: a public monument

---

[12] For a thorough description of the sixteenth-century heraldic funeral, see Gittings, *Death, Burial and the Individual*, 166–178.

made by the destruction of an entire town that was itself once full of public monuments, those buildings that give a town its identity (*Tam.*, 2:3.2.45b–46). All of this only anticipates the monument Tamburlaine plans for himself and Zenocrate eventually to share, describing it even as he defers constructing it: "Then in as rich a tomb as Mausolus' / We both will rest and have one epitaph" (*Tam.*, 2:2.4.133–134). According to Abbe Blum, "There would be no monument without the one who desires, views, needs to contain, and reacts to the monumentalized other."[13] For Marlowe's Tamburlaine, this is quite literally true. There will be no monument without him.

Unlike Tamburlaine, who has been closely acquainted with death his entire life, or Leontes, who asks to view the bodies of his wife and son, Herod shows no interest in his wife's corpse as funerary object. He gives no orders for the disposal of his wife's body, does not ask to see it and makes no plans to memorialize it. He fears the unfixed female body far more strongly than either of the others. Yet Herod too finds comfort in picturing his own tomb. He raves that he will bury his guilty self alive, and the play closes with his imagining that, some day in the future,

> A stone upon the vault someone shall lay,
> Which monument shall an inscription have,
> And these shall be the words it shall contain:
> Here Herod lies, that hath his Mariam slain.   (*Mariam*, 5.255–258)

Leontes, similarly, plans a monument to his wife that has his own abject self as focal point:

> Prithee, bring me
> To the dead bodies of my queen and son.
> One grave shall be for both. Upon them shall
> The causes of their death appear, unto
> Our shame perpetual. Once a day I'll visit
> The chapel where they lie, and tears shed there
> Shall be my recreation. So long as nature
> Will bear up with this exercise, so long
> I daily vow to use it. Come and lead me
> To these sorrows.   (*WT*, 3.2.232b–241)

---

[13] Blum, "Strike All That Look," 103.

Of the three, however, it is Leontes who most completely rejects what Michel calls "the idea of a perfect, eternal sepulchre that literally stands for social and ritual order."[14] As his advisors will make explicit in act 5, the grave of Leontes's wife and son signifies an unstable future for the state, a failure of order in the succession. Appropriately, his penitent self, visiting "Once a day," is the most vividly realized element of the monument Leontes conceives of here: a sign not of power and permanence but of weakness and loss. Nevertheless, Leontes is no more able than Tamburlaine or Herod to imagine a memorial for his wife that is not, at the same time, a monument to himself.

Furthermore, all three plays suggest that this imaginative limitation is nothing new in these men's lives; these husbands treat their wives' tombs—these women's new exteriors—in much the same way that they treat their wives' bodies—these women's old exteriors—when they are alive. Dead or alive, each husband, to some extent, requires that his wife's body stand in his presence as the image of his own power and identity. In the early days of Tamburlaine's relationship with Zenocrate, his opponent Bajazeth (Emperor of the Turks) gives to his Empress Zabina his crown to wear before battle; in response, Tamburlaine gives his own crown to Zenocrate. Both men thus cast their women (wife in Zabina's case, betrothed in Zenocrate's) as stand-ins for themselves. Tamburlaine further dramatizes his view of Zenocrate as a reflection of his own power when he requires her treatment of Zabina to mirror his own treatment of Bajazeth: the two women must trade words while their men trade blows (*Tam.*, 1:3.3.130–131). However, in both these situations Zenocrate is quite active and vocal. Activity and vocality are less safe choices for either Mariam or Hermione; the demand for wives, in whom they can see reflected the image of their ideal selves, is much more unyielding in Herod's case and in Leontes's than in Tamburlaine's. Herod calls Mariam a "precious mirror" on which his "dazzled eye might rest" (*Mariam*, 2;5.125, 124), valuing only her static appearance, not her ability to speak. Similarly, Hermione's ability to converse persuasively with Polixenes leads Leontes to see the two of them as "making practised smiles / As in a looking-glass" (*WT*, 1.2.118–119). Not only does the simile suggest deceit and vanity, but it also exposes one of the sources of Polixenes' anxious envy: he himself wants to look at Hermione "As in a looking-glass," and see himself in her, looking back only at him. Although Leontes seeks comfort in the idea that Hermione has produced a son who is the mirror image of himself (but more innocent), it is

---

[14] Michel, "Monuments," par. 3.

in Hermione's eyes, even more than in Mamillius' face, that he needs to find an idealized image of himself.

Leontes and Herod are primarily administrators who perform their claims to power by staging iterative illusions of both personal and political stability. Tamburlaine, by contrast, performs his claim to power through battle; as a soldier, therefore, his business is death and change. At the onset of his final illness he does brag that "Sickness or death can never conquer" him (*Tam.*, 2:5.1.220), but constant violent action is almost as satisfying proof of this to him, as images of unchanging stability are to Herod. Optimistically Tamburlaine calls Callapine's attack "A present medicine to recure my pain!" (*Tam.*, 2:5.3.106). Thus, Tamburlaine has more tolerance than Herod for the constant flux that is the symptom of personal and political mortality, and this, perhaps as much as the earlier date of Marlowe's composition, makes Tamburlaine a different kind of husband as well as a different kind of king. At the end of the *First Part*, Tamburlaine describes the corpses of those he slaughters in his conquests as "objects … / Wherein as in a mirror may be seen / His honour, that consists in shedding blood" (*Tam.*, 1:5.1.474–476). In the final act of *Part Two*, he exults in his ability to destroy those very things that were intended by their builders to memorialize the stability of their reign and its timeless foundations:

> The stately buildings of fair Babylon,
> Whose lofty pillars, higher than the clouds,
> Were wont to guide the seaman in the deep,
> Being carried thither by the cannon's force,
> Now fill the mouth of Limnasphaltis' lake
> And make a bridge unto the battered walls.
> Where Belus, Ninus, and great Alexander
> Have rode in triumph, triumphs Tamburlaine.   (*Tam.*, 2:5.1.63–70)

Just as he glories in the wounds and scars that memorialize sudden and violent change to his own body, Tamburlaine glories in his vision of history as subject to sudden violent change at his own hands.

Herod, however, cannot tolerate any suggestion of mutability in either his kingdom or himself. He, too, has killed for power, but by indirect methods he prefers not to acknowledge. Consequently, he must be surrounded by emblems of permanence and stability: monuments to himself and his eternally legitimized reign, chief among which must be Mariam. This is because she is not only his wife but also, as his wife, the source of his best claim to the throne. As Cary explains, "This Mariam had a brother called Aristobulus, and next him and Hircanus, his grandfather, Herod in his wife's right had the best title. Therefore to remove them, he charged the [second] with treason: and put him to death; and drowned the [first] under colour of sport" (*Mariam*, Argument). In act 1 we learn that Herod has been called to Rome, where Caesar has recently overthrown "Anthony, his great friend," and that "In his absence, news came to Jerusalem that Caesar had put him to death" (*Mariam*, Argument). Yet, as we learn at the end of the third act, the rumours are false, and act four witnesses Herod's return to Jerusalem. On this occasion he insists on being able to read both the city and his queen as reflections of his triumphant happiness:

> Hail happy city! Happy in thy store,
> And happy that thy buildings such we see;
> More happy in the temple where w'adore,
> But most of all that Mariam lives in thee.
> … … … … … … … … … … …
> Oh haste thy steps rare creature, speed thy pace,
> And let thy presence make the day more bright,
> And cheer the heart of Herod with thy face.   (*Mariam*, 4.1.1–4, 10–12)

To be able to lay his eyes on her beautiful face is, he would have her and himself believe, all that his happiness requires. However, as we learn upon Mariam's appearance, she must do more than appear. She must resemble the buildings Herod associates with her; she must be one who is more monument than woman and one, furthermore, who looks both at him and to him exactly as she looked before he left.

In fact, Herod has returned from Rome with a fantasy that involves Mariam's body offering itself to his eye, a singular "eye" that to him suffices to signify his "I":

But when I am with Mariam, time runs on,
Her sight can make months minutes, days of weeks:
An hour is then no sooner come than gone
When in her face mine eye for wonders seeks.
You world-commanding city, Europe's grace,
Twice hath my curious eye your streets survey'd,
I have seen the statue-filled place,
That once if not for grief had been betray'd.
I all your Roman beauties have beheld,
And seen the shows your ediles did prepare;
I saw the sum of what in you excell'd,
Yet saw no miracle like Mariam rare.
The fair and famous Livia, Caesar's love,
The world's commanding mistress did I see:
Whose beauties both the world and Rome approve,
Yet, Mariam, Livia is not like to thee.
Be patient but a little while, mine eyes,
Within your compassed limits be contained;
That object straight shall your desires suffice,
From which you were so long a while restrain'd.
How wisely Mariam doth the time delay ... . (*Mariam*, 4.1.17–37)

Herod longs to see Mariam, but he particularly longs to see her as a carefully controlled spectacle. Urging his eyes to be patiently "contained" within their "compassed limits," he chooses to assume the fixed position of Dürer's artist, whose single eye, contained within the compass of the instrument through which it peers, comprehends everything the scene before him contains (Fig. 15.1). Herod anticipates that, by viewing Mariam in this way, his "desires" will be consequently satisfied, and not otherwise.[15] When Herod speaks of the time for which he longs, "When in her face mine eye for wonders seek," it

---

[15] Nancy Gutierrez identifies the last fourteen lines of this scene, 29–42, as a sonnet. Since the entire script is written in abab quatrains, I am not sure that the fact this scene ends in a rhyming couplet entirely justifies the label. Nevertheless, her point that Herod here "voices several Petrarchan conventions: the beauty of the lover's mistress when compared to other famous beautiful women (ll. 1286–89 [29–32]); the impatience of the lover to see his mistress (ll. 1290–97 [33–40]); and the need for the lover to hide his emotions from the world (ll. 1298–99 [41–42])" is a valid and important one. See "Valuing *Mariam*," 240.

may well be that the wonder he seeks most to see in her face is himself as she sees him (*Mariam* 4.1.20). So that all may be perfectly ordered, Mariam must memorialize no one else but him.

The way Herod plans to view Mariam is one that confines her within "compassed limits" as inevitably as it does his own eyes. Herod gets to fix the frame; Mariam must fill it. In assuming the position of the artist with the authoritative gaze, in other words, Herod requires that Mariam assume the position of the artist's model. As such, she must do her best to resemble (at once to recall and to anticipate) the work of art that Herod wants to see in her. It is statues, not living women, that head Herod's list of Rome's "beauties." He does proceed to add Livia to the list, but including both her and Rome's statues under the ambiguous term "Roman beauties" suggests his reluctance to acknowledge any significant difference between statue and woman. Thus, although Herod cites the "beauties" of "statue-filled" Rome in order to assert that Mariam's face is the greater wonder, the comparison also reveals that the marble statue is the ideal against which Herod measures his memory of Mariam's real self.

There is one miracle that, according to Herod, such wonders can work. However, it is one not of healing or of transformation, but of preservation. Herod repeatedly credits Mariam with power over time itself: quite a different sort of magic from what one might ask of a saint's relic. When he is with her, Herod says, "time runs on"; he commends "How wisely Mariam doth the time delay." Although this last comment literally refers to her delaying the moment of her arrival in his sight, its phrasing underscores Herod's need to construct Mariam as one who can work the "wonder" of defeating time itself, on his behalf. Like that of a statue, the face Herod has "beheld" in the past is exactly the same one he anticipates seeing imminently. When Mariam looks at him with the unblinking gaze of Galatean love, he feels himself to be immune to time's ravages: "Her sight can make months minutes," Herod claims. The ambiguous syntax of this assertion also elides the difference between his act of viewing Mariam and her act of viewing him. All the perfect woman can see is him seeing her: a continuous replay of the moment in Arthur Golding's 1584 version of the Pygmalion myth, when the waking statue first opens "Hir eyelidds up, hir Lover and the light at once" to "spye."[16] Such a face cannot be merely mortal. It must be both more and less than mortal: still, unchanging, more statue than woman. No wonder

---

[16] Ovid, *Metamorphosis*, X. 320.

Herod makes no reference here to enjoying Mariam's company, her words or her actions, only to her face. What he sees must be everything she is, and everything she is must reinforce his power.[17]

It was not always quite thus, however.[18] Herod has just returned from a brush with death, where he was confronted with the facts of his subjection both to Caesar and to mortality, and his tolerance for reminders of either is at a new low. Clearly, his experience, in that city filled with images of its permanence and mastery, haunts his memory as much as Mariam's face. Now he needs the latter somehow to redeem the former—by being picture-perfect and silent, by giving no sign of that flux which threatens the integrity of bodily borders and warns of "self-dissolution."[19] Later in this act, Herod does offer praise to Mariam's verbal skills, but he places her exercise of them firmly in the past:

> HEROD. But have you heard her speak?
> SALOME.   You know I have.
> Herod. And were you not amaz'd?
> SALOME.   No, not a whit.
> HEROD. Then 'twas not her you heard; her life I'll save,
>   For Mariam hath a world-amazing wit.   (*Mariam*, 4.7.
> 424–428)

To be "amazed" is to be lost, bewildered, unable to purposefully proceed. It is thus but a small step from Herod's proud and loving amazement of yesterday to his fearful question of today, "Can human eyes be daz'd by woman's wit?" (*Mariam* 4.7.496). Of course, Salome helps her brother Herod take that small step by playing on *amazing*'s connotations of *unnatural* and *destabilizing*. She does this by emphasizing Mariam's "tongue" and her "mouth": evidence that,

---

[17] Quilligan makes a similar observation, although she considers speech only and not looks as well: "The role of wife is one in which a woman exercises her self only to erase her self so that her husband may have a self. She is not to be mute, but to provide a 'conversation' out of which he will construct his self. What she says, she says *only* to him." See "Staging Gender," 227.

[18] Although Herod's change in attitude is significant, however, it represents less a sea-change than a slight shift in emphasis, one that exposes the violence always inhering in the dominant discourse of the culture Mariam has grown up in.

[19] Zimmerman, *Early Modern Corpse*, 5.

unlike a painting or a statue, the face is not a coherent impermeable surface. Rather, Mariam's face contains an orifice, both point of entry and source of outflow. Salome emphasizes this in her response to Herod's praise:

> SALOME. She speaks a beauteous language, but within
> Her heart is false as powder: and her tongue
> Doth but allure the auditors to sin,
> And is the instrument to do you wrong.
> HEROD. It may be so; nay, 'tis so: she's unchaste,
> Her mouth will ope to ev'ry stranger's ear:
> Then let the executioner make haste,
> Lest she enchant him, if her words he hear.　(*Mariam*, 4.7.
> 429–436)

On these terms, if Herod has been *amazed*, it is because of Mariam's *allure*, a word that suggests both beauty and the willful practice of black arts, namely *enchantment*. The thought of Mariam exercising her wit now, or in the future, and the thought of Mariam's open mouth, a sign of her body's permeability and a reminder of how much there is to her that he cannot see, turns Herod's remembered amazement into present terror, a terror that his sight will be dazed or rendered unreliable. This is a sense that, increasingly, Herod cannot afford to doubt.

Leontes faces a similar crisis, symbolically if not literally, at the opening of *The Winter's Tale*. He is not a usurping tyrant, like Herod; he has not had to confront Caesar and face death; he has only had to enjoy the company of his best friend for nine months. Leontes and Polixenes have been occupying the same ground on the friendliest of terms. Nevertheless, occupation is very near to being possession, and possession is, for Leontes at least, figured in terms of the female body. Thus Polixenes, although not yet apprised of his host's suspicion, is correct when he comments, "The king hath on him such a countenance / As he had lost some province, and a region / Loved as he loves himself" (*WT*, 1.2.369–371a). It is not in the early modern order of things for a king to share his home with another king. This is the context in which Hermione's accustomed liberties of speech suddenly no longer charm.

It is, furthermore, a time in which Leontes cannot possibly expect to find in his wife a reassuring image of his own stable power, whatever may prompt him to wish to do so. She is visibly pregnant, close to full term. Thus she flaunts perforce a body that changes too rapidly to ignore, a body without reliable boundaries between self and other, between inside and outside. Leontes cannot look at Hermione without seeing proof that his wife's body is sexual, changeable and beyond his control: "From east, west, north, and south, be it concluded, / No barricado for a belly. Know't," he pronounces (*WT*, 1.2.204–205). Consequently, Leontes needs to invent an imaginary version of this woman that he *can* fix—in mind. In this creative act, he is highly successful, as Camillo warns Polixenes. No one can "shake / The fabric of his folly, whose foundation / Is piled upon his faith, and will continue / The standing of his body" (*WT*, 1.2.428–430a). At the end, Leontes must not only suffer the Oracle of Apollo to shake the fabric of this particular folly to its foundation, but must also give up the folly of believing that any body can continue to stand unshaken over time.

Such challenges do not apply only to crowned rulers, either, as Cary makes clear, for her portrayal of the other husband in the *Tragedy of Mariam*, Constabarus, shows how closely imbricated can be a husband's desire for political, or psychological, stability and for his wife's body to be well ordered. In a well-known passage, Constabarus expostulates to Salome:

> Are Hebrew women now transformed to men?
> Why do you not as well our battles fight,
> And wear our armour? Suffer this, and then
> Let all the world be topsy-turvèd quite.   (*Mariam*, 1.6.47–50)

According to him, the stability of the entire world depends on Salome's compliance with his demands and their country's laws. However, the status he wishes to demonstrate and preserve is, as the following oath suggests, an unattainable, inhuman stability:

> Now by the stately carvèd edifice
> That on Mount Sion makes so fair a show,
> And by the altar fit for sacrifice,
> I love thee more than thou thyself dost know.   (*Mariam*, 1.6.9–12)

The "stately … edifice / … on Mount Sion" that Constabarus swears by is, of course, Jerusalem's temple, central to both Jewish culture and Jewish history. Here, then, Constabarus identifies himself with his ideal: the holy building that never changes. He swears by it, but with his oath also places himself "by" it, appropriating its holy permanence metonymically. However, we may note that at the heart of his oath is the word "altar": a homonym for that which Constabarus fears the most: the human tendency to "alter."

In rebuttal, Salome also uses the discourse of building, but she does so in order to emphasize the impermanence characteristic of Constabarus's own life, as well as to claim responsibility for his present elevated status. "Did I for this *uprear* thy low estate?" Salome demands. "This hand of mine hath lifted up thy head, / Which many a day ago had *fallen* full low" (*Mariam*, 1.6.23, 27–28, emphasis added). Walls, like men, can be raised up and can fall, and so, in reminding us that Constabarus was not always as powerful as he is today, Salome indirectly reminds us that even the temple, built, fallen and rebuilt, has not always stood as today it stands. Her challenging response provokes Constabarus to admit and deny the changeability of his nature simultaneously: "You have my patience often exercised," he accuses her. But, he adds, "Use makes my choler keep within the banks" (*Mariam*, 1.6.31–32). In acknowledging his all-too-human temper, Constabarus makes Salome responsible for it, while crediting himself with its management. That essential fluid choler, in his view, is like floodwater associated with devastation and chaos; any change he does not feel he controls, whether emotional or climatic, threatens to make his world "topsy-turvèd quite." And it is caused by women; it has nothing to do with his essential masculine nature.

After invoking the temple, Constabarus further buttresses his defenses by invoking Jewish history, but his version of it denies the destruction and rebuilding of the former and the general turbulence of the latter:

> Since mildest Moses, friend unto the Lord,
> Did work his wonders in the land of Ham,
> And slew the first-born babes without a sword,
> In sign whereof we eat the holy lamb;
> Till now that fourteen hundred years are past,
> Since first the Law with us hath been in force:
> You are the first, and will, I hope, be last,
> That ever sought her husband to divorce!   (*Mariam*, 1.6.71–79)

Before mentioning Salome's particular rebellion (seeking divorce), Constabarus must first insist on the "force" of "the Law," emphasizing its impersonal and timeless authority over Salome. Yet surely Constabarus's identification of the inauguration of Mosaic Law with the slaughter of infants—as the only example provided here of Moses's mildness—calls the mildness of that "Law" into question. Constabarus's insistence on the absolute authority of Mosaic Law is further undercut by the fact that the situation to which he and Salome are presently responding, namely Herod's supposed death at Cæsar's command, demonstrates the lived reality that all in Judea are subject to Roman law. His insistence that the Law is absolute, unchanging and uncontested thus reveals itself to be more an expression of fantasy than a statement of truth.

Although Salome is, in many ways, Mariam's opposite, the two are alike in that both are married to men who expect them to perform the stability of the entire state with their bodies. Whereas Tamburlaine revels in his power to make and unmake rulers and ruled, such men as Herod and Constabarus deny any understanding of history as a chronicle of hierarchies turned topsy turvy, of relationships and allegiances made, unmade and remade. Any evidence of impermanence, all threats or reminders that their positions are assailable, become the responsibility of their wives. The more shaky they feel, the more they demand that their power be iteratively performed and witnessed.

Herod makes this expectation clear as soon as his long-awaited Mariam appears. She is beautiful as ever, but sombre, and this is not good enough; she must let him see her seeing him with approval. In this, Herod resembles Shakespeare's Claudius, another murderous king who inaugurates his regime by requiring of his court and his step-son a forced exchange of smiles. Like Claudius, Herod demands that his sombre relation put off what he refers to as her "dusky habits" (*Mariam*, 4.3.4):

> This froward humour will not do you good:
> It hath too much already Herod grieved
> To think that you on terms of hate have stood.
> Yet smile my dearest Mariam, do but smile,
> And I will all unkind conceits exile.   (*Mariam*, 4.3.53–57)

Herod insists upon being unconditionally loved, and his happiness at Mariam's sight depends on her performing total happiness with him. It is not clear how fully Mariam ever comes to understand the impossibility of performing any kind of perfect consistency; in this she resembles Webster's Duchess of Malfi, who, as Theodora Jankowski convincingly argues, fails to acknowledge that no woman's body can, or should, be "marble-constant," and consequently develops "a system of rule in which she fails to consider her body's potential [for change], either as a means to power or a means by which she can lose power."[20] Mariam does, however, understand the significance of the smile that Herod demands, as she explains to Sohemus: "I know I could enchain him with a smile / And lead him captive with a gentle word" (*Mariam*, 3.3.45–46). But the question of whether to do so is, in her mind, also the question, "And must I to my prison turn again?" (*Mariam*, 3.3.33). Fixing her body into that permanent smile makes her as much a "captive" as it does him, for the smiles that such kings demand participate as much as marble monuments do in the erasure—or reconstruction—of history. In asking Mariam to forget the dead, Herod is also asking her to reconstruct her identity as depending on her relationship to him rather than on her relationship to her grandfather and brother, whose deaths he arranged. To smile in such a situation, as Hamlet and Mariam both see it, is to betray not only the dead but also oneself.

This, I would suggest, helps to explain why Cary has to keep Mariam off stage in her play's final act. As Sawday points out, corpses in anatomy books of the period tended to be gendered female,[21] and corpses often were represented as willingly offering themselves to the viewer's gaze, offering thereby the illusion of authoritative mastery over death and the female body both at once. In the years between Marlowe's writing of *Tamburlaine* and Cary's writing of *Mariam*, the emerging study of anatomy, as well as the emerging and related field of perspectival art, led toward what I consider a significant decrease in tolerance for what Nancy Vickers refers to as the "poetry of tension, of flux, of alternation between the scattered and the gathered."[22] This increasing intolerance for the unfixed found its expression, in British representations of the female body at the turn of the seventeenth century, in an increasing commitment to an art of fixation, in which the female body is not so much "scattered and gathered" as it is anatomized and

---

[20] Jankowski, *Women in Power*, 156, 151.

[21] Sawday, *Body*, ch. 3, ch. 6.

[22] Vickers, "Diana," 107.

inventoried. Despite being in many ways a captive, Marlowe's Zenocrate travels widely with Tamburlaine; she is unusually mobile, and she never encounters jealousy. However problematic, hers is not a marriage in which perfect fixity is the ideal. In the later *Tragedy of Mariam*, on the other hand, Cary both acknowledges and critiques the previous decade's trend towards fixation.

Of course, scholars before me have noted Cary's concern with mobility and confinement, pointing for instance to Mariam's lament that Herod's confinement first taught her heart to "range" metaphorically, and to the act one Chorus's passing judgment on any woman who seeks "variety."[23] What I would add to this discussion is that Cary depicts Herod's Palace as a sort of proto-Panopticon, thereby dramatizing the effects on her female characters of living under this new scopic regime.[24] Yet at the same time, Cary's play denies her audience the pleasure of seeing Mariam's dead body on display as either commodity, anatomy lesson, or monument, thereby staging for us as for Herod the unsettling experience of having one's demand for a certain kind of spectacle remain unmet.

The marriage Marlowe stages features a husband who gains his sense of power, over himself and others, from his ability to create violent change. When his wife dies, he cannot conceive of a single satisfactory monument, but nor does he try to make one of her in life. Cary, however, stages marriages much like that which Shakespeare stages in the *Winter's Tale*, featuring a kind of husband who copes with an unbearable degree of uncertainty and flux by projecting what he fears in himself and his environment onto the body of a woman, over which he then strives to perform the mastery of the artist and of the anatomist. Her body must be perfectly legible, but can only be so if perfectly still, and if perfectly in agreement with the viewer's ideal image of himself. In Shakespeare's *Winter's Tale*, Leontes only gets his wife back after he proves himself able to resist the "impulse to monumentalize," which Blum defines as the impulse to commemorate something or someone of value, often by "altering, idealizing, [or] idolizing the original proportions."[25]

---

[23] Cary, Chor. 1.19. See Hodgson-Wright's review of the criticism (Introduction, 20–23).

[24] Compare Michel Foucault's description of the prisoners' cells in Jeremy Bentham's Panopticon: "like so many cages, so many small theatres, in which each actor is alone, perfectly individualized and constantly visible" (*Discipline and Punish*, 200).

[25] Blum, "Strike All That Look," 99.

Because the statue Paulina shows Leontes has aged "by some sixteen years," it commemorates by altering, but not by idealizing (*WT*, 5.3.31). The statue therefore denies Leontes the opportunity to idolize Hermione's "original proportions," and Shakespeare suggests that it is his acceptance of this loss that completes Leontes's redemption. Quite simply, he could have been critical, could have complained that the statue were not better done, could even have demanded one more beautiful. The final test of whether he has profited from Paulina's years of tuition is whether he can cherish the changes Hermione has already undergone; otherwise, how is he fit to be a husband to the woman Hermione will change into in the future?

Evidence that he is ready, according to the internal logic of the play, may be found in the fact that Leontes can now recognize and welcome resemblance without identity, consistency in alteration. In the first half of the play, this is not the case. He is told how much his children, Mamillius and Perdita, look like him, but cannot acknowledge it.[26] Nor can he bear to see that his pregnant wife is not even identical with herself.[27] To make matters worse, Polixenes was once himself indistinguishable from Leontes; as boys they "were as twinned lambs that did frisk i' th' sun" (*WT*, 1.2.69). In the face of such a proliferation of resemblances, Leontes cannot recognize his faithful wife, himself, or anyone. In every face he reads only deception and betrayal. How different, then, is his response to Florizel and Perdita in act 5. In them he recognizes the images of his son and daughter as they could have been but—as far as he knows—never were, while at the same time seeing in Florizel his "father's image … , / His very air" (*WT*, 5.1.126–127). Finally, in Hermione he loves and honours a statue that looks exactly like the aged wife he has never seen, and also exactly like the young bride she was "when first" he "wooed her" (WT, 5.3.36). Such a proliferation of doublings elicits from him, this time, wonder and humility rather than rage.

These many doublings thematically enhance the central binary of the statue scene, which is stone *versus* wavering flesh. Leontes asks whether the stone "Does not rebuke" him "For being more stone than it," and observes his "admiring daughter … / Standing like stone" at the sight of her mother's statue (*WT*, 5.3.37–38, 41–42). Remarkably, this inability to distinguish, at such a fundamental level, causes him no anxiety. Shortly afterwards, Paulina

---

[26] See Shakespeare, *WT*, 1.2.121–162a and 2.3.93b–132a.

[27] Not only is her pregnant body changed and changing, but it is also two people in one, another kind of doubling.

exhorts the statue to "Bequeath to death your numbness, for from him / Dear life redeems you" (*WT*, 5.3.102–103). This is appropriate, because Leontes can now recognize and welcome resemblance without identity, consistency in alteration. In Cary's *Mariam*, those who cannot accept this are tragic figures. But Leontes no longer requires a marble-perfect wife nor prides himself in his own stony heart. He accepts Paulina's lesson that a distinct and coherent identity is impossible, and that there is nothing more paradoxical than integrity.

The Winter's Tale also resembles Cary's tragedy in that both withhold from their audiences the suspect pleasure of the authoritative gaze. Even though the statue scene is satisfyingly spectacular, Shakespeare's romance nevertheless invites us to participate in the pleasures of undecideability. Pointing out that "there is clear textual evidence that Shakespeare wrote doubled roles into his plays," John C. Meagher argues that "Shakespearean dramaturgy, while being embedded in staffing constraints, *takes advantage* of what happens when he has to double roles."[28] In the case of *The Winter's Tale* specifically, Meagher argues that Leontes's surprising proposal that Paulina marry Camillo at the end "is not so abrupt after all," if we assume "that the same actor played both roles" of Camillo and Antigonus, Paulina's lost husband. If this is indeed the case, then "at another dimension of dramatic illusion, Antigonus has broken his grave and Paulina has recovered her long-lost mate about as surely as Leontes has been reunited with Hermione."[29] By her inventive powers, through loyal criticism and faithful deception, Paulina brings Leontes and Hermione back to "Dear life." By his inventive powers, through doubling, Shakespeare "delivered dramatic satisfaction to his audiences."[30] But to enjoy this satisfaction, we too must give up the satisfaction of being able to identify any body with certainty.

Shakespeare's Hermione, then, resembles Cary's Mariam and Salome, in that all three are married to male authorities (primarily heads of state but also heads of families) who know the need for their power to be iteratively performed and witnessed, who constantly require reflections of their power, and who understand such monumental reflections to guarantee their own physical stability and the stability of the entire state both at once. Although not as obviously constrained as is Tamburlaine's captive bride

---

[28] Maegher, *Shakespeare*, 102, 103, original italics.

[29] Maegher, *Pursuing*, 221.

[30] Meagher, *Pursuing*, 222.

Zenocrate, Cary's and Shakespeare's wives exist under a kind of surveillance that Marlowe's theatre could not even stage. Yet, in *The Tragedy of Mariam* and *The Winter's Tale*, Cary and Shakespeare both offer important critiques of the emerging scopic regime, and stage important interventions in the post-proscenium construction of gender. All three playwrights, furthermore, suggest that there is no more "holy, time-honoured" object than the human body marked by the passage of time.

University of North Alabama

Cited Works

Blum, Abbe. "'Strike All That Look upon with Mar[b]le': Monumentalizing Women in Shakespeare's Plays." In *The Renaissance Englishwoman in Print: Counterbalancing the Canon*, eds. Anne M. Haselkorn and Betty S. Travitsky. Amherst: University of Massachusetts Press, 1990, 99–118.

Cary, Elizabeth. *The Tragedy of Mariam*, ed. Stephanie Hodgson-Wright. Peterborough, ON: Broadview, 2000.

Foucault, Michel. *Discipline and Punish: the Birth of the Prison*, trans. Alan Sheridan. Vintage. New York: Vintage / Random House, 1995.

Gittings, Claire. *Death, Burial and the Individual in Early Modern England.* London: Routledge, 1984.

Gutierrez, Nancy. "Valuing Mariam: Genre Study and Feminist Analysis." *Tulsa Studies in Women's Literature* 10:2 (1991): 233–251.

Hodgson-Wright, Stephanie, ed. Introduction. *The Tragedy of Mariam*, by Elizabeth Cary. Peterborough, ON: Broadview, 2000.

Houlbrooke, Ralph. *Death, Religion and the Family in England, 1480–1750.* Oxford Studies in Social History, gen. ed. Keith Thomas. Oxford: Clarendon Press, 1998.

Jankowski, Theodora A. *Women in Power in the Early Modern Drama.* Urbana: University of Illinois Press, 1992.

Kurth, Willi, ed. *The Complete Woodcuts of Albrecht Dürer.* Trans. Silvia M. Welsh, introd. Campbell Dodgson. London: Foyle, 1927; rpt. New York: Dover, 1963.

Meagher, John C. *Pursuing Shakespeare's Dramaturgy*. Madison and Teaneck: Fairleigh Dickinson University Press / London: Associated University Presses, 2003.

_____. *Shakespeare's Shakespeare: How the Plays Were Made*. New York: Continuum, 1997.

Marlowe, Christopher. *Tamburlaine the Great, Parts I and II*. In *Dr. Faustus and Other Plays*, eds. David Bevington and Eric Rasmussen. Oxford Drama Library. Oxford: Clarendon Press, 1995, 1–136.

Michel, J.Y. "Monuments in Late Elizabethan Literature: A Conservatory of Vanishing Traditions." *Early Modern Literary Studies* 9.2 (2003): 4.1–53. http://purl.oclc.org/emls09-2/michmonu.html.

Orgel, Stephen and Roy Strong. *Inigo Jones: The Theatre of the Stuart Court*. 2 vols. Sotheby Parke Bernet: University of California Press, 1973.

Ovid. *The XV Bookes of P. Ouidius Naso, entituled, Metamorphosis …* , trans. Arthur Golding. London: Iohn Windet and Thomas Iudson, 1584. Early English Books Online.

Panofsky, Erwin. *Perspective as Symbolic Form*. [Originally published as "Die Perspektive als 'Symbolische Form.'" *Vorträge der Bibliothek Warburg* 4 (1924–25): 258–330.] Trans. and introd. Christopher S. Wood. Cambridge, MA and London: MIT Press, 1991.

Peterson, Lesley. "The Source and Date for Elizabeth Tanfield Cary's Manuscript *The Mirror of the Worlde*." *Notes and Queries* 51.3 (2004): 257–263.

Quilligan, Maureen. "Staging Gender: William Shakespeare and Elizabeth Cary." In *Sexuality and Gender in Early Modern Europe: Institutions, Texts, Images*, ed. James Turner. Cambridge, UK: Cambridge University Press, 1993, pp. 208–232.

Sawday, Jonathan. *The Body Emblazoned: Dissection and the Human Body in Renaissance Culture*. London and New York: Routledge, 1995.

Shakespeare, William. *The Winter's Tale*. In *The Norton Shakespeare*, eds. Stephen Greenblatt et al. 2nd ed. New York: Norton, 2008, 2881–2962.

Stallybrass, Peter. "Patriarchal Territories: The Body Enclosed." In *Rewriting the Renaissance: Discourses of Sexual Difference in Early Modern Europe*, eds. Margaret W. Ferguson, Maureen Quilligan, and Nancy J. Vickers. Chicago: University of Chicago Press, 1986, 123–42.

Vickers, Nancy J. "Diana Described: Scattered Woman and Scattered Rhyme." In *Writing and Sexual Difference*, ed. Elizabeth Abel. Chicago: University of Chicago Press, 1982, 95–108.

Zimmerman, Susan. *The Early Modern Corpse and Shakespeare's Theatre.* Edinburgh: Edinburgh University Press, 2005.

Anne Wentworth's Apocalyptic Marriages: Bigamy, Subjectivity, and Religious Conflict

William E. Smith III

On 3 January 1670 the world changed; or at least Anne Wentworth's world did.[1] According to her autobiographical and polemical *A Vindication of Anne Wentworth* (1677), she underwent a mystical experience involving Jesus that seems to have simultaneously aided her to recover from an illness, which she claims her husband's abuses induced, and that affirmed her sense of election and salvation, as well as revealed a divinely ordained prophetic commission. There is, however, another crucial element packed into this already complex "Heavenly Vision" (*Vindication*, 5). Anne Wentworth, a Particular Baptist living in London, found herself married to Jesus.

This wedding was no straightforward affair. To understand this matrimony, the text can be read in two different interpretative directions: the metaphorical and the literal. "Then was the full communion between Christ and my Soul," Wentworth records, "the Love knot, the comly bands of Marriage; then did he espouse me unto himself for ever, and enable me to follow him" (*Vindication*, 12). The sentence, up to the semicolon, reads like a metaphorical *sponsa Christi* description of a *unio mystica* (mystical union) that could serve as a Puritan sign of election. Parsed this way, Wentworth expresses the requisite evidence of unmerited divine favour in marital trappings.

Yet, the remainder of the sentence leads in a different direction. The "then" introduces a sequence of events that links the act of marrying with a post-wedding night life. In *A Vindication*, Wentworth elaborates on being Christ's wife. At one point, she boldly declares, "My heavenly Bridegroom is come, and has given me courage" (*Vindication*, 9). As Richard Rambuss

---

[1] For ease of reference I retain Wentworth's dating system, which is based on the Julian calendar, since she dates things frequently. Under the current Gregorian calendar, the mystical experience would have occurred on 13 January 1671. I also incorporate parenthetical references to Wentworth's writings directly into the text, citing the work's short title and the page reference.

comments, "she doesn't appear to be talking metaphor."[2] According to her four autobiographically driven prophetic treatises published in the late 1670s, Wentworth claimed to have had two different heavenly visions and that Jesus frequently spoke to her in very articulate auditory revelations throughout the 1670s. He also sent two angels and a mysterious woman to her, conveying messages relevant to Wentworth's life and new prophetic mission. In Wentworth's account of her life, being *sponsa Christi* means bearing an apocalyptic message about England's, and the world's, impending judgment. So far Wentworth is very much in line with the prophetic female tradition, which featured such notables as Bridget of Sweden and Anna Trapnel, that spanned from the late medieval period through the end of the seventeenth century, as scholars such as Diane Watt have demonstrated.[3] But it is also expressed in more personal, even if not always pleasant, ways. Wentworth's literalization of her divine marriage partially manifests itself in struggles for domestic domination and in violence. Often she frames these conflicts in terms of uxorial submission and obedience.

There remains, however, the intractable presence and problem of Wentworth's other husband, as her domestic story and apocalyptic theology frequently remind the reader. It turns out that Wentworth is a bigamist. In this arrangement and in some of her literalizing strategies, Wentworth is most comparable to Margery Kempe, a fifteenth-century English visionary mystic who modified her marriage to John Kempe so as to accommodate her marriage to God.[4] Some scholars working on Wentworth have tried to resolve the problem of her two spouses by getting rid of William Wentworth in one fashion or another. Rambuss argues that Wentworth is developing the "biblical stricture of monogamy" found in writings by Puritans such as Francis Rous and An Collins. This move allows Wentworth to present "herself as having exchanged husband for husband," even as Rambuss acknowledges that Wentworth does leave open a window of opportunity for Mr. Wentworth's return.[5] Recently, Francis Dolan, while likewise noting the possibility of reconciliation with the husband, claims Wentworth metaphorically kills him. Taking her cue explicitly from Rambuss's position on monogamy, Dolan makes this metaphorical death "the precondition of [Wentworth's] union

---

[2] Rambuss, *Closet Devotions*, 80.

[3] Watt, *Secretaries of God*.

[4] Lipton, *Affections of the Mind*, chapter four.

[5] Rambuss, *Closest Devotions*, 80, 81.

with Christ and consequent salvation."[6] The reasons for insisting on Mrs. Wentworth's success in killing off her husband remain unclear, however, since all her dissenting actions against him appear to date after her 1670 mystical encounter.

The account of Mr. Wentworth's death or displacement seems compelled by the critics' assumption that Anne Wentworth was committed to a monogamous ideal, which Rambuss grounds in "biblical stricture." In other words, if Anne married Christ, she could not also be married to William; one male must necessarily replace the other. Yet, the Bible also preserves cases of divinely licensed polygamy, as evidenced by the Patriarchs. And those caveats about Wentworth possibly taking back her first husband remind us that she never stopped thinking of William as her husband. Therefore instead of a champion of monogamy, I contend that Wentworth's writings preserve a vision of herself in a polyandrous marital arrangement.[7]

But what difference does recognizing Wentworth's bigamy make in reading her texts and life? The presence of multiple spouses escapes Dolan's foundational equation of spousal relations that she develops in *Marriage and Violence*. "The marital economy of scarcity," which, as Dolan convincingly argues, underpins many conceptions of early modern marriage, operates so that the marital union of two persons demands the functional absorption, or annihilation, of one member's subjectivity.[8] As Dolan notes, "the problem is a conception of marriage that can accommodate only one 'individual.'"[9] But, if this husband refuses to die, as I suggest, and keeps imposing himself upon Wentworth, how can she preserve herself — as she clearly does — in the face of his continued onslaughts? She marries again.

In the role of second husband, Christ, in effect, serves as a subjective counterweight to the first husband and provides a means for Wentworth to rear her symbolic head. James Holstun argues that often seventeenth-century women found agency in the space that emerged between two competing

---

[6] Dolan, Marriage and Violence, 60.

[7] In his recent article, Warren Johnston comes closest to my argument. Ultimately, however, he describes the divine marriage as replacing the human one and, thus, returns Wentworth to monogamy during the latter half of the 1670s (Johnston, "Prophecy, Patriarchy, and Violence," 353–355).

[8] Dolan, *Marriage and Violence*, 3.

[9] Dolan, *Marriage and Violence*, 6.

groups, which he illustrates with reference to interdenominational conflicts.[10] Positioned between two husbands with conflicting demands, Wentworth exemplifies this principle on the domestic level, albeit one that ultimately has denominational and national implications. Indeed, her uxorial domestic self and her prophetic self, in a sense, are two sides of the same coin. But these roles, and the range of activities and speech they legitimize, became possible because of her bigamy.

Wentworth's polyandry also shaped the contours of her apocalyptic message. Because she saw her marriages as the linchpin of England's apocalyptic future, Wentworth adds a provocative case study to current efforts to reassess the state of English apocalyptic thinking and activity after the Restoration by religious dissenters, especially among the Particular Baptists.[11] In Wentworth's writings, this sect becomes the target of apocalyptic fury, rather than the heralds of it. Indeed, these Baptists, a seventeenth-century English sect notable for combining adult baptism with a theology of limited atonement, were her major denominational enemies. And importantly, her other chief object of prophetic damnation, William, remained a loyal Baptist congregant even after Wentworth ceased associating with the sect.[12] In her deferential obedience to her second husband, she pursued a series of religious activities and took up certain ideas that, in turn, her human husband opposed by all available means. This ongoing conflict provides the conditions for Wentworth to work out her interrelated prophetic and uxorial identities. Caught between the demands of two husbands (and both were demanding), Anne Wentworth found her voice.

Domestic Disturbances: Prophetic Mysticism and Religious Conflict

Anne Wentworth never fully escaped abuse, be it physical or psychological. In her writings, marriage — human or divine — includes violence. Ultimately, it did not destroy her, but created the conditions necessary for her relative domestic independence. Along with the eventual strength to resist her husband and reside separately from him, Wentworth gained a prophetic voice. This is not to suggest that she wanted to bear such oppressive attention; indeed she

---

[10] Holstun, *Ehud's Dagger*, 257–258.

[11] For two examples, see Bustin, "Papacy, Parish Churches, and Prophecy," and Cogley, "The Fall of the Ottoman Empire."

[12] White, *The English Baptists*.

made the most of opportunities to escape from it. Violence, for Wentworth, is part of the world. The trick, then, was for Wentworth to make this hostility productive in ways favourable to her, rather than be annihilated by it. As part of her strategy of redeployment, Wentworth advanced what I call her "conjugal epistemology," which linked William's violence to the state of his soul, in an effort to undermine her husband in the eyes of his coreligionists. Wentworth also gains an ally in Jesus, who interrupts the dynamics of her first marriage and sets her off on a path that she finds more suitable. The heart of this entire struggle lies over the control of Wentworth's self, her domestic conditions and the wifely identities tied into them. It is through these material battles — over her body, domestic space and prophetic speech — that Wentworth literalizes her marriage to Christ.

Wentworth seems to have married William around 1652. Quickly, he proved to be an unpleasant character, whom at one point Wentworth describes as "a scourge and lash to me" (*A True Account*, 8). Frequently she complains about her husband's abusive behaviour toward her, spanning eighteen years before her "Heavenly Vision." Wentworth preserves her fear that he would kill her during these years in *A Vindication*. "He has in his barbarous actions towards me, a many times over-done such things, as not only in the Spirit of them will be one day judged a murdering of, but had long since *really* proved so, if God had not wonderfully supported, and preserved me" (*Vindication*, 4).[13] As Wentworth narrates it, this cruelty peaked with a particularly intense near-death experience in 1670. Wentworth claims she suffered from a life-threatening case of "hectick Feaver," caused by her years of abuse, which required Wentworth to be "raised from the Grave" by God (*Vindication*, 12; *Spiritual Pill*, 4).

It turns out, though, that the divine intercession of 1670 did not end the marital strife between the two human spouses. Instead, it actually created some of the conditions for its continuation. At some point between 1670 and early 1674, Wentworth fled to a friendly widow's house because she feared "my Husband's wrath, his terrible behavior towards me" (*Spiritual Pill*, 7). According to Wentworth, her attempt to obey an unspecified demand by God required her to disobey William. This act ignited William's abusive rage.

Wentworth locates the problem of her husband's abuse not in his violence per se. It appears, rather, in his having "many times over-done such things." She is portraying him, here, as a person who could not control

---

[13] Throughout this article, all emphases are as in the original text.

himself, placing his self-mastery in doubt by asserting that he went beyond the acceptable limits of domestic discipline. Wentworth implicitly accepted that her husband had the right to limited physical chastisement by finding fault in the degree of violence, rather than in the violence per se. She matches this excessiveness, but in a way that casts herself in a favourable light. She claims she is a paragon of patient submission. "I had spent out all my natural strength of body in obedience to satisfy the unreasonable will of my earthly Husband and laid my body as the ground, and as the street for him to go over for 18 years together, and keep silent" (*True Account*, 8). In other words, Wentworth portrays herself as the long-suffering wife, who only reluctantly, and at the last possible moment, resists her abusive husband.

This type of framing aligns Wentworth's experiences with the general rhetorical strategies wives used against their husbands in accounts of domestic conflict, especially at court. In her study of late seventeenth- and early eighteenth-century wife beating, Margaret Hunt points out, "Wives' testimony in divorce cases on the one hand asserted their virtue, obedience and commitment to male supremacy and on the other protested their husband's abuse of his authority and refusal to fulfill his obligations."[14] Only when domestic violence reached life-threatening levels could a woman use it as grounds for divorce.[15] As Francis Dolan has shown, accounts of husbands' murdering their wives increased dramatically after 1650, and were part of a broader cultural criticism of abusive husbands without, however, fundamentally challenging the social order.[16] While not pressing for a divorce, Wentworth employed similar sympathy-generating rhetorical tools in her presentation of her marital conditions.

Yet, Dolan's study revealed that pamphlets and ballads about murderous husbands "present the murders of wives as abuses not only of authority but of intimacy."[17] Whereas familiarity between spouses was perverted in these accounts, so that the husband could slay his wife in a particularly cruel way, Wentworth argues that her domestic proximity to her husband and his violence exposes an aspect of his religiosity otherwise unavailable to his Baptist comrades. In *A True Account*, Wentworth asserts that her husband's fellow Baptists see a person who is "a moral honest, just-

---

[14] Hunt, "Wife Beating," 15.

[15] Gowing, *Domestic Dangers*, 206–208.

[16] Dolan, *Dangerous Familiars*, 89–99.

[17] Dolan, *Dangerous Familiars*, 99.

dealing man," like themselves. She adds that she is aware of "no gross sin that he is addicted too." Therefore these people understandably support him. But it turns out that these externally visible behaviours, which are highly valued by those who are only nominally Christian according to Wentworth, are merely a masquerade. Alluding to Matthew 23:25–26, which compares the "scribes and Pharisees" to a cup that is only washed on the outside, Wentworth describes her husband as a person who is only clean, pure and good on the surface, but whose "soul was never yet washed from the filth of his inbred natural corruption." She is able to know this because his true spirit has been exposed to her over the course of their marriage, rather than in "his carriage to the World." Although William had been a Particular Baptist since before their marriage, and thus presumably well known to that community, Wentworth insists she has a better understanding of his real *inner* self, and it is not fit to be counted among the saints (*True Account*, 7).

Wentworth operates under the assumption that a person's behaviour will, over time, reveal its true inner-self when "out of sight" of the broader community. Given that Wentworth claims she alone is aware of this knowledge about Mr. Wentworth, she also suggests that this epistemology depends on conjugal familiarity. Wentworth knows from daily and prolonged exposure how he treats his metaphorical other half. She also knows that there is a cruel, unloving side to this man who, as Jesus describes it in a revelation to Wentworth, "wounded thee to thy heart on thy Wedding day" (*Spiritual Pill*, 46). Her marital relationship, in other words, constitutes the vantage point from which she can, so to speak, see into his soul.

Revealing her husband's unregenerate soul — if they accepted the claim — should make the Baptist community second guess their support for her husband. Therefore, Wentworth may be attempting to influence how her husband's Baptist allies would respond to her exposé of her domestic situation in order to divert support away from her husband to herself. She purports to desire her human husband's internal regeneration, or "the spirit of God in him," and thus his fundamental comportment toward her, over any worldly status or material gain (*True Account*, 8). By presenting herself as a person willing to reconcile with, and submit herself once more to, her husband if he reforms, she insists that she is not being stubborn. It is, instead, William who needs to change, and Wentworth, who stopped attending Baptist meetings soon after her mystical marriage, implies it is her former congregants' job to rebuke him.[18]

If garnering this type of sympathy was one of her goals in telling her life story, then Wentworth appears to have failed. Her refusal to obey Mr. Wentworth, and her insistence on speaking out publicly against her husband, upset the Baptist community, which, in her account, sided completely with her husband throughout the 1670s. In 1673, for example, several major Baptist ministers made a house call, in order to convince Wentworth to submit to her husband again. This encounter, especially these men's "torment[ing]" her about her writings, upset Wentworth terribly and, in the final retelling of this visitation, she claims their chastisements drove her to her prayer closet because she "knew not what to do, nor how to answer them."[19]

But William held no monopoly on religiously motivated domestic violence in Wentworth's world. In the wake of the wedding vision, Jesus reveals himself to be more than willing to beat Wentworth into submission and obedience, and does so in ways disturbingly similar to those of her first husband. "Domestic violence," Rambuss points out, "evidently has its place even in the marriage to God."[20] Interestingly, though, Wentworth did not accuse Jesus of excessive violence, as she did with William. Wentworth never presents Jesus as out of control. His disciplinary violence is strictly intended to convince her to accept her role as his earthly prophet. Once accomplished, the violence ends.

Near the beginning of *A Vindication*, Wentworth elaborates on her need to obey God, who can kill both body and soul, over her human husband. This "Heavenly Bridegroom" "call'd and commanded me (in a way too terrible, too powerful to be denyed) to undertake and finish a work" (*Vindication*, 4). This "terrible" calling really did seem to be truly terrifying for Wentworth. Fearing to follow her divine husband, because it would "inrage my Husband and all his Brethren," Wentworth resisted taking up the prophetic aspects of

---

[18] Although coming from slightly later dates, there is evidence in Baptist documents that show that congregations were willing to reprimand husbands whom the congregation felt were mistreating their wives. See the Edward Gaines case of 1685 in the Warboys's Church book (*Records of the Churches Gathered*, 281), and Patricia Crawford mentions that the Cripplegate congregation reproved a man for excessive wife-beating in 1697 (*Women and Religion*, 201).

[19] Wentworth, *Spiritual Pill*, 7, on 6 she names Hanserd Knollys, William Dickes and Thomas Hicks as the three visitors.

[20] Rambuss, *Closest Devotions*, 82.

her new marital duties for "Eleven Months" (*Spiritual Pill*, 5). Apparently losing patience, God began "breaking [her] all to pieces in [her]self, and ... has by many and great Tribulations been *bowing* [her] own will" so that she would "tremble at his *word*" (*Vindication*, 3). God has no qualms in coercing his spouse into submission.

While Wentworth eventually concedes to her new husband's demands, it takes a very dramatic intervention by God to complete his "breaking" of her will. Seemingly exasperated by her insubordination, God attacks her on two fronts. On the one hand, he turns her into an insomniac ("took away my sleep from me") and, on the other, sends an "Angel from Heaven," who threatens to kill her. This combination leads Wentworth to capitulate; "And then the *terrors* of the Lord forced me to obey the command [to be his prophet]" (*Vindication*, 7). God's violence against Wentworth ends with her submission. God's domestic abuse, therefore, succeeds in transforming Wentworth into the docile wife that her human husband's actions failed to secure.

Whereas William's ill behaviour is ongoing, God begins to treat Wentworth better after she submits and assumes her prophetic mantle. In an experience dated to April 1678, for example, Wentworth records her only overtly erotic encounter with the divine. One night, while in "bed," her "Souls husband" comes and speaks things "delightfull to [her] ear." The divine presence, marked by God's voice, proves "sweet to [her] taste," made her "smile" and "laugh." Wentworth insists her spouse "shall lye all night betwixt my breasts: and he did lye all night teaching and speaking comfortably unto me." And speak her divine husband does; his very precise and explicit message that follows this physical description takes up two pages.[21]

Perhaps the clearest case where Jesus acts as the good, kind spouse occurs during a prolonged episode in Wentworth's life, during which William shows his cruelty once more. This time the first husband's abuse is aimed not at Anne's body, but her abode. In "Mid-Summer" 1677 William left the couples' home "in *Kings-Head Court* in *White-Cross-street* neer *Cripple-Gate*," where Wentworth records she had lived since roughly 1666, and he moved to Hoxdon (*True Account*, 22; *Spiritual Pill*, 17). Wentworth refused to depart with him. Mr. Wentworth then rented the house from under her, but Anne would not vacate. In an effort to force her to leave, he "took away the Goods and left me neither Bed, nor any thing to sit on; Nor no meat, drink or money" (*Spiritual Pill*, 16–17). But even this failed to get Wentworth to budge. Finally

---

[21] Wentworth, *Spiritual Pill*, quotations on 19; the divine message, 19–21.

William "sent three of [her] Cousins, to come and take [her] out," which they did and "carried [her] in a Coach to *Hoxdon*" (*Spiritual Pill*, 17).

Wentworth's initial refusal to leave her home, she informs the reader, is because Jesus told her to wait until she was forced out. In fact, Jesus is intimately concerned with this entire domestic affair. He guarantees Wentworth that she will retake possession of her old home in midsummer 1678. But she is not to live there alone; Jesus plans on cohabitating with her. In a message Wentworth claims he repeated frequently during this period, Jesus says, "Thou shalt abide with me, and I will abide with thee, and come and sup with thee and make my abode with thee" (*Spiritual Pill*, 18). In order to bring about this domestic restoration, Jesus, who reminds Wentworth that he is "thy beloved Husband," will get some "saints," unknown to Anne, to aid her in regaining the old home (*Spiritual Pill*, 20). These mysterious "saints" materialize, according to "A.B.," who writes "An Admonition to the Reader" contained in *England's Spiritual Pill*, and who claims to be an eye witness to Wentworth's homecoming.[22] These people, who all remain "strangers," aid Wentworth to seize control of her old home, as well as provide her with material goods, such as "furniture" and "linnen," and to give her "money," thus allowing her to pay the rent (*Spiritual Pill*, 33). Therefore, unlike Wentworth's "unnaturall Husband" who is "wanting in his duty" to her, Jesus treats Wentworth as a good husband should treat his wife.[23]

Jesus' intervention into his wife's domestic affairs is not an act of pure altruism. Not only is the husbandly character in question here, but this repossession of the marital home is actually supposed to stand as "a sign, that he, the Lord hath sent her, to give warning to the Nation" (*Revelation*, 22). The prophecy, thus fulfilled, operates as a sign of divine approval that affirms Wentworth's status as Jesus' prophet. By being a good husband to Wentworth, Jesus aids her in fulfilling the prophetic labour he has assigned her. Tying these two identities together makes sense because Wentworth situates their origins in the same event, namely the "Heavenly Vision."

---

[22] Wentworth, *Spiritual Pill*, 33–35. A.B. claims to have talked to Hanserd Knollys in 1677 to check Wentworth's reputation "upon our first acquaintance with Mrs. *Wentworth*" (34). A.B. also wanted to help secure the return of Wentworth's "book of experiences," which was seized by her husband in 1677. This may mean A.B. is one of the authors of a letter preserved in CSPD (435–436).

[23] Wentworth, *Spiritual Pill*, 24, see also 25 where Jesus compares himself explicitly to William Wentworth, and the "conclusion" added to *Revelation* (22–23) apparently by "A.S." (*Spiritual Pill*, 2).

In *A Vindication*, Wentworth understands her marriage to Christ as initiating her prophetic career. Explaining the implications of this marriage, and the importance of her life to him, Jesus informs Wentworth that, in the end, her human oppressors will lose their power over her because of his intervention. But he has come not only to offer protection. "And he afterwards revealed to me, (what I did not then know) that my *oppressions* and *deliverance* had a *Public Ministry* and *meaning* wrapt up in them" (*Vindication*, 12). As part of this mission, she was "to bear witness against him that has wounded and oppressed me for 18 years" (*Vindication*, 13). It is not surprising that her human husband acts in this passage as a central and condemned figure, since her personal life story of captivity and liberation is crucial to the message she is obliged to pronounce. In obedience to the divine, Wentworth entered the public phase of her life. Besides publishing texts in which she elaborates on William, she sent two vague, but ominous, apocalyptically themed letters to Charles II and the Lord Mayor of London. Wentworth may have even partaken in some public preaching. Thomas Barnes, a state agent who also commented on international affairs, mentioned in a missive, "The predictions of Mrs. A. W[entworth] are to be heard next week by some in town. Several papers are dispersed about it, which, as soon as I can get, I may send. There is much talk of it."[24]

Firmly ensconced in her divine domestic role as Jesus's uxor, Wentworth feels not only compelled but empowered, in body and voice, to go beyond the residential threshold within which William tried to restrain her. Securely based in the domicile, which, by 1678, was solely in her and Jesus's possession, Wentworth finds the house is not the site of confinement but a base from which she fulfills her prophetic mission and a key site in which she can perform this work. Standing at the door that she controls, Wentworth saw a world that needed her.

---

[24] CSPD, 411. Barnes's interest in Wentworth may originate from her political letters, which are the oldest epistles related to Wentworth's case in the CSPD. Barnes's entries stop when what broader support Wentworth initially mustered began to dissipate near the end of 1677 (478).

Domestic Policies: Wentworth as Apocalyptic
Prophet and Fate of the Nation

In fulfilling her divinely mandated ministry, Wentworth spreads a necessary warning about the imminent end of the world. It was this aspect of her calling that caused her to attempt to contact the aforementioned English political figures. Yet, even at arguably her most universal level, Wentworth continued to promote a worldview that ultimately centred on her personal life. Cataclysmic changes were imminent on an international scale, but England's specific fate in this looming tumult was partially dependent on whether or not Wentworth's husband and his allies dramatically altered their treatment of her. As Jesus reveals more to his prophet-wife about these apocalyptic matters, however, she comes to understand better her predestined role in salvation history. And as she begins to comprehend her and William's particular and peculiar relationship to the figures of Zion and Babylon, it becomes apparent that England is in dire straits, indeed.

Near the opening of *A True Account* (1676), Wentworth pleads for people to "examine [their] hearts," to make sure that as many as possible "turn onto the Lord, and know whether God be in us" or not "*because the days are few and evil* that we have here to live" (*True Account*, 2). Wentworth makes clear in her writings that this is no mere *momento mori*. In a rare moment of precision regarding her apocalyptic message, Wentworth prophesizes a firm date for Christ's return. In her letter to the Lord Mayor, she claims that "the judgements of God that will come on the nation" have their "beginnings … before next New Year's Day," which would be near the end of 1677 (CSPD, 279). She repeats the apocalyptic centrality of New Year's Day in *A Vindication*, especially as the period when God will "pour thy Plagues on that great *Whore / Babylon*, for her sin" (*Vindication*, 20; see also 21 and 22). By 1679 the world situation had not noticeably changed, as her New Year's Day prediction had suggested. Wentworth, however, takes this temporal issue into account in *The Revelation* of that year. Jesus tells Wentworth that the original date was correct, in that it was when "*The Great Disappointment and Overturning*" began, and "*will now very shortly follow*" its fulfillment.[25]

This apocalyptic understanding of the late seventeenth century as the final period of time before Christ comes in judgment informs

---

[25] Wentworth, *Revelation*, 21. Interestingly this New Year's Day issue does not appear in *Spiritual Pill*.

Wentworth's overall message. She claims she has information regarding it, not by providing a better reading of the relevant biblical passages, as her Baptist opponent Hanserd Knollys does in his own apocalyptic writings, but through direct revelation.[26] It is on this basis that, in 1677, she was able to garner some public support.[27] After sending her letters to the King and Lord Mayor, some unnamed "serious Christians" attempted to convince Mr. Wentworth and his fellow Baptists to release Mrs. Wentworth's seized writings. These anonymous Christians did this, they asserted, because they wanted the information contained in them about "a dreadful judgement against the whole nation" that has been "made known to her by special revelation." In their eyes, this was all the more urgent since they "hear almost daily the loud echoes of many witnesses and faithful watchmen of God, whom he hath sent with the same message to warn us to prepare for the severe visitation" (CSPD, 435–436).

While the authors of this letter were correct to mark England or "the whole nation" as a central object of concern in Wentworth's message, she insists that England's borders do not delimit the coming apocalypse. In *The Revelation*, for example, Wentworth records that when "*Babylon* will be burnt" this will take place not just in England, but across "*All Europe*" and she notes that there will be "No safety upon Earth" except for being part of "the Covenant of Grace" (*Revelation*, 5). In *A Vindication*, Wentworth writes, "the indignation of the Lord should end in the utter desolation, Ruine and confusion of the *Prophane world* and *grosser Babylon*" (*Vindication*, 2).

Still, an anglo-centrism guides her thinking in this area. Earlier in *The Revelation*, Jesus points out that he is "*ready, to execute my righteous Judgments upon* England, *for their abominations are great*" (*Revelation*, 1). When Wentworth decries the "Crown" and "England" for "thy blinde zeal of formal Religion" she may have various State efforts to impose religious uniformity during the 1660s and 1670s in mind.[28] No matter what particular "abominations" constitute England's guilt, it is certain that the "*English people*" are "given up for destruction" (*Revelation*, 3). As Babylon undergoes annihilation by Jesus, "*Thousands and thousands* [will be] *undone in poor*

---

[26] For two examples, see Hanserd Knollys's essays *Apocalyptical Mysteries* and *An Exposition of the Eleventh Chapter of the Revelation*.

[27] For more on this, see n. 24.

[28] Wentworth, *Spiritual Pill*, 12. For a history of how the State's actions affected various religious dissenters, see Greaves, *Enemies Under His Feet*.

England."[29] As part of her closing remarks in *A Vindication*, Wentworth warns, "For woes upon England will certainly come" (*Vindication*, 22).

While Wentworth presents England as central to Christ's second coming, and is clear that this return is imminent, she remains less precise about what the English can do to survive the upcoming turmoil. Part of the reason for this vagueness is that, strictly speaking, the English people in general are not the ones who matter on this front. In her July 1677 letter, Wentworth does inform Charles II that everyone should "forsake sin and be humble and fall to weep and mourn" (CSPD, 279). Obviously, if a person were part of the invisible Church, or "covenant of Grace," they would likely survive.[30] Yet, in a letter to "dear Christian friends," Wentworth formulates England's collective fate as one wrapped up with her husband and his allies. She asks, "Must all England smart for them, for so great a cry that is ascended up against hypocrisy, oppression and unjust dealing?" (CSPD, 435). Wentworth's question implies that England's future suffering might not occur, or be so severe, if Wentworth's current "domestic" persecution were to end.

The cessation of *her* trials lies primarily in the hands of her husband and his Baptist allies. But given that Wentworth tends to apply phrases such as hard-hearted to these people, she remains rather pessimistic about their radical reformation, even though she leaves the door to repentance open. In *A True Account*, for example, Wentworth defends herself from the charges of Mr. Wentworth and company that she is "deceived," "deluded" and suffers from "whimsies," by insisting that they are the ones under the power of the "Father of lies." She then lists a number of biblical comparisons. Her enemies, she informs the reader, "might as well accused *Abigail* for saying her Husband was a churlish *Nabal*, and folly was with him, and have reproved *Moses* for writing that King *Pharaoh* was an oppressing King" (*True Account*, 11–12). She also brings up Mordecai and Haman. Clearly, Wentworth's main reason for turning to these biblical characters is to align herself with the heroes in order to solidify her claims to veracity. But her choices are interesting in another respect. Pharaoh was hardhearted, and, like Nabal and Haman, died without reforming. Wentworth concludes these remarks by asking, "How can

---

[29] Wentworth, *Revelation*, 15. The subsequent lines suggest Wentworth means these people are sent to hell or a similar fate.

[30] Wentworth appears to mean the invisible Church. In *Spiritual Pill*, for example, she explicitly condemns all the major forms visible ecclesiology then present in England, from Catholicism to the Quakers (17).

any proud man upon earth bear such a thing" (being spoken against, even truthfully).[31]

Previously in this treatise, Wentworth expresses hope that God will "soften [her husband's] heart, and humble his proud spirit" (*True Account*, 8). But such desired personal transformations never appear to materialize. In 1677 she still had some optimism. Wentworth expresses hope that "the Eyes of all my persecutors may be opened" in *A Vindication*. Wentworth believes that, with God's activity and the message he is spreading through her (and about her), some will cease their oppressive behaviour and support her. Indeed, she speculates that a select few among her opponents are really part of the true Church: "some of which [i.e. her current opponents] I judge to be the Lords People, however acted in this matter by a *Zeal without knowledge*" (*Vindication*, 4).

This type of statement does not appear in her latter publications. Apparently she had not noticed a change in their disposition by the time she published *The Revelation* and *England's Spiritual Pill*, in which threats of judgment against her enemies only increase.[32] If anything, Wentworth sees the possibility for a change of heart in these people as lessening with the passage of time. In *The Revelation* she singles out Mr. Wentworth, Thomas Hicks, William Dicks, and Hanserd Knollys, whom she calls "Traytors," as unlikely to repent before death, and says that Jesus will drop "the Ring-leader of them all" into the "pit" (*Revelation*, 10). In the revelation of 20 July 1679, Jesus indicates that those who "mocked and oppressed" Wentworth were among those who "will not awake" and he "will severely punish them" (*Revelation*, 13). In *England's Spiritual Pill*, Jesus promises to "come and send a Fire upon" these "four Men" and "their Churches," which are part of "*Babilon*" (*Spiritual Pill*, 9).

If the window of opportunity for repentance was closing for Mr. Wentworth's supporters by 1679, then it may be that Mr. Wentworth's own chance to change was a foregone conclusion. Of course, theoretically, his "hard" heart could soften. But, like the Pharaoh of Exodus, God appears disinclined to perform any mollifying intervention out of providential necessity. Indeed,

---

[31] Wentworth, *True Account*, 12. In *Revelation*, Mordecai and Haman reappear during a revelation in which "the Hypocrites in *Zion*" and "*Babylon*" face imminent and violent destruction (4).

[32] For two claims that divine punishment awaits her opponents for oppressing her, see *Revelation*, 2 and 8.

Wentworth claims Jesus was "strengthening of my Husbands hands against me, and hardening his heart more then ever King Pharoahs was" (*Spiritual Pill*, 16). On 31 March 1679, Jesus "shewed [Wentworth] why the people did not understand [her], nor [her] work." They "blind themselves" by focusing so much on the disputing spouses and charge Wentworth with "delusions and disobeying of thy Husband." By reading this marital conflict in this manner, they fail to "see, how I [Jesus] have placed the two Spirits in a Man and his wife, to figure out Zion and Babylon." As this revelation makes clear, Wentworth embodies the spirit of Zion, and her husband that of Babylon. While neither person solely constitutes the citizenship of these biblical cities, they are their most important living residents. Indeed, Jesus informs Anne that this relationship between the Wentworths — their respective possessions of the two spirits and the conflict it engenders — was "purposed before the beginning of the World, after the counsel of my own will, before I formed thee in the womb." In other words, Mr. Wentworth appears to have been providentially fated to "be" Babylon.[33]

It is not just that Mr. Wentworth bears the spirit of Babylon, but that the battle ragging between the spouses becomes the occasion for Christ's second coming. Jesus lets Wentworth know that she is to have a "hand in *Babylons* Ashes" (*Revelation*, 9). In fact, a primary reason why Jesus "took [her] from the Grave," which occurred on that night in 1670 when he miraculously healed her, is to see the destruction of Babylon. Jesus promises to "strike a blow, and all of them [Wentworth's "enemies"] will I hit. / From Heaven will I the Lord come to appear, / For to make them all my own voice to hear" (*Revelation*, 10). The battle lines for this cataclysmic event are drawn most clearly by how people relate to her. Since, as Zion, she is "a *figure of* [Jesus'] *Church*," no one who persecutes her can be part of it (*Spiritual Pill*, 29). Instead, she claims they are part of the "Antichristian faction" (*Spiritual Pill*, 40). In this account, then, the Wentworths' preordained marriage marks a transformational turning point in salvation history. This marriage is nothing short of apocalyptic.

But then again, strictly speaking, it is not the only one. We must not forget that Anne Wentworth was a bigamist. Jesus himself returns the focus to his marriage to Wentworth in this revelation. By mentioning the miracle healing, Jesus is also recalling the night of that "Heavenly Vision,"

---

[33] Wentworth, *Revelation*, 9. Whereas this claim is only made once in *The Revelation*, it occurs numerous times in *England's Spiritual Pill*.

when he and Wentworth wed. Wentworth, moreover, performs her double identity as prophet-spouse by relating this knowledge in the form of one of her many divine revelations.[34] After all, it is Jesus, her heavenly spouse, who comes many a night with divine messages that fuel her prophetic mission. As part of this role, Wentworth forges a self that seeks to change the world. In the face of Particular Baptist opposition and, especially, her husband's violence, Wentworth constructs a history and future in which their dominance not only will be overturned in the approaching apocalypse, but is currently insecure, as her victory in the London house dispute of 1677–78 attests. Through her first marriage, Wentworth helps initiate the end of the world. By means of her second, simultaneous marriage, and all the work she does in its name, she believes that she aids her fellow inhabitants of the spiritual Church to enter into the new world, a world without Babylon and its many Particular Baptist inhabitants, and so a world, in other words, without her human husband and, thus, she will no longer be living in bigamy.

INDIANA UNIVERSITY

CITED WORKS

Bustin, Dennis. "Papacy, Parish Churches, and Prophecy: The Popish Plot and the London Particular Baptists — A Case Study." *Canadian Journal of History* 38.3 (2003): 493–504.

Cogley, Richard W. "The Fall of the Ottoman Empire and the Restoration of Israel in the "Judeo-Centric" Strand of Puritan Millenarianism." *Church History* 72.2 (2003): 304–332.

Crawford, Patricia. *Women and Religion in England, 1500–1720*. London and New York: Routledge, 1993.

CSPD = *Calendar of State Papers, Domestic Series. March 1st, 1677, to February 28th, 1678*, ed. Daniell, F.H. Blackburne. London: His Majesty's Stationery Office, 1911.

---

[34] Revelation VIII of *England's Spiritual Pill*, for example, frames her prophetic mission explicitly in terms of Wentworth being Jesus' specially "chosen" and reminds her that he "*Married thee unto my self*" (28).

374 *Marriage in Premodern Europe*

Dolan, Frances F. *Dangerous Familiars: Representations of Domestic Crime in England, 1550–1700*. Ithaca and London: Cornell University Press, 1994.

_____. *Marriage and Violence: The Early Modern Legacy*. Philadelphia: University of Pennsylvania Press, 2008.

Gowing, Laura. *Domestic Dangers: Women, Words, and Sex in Early Modern London*. Oxford: Clarendon Press, 1996.

Greaves, Richard L. *Enemies Under His Feet: Radicals and Nonconformists in Britain, 1664–1677*. Stanford: Stanford University Press, 1990.

Holstun, James. *Ehud's Dagger: Class Struggle in the English Revolution*. London and New York: Verso, 2000.

Hunt, Margaret. "Wife Beating, Domesticity, and Women's Independence in Eighteenth-Century London." *Gender & History* 4.1 (1992): 10–33.

Johnston, Warren. "Prophecy, Patriarchy, and Violence in the Early Modern Household: The Revelations of Anne Wentworth." *Journal of Family History* 34.4 (2009): 344–368.

Knollys, Hanserd. *Apocalyptical Mysteries, Touching the Two Witnesses, the Seven Vials, and the Two Kingdoms, to wit, of Christ, and of Antichrist Expounded*. London: 1667.

_____. *An Exposition of the Eleventh Chapter of the Revelation*. London: 1679.

Lipton, Emma. *Affections of the Mind: The Politics of Sacramental Marriage in Late Medieval English Literature*. Notre Dame: University of Notre Dame Press, 2007.

Rambuss, Richard. *Closest Devotions*. Durham and London: Duke University Press, 1998.

Records of the Churches Gathered at Fenstanton, Warboys, and Hexham, 1644–1720, ed. E.B. Underhill. London: Hanserd Knollys Society, 1854.

Watt, Diane. *Secretaries of God: Women Prophets in Late Medieval and Early Modern England*. Cambridge: D.S. Brewer, 1997.

Wentworth, Anne. *A True Account of Anne Wentworths Being cruelly, unjustly, and unchristianly dealth with by some of those people called Anabaptists*. London: 1676.

_____. *A Vindication of Anne Wentworth*. London: 1677.

_____. *England's Spiritual Pill Which will Purge, Cure, or Kill*. London: 1679/80 (?). Available in *Miscellaneous Short Poetry, 1641–1700*, ed. Robert C. Evans, The Early Modern Englishwoman: A Facsimile

Library of Essential Works, ser. II, Printed Writings, 1641–1700: Pt 3, vol. 4. Aldershot and Burlington: Ashgate, 2006.

————. *The Revelation of Jesus Christ*. London: 1679.

White, B.R. *The English Baptists in the Seventeenth Century*. London: The Baptist Historical Society, 1983.

3.1 Detail showing the Ducal Palace in Mantua with the addition of the Palazzina Paleologa, built by Giulio Romano, from a modern reproduction of the map of Mantua engraved by Pierre Mortier in Amsterdam, 1704. Photo: author.

3.2 One lira coin, issued 1562, Casale Monferrato, with the portraits of
Guglielmo Gonzaga and Margherita Paleologa, in widow's veil, inscribed
"MARG ET GVL DVCES MANT ET MAR MONT F." Motto on verso:
"NON IMPROVIDIS." I thank Dr. Roberto Maestri, Circolo Culturale i
Marchesi di Monferrato. "I Marchesi di Monferrato," (html//www.marchi-
monferrato.com) for his kind permission to use this image.

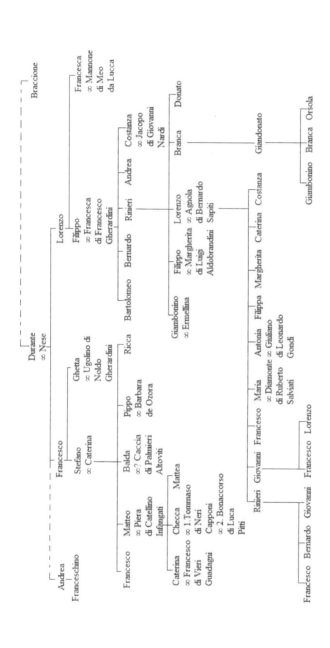

7.1 Selected genealogy of the Durante branch of the Scolari family. The 'm' preceding a name indicates "messer". The genealogies are based on primary archival sources.

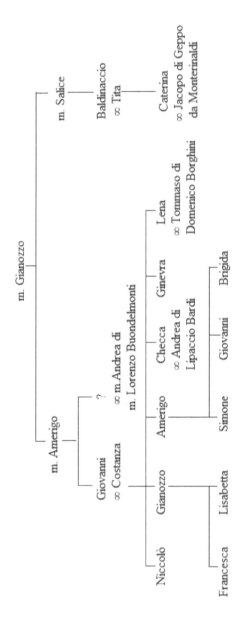

7.2 Selected genealogy of the Giannozzo branch of the Cavalcanti family.

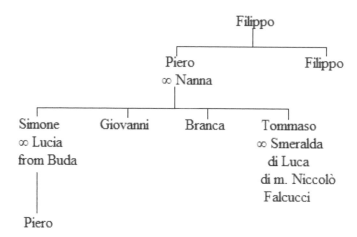

7.3 Selected genealogy of the Filippo branch of the Melanesi da Prato family.

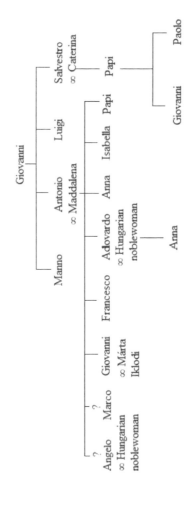

7.4 Selected genealogy of the Mannini family.

3750 - ROMA - Gall. Colonna - Alunno del Ghirlandaio - Ratto delle Sabine - (Stab. D. Anderson - 1934).

9.1 Bartolommeo di Giovanni, *The Rape of the Sabine Women* (1488). Galleria Colonna, Rome. Courtesy of Alinari / Art Resource, NY.

9.2 Bartolommeo di Giovanni, *Peace between the Romans and the Sabines* (1488). Galleria Colonna, Rome. Courtesy of Alinari / Art Resource, NY.

12.1 Bartolomeo Passerotti, *Family Portrait* (ca. 1575). Gemäldegalerie Alte Meister, Dresden, Germany. By permission.

12.2 Leandro Bassano, *Portrait of a Widow at her Devotions* (ca. 1590-1600). Private collection. By permission.

15.1 Albrecht Dürer, *An Artist Drawing a Recumbent Woman*, 1538, woodcut in *The Art of Measurement*. From Willi Kurth, *The Complete Woodcuts of Albrecht Dürer* (London: W. & G. Foyle, 1927), no. 340 (from the collection of the Centre for Reformation and Renaissance Studies)

INDEX